# OUT
## OF THE
## MOUNTAINS

———

# OUT
## OF THE
# MOUNTAINS

———

## THE COMING AGE OF THE URBAN GUERRILLA

### DAVID KILCULLEN

OXFORD
UNIVERSITY PRESS

# OXFORD
## UNIVERSITY PRESS

Oxford University Press is a department of the University of Oxford.
It furthers the University's objective of excellence in research, scholarship,
and education by publishing worldwide.

Oxford   New York
Auckland   Cape Town   Dar es Salaam   Hong Kong   Karachi
Kuala Lumpur   Madrid   Melbourne   Mexico City   Nairobi
New Delhi   Shanghai   Taipei   Toronto

With offices in
Argentina   Austria   Brazil   Chile   Czech Republic   France   Greece
Guatemala   Hungary   Italy   Japan   Poland   Portugal   Singapore
South Korea   Switzerland   Thailand   Turkey   Ukraine   Vietnam

Oxford is a registered trade mark of Oxford University Press
in the UK and certain other countries.

Published in the United States of America by
Oxford University Press
198 Madison Avenue, New York, NY 10016

© David Kilcullen 2013

First issued as an Oxford University Press paperback, 2015.

Library of Congress Cataloging-in-Publication Data
Kilcullen, David.
Out of the mountains : the coming age of the urban guerrilla / David Kilcullen.
pages   cm
ISBN 978-0-19-973750-5 (hardback); 978-0-19-023096-8 (paperback)
1. Guerrilla warfare. 2. Urban warfare.
3. Low-intensity conflicts (Military science)
4. Conflict management.
5. Non-governmental organizations. I. Title.
U240.K493   2013
355.02'18091732—dc23      2013014396

1 3 5 7 9 8 6 4 2

Printed in the United States of America
on acid-free paper

# CONTENTS

---

# ACKNOWLEDGMENTS

———————

I CALLED THIS BOOK *Out of the Mountains*, but I might just as easily have called it *Back to the Future*, since the issues I examine here—centered on conflict in the urbanized, networked littorals of an increasingly crowded planet—were already well understood by the end of the last century.

Marine Corps general Charles Krulak said in 1996 that "the future may well not be 'Son of Desert Storm,' but rather 'Stepchild of Somalia and Chechnya.'" Ralph Peters, Robert H. Scales, Alan Vick, Roger Spiller, Russell Glenn, Paul Van Riper, John Arquilla, Michael Evans, and Justin Kelly had all written extensively by the late 1990s on urban operations in coastal cities. By 2000, Dave Dilegge—later a torch-bearer for the insurgency of ideas through the *Small Wars Journal*—had founded a community of interest around his *Urban Operations Journal*. At the same time, Duane Schattle, Dave Stephenson, and Frank Hoffmann were thinking through the challenges of urban operations against hybrid threats. Military forces in several countries were expanding their amphibious and urban capabilities, while police services, aid agencies, and some NGOs were considering governance and human security in marginalized urban areas. I myself had written a series of papers on urban tactics and amphibious operations, informed by the experience of late-1990s peace enforcement in coastal environments.

But much of this thinking on urban littorals, an already very well established set of ideas by 2001, was sidelined by urgent military necessity after the horrendous Al Qaeda terrorist attacks of 9/11. We found ourselves (not by choice) involved in a landlocked, rural insurgency—far from cities or coastlines—hunting guerrillas in mountain valleys, trying to work with and protect the remote tribal communities in which they nested and on which they preyed. As Iraq descended into chaos after 2003, we were drawn into intense urban counterinsurgency—but, again, we were far from the coast. For a decade since then, the vibrant civilian and academic discussion about future challenges in coastal megacities has gone on without much input from those who have been fighting the war. Bing West, with his closely observed studies of urban combat in Iraq, and Lou DiMarco, with his survey of urban operations since Stalingrad, are two outstanding exceptions to this rule—but even their work has had less impact on the debate than it deserves.

That civilian debate, however, has been enormously productive. Diane Davis, Stephen Graham, Jo Beall, Mitchell Sipus, Saskia Sassen, and Mike Davis, among many others, have added immensely to our understanding of development and conflict in connected cities. Policing and crime thinkers such as John P. Sullivan and Diego Gambetta, and urban sociologists such as Sudhir Venkatesh have studied the challenges of criminal insurgency in large cities and explored the ways in which underworld networks communicate. Institutions such as the World Bank, the United Nations, and the Asian and African Development Banks, along with firms such as IBM and McKinsey, have studied the problems of future urbanization. Universities including the London School of Economics, the Massachusetts Institute of Technology, Columbia University and the Harvard Graduate School of Design, among many others, have established cities programs, while think tanks such as the Brookings Institution (with its Global Cities Initiative) have examined the problems of urban growth, littoralization, and connectivity. Architects such as Oystein Gronning and Eyal Weizman have applied spatial design thinking to urban conflict.

Now that the war in Afghanistan is beginning to wind down, it's time for the military to reengage with the challenge of irregular conflict in the urban littoral. When the dust eventually settles and our generation, the generation that fought the war, shakes itself off and turns from the moment-by-moment challenge of the war to once again consider the future environment, we'll find that the same old challenges of the urbanized littoral remain, but that much of what we thought we understood has changed. Not only have enormous advances been made over the last decade in cloud computing, complex systems theory, big data analysis, remote observation, and crowd-sourced analytics—allowing new insights into old problems—but vast amounts of real-time data are now available to inform our thinking. Most important, the environment itself has changed. The level of connectivity and networked interaction (among populations all over the planet, and between and within coastal cities) has exploded in the last decade, and it's time to bring this new understanding to bear on the problems of urbanization and conflict. What we may find—and what this book tentatively suggests—is that things aren't where we left them when we headed off into the mountains after 9/11.

In writing this book, I've benefited from the thinking and research of all these individuals and institutions, and also from the unstinting and generous help of friends, colleagues, and family across the whole world. Professor Tammy Schultz read and carefully critiqued every chapter. Dr. Erin Simpson kept me focused on the big issues and helped sharpen the argument over many discussions in the field and over the map. Greg Mills, Oyeshiku Carr, John Pollock, Claire Metelits, Satish Chand, and Amit Patel contributed foundational ideas, as did Leah Meisterlin, Steve Eames, Nigel Snoad, Oystein Gronning, Antonio Giustozzi, Claudio Franco, Andrew Exum, Gordon Messenger, and John Sullivan. Stacia George, Alex Hughes, Jason Knobloch, Matt McNabb, Richard Tyson, and Will Upshur at Caerus designed and led community-participative mapping programs in some extremely challenging urban environments—and developed crowd-sourced analytics and remote observation tools that made it possible to see the patterns discussed in this book. Likewise, Anna Prouse, Nate Rosenblatt, Jacob Burke, and Omar Ellaboudy pioneered field research techniques to map the virtual/human network overlaps that turn out to be critical in this environment. Nate Rosenblatt, in particular, provided many insights and key sources that proved critical to understanding the Arab Awakening, while Anna Prouse fearlessly walked the streets of several hostile cities (not just in Africa) as we figured things out. Christian Chung and Scott Long did the initial desktop analysis on Jamaica and Sri Lanka that helped me to do effective fieldwork later. Michael Stock, Randy Garrett, Ben Riley, John Seel, Pat Kelleher, Nadia Schadlow, Marin

Strmecki, and Dan Ermer provided guidance, insight, funding, and moral support—not necessarily in that order of importance—that made this research possible. Ben Fitzgerald and his team at Noetic were essential partners in the effort, and the Smith Richardson Foundation gave generous financial and intellectual support to field research and tech platform development. To the extent that this work has any merit, it derives in large measure from the wisdom of this great community of research and program partners; the errors, omissions, and misstatements, of course, are mine alone.

At Oxford University Press, David McBride and Sarah Rosenthal were cogent, insightful, and supportive through multiple delays, rewrites, and email absences as we pulled the manuscript together, while Kim Craven and Christian Purdy were helpfully (but not endlessly) patient. At Hurst & Co. in London, Michael Dwyer provided extremely helpful inputs at critical times, and Jon de Peyer kept me focused on the timeline, as did Henry Rosenbloom at Scribe Publications in Melbourne. My parents, John and Anne Kilcullen, my sister Janet, and my whole American family—including Ken Schoendorf and Jennifer Parker, Jimmy Davidson and Melanie Pease, Jim Davidson and Sarajane Wallace, and Patrick and Roberta Davidson—gave me vastly more than moral support: their edits, ideas, and perspectives (not to mention a succession of kitchen tables, sofas, and desks on which to perch my laptop while I wrote the manuscript) were incredibly helpful. Finally, as an intellectual partner, a critical sounding board, a perceptive editor, and an emotional rock, I can only humbly thank my beautiful wife, Janine, and promise to be calmer (and hopefully less absentminded) now that the bloody thing is finally done.

Washington, D.C.
April 2013

# OUT
## OF THE
## MOUNTAINS

———

# Introduction

## Ambush in Afghanistan

I

*3:45 p.m., September 10, 2009*
*Dara-i-Nur District, Nangarhar, Afghanistan*

The bridge gleamed in the afternoon light. In two hours the temperature would plunge as the sun sank behind the mountains, casting the valley into shadow. But for now the air was warm, with the chill edge of eight thousand feet of altitude. The sun heated the stunted pines, filling the valley with scent. It warmed the men who lay in the pine needles, among gray rocks, two hundred yards up the hillside, overlooking the road.

The road was an oily two-lane blacktop, newly made, that followed the valley floor. Below the bridge, the valley opened up into fields and orchards, with gray stone and mud-brick villages set back from the road among the trees. The open ground below the bridge gave scope for evasive maneuver, so this was the last spot where you could hope to ambush a patrol coming out of the mountains with any real chance of pinning it down.[1]

As our column snaked down the valley, a car going the other way pulled onto the dusty shoulder of the road. We were lumbering along in a slow-moving convoy of mine resistant vehicles called MRAPs that look like huge coyote-brown garbage trucks.[2] A yellow bicycle leaned against the concrete barrier on the left-hand side of the bridge, no owner in sight.

The leading MRAP reached the bridge, drew level with the bike, and passed it.

At that instant the ambushers opened fire from the hillside with rocket-propelled grenades, long bursts from two machine guns, and rifles firing in support.[3] They concentrated on the head of the column, most likely trying to disable the leading vehicle, block the bridge, and trap us. Had they succeeded, we would have had a bad day out. Strung out on the valley floor, we could not have maneuvered: they could have worked us over at leisure until nightfall let them slip away. Exactly this had happened to two of my friends in the past couple of years; it was something of an occupational hazard in the Afghan hills, where a sparse road network and mountain terrain made our movements predictable.

The RPGs passed close to the cab of the front gun truck but exploded harmlessly in the creek bed. Having failed to stop us in the first burst, the attackers had lost the element of surprise. Our patrol was now fully alert, laying down heavy suppressive fire as it rolled across the bridge. The ambushers had lost any chance of blocking the road.

Our column brushed past the ambush at a steady pace, neither pausing nor hurrying. The gunners traversed right, angled up, then fired, each vehicle hosing the ambush down as it moved through the killing area. Long streams of red tracer fire slid across the valley in a flattened arc, splashing onto the hillside. The enemy shooters fell silent, the dry grass and pine scrub caught fire, and smoke obscured the hill, ending the fight before it had properly begun. Our leading MRAP was hit by rifle fire but suffered no other damage, and we lost nobody killed or injured. The whole thing was over in less than three minutes. It was all very halfhearted: in fact, by the standards of eastern Afghanistan in the early autumn of 2009, it barely even qualified as a firefight at all.

It wasn't a great ambush site, either. I say this as something of an involuntary connoisseur: in Iraq and Afghanistan I'd seen ambushes of varying severity, including so-called complex attacks that combined bombings with ground assaults. Earlier, as an Australian officer seconded to teach tactics at the British Army's School of Infantry at Warminster in the mid-1990s, I'd taught ambush and counterambush techniques on a series of intensive four-month battle courses for infantry platoon commanders.

If these guys had been my students on the battle course, I would have failed them on their ambush plan. The ambush was too far down the valley to be sure of stopping us, too far from the road for the RPGs to be accurate, too high above the killing area for the machine guns to achieve a flat field of fire. The ambushers made no serious attempt to block the road, they sited themselves on a forward slope that made withdrawal impossible once things began to go wrong for them, and they had no cut-off, early warning, or backup. Their choice of a site on the forward slope meant that the ground rose up behind them, so there was no clear back-blast area for their RPGs. The dust that the RPGs kicked up made their position very obvious and probably cost them several dead and wounded. It was all rather incompetent.

Thirty minutes later and five miles farther down the road, we circled the wagons among the gray pebbles and scrappy trees of the riverbed and got out to wait for the helicopters.

The patrol was from the Provincial Reconstruction Team (PRT) in Jalalabad, capital of Nangarhar province. They'd been in-country just over two months, and this was their first significant firefight. The guys were clearly relieved to have made it through unscathed, and to have acquitted themselves well. The presence of news media—the experienced war correspondent Lara Logan, her producer, Howard Rosenberg, and a *60 Minutes* film crew were there, along with Ambassador Hank Crumpton, the legendary CIA officer who'd masterminded the 2001 invasion—probably elated them further, and they talked over the firefight with excitement. Listening to the discussion, I was reminded of Winston Churchill's comment on a cavalry patrol he watched returning from an ambush in the Mamund Valley, thirty miles east of here, in September 1897: "They were vastly pleased with themselves. Nothing in life is so exhilarating as to be shot at without result."[4]

"How many Taliban do you think we killed?" one of the drivers asked his gunner as they sat smoking. I was five feet away, leaning back against the riverbank to take the weight off my assault vest, and taking a long drink from my Camelbak.

"I don't know, five to seven? We'll know for sure when we get back and clear the site."

"How do you know they were Taliban?" I asked the soldiers, who both seemed to be in their early twenties.

They looked at me.

"Dude, they were *shooting* at us."

"Fair enough."

## II

The two Black Hawks popped over the skyline with a sudden rotor thump, flaring to land on the dry watercourse in a cloud of grit and pine needles. Over the engine noise, we shouted our goodbyes and I headed for the rear aircraft, crouching with eyes half closed in the instant dust storm.

Flying back to Kabul, we followed the stupendous southern edge of the Hindu Kush, our minuscule helicopters hugging the giant mountains like dragonflies skirting a rockpile. We dropped down into the Alishang Valley, following the terrain, picked up the Kabul-Jalalabad road, then flew above it, the pilots using the highway as a handrail to guide us home. The sun was setting, and I gazed out the helicopter door, arms tightly folded, chin tucked into my chest against the cold, watching the clean rock of the mountaintops scroll beneath my climbing boots. The peaks threw long, sharp shadows in the clear tawny light of late afternoon. They seemed close enough to touch.

Something didn't add up. Despite what the MRAP crew had said, the more I thought about it, the less this seemed like a Taliban ambush. I couldn't quite put my finger on it, but something was wrong with the picture.

For a start, Dara-i-Nur district, where the firefight happened, is 99 percent Pashai. The Pashai aren't Pashtun; they speak their own language and keep to themselves. They're not aligned with the government (that deep in the Afghan countryside, virtually nobody is "aligned" with anyone but themselves), but neither do they support the mainly Pashtun Taliban. In fact, like mountain people all over the world, the Pashai are militantly self-sufficient and can be suspicious and hostile toward outsiders, whatever their origin. This district, though only fifteen miles from the Pakistani frontier, had seen little Taliban activity to date, and it was a part of Nangarhar province that never really supported the Taliban even when they were in power during the late 1990s. Of course, Taliban fighters could have slipped in without the locals' knowledge, but that would have been unusual this late in the season—there were only a few weeks left till the first snowfalls began to close the highest passes, making it harder for guerrillas to move in the mountains or cross over from their safe havens in Pakistan.

For another thing, these weren't the usual Taliban tactics. The insurgents were creatures of habit—they set patterns, doing things the same way over and over again.[5] But within the bounds of their tactical repertoire, they were tough and competent. In any serious ambush, a Taliban main force column, even just a local guerrilla group (known as a *delgai*), would first have blocked the road, blowing the bridge or blocking it with a vehicle, then shot us up with RPGs and machine guns from the crest line and mortars from the valley behind, perhaps with a ground assault force waiting in reserve behind the crest.[6] They'd done it this way a hundred times—but not today.

Some of our group had speculated that the car that pulled off the road, or the bicycle on the bridge, might have concealed a roadside bomb that had failed to explode. Nobody stopped to check, of course, as we were focused on "getting off the X," but it didn't seem all that likely. Suicide car bombs weren't uncommon in Afghanistan, of course, but they were more an urban than a rural thing at this time—in the countryside it was more usual to see homemade fertilizer bombs, clusters of Russian mortar bombs, or stacks of Italian antipersonnel or antitank mines buried in the roadway or dug into the side of a cutting. And the bike, even with a pannier, would have been too small to hide the size of improvised explosive device needed to blow the bridge or disable an armored vehicle.

No, the bicycle was either a coincidence or just an aiming point—a distinctive object placed at a known distance to help the ambushers set the range for their weapon sights.

And it was unlike the Taliban to site an ambush so poorly, on the forward slope of the hillside, with no escape route. With their Pakistani advisers, decent equipment, and years of practice, the Main Force Taliban in eastern Afghanistan were getting pretty good by this stage of the war. The previous year, just northeast of here, they'd mounted a sustained assault with two hundred fighters, foreign advisors, the collusion of village elders, and supporting fire from the local Afghan National Police detachment against an outpost of the 173rd Airborne Brigade near the village of Wanat in the Waygal Valley. The attack killed nine Americans and wounded twenty-seven, along with four soldiers from the partnered Afghan National Army unit, and turned out to be one of the most intense and sustained fights of the entire war. Taliban positioning of support weapons at Wanat had been textbook perfect, and their maneuver had been aggressive, competent, and determined—nothing like the amateurish effort we'd just brushed off.[7]

So, on balance, the evidence suggested this probably wasn't a Taliban ambush. What was it, then? Perhaps, I thought, it might have had something to do with what the patrol had been doing that day.

Provincial reconstruction teams were specialized units created for reconstruction and stabilization purposes early in the wars in Afghanistan and Iraq. They typically included three or four civilian experts, a combined civil-military command group, military reconstruction specialists, and fifty to seventy soldiers to provide protection, mobility, and logistical support. The first teams emerged in an ad hoc way in late 2002, but by 2009 they were part of a sophisticated, multinational reconstruction infrastructure; in Afghanistan there were twenty-seven teams at this time, twelve of which were American-led. PRTs were usually based in the provincial capital and were responsible for projects across the whole province. That afternoon we'd visited two such projects: a micro-hydroelectricity plant and a slaughterhouse. Both were highly impressive feats of engineering.

Despite the name, there was nothing exactly "micro" about the hydro plant in the village a few miles up the valley. On the contrary, it was a major construction effort, built into the side of a ravine, with a catchment canal and holding tank at the top of the hill to contain snowmelt diverted from upriver. Water flowed down the canal into a stone basin the size of a small house, then fed into a pipe that dropped one hundred feet straight down into the gorge, to a turbine shed housing a forty-kilowatt generator. The orange turbine, about the size of a ride-on lawn mower, produced enough electricity to light more than half the village. I scrambled down the precipitous hillside to look at the turbine, climbing carefully over boulders, scree, and dirt, dazzled by the sun, with trickles of sweat itching inside my body armor in the afternoon air. Troops from the PRT perched behind trees and rocks on top of the hill, scanning the other side of the valley through their weapon sights.

After a few minutes the Afghan engineer who supervised the project joined me, followed by Lara Logan and Ambassador Crumpton. All of them were dusty from the climb into the ravine, and the engineer carefully wiped his shiny black oxford shoes before describing the design of the micro-hydro turbine and generator system. He explained that the project had taken eighteen months, cost more than a million dollars, and employed twenty local men. He was rightly proud: the thing was beautifully engineered, and it was constructed to exacting standards. This engineer had built hydro plants all over Afghanistan, mostly for the narcotics affairs section at the U.S. mission. Installations such as this were part of a set of projects designed to offer alternative livelihoods to farmers who stopped growing opium poppies, and so were funded with counterdrug money.

A few miles farther down the road, the slaughterhouse had just been completed. It was the main project in this area for an agribusiness development team (ADT) of the Missouri National Guard. ADTs were small units that usually cooperated with the PRT in their province, came from National Guard units in farming areas of the United States, and had a relationship with a land grant college or agricultural university in their home state. The teams made a practice of rotating back to the same area on every tour, and as farmers themselves, team members could bond with local farming communities. The ADTs' parent National Guard units, hometowns, state governments, and universities often struck up partnerships with Afghan districts or colleges, making the ADT program useful both in a practical sense and for the political goodwill it generated. In the case of Nangarhar, where the Missouri National Guard pioneered the ADT concept in Afghanistan, the State of Missouri had committed to a five-year collaborative program that included a partnership with Nangarhar University, in Jalalabad, and dozens of projects across the province.

This particular project aimed to improve hygiene and efficiency in local livestock markets. In Afghan villages, you often see butcher shops or market stalls with bloody cuts of meat—even whole goats or sheep—hanging in the window. In this valley, the ADT had seen animals slaughtered in the open and then butchered on the bare earth. This traditional practice covered the meat in dirt, attracted flies, and left large standing pools of blood, creating a disease hazard. Community leaders agreed that it wasn't ideal, but they pointed out that lack of water or a suitable slaughterhouse meant that there was no practical alternative.

So, with considerable ingenuity, the ADT designed and helped build a slaughterhouse near the main road, with a rainwater tank and an animal holding pen alongside. The new slaughterhouse took months to construct. It used solar panels made by a local Afghan company to generate electric power for lighting, water heating, and cold storage, and applied techniques to minimize the use of precious water. Working with the PRT and the community, the agriculture team helped secure land for the site, and helped the local butchers' association negotiate an agreement so that butchers in the area could share the slaughterhouse, each using it in turn to slaughter animals under hygienic conditions. A local mullah inspected and certified the facility for compliance with Islamic religious requirements. Today, the district governor, elders, and religious leaders from the local community had come for the formal opening. The building was cool, well lit, and spotlessly clean. Our patrol stopped at the site for almost an hour while the governor made a speech, and the elders responded. It was only a few minutes after leaving the slaughterhouse that we were ambushed as we moved down the valley.

What might these projects tell us about the ambush? Was there a connection? If the ambushers weren't Taliban, who were they?

People near the ambush site lived closer to the district center than to either of these two projects. But other villages, farther up the valley, had gotten significant economic benefits—electric light and the slaughterhouse—from foreign assistance. It's quite possible that people down the valley felt cheated when the other villages got these lucrative projects. People had seen our column heading up the valley earlier in the day, and the ambushers must have known that, with our heavy road-bound gun trucks, we could only come back out along the same route. They may have seized the opportunity while we were up the valley visiting the micro-hydro plant and the slaughterhouse to set up a hasty ambush on the bridge and hit us on the way out. Hastiness in setting up the ambush would explain its poor positioning and the lack of a roadside bomb; if the attack was intended mainly to send us a message rather than kill us, this would also explain its halfhearted nature; and if the attackers were local men rather than members of a full-time Taliban column, this would explain their amateurish technique.

To someone unfamiliar with Afghanistan, ambushing a heavily armed patrol over something as minor as the placement of an aid project might seem like a ridiculous (and highly risky) overreaction, but this wouldn't be the first time that perceived injustice led Afghans to take up arms against foreign aid projects or outside contractors. In one incident a year later in Helmand province, in Afghanistan's southwest, insurgents attacked security guards working for a local contractor, killing twenty-one people. The project involved constructing a road to link the towns of Sangin and Gereshk. In media reporting it emerged that Taliban opposition to the road, which would bring security forces into an area they'd previously dominated, "meshed with opposition from villagers, who were upset that the contractor had not consulted them about building the road or asked what services they needed, nor offered local people jobs on the project."[8]

> "One of the big problems that the contractors face and one reason they get attacked is because they bring people from other villages as laborers and security guards," said Haji Abdul Ahad Khan, an elder who on Friday was attending the funeral of one of the slain security guards. "They do not ask our villagers to participate in these projects or hire them to do any of the labor. This makes our people angry," he said. "And they start projects in our area without consulting the village elders. They start cleaning our canals for us, or building a road for us. I don't want a road, why would you build that? We need a school or a clinic."[9]

In other words, both the insurgents and the local population had a common interest in disrupting the road project. In addition to his rather entitled attitude, it's interesting to note that the local elder, Abdul Ahad Khan, implies (though he's careful not to say so directly) that the elders' anger against outside contractors may actually have led to the attack. The Taliban may have been responding to popular grievance and economic discontent, they may have acted on the basis of a shared interest with the community in stopping the road from coming into their area, or the elders may have actually asked the insurgents to mount the attack or struck a financial deal with them to drive out the contractor.

Something like this may also have happened during the battle of Wanat, which I mentioned earlier. An investigation by the U.S. Army's Combat Studies Institute found that the Waygal elders might have deliberately drawn out a meeting that had been called to discuss the site for the new American outpost, keeping the officers from 173rd Airborne talking long enough for an ambush to get into place to attack the Americans as they left.[10] The same study found that the local community, for historical, ethnic and economic reasons, had a strong incentive to stop the U.S. Army building a road into their valley—a traditional buffer zone between two antagonistic local population groups, Nuristanis and Safi Pashtuns, who competed politically and economically and had a long history of violent conflict.[11]

As in Helmand, the Waygal elders and the insurgents had a common interest in preventing the road project. The elders opposed the road because it would have connected them to ancestral enemies, undermining their safety and autonomy, while the Taliban and their sponsors in Pakistan opposed it because it brought our troops within striking distance of the major infiltration routes from their bases across the frontier. The army's report found evidence that the elders might actually have instigated the Wanat attack or at the very least might have been fully aware of it ahead of time, and perhaps their local men played a supporting role in the fighting. One of the first warning signs that something was wrong at Wanat came five days before the battle, when the Pashtun contractor from Jalalabad hired to construct the defenses (but intimidated by previous attacks on his people and equipment) failed to even turn up—a win for the Nuristani elders, who strongly opposed outside contractors, especially those using labor from the rival ethnic group rather than their own young men. During the battle, the Wanat police detachment was also suspected of providing covering fire to the Taliban attackers from within the grounds of their compound. These police were mostly young men from the village or the local district, so their loyalty to local elders (rather than the Taliban) may have played a role in their decision to support the insurgents against both the Americans and the Afghan National Army.

Economically driven incidents of violence have, unfortunately, become extremely common across the south and east of Afghanistan, while even in the relatively quiet north a provincial governor half-jokingly told the German commander in his area, "The Pashtuns in the south shoot at you, and you give them money. Here we support you, and we get nothing. Who do we have to shoot to get some aid around here?"[12]

This pattern isn't unique to Afghanistan. In Iraq in 2007 I spent a little time with a reconstruction liaison team (RLT), a specialist team that monitored infrastructure projects. RLTs in Iraq were fielded by Aegis, the British security and consulting firm, by far the most competent and enlightened of the many security companies operating in Iraq—or, indeed, anywhere I've worked. Aegis teams worked for the U.S. Army

Corps of Engineers. Each comprised eight people in two vehicles, and always included a mix of Iraqi nationals with expatriate drivers and radio operators. The Iraqis took the lead in consultation with local communities, with the expats hanging back and keeping a low profile. The proof of this low-key approach was in the results: at a time when aggressive, heavily armed security contractors were getting into firefights every day, killing dozens of innocent Iraqi civilians, the Aegis RLTs pulled off more than three hundred successful operations, in the most dangerous parts of Iraq, without ever getting into a firefight, killing a single Iraqi, or losing a team member.

The RLT leader I was with, a cool and unflappable former German paratrooper, told me of an incident at a forward operating base in northern Iraq. A U.S. Army unit had just rotated into the area and was being mortared from a district that, until then, had been perfectly quiet. Suspecting the insurgents had sent fighters into the area, the Americans were considering a cordon-and-search operation, but first asked the Aegis team to check things out. In their quiet way, with Iraqi team members discreetly engaging the community, the RLT quickly had an answer: the local sheikh ran a construction company, and he'd been promised a contract by the outgoing unit. During the changeover between the two U.S. units, this seemingly minor detail had somehow slipped through the cracks. The new unit, unaware of the commitment, had given the contract to another company, so the sheikh was mortaring the base—in order, he said, to get people's attention and avenge the injustice.

Again, mortaring the base might seem like a risky overreaction to a mere contracting glitch. But the sheikh, whatever his feelings toward the coalition, had little choice: failing to avenge the slight would have undermined his authority, making him, his family, and his tribal group less safe. The loss of prestige would have weakened his ability to prevail in local disputes and negotiations, ultimately depriving his group of access to resources—and in a chaotic country with little rule of law and no welfare safety net, that was a potential death sentence. Thus what might look like a minor issue, and in fact *was* quite minor in itself, had major implications for this local leader and thus, by extension, for the American unit. It would have dishonored the sheikh to take a gentler approach (say, a phone call or a visit to complain to the new unit), since he couldn't afford to be seen as a supplicant. Prestige was the one essential currency he had, and he had to act to preserve that prestige: he really did have no choice. He hoped the Americans would understand, he told the Aegis team, that it was just business—nothing personal. Sure enough, when the new unit, acting on the RLT's advice, resolved the contracting issue, the mortaring stopped overnight.[13]

## III

We'll never know for certain the background to this very minor firefight in Dara-i-Nur, just one of dozens of combat incidents that happened across Afghanistan that day in September 2009. Perhaps my guess, as I pondered the attack on the helicopter ride back to Kabul, was right, and the halfhearted ambush was part of the broader aid-and-contracting-driven pattern of violence that I and many others have observed elsewhere in Afghanistan, and that the Aegis team experienced in Iraq.

Perhaps it had nothing to do with the Taliban and everything to do with perverse incentives created by rapid and uneven development in a tribal society whose economic, social, and agricultural systems have been wrecked by decades of war. No external aid is neutral: a sudden influx of foreign assistance creates a contracting bonanza, benefiting some at others' expense, and in turn provoking conflict. Likewise, it creates spoils over which local power brokers fight for personal gain, to the detriment of the wider community, and can contribute to a sense of entitlement on the part of locals. Access to foreigners, who have lots of money and firepower but little time or inclination to gain an understanding of local dynamics, can give district power brokers incredibly lucrative opportunities for corruption. A tsunami of illicit cash washes over the society, provoking abuse, raising expectations but then disappointing them, and empowering local armed groups, who pose as clean and incorruptible, defenders of the disenfranchised, at least till they themselves gain access to sources of corruption.[14]

Then again, perhaps I was wrong—maybe the Taliban had already infiltrated the district by then, as they certainly did later, and for some reason the local fighters were just having trouble getting it together that day. Ambushes are complex enterprises, the most difficult task an infantry small unit can undertake, and they're won or lost in the first few seconds, with the outcome often decided in the very first burst of fire. Seemingly trivial details—the placement of a key weapon, the angle of the sun, a gust of wind, split-second timing in the moment of the first shot—can have disproportionately large effects. Maybe the ambushers did have a roadside bomb in place but it failed to go off, or perhaps they lacked time to put a bomb in. Another few inches to the left, and the first RPG would have hit the leading MRAP and disabled it in the middle of the bridge, with perhaps a far different outcome for the firefight. The quick response from the patrol—who, in their first real action, showed great composure and professionalism, calmly suppressing the ambush without overreacting— may also have had a lot to do with it.

Either way, it seems clear to me, as I'm sure it does to any reader, that "classical" counterinsurgency theory doesn't explain what happened here. Nor does it explain incidents like the Helmand road contractor attack, the Aegis team's Iraq experience, or the battle of Wanat. Counterinsurgency most certainly offers a partial explanation, and is demonstrably correct as far as it goes. But other factors were at work here, beyond solely the existence of "an organized, protracted politico-military struggle designed to weaken the control and legitimacy of an established government, occupying power, or other political authority while increasing insurgent control."[15] Indeed, it's impossible to determine what actually happened in any of these incidents on the basis of counterinsurgency theory alone.

Not only is it possible that, in all these incidents, local elders were in the driver's seat, not the insurgents, but it's also clear that particular acts of violence may be easier to explain through constructs like relative dep- rivation in aid programming, perceived injustice among ethnic groups or business networks, local and tribal rivalries, perverse economic incentives, and traditional modes of warfare (none of which are specific to counterin- surgency theory, or even to theories of conflict at all) rather than through a counterinsurgency lens.

That day in Dara-i Nur was just one of many days in the field when I've felt a sense of dissonance about our reliance on "pure" or binary the- ories that are framed around the nature of a specific threat group—in this case, a feeling that, for all its power in explaining certain types of conflict, counterinsurgency as a paradigm didn't quite fit the facts on the ground, and did not quite cover the full range of what we were experiencing. I first wrote about this in 2005, and again in 2006, but over time this feeling has grown stronger.[16]

In my work in Iraq, Afghanistan, Pakistan, Somalia, Sri Lanka, Colombia, Libya and other conflict zones over the past several years, I've been lucky enough to gather around me an eclectic (not to say eccentric) team of experts, with deep experience in conflict mitigation, development, diplomacy, rule of law, peace-building, urban design, human rights, community mapping, systems design, alternative energy, conflict resolution and mediation, and other disciplines. As our field teams work with NGOs, aid agencies, institutions like the World Bank, communities, businesses, and governments, our collective sense of unease has grown. More and more, existing models simply don't explain the full range of events we see on the ground. I've explored several frameworks, searching for ways to explain the complex patterns of violence we see in our work.

This book documents some of those attempts to go beyond classical counterinsurgency, in search of models that better explain how conflict happens on the ground, and how local patterns of conflict nest in a wider system of human activity and within broader trends that will shape our planet over the next few decades. This, then, is a book about what may happen after Western military involvement in Afghanistan comes to an end. It's a book about future conflicts and future cities. It's about the challenges and opportunities that population growth, coastal urbanization, and escalating connectivity are creating across the planet. And it's about what governments, cities, communities and businesses (and, of course, the military) can do to prepare for a future in which all aspects of human life—including, but not only, conflict, crime and violence—will be crowded, urban, networked and coastal.

My background is as a student, theorist, and occasional practitioner of guerrilla warfare. So, naturally enough, with a base of field research and personal experience largely shaped by war, I started this book with a focus on conflict, searching for a unified field theory to explain the disconnects I was noticing in places like Dara-i-Nur, and looking for some insight into conflicts involving non-state armed groups—the "forever wars" that drag on across the world, even as conventional wars among nation-states continue to decline.[17]

For various institutional reasons, governments, military forces, law enforcement agencies, and even (perhaps especially) university faculties tend to prefer theories of conflict framed around a single threat—insurgency, terrorism, piracy, narcotics, gangs, organized crime, and so on. This approach—which results in well-known concepts like counter-terrorism, counter-insurgency, counter-piracy and so on—might be fine in a binary environment, where one government confronts one threat at a time, but in the real world—the world of complex, adaptive social systems such as cities, trading networks, and licit or illicit economies—there never has been, and never will be, a single-threat environment like this. Rather, many different groups coexist, compete, cooperate, and clash (sometimes violently), overlapping in, and competing for control over, the same territory and population.

So I wanted to find a set of ideas that would do a better job at explaining the conflict ecosystem—the nonlinear, many-sided, wild, and messy world of real conflict—than do traditional binary paradigms such as counterinsurgency. I suspected such a unified theory might have something to do with the similarities we observe in the ways that nonstate armed groups of all kinds interact with populations they compete to control, and the way those populations manipulate and exploit nonstate armed groups in return. I began to call this set of ideas, which I describe in Chapter 3, the "theory of competitive control."

But as I worked on the theory, between teaching at a university in Washington, D.C., starting and running a strategic research and design firm in northern Virginia, and doing practical fieldwork with conflict-affected communities in many places around the world, I realized that the idea I was examining—a concept that took into account the four emerging megatrends of population growth, urbanization, littoralization, and networked connectivity—wasn't really a theory of *conflict* at all. It was much broader than that.

This is because these megatrends will affect all aspects of life on the planet in the next twenty to thirty years, not just conflict. And communities, companies, and cities that understand these trends, learn how to mitigate the risks they pose, and develop ways to maximize the opportunities they offer are quite likely to thrive in the future environment, while others may go under. My hope is that the reflections that follow, while often tentative or speculative, will at least help to begin a discussion on which others can build.

# I

## Out of the Mountains

According to his son, Omar, Osama bin Laden would routinely
hike from Tora Bora into neighboring Pakistan on walks that could
take anywhere between seven and 14 hours. "My brothers and I all
loathed these grueling treks that seemed the most pleasant of out-
ings to our father," Omar bin Laden later recalled. Bin Laden told
his sons they had to memorize every rock on the routes to Pakistan.
"We never know when war will strike," he instructed them. "We
must know our way out of the mountains."

—Peter Bergen, 2009

### I

One wet, chilly night in New York, I was hanging out with my friend
Steve Eames in the bar of the Bryant Park Hotel, in Manhattan's Fashion
District. It was October 2007, I was just back from Baghdad, and the dark,
crowded, hipster vibe of the place—not to mention the claustrophobic
feel of the enormous coastal city—was mildly freaking me out.

Steve and I joined the army together in 1985. We were classmates at
Duntroon, Australia's military academy; both of us graduated into the
infantry, and both of us served in airmobile light infantry units and military advisory missions across Southeast Asia and the Pacific. Steve did
a tour with the Special Air Service Regiment (Australia's top-tier elite
special operations unit, equivalent to the U.S. Army's Delta Force) before
leaving the army to become, by turns, an environmental activist, NGO
advocate, war correspondent, industrial security planner in North Africa,
and free trade zone developer in the Arabian Gulf. He eventually specialized in planning large-scale sporting events. Over a fifteen-year career
designing public safety systems for some of the world's biggest cities, he'd
worked several Olympics, Asian Games, and Commonwealth Games.

I was tired, after what turned out later to have been the worst months of the Iraq war, but relieved that the counterinsurgency techniques we'd designed under fire in Baghdad seemed to be working and were starting to save Iraqi and Allied lives. Over a nine-month period these techniques had brought civilian deaths in the city down from hundreds, sometimes thousands per week, in late 2006, to a few dozen at most by mid-2007—still tragic, but a massive drop in violence. I allowed myself to hope that we might have given Iraqis breathing space to pull back from what had been shaping up as an incredibly nasty sectarian genocide. Steve was unconvinced.

"You killed the city, mate. You know that, right?"

"What? Piss off."

"Seriously. All that barbed wire, concrete barriers, checkpoints. You shut the city down. You stopped it flowing—put it on life support. You stopped people getting around to do what they had to do. You cut the violence, sure, but you did it by killing the city."

"All right," I said, "you're so smart, how would you have done it?"

And Steve pointed out what every police officer, paramedic, traffic engineer, and social worker knows, and what should have been obvious to me all along: a city is a living organism that flows and breathes, and any public safety solution that no longer lets it flow is no solution at all.

In Olympic security, for example, Steve explained, it's not enough to make sporting venues safe: if spectators and players can't get to the events or people can't go undisrupted about their business in the wider city, that would be a fail. In urban counterinsurgency, just keeping people safe is a failure, too: true success involves achieving an agreed level of service—an acceptable minimum level of disruption that lets the city flow—while also getting violence down to a level that people can accept. Of course, in Olympic security, organizers set up a system of cleared zones, connecting corridors, charter agreements with local communities, and so on—a layered all-hazards defensive system that considers every risk and threat—not just, say, a terrorist attack. But it's usually temporary: after a few months, the organizers dismantle the system and let the city go back to how it was before.

We began to speculate. What if we could combine what I'd learned in Baghdad about protecting urban populations from extreme violence with what law enforcement agencies know about community-based policing, city governments know about maintaining a functioning urban environment, and the Olympic community knows about achieving security while preserving urban flow? Could we craft an approach that would replicate the security-plus-service model of a big sporting event, but on a permanent basis? Was that even feasible in a place such as Baghdad, or would traditional civilian methods just break down above a certain level of violence? Could we design into the city itself the public safety systems that would both keep people safe *and* keep the city flowing? Could we forge the same level-of-service agreements and security charters that people enter into for the temporary purpose of Olympic security, but keep them in place for the long term? Would communities agree to that, even given the alternatives? Could we build in what civic architects know about urban metabolism and create a community-based system to secure a city as a living organism, not just a piece of urbanized terrain? And if we could retrofit that system to an existing city, could we also build it in from the outset to a new city or industrial site?

None of these ideas is the slightest bit revolutionary: many cities in the developed world already embody just these kinds of systems. London, for example, has the world's most sophisticated wide-area television surveillance system, and many of the measures put in place for the 2012 Olympic Games remained afterward, despite controversies over lack of community participation in decisions on surveillance, security, and urban disruption.[1] Nor is this new: as any student of urban history knows, when you walk through the cityscape of Paris, for example, you're moving in an interlocked defensive system of urban zones, built around design principles that include securing the state against a restive population.

Central Paris was designed in the 1850s by Baron Georges-Eugène Haussmann. Haussmann was the prefect of the Seine *département* (and among other things, de facto chief of homeland security for Emperor Napoleon III). Haussmann's boss knew about urban uprisings: it was the 1848 revolution that prompted his return from exile to become president of the French Republic, and when he overthrew that republic and seized power as emperor in 1851, he had to put down an uprising led by, among others, Victor Hugo, author of *Les Misérables*. Haussmann's Paris was designed—consciously and intensively—to prevent a recurrence of the kind of unrest that had affected the city for generations. He laid out wide, straight boulevards that just happened to be exactly one cavalry squadron wide (rather handy, in the event of riots) and created spacious squares that dominated the boulevards so that the state could put artillery on each square (and, if needed, sweep the streets between them with grapeshot). He imposed architectural codes that ensured buildings were set back at an angle from street corners—creating a delightful sense of light and air at street level but also, incidentally, making it far harder for demonstrators to put up barricades. Haussmann resettled unruly populations away from traditional urban strongholds that were hard for troops and police to penetrate—Hugo called them "narrow, uneven, sinuous streets full of turns and corners . . . a network of streets more intricate than a forest"[2]—and moved them to outlying districts into which the French state could more easily extend its authority. Haussmann placed railway stations and bridges to help troops and police maneuver quickly around the city, to stifle any revolution. The completed "Haussmann system" transformed central Paris from a wild, jungle-like thicket into a formal, manicured garden: it facilitated state control of the capital, while the process of constructing all those boulevards, buildings, and squares created jobs for disaffected workers and thus acted as a safety valve for public unrest.

Many people are rightly concerned by the authoritarian tendencies that lie behind these kinds of urban systems, even while also recognizing that the alternative—as people had just lived it in Baghdad—might be even worse. In a free society, there's clearly a balance to be struck between the risk of violence from insurgency, crime, or social chaos (nonstate violence, if you like) and the risk of state repression. This was exactly the problem in Iraq, with ordinary people caught between nonstate violence from Sunni extremists, on one hand, and state violence from the Shi'a-dominated Iraqi National Police, on the other. Could we, then, help a neighborhood become self-defending against all comers, making people both safer from nonstate violence *and* harder for the state to oppress? Would it be possible, on the basis of a charter agreement co-designed with local inhabitants, to work with rather than against a community, to help people design security into the actual fabric of their urban landscape? This would not just make it harder for militias, gangs and insurgents to prey on people but also minimize the need for security forces to flood into a threatened area—a cure that many citizens might think was worse than the disease. In Baghdad, as in many places where Steve and I had worked, adding troops and cops wouldn't necessarily make people safer: it might just give them more opportunities to get shaken down. And for an overstretched police service or a military lacking the numbers for counterinsurgency, this system would allow a far smaller force to secure a much greater area, making better use of scarce assets.

Our brief drink became a long discussion: we cleared the whiskey glasses off the table, drew some maps and system diagrams, and tried to pull together the outlines of an approach. That first discussion became many more sessions, then structured design workshops over computer models and satellite photographs, then a long-term collaboration with Steve, my team at Caerus, software designers, architects, and an Oslo-based urban design firm. Over the years we've jointly developed a methodology that combines all the elements mentioned above, working on design solutions for cities as diverse as Kandahar, Muscat, and Rio de Janeiro, and developing community participative maps and urban violence models for cities in Liberia, Nigeria, and Honduras and for the U.S.-Mexico border area.

This chapter sets the scene for the rest of this book. It lays out some of the insights that emerged from these conversations, from the field experiments and projects that followed, and from the wider body of research on what things will be like on the future planet. It's an attempt to formulate what it is about the urban, networked environment that makes conflict there so different from conflict in places such as Dara-i-Nur, before we begin (in the chapters that follow) to describe how real-world conflict happens on the ground today.

## II

Since the start of this century many soldiers, diplomats, and aid workers have had their heads in the Afghan mountains. Governments have expended enormous effort on hunting down fast-moving, lightly equipped bands of guerrillas in the world's most forbidding terrain. Aid agencies have grappled with the need to stabilize and reconstruct the remote communities where these guerrillas operate. But if, as I'll show in this book, the future is actually going to be urban, networked, and coastal, then the issues that Steve and I were discussing—the need to ensure that cities can both meet their populations' needs and preserve people's safety—will be the main challenges of the next generation. To deal with them, we'll need to get ourselves, mentally and physically, out of the mountains.[3]

International troops have left Iraq, and most will leave Afghanistan by the end of 2014. But there will be strong elements of continuity after these conflicts wind down. Formally declared warfare among nation-states, for example, is likely to keep getting rarer, while violence involving nonstate armed groups (whether we call it "war" or "crime") will probably remain the most common and widespread form of conflict.[4] As just one example of this, we might note the long-standing historical pattern in which the United States conducts a large-scale or long-duration counterinsurgency or stabilization operation about once a generation and a small or short-term mission about once every five to ten years—far more often than it gets into declared wars against other nation-states.[5]

Since the mid-nineteenth century, in fact, the United States has been drawn into literally dozens of small wars and irregular operations. Even the few conventional wars during this period—including the U.S. Civil War, the Spanish-American War, the First and Second World Wars, and the Korean War—involved guerrilla conflict, stability operations, and postconflict nation building. The Spanish-American War, for example, triggered a drawn-out and controversial counterinsurgency campaign in the Philippines, and several follow-on operations in Cuba.[6] During the Korean War, which is generally regarded as "conventional," General Douglas MacArthur's landing at Incheon (discussed in the Appendix) stranded thousands of North Korean troops behind United Nations lines—they fought as guerrillas for several years, preying on local villagers, creating no-go areas, and attacking lines of communication. It took a major effort, over several years, to deal with this threat.[7] Likewise, the 1991 Gulf War, the quickest and most cleanly conventional of recent American conflicts, brought with it a long tail of humanitarian, enforcement, and stabilization operations. These included the northern and southern no-fly zones, a major U.S. Air Force effort intended to deter Saddam Hussein from reprisals against the Iraqi people, and Operation Provide Comfort, a humanitarian assistance effort that kept U.S. troops on the ground in Iraqi Kurdistan more than five years after the hundred-hour ground war was over.[8]

This pattern of frequent irregular warfare—the military term for conflict that involves nonstate armed groups—seems to be totally independent of policy makers' preferences.[9] In particular, presidential desire (or lack of desire) to carry out these operations has no detectable impact on how often they occur. President Lyndon Johnson, for example, considered Vietnam a distraction from his domestic goals, yet oversaw an escalation that drew almost six hundred thousand U.S. troops into the war at its peak in 1968. President Bill Clinton came into office with a similarly domestic focus and a desire to avoid overseas entanglements. He delayed committing troops to the Balkans and sidestepped Rwanda altogether, scarred by a failed intervention in Somalia. Yet he ultimately sent troops to Bosnia, Kosovo, Macedonia, Haiti, and Liberia, maintained no-fly zones against Iraq (including a major air campaign in 1998), and deployed ships and planes to support the Australian-led intervention in East Timor in 1999. As a presidential candidate, George W. Bush opposed stability operations and derided nation building. But as president, he led the United States into its largest war since Vietnam, its largest nation-building effort since World War II, and the largest NATO stabilization operation ever. He committed forces to not one but two simultaneous large-scale counterinsurgency campaigns, along with counterterrorism and nation-building interventions worldwide. None of these presidents had any subjective desire to get involved in irregular conflict: all of them did so anyway, and all at about the same rate as their predecessors.

In January 2012 President Obama became the latest in the long line of leaders to express a desire to avoid this kind of conflict. In his guidance to the Defense Department, the president signaled a rebalancing toward Asia and the Pacific in the aftermath of wars in Afghanistan and Iraq, and directed that U.S. forces "no longer be sized to conduct large-scale, prolonged stability operations."[10] If we leave aside the inconvenient reality that the Afghan war was, even at that time, far from over (and that conflicts were ongoing in Iraq, Syria, Yemen, Somalia, Mali, Nigeria, and the Congo), history suggests that the president's directive, even though undoubtedly sincere and well intentioned, won't change much. Leon Trotsky said, "You may not be interested in war, but war is interested in you." American policy makers clearly don't like irregular operations, and the U.S. military isn't much interested in them, either, as an institution.

But the deep structure of American engagement with the world, over at least the past 150 years, has meant that the military ends up doing these operations anyway, much more often than it does conventional state-on-state wars.

To be sure, new technologies—drones and offensive cyberwarfare, for example, both of which are discussed in Chapter 4—give policy makers ways to avoid putting boots on the ground, and we're already seeing more emphasis on what we might call remote warfare as part of what some have dubbed the "Obama Doctrine."[11] But literally dozens of new technologies have entered the arsenal over the past 150 years, without any detectable effect on the number of irregular operations. If anything, these technologies may make policy makers *more* likely to intervene in future conflicts, because they offer the tempting possibility of fewer troops deployed, fewer body bags coming home, and less political controversy, through the promise of a lighter "footprint."

This history suggests that there will be a strong, continuing demand into the foreseeable future for military operations against a variety of nonstate actors, and not just for the United States: in 2013 alone, the French undertook a major irregular intervention in Mali, British forces deployed to several countries in Africa and Asia, Australian troops were operating in East Timor and several Pacific islands as well as in Afghanistan, twenty-seven nations contributed ships to a naval anti-piracy task force in the Gulf of Aden, there were regional peacekeeping and counterinsurgency operations all over Asia and Africa, and many other countries were engaged in military operations against nonstate armed groups.

But the evidence also suggests that the future environment—the *context* for these operations—will differ radically from what we've known since 9/11. In particular, research on demography and economic geography suggests that four megatrends are driving most aspects of future life on the planet, including conflict. These are rapid population growth, accelerating urbanization, littoralization (the tendency for things to cluster on coastlines), and increasing connectedness. If we add the potential for climate-change effects such as coastal flooding, and note that almost all the world's population growth will happen in coastal cities in low-income, sometimes unstable countries, we can begin to grasp the complex challenges that lurk in this future environment.

*Crowded, Coastal, Connected Cities*

As I just noted, Western governments and militaries have focused since the turn of the century on wars like those in Afghanistan. This is the world of the Dara-i-Nur ambush I described in the preface: a place of mountain terrain, micropolitics, and remote villages, where outsiders move—only half understanding what they see—in a landscape defined by centuries of tradition and by a harsh and unchanging geography. The last decade has also, of course, seen intense urban fighting, mainly in Iraq—from high-intensity battles such as in Fallujah or Ramadi to urban insurgency in Baghdad or Basra.

Urban warfare in Iraq had a huge impact on the American military, but its international effect was far less pronounced. For one thing, although roughly the same number of governments sent troops to Iraq as to Afghanistan (fifty in Iraq versus fifty-one in Afghanistan), far fewer sent *combat* troops to Iraq, so a smaller number of countries bore the brunt of the actual fighting.[12] For another, the Iraq war was very concentrated in time and space. Almost all the fighting happened between 2004 and 2008, with by far the heaviest combat occurring from March 2006 to September 2007, the deadliest eighteen months in Iraq's modern history. During this period, as for much of the war, the violence was concentrated in Baghdad. In 2006, for example, almost twice as many civilians were killed in Baghdad city as in the rest of the country combined.[13] As I wrote while preparing to deploy to Iraq in January 2007, almost half of all combat incidents at that time happened within the Baghdad city limits, in a purely U.S.-Iraqi operational sector.[14] Thus Americans and Iraqis experienced sustained, heavy urban combat, but most others—with the sole significant exception of the British in Basra—were lucky enough to miss this experience, either because they didn't send combat troops or because their soldiers were in more rural, less violent areas outside the capital.

So, by default, Afghanistan has been the defining experience of modern conflict for many of the developed world's armies and air forces—the model, in effect, for twenty-first-century warfare. And the war in Afghanistan, unlike Iraq, is extremely diffuse. The conflict is spread across the country, and the heaviest fighting happens mostly in rural areas, far from Afghanistan's cities—which, for most of the war, have been far safer than the countryside. To be sure, as the counterinsurgency fight intensified in 2010–12, the Taliban shifted to urban attacks (bombings, drive-by assassinations, and raids) and the level of guerrilla fighting in the countryside dropped in relative terms. But in absolute terms, the war is still mainly one of small mountain villages, farming areas, and frontier valleys.

Also, in both Iraq and Afghanistan, the heaviest fighting was far from coastlines. Afghanistan, of course, is landlocked, and the parts of Iraq that saw the worst of the conflict were also a long way from the coast. Again, the British experience in the Faw Peninsula (discussed in the Appendix) and in the coastal city of Basra was the sole important exception to this pattern. It was an exception that proves the rule, though, since it only emphasized how rare coastal fighting has been for Western forces in twenty-first-century conflict so far. But the urban littoral will indeed be the arena for much of future conflict, simply because it will be where most people live, according to currently available data.

### Imagining Future War

These data don't permit specific predictions, of course—only general projections based on current trends. It's absolutely certain that there will be outliers, shocks, and nonlinear shifts. There will be disruptive technologies, political discontinuities, and "black swans."[15] Specific future wars will undoubtedly happen in a range of environments and conditions, and landlocked rural mountainous areas will of course continue to see a share of conflict proportional to their share of population. It's just that, since the population of the planet is shifting from rural to urban areas, that proportion will be a diminishing part of the whole.

Thus, just as climate projections don't say much about tomorrow's weather, projections of current trends say little about future wars. But they do suggest a range of conditions—a set of system parameters, or a "conflict climate"—within which those wars will arise. This is because, as the anthropologist Harry Turney-High suggested more than thirty years ago, social, economic, political, and communications arrangements influence war making so profoundly that "warfare *is* social organization."[16] Thus, the specifics of a particular war may be impossible to predict, but the parameters within which *any* future war will occur are entirely knowable, since wars are bounded by conditions that exist now, and are thus eminently observable in today's social, economic, geographic, and demographic climate.

If we accept this idea, along with the fact that war has been endemic to roughly 95 percent of all known human societies throughout history and prehistory, it follows that warfare is a central and probably a permanent human social institution, one that tends (by its very nature as a *human* activity) mainly to occur where the people are.[17] This is especially true of nonstate conflicts (guerrilla, tribal, and civil wars, or armed criminal activity such as banditry and gang warfare), which tend to happen near or within the areas where people live, or on major routes between population centers.[18] And it follows that since the places where people live are getting increasingly crowded, urban, coastal and networked, the wars people fight will take on the same characteristics.

We can summarize the conflict climate in terms of four drivers, sometimes called megatrends, that are shaping and defining it. These are *population growth* (the continuing rise in the planet's total population), *urbanization* (the tendency for people to live in larger and larger cities), *littoralization* (the propensity for these cities to cluster on coastlines), and *connectedness* (the increasing connectivity among people, wherever they live). None of these trends is new, but their pace is accelerating, they're mutually reinforcing, and their intersection will influence not just conflict but every aspect of future life.

Population growth and urbanization are closely related. More and more people are living in larger and larger cities, and the greatest growth is in the low-income (sometimes poorly governed) areas of Asia, Africa, and Latin America that are least equipped to handle it. This is easy to see if we just look at the numbers. At the start of the industrial revolution in 1750, world population was about 750 million. This population took 150 years to double, reaching 1.5 billion in 1900. It then doubled again in only 60 years, to reach 3 billion by 1960. This, of course, represents a sharp increase in population growth—one that occurred despite the enormous effects of the two world wars, which between them killed more than 70 million people.[19] Population growth kept accelerating after 1960, with the world population doubling yet again in only 39 years, to reach 6 billion by 1999, and adding another billion in just one decade to reach a total (in 2012) of about 7.1 billion. This growth won't continue indefinitely: global population is expected to level off at somewhere between 9.1 and 9.3 billion humans on the planet by about 2050.[20] Still, that's a lot of people—about a twelve fold increase in just three centuries.

As population has grown, urbanization has accelerated. In 1800, for example, only 3 percent of people lived in a city with 1 million inhabitants or more; by the year 2000, 47 percent of the global population lived in cities this size. In 1950, there were only 83 cities with populations over 1 million; by 2007, there were 468. By April 2008, the world had passed the 50 percent urbanization mark, and in December 2011, the world's most populous nation, China, announced that it had reached a level of 51.3 percent urbanization.[21] India, with the second-largest population on the planet, will not only overtake China's population by 2025 but will also undergo a radical shift in settlement patterns, going from approximately two-thirds rural in 2012 to two-thirds urban by 2040. Some Indian population centers will become megacities, and "according to one vision, India's entire western seaboard could turn into a single conurbation . . . within two decades India will probably have six cities considerably bigger than New York, each with at least 10 million people."[22] By 2050, roughly 75 percent of the world's population will be urbanized. In more immediate terms, about 1.4 million people across the world migrate to a city every week.[23]

This unprecedented urbanization is concentrated in low-income areas of Asia, Latin America, and Africa. Cities are expected to absorb *all* the new population growth on the planet by 2050, while simultaneously drawing in millions of migrants from rural areas. And this growth will be "concentrated in the cities and towns of the less developed regions. Asia, in particular, is projected to see its urban population increase by 1.7 billion, Africa by 0.8 billion, and Latin America and the Caribbean by 0.2 billion."[24] What this means is that population growth is becoming "an urban phenomenon concentrated in the developing world."[25]

To put it another way, these data show that the world's cities are about to be swamped by a human tide that will force them to absorb—in just one generation—the same population growth that occurred across the entire planet in all of recorded history up to 1960. And virtually all this urbanization will happen in the world's poorest areas—a recipe for conflict, for crises in health, education, and governance, and for food, energy, and water scarcity.[26]

I should mention that many places affected by rapid urbanization happen to be majority-Muslim, and that *takfiri* extremists—successors and imitators of Osama bin Laden—will undoubtedly keep threatening their own societies and the world at large. Indeed, the freedom from repression that emerged from the Arab Awakening—in itself an entirely positive thing—may have prompted a spike in violence in these parts of the world, at least for the time being. Thus the Muslim world certainly won't be spared the disruption we're discussing here; indeed, it may experience more conflict and unrest than other parts of the planet. But the challenges I'm describing will dwarf the terrorist threat of the last decade. If a city's infrastructure is collapsing—overwhelmed by a rapidly growing population, unplanned slum development, political instability, violent crime, conflict, disease, increased vulnerability to natural disaster, and shortages of energy, food, and water—then the fact that extremists are also out there will of course be highly unpleasant and dangerous, but it will be far from the main threat. Groups such as Al Qaeda will still exist and will pose a danger that needs to be dealt with one way or another. But the main cluster of threats, both for individuals (sometimes known as threats to *human security*) and from a collective standpoint (threats to *public safety* or *national security*), will come from the environment itself, not from any one group in it.

The next key trend in that environment is *littoralization*—an unwieldy word that just means the tendency for things to cluster on coastlines. Urban growth isn't evenly spread: rather, cities are concentrated in coastal (littoral) areas, within a few dozen miles of the sea. Already in 2012, 80 percent of people on the planet lived within sixty miles of the sea, while 75 percent of large cities were on a coast.[27] Of twenty-five megacities (cities with 10 million or more inhabitants) at the turn of the twenty-first century, twenty-one were on a coast or a major river delta, while only four (Moscow, Beijing, Delhi, and Teheran) lay inland.[28] By 2010, of the world's ten largest cities, all but two were on a coastline or coastal delta.[29]

Alongside the generic meaning of *littoral* as "coastal," the term *littoral zone* has a specific military meaning, defined by available weapon systems. In a military sense, a littoral zone is the portion of land space that can be engaged using sea-based weapon systems, plus the adjacent sea space (surface and subsurface) that can be engaged using land-based weapon systems, and the surrounding airspace and cyberspace. In other words, a littoral zone is the sea space you can hit from the land, the land you can hit from the sea, and the airspace and cyberspace above both. Obviously enough, the area you can hit depends on the weapon you're using, so as weapons get more capable and longer in range, the size of the area defined as "littoral" grows accordingly. Also, obviously, areas that are littoral for a military with long-range weapons and strike platforms may not be so for another military with shorter-range systems. However large or small littoral zones may be, the interaction among mutually influencing sea, land, air, and cyber spaces makes such zones highly complex systems that are vastly more dynamic than the sum of their parts.[30]

The presence of ever-larger cities in this zone, with increasing population density, more intensive land usage, heavier ground movement, and busier air and sea traffic, makes an already complex system even denser and more complicated. For this reason, operations in littoral zones are very different from either continental (entirely land-based) or maritime (purely sea-air) operations. The practical effect of all this is that a huge proportion of the world's population now lives in what we might call the "littoral influence zone"—a zone that, depending on available weapons, can stretch more than a hundred miles inland, and twice that distance offshore.

One illustration of this occurred on the night of November 25, 2001, when Marines commanded by then Brigadier General James Mattis seized America's first base in Afghanistan. This daring operation was the longest helicopter raid in history. It involved a night flight of 689 kilometers (370 nautical miles), from a ship at sea, by an assault force of Marines in troop-carrying helicopters, supported by attack helicopters and air-to-air refueling tankers. A team of Navy SEALs went in, four days before the assault, to conduct covert reconnaissance. The SEALs took real-time photographs of the site and emailed them back to the personal computers of planners on board the USS *Peleliu*, an amphibious assault ship operating in the Arabian Sea off the coast of Pakistan.[31] On the night of the raid, troop-carrying helicopters launched from *Peleliu*, refueled in midair en route to the objective, and captured the site—an airstrip in southern Afghanistan, later known as Forward Operating Base (FOB) Rhino—without opposition. Once the strip was secured, transport aircraft brought in follow-on troops and expanded the Marines' foothold. There is nothing obviously "coastal" about a remote, landlocked airstrip, far from the sea, in the middle of the Afghan desert. Yet the seizure of FOB Rhino was an outstanding example of littoral warfare—enabled by capabilities such as extended-range helicopters, air-to-air refueling, long-range communications and surveillance, and deep-penetration special operations. Modern naval forces can thus bring areas far from the sea into the littoral influence zone: the whole of Southeast Asia, the entire Mediterranean basin, and large parts of Australia, Africa, South America, and Central America are thus "littoral" in this sense, even when far from the sea.

At the same time, patterns of coastal urbanization suggest that the number of people on the planet who live in this littoral influence zone is very high and growing fast. In the Mediterranean basin alone, the urban coastal population grew by 40 million between 1970 and 2000, and three-quarters of that growth was in North Africa and the Middle East.[32] The Maghreb (Muslim northwest Africa), in particular, has exceptionally high rates of coastal urbanization, "striking examples being Libya (85 percent), Tunisia (70 percent), Morocco (51 percent) and Turkey (52 percent)."[33] The two most urbanized of these countries (Tunisia and Libya) were also the most heavily affected by revolutions during the Arab Spring of 2011, while the uprisings in Egypt occurred almost entirely in a triangle of cities that all lie within a hundred miles of the sea, squarely within the littoral influence zone of the Mediterranean.

These uprisings also saw the use of cell phones, social media, and text messaging as organizing tools, along with cross-pollination among activists in neighboring countries and the involvement of international media (all of which are described in detail in Chapter 4). This highlights the third major trend in the future environment: the world's newly urban populations are highly connected and networked.

This *connectedness* is both an internal and external feature of coastal cities, and it's an entirely new phenomenon. As I noted in the introduction, factors such as population growth and coastal urbanization were very well understood in the 20th century—in the 1990s, many military theorists and urban planners were writing and speaking about the planet's emerging urban littorals. But this was in the pre-cellphone area, before Internet access became common in the developing world, before satellite TV was widespread. What's new today is the entirely unprecedented level of connectedness that these tools allow—and this changes the picture in some very important ways. In particular, connectedness has expanded dramatically, and is continuing to expand, not only within coastal cities but also between them and their hinterlands, from city to city, and between home populations and global networks, including diaspora populations.

If you fly in a helicopter above any coastal city or slum settlement in the developing world, the most obvious rooftop feature is the forest of satellite dishes, TV antennas, and radio masts. This is just the most prominent visual indicator of how connected these areas are becoming. Indeed, in transitional and periurban areas (the informal settlements, slums, and townships that aggregate around the margins of cities and absorb a high proportion of new immigrants from the countryside) people can connect with national and international information flows to an unprecedented degree, however ineffective their government.

For example, a 2011 study found that Somalia, a country that has experienced near-anarchy and state collapse for twenty years, has rates of cell phone usage approaching 25 percent—far greater than its neighbors, including relatively well-administered Ethiopia—and that there has been a remarkable proliferation of telecommunications companies offering "inexpensive and high-quality services . . . including internet access, international calls, and mobile connectivity. Some of them are closely connected with the remittance industry."[34] This vibrant remittance system is another major indicator of the connectivity between coastal cities such as Mogadishu, Somalia's largest urban area, and the Somali diaspora (roughly 800,000 people worldwide—about 10 percent of the total Somali population).[35] As one visitor to Mogadishu noted in 2011, "older parts of the city were falling apart, but the people there were still connected to the outside world via satellite dishes that were installed on roofs that leaked. In fact, one of my most enduring memories of Mogadishu is that of satellite dishes everywhere, even in areas that were heavily-controlled by militia."[36] This connectivity lets urban Somalis tap into global networks for the exchange of money and information, allows them to engage in trade, and lets them pursue legitimate business (such as mobile phone companies).[37]

Of course, people who live in rural areas without cellphone coverage can't access these connectivity-enabled overseas sources of support. Thus, greater access to global systems of exchange—something that's available only from well-connected urban locations—has become a major reason for people to migrate to cities, increasing the pace of urbanization. This is just one part of a broader pattern of economic change, driven by increasing global connectedness, that has seen investment by diaspora networks replace agricultural surplus as one of the main drivers of rural-to-urban migration in low-income countries.[38]

The same connectivity that drives diaspora investment and licit trade, of course, also enables illicit flows such as people smuggling; the trafficking of weapons, drugs, and other contraband; piracy; and terrorism. One example of an illicit flow is charcoal export from Somalia—an environmentally devastating activity that destroys precious tree cover in sparsely vegetated semidesert areas. The United Nations banned the trade in February 2012, due to its connection with interclan violence and the Shabaab terrorist group: clans were basically fighting each other for the right to burn off Somalia's few remaining trees and sell the ashes to foreigners. This destructive trade exploits the connectedness among coastal cities in the Horn of Africa, throughout the Arabian Gulf, and in the Red Sea. It relies on Somali and Arab coastal shipping and on groups such as Shabaab, which seek access to funds and are willing to trade (on any basis, licit or illicit) in order to get it.[39] In a failed state—as Somalia was for the past two decades—concepts such as "illicit networks" ring hollow anyway, since no authority exists to declare things licit in the first place.

In a deeper sense, networks themselves, by definition, are neither licit nor illicit. *Behavior* may be licit or illicit; networks just are. People self-organize in networks of all kinds, and they use those networks to engage in complex hybrid patterns of illicit *and* licit behavior. In this context, in common with researchers such as Sean Everton, I prefer to think of "dark networks"—dark in the sense that they are invisible to the naked eye.[40] We might think of them as subterranean rivers of connectivity that run below and between the elements of the world we see. They can't be observed directly unless we do something to stimulate the network, drawing a detectable response that illuminates it. The mere fact that a network is "dark" just means it's not immediately visible—a systems characteristic that implies no value judgment on what the network does. In particular, the fact that a network is dark doesn't mean it's nefarious, nor that it's engaged in harmful activity: indeed, in the real world, dark networks engage in many kinds of activities, beneficial, neutral, and harmful, all at the same time. Understanding the presence of these networks, their multipurpose nature, and the way their flows intersect is one of the key things we need to do if we hope to understand the future environment.

Obviously enough, urbanization increases connectedness: as rural-to-urban migration continues, the newly urbanized populations that cluster in periurban settlements around an older city core may look marginalized (they literally live on the city's margins, of course, and they may be sidelined in economic and social justice terms), but electronic communications, media, and financial systems connect them with people in their home villages and with relatives and friends overseas. And because large transportation nodes (such as airports, container hubs, or seaports) are often in transitional or periurban areas and tend to draw much of their workforce from these areas, periurban populations are closely connected with international trade and with transportation and migration patterns, both internal and external. This is especially true in coastal cities: as the economic geographer Gordon Hanson argues, "when joined with globalization and developments in export-led manufacturing, coastal ports and nearby cities have greater access to international markets, thus providing key advantages for economic growth."[41] This means that the apparently marginalized populations of the new coastal urban sprawl aren't really marginal at all: on the contrary, they're central to the global system as we know it.

At the city level, workers from periurban areas often do the menial, manual, technical, or distasteful work that keeps an urban core functioning, and they sit astride key communication nodes that connect a city to the external world as well as to its food, energy, and water supplies. Wealthy neighborhoods tend to rely on services provided by workers who can't afford to live in the upscale areas where they work, and who thus commute from outlying or transitional areas. Periurban areas therefore represent a kind of social connective tissue between a country's urban centers and its rural periphery, connect that periphery to international networks (much as, say, the port facilities in the coastal city of Karachi connect Pakistan's hinterland with the enormous Pakistani diaspora), and at the global level play a connective role in patterns of transportation, migration, finance, and trade. This exact phenomenon, as we shall see in Chapter 4, lay behind the rapid spread of uprisings during the Arab Spring.

### Getting Swamped

Taking these four megatrends together, we can see a clear pattern. Rapid urban growth in coastal, underdeveloped areas is overloading economic, social, and governance systems, straining city infrastructure, and overburdening the carrying capacity of cities designed for much smaller populations. This is likely to make the most vulnerable cities less and less able to meet the challenges of population growth, coastal urbanization, and connectedness. The implications for future conflict are profound, with more people competing for scarcer resources in crowded, underserviced, and undergoverned urban areas.

Lagos, capital of Nigeria, is one city that exemplifies both the positive and negative aspects of this kind of rapid urban growth. As the visiting journalist Josh Eells noted in May 2012:

> In the past five years, Lagos has exploded. Current estimates put the population somewhere between 15 and 18 million, with an annual growth rate of around 6 percent—one of the fastest-growing cities on the planet. By 2025 it's expected to top 25 million, making it the third-largest city in the world, after Mumbai and Tokyo. The result is a place stretched to its breaking point: a Dickensian conurbation of overcrowded slums and nonexistent services. It's also in some ways a city of the future: what happens when democracy, industrialization, and unchecked population growth collide in the developing world.[42]

Lagos has the population of a megacity but the infrastructure of a mid-sized town. The city has only sixty-eight working traffic lights, making traffic "a force of nature"—"Lagosians have words for traffic the way Eskimos have words for snow: congestion, logjam, lockdown, holdup, gridlock, deadlock, and the wonderfully evocative go-slow. Horror stories abound: police attacking motorists with bullwhips, taxi drivers getting into fistfights, angry commuters backing over policemen with their SUVs."[43]

It's not all bad: Lagos is also a city with an amazing capacity for community-driven innovation and self-organization. It has radio stations that specialize in reporting traffic, crime, and road conditions in particular districts, drawing on self-synchronized networks of motorists and road users who text and dial in, to create locally tailored networks that help people navigate complex conditions safely.[44] *Lagos* is Spanish for "lakes," of course, and the city is an exemplar of the future in this way, too: it's built around a series of coastal swamps, low-lying islands, and lagoons—and no part of the city is more than sixteen feet above sea level. The implications for Lagos of climate change and a rise in sea level are thus potentially profound.

The Asian Development Bank estimated in 2011 that drought, desert-ification, and soil salinity, exacerbated by climate change, will prompt millions of rural people to migrate to cities over coming decades across Asia and the Pacific alone. As the bank's researchers noted, "the region is home to more than 4 billion people and some of the fastest growing cities in the world. By 2020, 13 of the world's 25 megacities, most of them situated in coastal areas, will be in Asia and the Pacific. Climate change will likely exacerbate existing pressures on key resources asso-ciated with growth, urbanization and industrialization."[45] A growing body of research is emphasizing the implications of climate change for coastal urbanization, where the slightest rise in sea level can cause major disruption.[46] Whether or not you believe in human-made climate change, the fact is that even without any sea level rise, coastal urbani-zation will, by definition, put more of the world's population at risk of flooding, creating greater demand for flood-related disaster relief (as we'll see in the case of Dhaka, Bangladesh, in Chapter 5). Floods are already the most common natural disaster in the heavily urbanized Mediterranean basin, for example, and by far the most frequent natural disaster to which aid agencies and donors such as the World Bank have to respond—and as more people cluster in coastal cities, this will only increase.[47]

Another side effect of the combination of climate change, coastal urbanization, and connectedness is a rise in infectious disease. Several studies have correlated slum settlements (particularly those created through rapid unplanned urbanization) with increased risk of insect-borne diseases such as malaria.[48] Infectious diseases are more prevalent in urban areas, and seasonal flooding—which happens more often in coastal cities, of course—has been suggested as a major cause of increased disease transmission risk.[49] At the same time, megacities create global population-mixing effects, and this makes traditional local-level approaches for disease surveillance, response, and public communication much less effective.[50] People who live in transitional or periurban areas interact with residents of the densely populated urban cores where they work, and with users of public transportation systems, airports, and seaports. Combined with the global transmission belt of increased world-wide air and sea travel, and greater connectivity across the planet, this creates pathways for the extremely rapid global spread of infectious or exotic diseases—something that was seen in recent pandemic influenza episodes and in cases of bird flu.[51]

The food security effects of coastal urbanization are equally severe. Increased pollution from growing coastal cities depletes fish stocks. Fisheries that were once key sources of food for coastal towns begin to collapse under the pressure of unchecked population growth, bringing increased pollution and overfishing. This is particularly severe in low-income countries, where coastal megacities lack effective wastewater treatment systems, so enormous amounts of raw sewage flow directly into rivers and the sea. At the beginning of the twenty-first century, for example, Pakistan's largest coastal city, Karachi, generated a million cubic meters of sewage every day, creating a massive amount of coastal pollution.[52] Karachi (discussed in Chapter 2) has the largest fishing fleet in Pakistan, mainly comprising small boats that operate close to the coast, so increased coastal pollution prompted by urban growth could put a serious dent in Pakistan's fisheries and in the livelihoods and diets of Karachi's inhabitants.[53]

Onshore, meanwhile, the newly urbanized areas that surround an older city core absorb territory that was once occupied by farmland, market gardens, and orchards. As slums and unplanned housing developments expand into this space, the distance between a city's population and the food sources on which it depends increases significantly. Food has to be produced farther away and transported over ever-greater distances, increasing transportation and refrigeration costs, raising fuel usage, exacerbating pollution and traffic problems, and creating "food deserts" in urban areas. In a more general sense, "as societies urbanize and modernize, so their populations become ever-more dependent on complex, distanciated systems . . . to sustain life (water, waste, food, medicine, goods, commodities, energy, communications, transport, and so on)."[54] Food insecurity resulting from urban expansion is thus just one facet of a pervasive urban problem: reliance on complex infrastructure subsystems with many moving parts, all of which have to work together for society to function, and which require stable economic and political conditions.

Local armed groups can exert a chokehold on these systems, including a city's food supply, by preying on the transportation flows that connect the city to its hinterland: setting up illegal checkpoints, robbing travelers, or extorting protection money from farmers who need the road to get their food to market. In Kenya's capital, Nairobi, for example, gangs such as Mungiki have exploited their location astride the city's food transportation routes (as well as their relationships with figures in the Kenyan political elite) to prey on the *matatus*—the brightly colored, privately owned minibuses that connect outlying suburbs with downtown areas—extorting as much as 1.1 billion Kenyan shillings (US$13 million) per year from transport operators.[55] Nairobi's population is 3.5 million today, and it's expected to reach 8 million by 2025, with more than half the city's inhabitants crammed into only 1 percent of its land area, clustered in crowded shantytowns and slums around the old city core.[56] The ability of Nairobi's gangs to interdict the city's transport and food lifelines thus gives them immense influence and makes dealing with them particularly problematic.

Perhaps the most severe impact, however, is that many cities risk running out of water as they expand into the catchment areas from which they traditionally drew their supply. This problem will only get worse as populations swell and urban settlements cover rainfall catchments and exhaust the replenishment capacity of river systems, pushing cities further from clean groundwater sources. The effects of water shortage in Syria and Libya are discussed in Chapter 4, but even in developed democracies such as Australia and the United States, analysts have argued convincingly that the pace and scale of urban development have reached a point where the ecological carrying capacity of the water cycle is just no longer sufficient for sustainable urban growth.[57] In developing countries this problem is even more severe, leading Chinese researchers to suggest that many Chinese cities will struggle with water shortages in the future.[58] In rich and poor countries alike, water supply and wastewater disposal are two of the most demanding aspects of urban governance, particularly in outlying areas. As one study pointed out in 2000, "for many megacities . . . access to piped water generally decreases towards the city periphery. In Mexico City, for example, piped water service declines from 45 percent in the urban core to 27 percent in the perimeter, dropping close to zero in squatter settlements."[59] In Mumbai, a population the size of greater London's lives in slums where government planners consider a ratio of one toilet to fifty people to be an "adequate" level of sanitation; the actual ratio in 2010 was one to six hundred.[60]

Likewise, the growing size and complexity of cities is straining the carrying capacity of governance systems such as police, emergency responders, courts, district administrators, hospitals, schools, and maintenance services. Government presence may be extremely limited in marginalized areas, even those that are geographically close to the seat of government. Gaps in government presence and authority—urban "no-go areas," as they're sometimes called—can then emerge. These allow safe havens for criminal networks or nonstate armed groups, creating a vacuum that is filled by local youth who have no shortage of grievances, whether arising from their new urban circumstances or imported from their home villages. As the international development researchers Kees Koonings and Dirk Kruijt pointed out in 2009, urban violence makes every other problem worse:

> Organized urban violence, in the form of often heavily armed territorial gangs and militias, brings together all the syndromes of urban exclusion: lack of "normal" livelihood opportunities, physical and infrastructural neglect of shanty towns, absence of the state and its public functions and moral and cultural disdain by the middle and upper classes towards the poor and excluded. It locks the urban excluded in a cul-de-sac.... Here we see a particularly harmful blurring of formal and informal, legal and illegal, civil and uncivil spheres. The police alternate between random violence against the shanty-town inhabitants and involvement in violent crime itself. Drug gangs defy the law and impose their own, but also maintain dyadic relations with the world of politics. Private militias, with ties to the official security services, pretend to defend law and order in *favelas* by imposing their own regime of extortion and intolerance.[61]

In Kingston, Jamaica, urban garrison districts have emerged over the past generation of rapid coastal urbanization, creating no-go zones where organized crime networks and local populations collaborate to exclude government presence, even as they benefit from patron-client relations with national political figures.[62] These are discussed in detail in Chapter 2, but even in developed cities such as Paris and London, rioting, youth unrest, and crime in periurban districts reached significant levels on several occasions over the past decade—and in low- and medium-income countries the problem is even worse.[63]

*The Microecology of Urban Violence*

If you're one of the many soldiers, aid workers, and diplomats who got to spend a lot of the last decade in some little plywood-and-sandbag firebase, up a winding dirt road, hunting terrorists through the mountains, or trying to connect with a population in a remote Afghan valley, then some of this might be new for you. For pretty much everyone else, it's very familiar, well-known stuff that urban theorists (including Mike Davis, Stephen Graham, Mitchell Sipus, Saskia Sassen, and Diane Davis, to name just a few) have been looking at for a long time—though not always through the lens of irregular warfare or systems theory, as we're doing here.[64] Likewise, for obvious institutional reasons, organizations such as the Australian Army, the British Royal Marines, and the United States Marine Corps have written extensively on these issues since the turn of the century.[65]

There's also a long-standing tradition in several academic disciplines that conceives of cities as systems: in particular, as biological systems, ecosystems, or even single organisms.[66] Central to this approach is the idea of *urban metabolism*, adapted from the concept of metabolism in biology—the "physiological processes within living things that provide the energy and nutrients required by an organism."[67] Metabolic processes transform inputs such as sunlight, food, water, and air into energy, biomass, and waste products. Urban historians and ecologists have long applied the notion of urban metabolism to understand the environmental history of cities.[68] "Just as living things require the inputs mentioned above, so do cities. That is, cities cannot exist without those inputs— urbanites require clean air, water, food, fuel, and construction goods to subsist while urban industries need materials for production purposes. These materials may initially come from the area of the urban site itself, but increasingly over time they are derived from the urban hinterland or even farther. That is, as the city grows, it extends its ecological footprint deeper and deeper into its hinterland."[69]

The idea goes back at least as far as Karl Marx, who wrote in the 1840s about the "metabolic rift" created by urbanization, which, as we noted earlier, accelerated dramatically during the industrial revolution.[70] Marx, of course, was writing in Europe at the end of the first hundred years of the industrial revolution, and talking about cities that had experienced a century of rapid urbanization and population growth, producing many of the same stresses, strains, and systemic breakdowns we're discussing here. In modern times, the idea of urban metabolism was repopularized by Abel Wolman's 1965 article "The Metabolism of Cities," and his notion that researchers can understand a city as a system by looking at its metabolic flows, via what is known as a *material flow analysis*, has since become a standard academic approach.[71] It's usually applied to the ecological sustainability of cities (that is, the way cities use and transform inputs of water, carbon, air, food, and fuel, then deal with the resulting waste products). The idea is that urban systems need enough carrying capacity to absorb, process, and deal with inputs and to process (metabolize) waste products, otherwise toxicity develops in the system and it begins to break down.

In recent years, though, people have started applying this concept more broadly, looking at nonmaterial flows and systems in cities as a way to examine the "relationships between social and natural systems, cities and their hinterlands (both immediate and global) and sustainability and social justice in urban areas."[72] Researchers in the fields of human geography and political ecology have built what we might call "urban social

# The Coastal City as a System

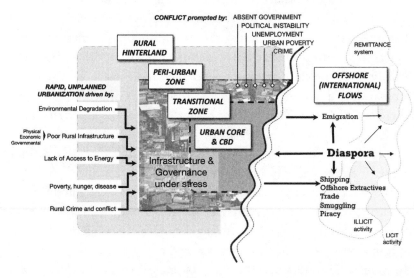

Figure 1.1

metabolism" models, which explore flows of population, money, trade goods, and information into a city, trying to understand how the urban area transforms these inputs, and analyzing the ways that cities manage the by-products of that transformation—including economic inequality, crime, conflict, social disruption and exclusion, political alienation, social injustice, violence, and unrest. Analyses of this sort help us understand the carrying capacity of a city's governance systems, along with its physical infrastructure, and in turn to understand the city's stability, sustainability, and resilience. This approach also helps illuminate what we might call the territorial logic—more broadly, the *systems logic*—of urban environments, and in turn helps us think about the sustainability of urban systems.[73]

Much as political geographers and ecologists have applied metabolism models to cities, military theorists have conceived of conflict (especially insurgency) as sharing many characteristics of biological systems. In 2003, for example, I proposed in *Countering Global Insurgency* that we might consider insurgencies as biological systems, thinking of an insurgent theater of operations (and the virtual theaters connected to it by global information and material flows) as a conflict ecosystem. In particular, I suggested that, far from being a discrete entity, separate from its environment, an insurgency is in fact a system state within that environment, a dissipative structure within a complex flow system, and thus inseparable from the ecosystem in which it occurs.[74] If we apply this notion to the urban environment, noting that (as I mentioned earlier) the primary threat in this environment comes from nonstate armed groups, we can start to see what an urban conflict ecosystem looks like, and to develop an understanding of what we might call the *microecology of urban violence*—the ways in which broader patterns of conflict play out in the dozens of microhabitats that make up a city under stress.

At a more macro level, we might think of rural-to-urban migration—driven by rural problems such as environmental degradation, energy poverty, famine, drought, or conflict—as one side of a population flow system that connects the city to its hinterland and creates a need for the city to deal with a complex array of problems such as informal settlements; economic, governance, and transportation overstretch; pollution, traffic, and border security; and food, water, fuel, and electricity shortages. Just as an urban metabolism model helps ecologists analyze material flows into and through the city, this kind of systems model can

## Urban Metabolism: the City as a System

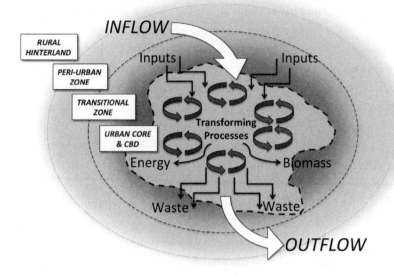

Figure 1.2

help us understand how the city transforms nonmaterial flows and how it deals with by-products such as crime, conflict, social injustice, or political unrest. This approach also helps us analyze how a city's ecosystem nests, in turn, within a larger national and global system. It allows us to understand how coastal cities (in particular, the ports and airports that connect them to the outside world) function as exchange mechanisms that connect rural populations with urban ones, and local networks with international networks. Putting this all together, we can start to see what is happening in a city under stress.

In this model, a coastal city's ecosystem lies at the center of a larger pattern of flows, with rural factors in the city's local or international hinterland—things such as environmental degradation, poor rural infrastructure, and rural conflict—prompting population flows into the urban area, which in turn contribute to rapid urbanization. Along with material flows (food, air, water, electrical power, and fuel), economic flows (construction materials and other commodities both licit and illicit; ground, sea, and air traffic; and money), and informational flows, these flows of population contribute to the creation of informal periurban settlements.

An accretion of slums, squatter settlements, and shantytowns grows in a transitional zone around the old city core, displacing land that was once used to provide food and other goods and services to the city, and covering the rainfall catchment area for the city's water supply. The city's growth puts its infrastructure under stress, so systems of governance, both within the old urban core and in newer outlying areas, now lack the carrying capacity to support the scale of the population and other inflows they are experiencing. The city's systems lack the carrying capacity to metabolize these inputs and become overwhelmed, and this leads to a buildup of toxic effects such as urban poverty and exclusion, disease, unemployment, social injustice, and ethnic dislocation. These in turn give rise to violent crime, social and political unrest, and—in severe cases—organized conflict. Shortages of food, fuel, electricity, and water exacerbate these problems, and urban violence in turn makes it harder to deal with these shortages. The city's connectedness (via information and money flows, and through transportation hubs such as seaports and airports) allows its population to participate in licit and illicit activities offshore, to influence (and be influenced by) conditions in the rural hinterland, and to connect with global networks, including diaspora populations. This set of interactions affects both local and international conflict dynamics.

*Violent Ecosystem: San Pedro Sula*

If this all sounds very abstract and theoretical (and I'm afraid it does), then it might help to describe a specific city by way of example. The city I have in mind is San Pedro Sula—the second city of Honduras—where, in early 2013, a Caerus team led by Stacia George conducted field research aimed at building a systems model of violence in what has become unflatteringly known as "the most dangerous city on the planet," a city that happens to exemplify all the main trends we have been discussing.[75]

The Republic of Honduras is smack in the center of the Americas. It's bounded on the east, southwest, and west by Nicaragua, El Salvador, and Guatemala, with the Pacific Ocean to the south and the Caribbean to the north. It has a population of just over 8 million, and its two major cities—the administrative capital, Tegucigalpa, in the south, and the commercial capital, San Pedro Sula, near the north coast—together account for almost a third of the total population. San Pedro Sula, for several years running, has topped the list of the world's most violent cities, with an astonishingly high murder rate of 169 homicides per 100,000 inhabitants.[76] (For comparison, even at the height of the Iraq War, Baghdad had a violent death rate of only about 48 per 100,000; New York's is 6.2; Sydney's is 1.0; London's is 1.2. Even Moscow, one of Europe's most violent cities, has a rate of only 9.6.)[77]

Collaborating closely with local community organizations and civil society groups, and using tools and techniques developed by Caerus teams in Africa, Asia, and Latin America over the past several years, Stacia's group tried to figure out what was driving this extraordinarily intense violence, through fieldwork aimed at developing a metabolic model of the city. The results were compelling.[78] What seemed on the surface to be a chaotic pattern of violence among a multiplicity of local gangs, narco-traffickers, and other groups turned out to be the result of a small number of macro-level flows that have accelerated over the past decade. These flows, along with the city's spatial layout, its geographic location as the country's main economic and transportation hub, and local conditions in a series of urban microhabitats, account for virtually all of the observable violence in San Pedro Sula.

Honduras has only one major seaport, Puerto Cortés, about forty-five minutes from downtown San Pedro Sula and part of its greater peri-urban area. The vast majority of the country's sea traffic passes through this port, and the only way to get to the port is through San Pedro Sula. Likewise, the only major road out of Honduras to the north and west passes through San Pedro Sula and Puerto Cortés before crossing into Guatemala, making San Pedro Sula the key chokepoint in the country's entire economic and transportation system. Because of its proximity to land and sea transport hubs, Morales Airport, outside San Pedro Sula, is also by far the country's busiest airport. In effect, the entire Honduran economy flows through San Pedro Sula, explaining the city's very high rate of growth (in economic and population terms) over the past decade. In terms of urban flows, the main impact of this economic growth is mass population movement: every day, several hundred thousand people flow into and out of San Pedro Sula in order to do business in the city itself or its surrounding areas. This huge flow is hard to understand, let alone protect, because San Pedro Sula's central location means that it has a multiplicity of entry and exit routes by sea, air, and land.

The city's licit economy has been booming since at least 2005, with textile factories (*maquilas*) being constructed in districts on the northern side of the city, closer to the port. The *maquilas* are in tax-free zones on the city's outskirts, between the port and the old urban core, which is now the city's downtown area. They import yarns and textiles from the United States, turn them into finished clothing for companies such as Gap, Nike, and Adidas, and then reexport the finished products back into the U.S. market. Both the inflow of raw materials and the outflow of finished clothes rely on shipping and port facilities, making the San Pedro Sula– Puerto Cortés corridor the most valuable piece of economic terrain in the entire country. The city itself is shaped like a flattened arrowhead pointing at the port, with inflows of people, goods, money, and traffic coming from the southeast, south, and southwest, and the major outflow to the north toward Puerto Cortés. Anyone dominating this intersection has a choke-hold on Honduras's economy—and, unsurprisingly, a large proportion of violence in the city turns out to be among gangs that are fighting each other for control of this critical economic terrain. Scattered across dozens of microhabitats (the central bus station, the nearby outdoor drug market, the food markets, the small businesses lining the bus routes, and the alleys and periurban slums on either side of the main roads into and out of the city), the violence can look chaotic, but in fact it revolves around a competition for control over economic terrain and over an extortion racket targeting small businesses.

Beside the violent struggle to control the legal economy, the competition to control illicit trade is even more violent. The major illicit flow into San Pedro Sula is the influx of cocaine, coming from South and Central America and the Caribbean by land, air, and sea. The drug trade is dominated by groups such as Mexico's Sinaloa cartel and Las Zetas, both of which subcontract Honduran gangs to move drugs for them. The Sinaloa cartel tends to dominate ground-based trafficking into Guatemala and on to Mexico, while sea-based smuggling currently seems to be dominated by the Zetas. The cocaine trade, with its associated flows, has transformed the patterns of violence in San Pedro Sula. Narco-trafficking gangs have displaced traditional street gangs based on local turf identities and known as *pandillas*. The *narcos* use the city (with its central location, transportation links, and excellent access to the U.S. market) as a smuggling hub. This pattern spiked in 2004–5 as cocaine traffickers responded to counternarcotics successes in Colombia and the Caribbean by opening new Central American routes, taking advantage of the existing gang structure in Honduras, and hiring local groups as enforcers. The cartels pay local gangs in cocaine, creating a domestic drug market in the city, and competition to control this new domestic market accounts for another large part of the city's violence.

Another key illicit flow is that of money. Narco-traffickers such as the Mexican Sinaloa cartel came to San Pedro Sula in the mid-2000s in part because it was an ideal money-laundering location. The opportunities afforded by legitimate businesses, the city's prime location astride the major licit and illicit flows into and out of Honduras, and a weak government that could be co-opted for money laundering led to a rapid deterioration in the city's governance institutions, further increasing opportunities for money laundering.

An influx of deportees from the United States is another key driver of violence. In 2012 alone, the U.S. government deported more than thirty-two thousand Hondurans, of whom almost half were violent criminals (many were gang members belonging to groups such as MS13 and the 18th Street gang), and all arrived by air in San Pedro Sula. This has been happening for several years, and it creates an enormous inflow of trained, blooded, organized violent criminals who fit directly into the gang structure of the city. In many cases, gang members who have already been deported are on hand to meet deportees as they arrive at the airport, and embed them straight into the local gang system. MS13 and 18th Street are United States gangs (both originated in Los Angeles) that were involuntarily transplanted to Honduras through deportations, reconstituted themselves from the flow of deportees, expanded to control drug trafficking routes, and together with Los Olanchanos, the third major gang in the city, have come to dominate the system of violence in San Pedro Sula.

Violence has surged as all these groups—local gangs, *narcos*, and deportees from North American gangs—have responded to the strong incentive of controlling territory and dominating key nodes in the city's flow system, especially transport routes and hubs. Controlling territory is the key to exploiting the city's licit economy (the flow of textiles in and finished clothing out), taking advantage of the city's central position in the Honduran economy, and dominating its illicit economy (the flow of transnational cocaine through the city, as well as the local drug smuggling, money laundering, and extortion rackets). The violence is increasing, in part, because this competition is relatively new, so a pecking order has yet to emerge and gangs haven't yet settled into defined spheres of influence or territorial control. Another key factor is that since this is an open system with a continuous inflow of weapons and fighters, there's no prospect that the competition between gangs will burn itself out. At the same time, the gangs' growing income lets them buy more sophisticated and powerful firearms. As a result, the microhabitats where gangs actively compete—the bloody boundaries of gang turfs—are by far the most violent in the city. Much of this is gang-on-gang violence: apart from kidnapping and extortion, the major risk to ordinary citizens is that of being caught in the crossfire.

For its part, the city's government doesn't have the capacity to handle the massive influx—thousands of weapons and new gang combatants per year, along with billions of dollars in cocaine—as well as to sustain a city whose population and area are rapidly growing but which lacks key infrastructure, resources, and support systems. In particular, city leaders have limited influence over the Honduran criminal justice system, which is run by the central government (based in Tegucigalpa, on the other side of the country) to suit its own interests rather than those of the city. For example, the *mano dura* policy of 2003–4, driven by elite-level politics at the central government level, involved an aggressive crackdown on gangs. This dramatically backfired, increasing violent activity and driving gangs underground. It turned the gangs into dark networks that were much harder to see and deal with, and created prison fraternities that became training and radicalization engines for the gangs, so they were primed for action just in time to exploit the influx of drugs when it began to spike in 2005.

In urban metabolism terms, violence in San Pedro Sula can be seen as a toxic by-product of this massive influx of drugs, weapons, money, and deportees, on top of existing licit economic flows driven by the city's role as a key littoral and business hub, which were already straining the limited carrying capacity of the city's governance and infrastructure. San Pedro Sula's metabolism has been overwhelmed: the city is simply unable to absorb and metabolize these inflows. The resulting toxicity is seen in symptoms such as urban dislocation, violence, crime, and social breakdown. It's important to note that these toxic effects aren't evenly spread: they're concentrated in at least a dozen microhabitats that Stacia's team studied on the ground, with some city sectors relatively peaceful and quiet, others the scene of intensely violent competition for control among the various nonstate groups, and yet others effectively autonomous and outside all government control.

San Pedro Sula, then, is a good illustration of how urban metabolism models, and an approach that views the city as a complex flow system (or, more accurately, a system-of-systems nested within larger regional, national, and transnational flows) can be applied as a way of understanding conflict dynamics.

## III

All this goes to highlight what Steve was pointing out that night in the bar of the Bryant Park Hotel: the environment is shifting, and we need to think of cities as living, breathing organisms if we want to understand the direction in which that shift is taking us. The megatrends of population growth, urbanization, littoralization, and connectedness suggest that conflict is increasingly likely to occur in coastal cities, in underdeveloped regions of the Middle East, Africa, Latin America, and Asia, and in highly networked, connected settings. We're still likely to experience wars between nation-states, and conflict in remote areas such as mountains, jungles, and deserts will still undoubtedly occur. But the trends are clear: more people than ever before in history will be competing for scarcer and scarcer resources in poorly governed areas that lack adequate infrastructure, and these areas will be more and more closely connected to the global system, so that local conflict will have far wider effects.

The implications are profound. In the first place, it turns out that what I've outlined here is far more than a theory of future conflict—indeed, it's a "theory of everything" in the sense that these drivers will affect every aspect of life on the planet in the next few decades, not just conflict. The city-as-a-system approach we've explored here can be applied to many complex problems that may appear unrelated—rural soil salinity, urban crime, water or fuel shortages, offshore piracy, social injustice, or racial exclusion, for example—to understand how they interact in a given city or network.

Taking this approach may help us identify emergent patterns within a city system, make sense of its system logic, reveal the flows within it, and thus begin to design tailored interventions that can both keep a city safe *and* allow it to flow and breathe. As the urban metabolism model suggests, and as discussed in greater detail in Chapter 5, we can break such approaches down into *supply-side interventions* (which help ameliorate some of the causes of rapid, unplanned urbanization and thus relieve some of the pressure on a city and its infrastructure), *demand-side interventions* (which help improve the city's resiliency and thus its ability to cope with the pressures on its systems), and *framing system interventions* (which seek to alter the context within which the city develops, by changing its interaction with larger national and transnational systems).

To fully understand these kinds of potential interventions, however, we first need to take a much more detailed look at the range of threats that affects this environment, and the ways in which particular threat groups operate—both at the local level (where, like the gangs of San Pedro Sula, they compete for control over population or territory) and in terms of their connectivity with the wider world. The next three chapters seek to add this detail. Chapter 2 looks at three examples of conflict over a spectrum from transnational terrorism through insurgency, civil war, and criminal activity, and it seeks to understand the complex ways in which these conflicts interact with overstressed urban environments. Chapter 3 explores the way that nonstate armed groups compete for control over populations and terrain at the hyperlocal level, and Chapter 4 examines (through the lens of the Arab Spring uprisings) the way that enhanced connectivity allows local actors to draw on worldwide networks. Taken together, these chapters provide the deeper context that will allow us, in Chapter 5, to draw some tentative conclusions and begin to think about ways in which we might deal with the crowded, coastal, urban environment of future conflict.

# 2

## Future Cities, Future Threats

> Imagine a great metropolis covering hundreds of square miles. Once a vital component in a national economy, this sprawling urban environment is now a vast collection of blighted buildings, an immense petri dish of both ancient and new diseases, a territory where the rule of law has long been replaced by near anarchy in which the only security available is that which is attained through brute power. Yet *this* city would still be globally connected. It would possess at least a modicum of commercial linkages, and some of its inhabitants would have access to the world's most modern communication and computing technologies. It would, in effect, be a feral city.
>
> —Richard Norton, 2003

### I. Sixty Hours in Mumbai

As dusk fell on November 21, 2008, the MV *al-Husseini*, an unremarkable coastal freighter a little larger than a fishing trawler, left its berth in the harbor of Karachi.[1] The *Husseini* steamed into the gathering darkness, blending in among a mass of small craft, fishing trawlers, container vessels, and passenger ships. The ship sailed out into the Arabian Sea, bound for the Indian city of Mumbai, five hundred nautical miles to the southeast. On board, a raiding party of the Pakistani terrorist group Lashkar-e-Taiba (LeT) prepared for the most audacious maritime terrorist attack in India's history.

The events that were about to unfold are worth examining in detail, since—along with the other examples we'll look at in this chapter—they help to illustrate the range of threats that will exist in the urban, networked, littoral environment of the future.

The assault team had received thirteen months of training from LeT instructors, as well as from retired (and, allegedly, active-duty) members of Pakistani Special Forces and Inter-Services Intelligence (ISI), at a camp near Muzaffarabad in Pakistani-administered Kashmir. One trainee later testified that the camp was run by LeT but was near a military base, was guarded by Pakistani troops, and received ammunition and weapons from the army.[2] The raiders' preparation included ideological indoctrination, weapons and tactics instruction, assault training, and amphibious raiding exercises using inflatable boats on the Mangla Dam reservoir in Kashmir. Seven trainees were chosen from an initial batch of thirty-two, recruited from urban areas in Pakistan by LeT and its political wing, Jamaat ud-Dawa. After selection was complete, three experienced LeT operatives came in to take charge of the group.[3] The team commander, using the nom de guerre Abu Dera Ismail Khan, divided the ten-man team into five pairs, assigning each to a target in the waterfront area of South Mumbai.[4]

Throughout 2008—according to evidence given during his terrorism trial—the American-born, ISI-trained Pakistani intelligence agent David Coleman Headley (Daood Sayed Gilani) had made a series of trips to scout the target locations, passing detailed geographical information to his ISI handler, Major Iqbal.[5] At the same time, LeT had established a network of up to forty local sympathizers in and around Mumbai.[6] Along with other spies, Headley (who was convicted on terrorism charges in January 2013, for this and other operations) had generated a detailed picture of the environment, helping planners in Pakistan understand the layout of streets and buildings and the flow of people, traffic, and commodities in the crowded urban peninsula of South Mumbai, a complex and densely populated area in which coastal slums, warrens of narrow alleyways, and residential housing were intermixed with office buildings, public spaces, and high-rise luxury hotels.[7]

On board the *Husseini* the raiders were busy examining the reconnaissance data, poring over Google Earth images to study their targets, confirming routes of attack, and ensuring they knew how to navigate the complex urban terrain in which they would be operating. Each man was issued a Russian AK-47 or Chinese Type 56 assault rifle, a Pakistani-made copy of a Colt automatic pistol, two clips of 9 mm pistol ammunition, six hundred rounds of rifle ammunition, and eight to ten Chinese-made Type 86 hand grenades.[8] Some raiders were given packs of military-grade RDX explosive, Garmin GPS satellite navigation devices, and cellphones. Three carried extra SIM cards of Indian and U.S. origin for the attack, and at least one had a Thuraya satellite phone. The terrorists loaded their combat equipment into backpacks along with water, emergency rations, a change of clothes, false ID cards, Indian cash, credit cards, and detailed maps of their targets.[9] They also packed cocaine, LSD, and steroids, probably to keep themselves awake during the raid: Indian police later found high concentrations of these substances in the blood of several dead attackers.[10]

Their journey to Mumbai took roughly thirty-six hours. On the night of November 23, the terrorists hijacked an Indian fishing trawler, the MV *Kuber*, far out in the open sea. They transferred four crewmembers to the *Husseini* as they seized the vessel, and then ordered the captain, Amar Narayan Solanki, to sail to a position a few miles offshore of Mumbai. Sometime after this—exactly when is unclear, since there are no surviving witnesses—the four crewmembers on board the *Husseini* were murdered. As *Kuber* sailed toward Mumbai the raiders checked in with their handlers in Pakistan using satellite phones, carried out final rehearsals and briefings, and assembled their explosives, fuses, and timers into a series of improvised bombs with which they would later create havoc on the streets of Mumbai. The precise sequence of events on board *Kuber* is also unclear, as all but one of those involved was also dead within a few days. But at least one source has suggested that Solanki, who had a history of involvement in coastal smuggling and illicit trafficking, and wouldn't have known that his crew were already dead, didn't resist the terrorists because he mistakenly believed they were smugglers of the kind who normally operate in these waters.[11]

At dusk on November 26, *Kuber* was about four nautical miles off Mumbai. On instructions received via satellite phone from their handlers in Pakistan, the raiders seized the captain, tied his arms and legs, cut his throat, and threw his body belowdecks.[12] They cross-decked from the fishing trawler into three military-grade Gemini rigid-hull inflatable boats—a difficult operation at night, out of sight of land, with a three-foot coastal swell running—then abandoned the *Kuber* and set off toward Mumbai in the inflatables.[13]

### Nightfall in Mumbai

The assault teams landed in two separate locations, near the fishing colony of Badhwar Park and Machhimar Nagar, in the Colaba waterfront area of South Mumbai. Unlike the upscale residential neighborhoods, hotels, and high-rise office complexes that dominate the rest of this area, the landing sites the terrorists chose were dense, complex informal settlements—coastal slums made up of thousands of tiny shacks, fishing huts, and moored boats.[14] Local people noticed both landings. In one case the terrorists, who were well groomed and wore neat Western-style clothes, successfully explained themselves as "students"; in the other they intimidated local fishermen (who, like Solanki, probably thought they were smugglers or members of local organized crime groups) by pointing to their weapons. Though the locals saw the team land, none of those who spotted the terrorists reported them to the police—probably because of the lack of police presence (or government services generally) in this part of Mumbai.[15] Just as the raiders had slipped out of Pakistan by nesting within the coastal traffic of Karachi, they had now entered India under cover of the normal background clutter of licit and illicit flows in and around the slums and port of Mumbai.

By 8:30 p.m. the full team of ten had landed and split into five pairs. Two of these pairs, guided by GPS, moved on foot to attack their previously assigned objectives. Each of the remaining three pairs hailed one of Mumbai's black-and-yellow Fiat taxis and blended into the heavy waterfront traffic to move to their targets; two of these placed an improvised explosive device under the seat of their taxi as they left it, having set the device on a timer to explode later, create confusion, and tie up the Indian emergency services.[16]

From their tactical operations center in a Pakistani safe house in Karachi, a team of attack controllers led by Sajid Mir of LeT, along with Hafiz Mohammed Saeed (the head of Jamaat ud-Dawa), Major Iqbal of ISI, and other Pakistani military and intelligence officers monitored the situation by using cellphones and satellite phones and by tracking Twitter feeds, Internet reports, and Indian and international news broadcasts.[17] Using Skype, SMS text messages, and voice calls, the control room fed a continuous stream of updates, instructions, directions, and warnings to the attackers at each stage of the operation, gathered feedback on the Indian response, and choreographed the assault team's moves so as to keep it from being pinned down by Indian security forces.[18] Zakiur Rehman Lakhvi, the overall planner and tactician of the raid, was also in the ops room; over the past few months he had acquired several Voice-Over-Internet-Protocol (VOIP) telephony accounts (similar to Skype) as well as phone accounts in the United States, Austria, Italy, and India, to main-tain connectivity with the raiders.[19]

Lakhvi had designed the first assaults as diversionary attacks to draw off Indian police and emergency services, forcing them to deal with mul-tiple simultaneous incidents across the city, while the main assault force headed for its true objectives: a Jewish community center and two luxury hotels, all in the waterfront area. Shortly after 9:35 p.m., the first assault pair burst into the Leopold Café, a popular drinking spot for foreign tourists, about two blocks from the Taj Mahal Hotel. The two assaulters threw grenades, and then fired into the crowd, killing eleven and injuring many others before withdrawing into the street. They then moved the short distance to the Taj Mahal Hotel, firing as they went along a crowded alleyway, killing another thirteen civilians en route.[20]

With chaos descending on the vast city's waterfront as the Mumbai police responded to the first attack, the other raiders were moving to their targets. Besides the team that was already shooting its way toward the Taj Mahal from the Leopold Café, another pair was headed for the same hotel. One assault pair was moving to the Oberoi Trident Hotel, and one to the Chabad Lubavitch Jewish cultural center at Nariman House. The final pair consisted of Mohammed Ajmal Kasab and the raiding group's ground commander, Abu Dera Ismail Khan. The two men took a taxi to Chhatrapati Shivaji Terminus, the magnificent colonial-era central railway station in downtown Mumbai.

Kasab and Khan slipped into the enormous passenger hall of the great station. After observing the flow of commuters for a time, and noting the positions of the lightly armed police and Railway Protection Force officers in the building, they opened fire into the crowd on Platform 13. Firing long bursts from their AK-47s and throwing hand grenades, they killed 52 people, wounded 108, and created a mass panic. After an attack lasting almost ninety minutes, the two terrorists withdrew from the terminus and headed on foot for the Cama and Albless Hospital, a women's and children's hospital two blocks from the station. Arriving, they opened fire, but inflicted no casualties on the hospital's 180 patients: the nursing staff, hearing the firing and explosions at the railway station, had locked the building's metal doors and guided their patients into back rooms. The attackers did kill two security guards, Baban Ugre and Bhanoo Devu Narkar, but were forced to flee without getting inside the hospital.[21]

Though the two terrorists failed to kill any patients, the Cama Hospital attack was a turning point in the raid, because as they fled the scene Kasab and Khan succeeded—through pure luck—in killing the senior Indian counterterrorism police officer in Mumbai.

Hemant Karkare, joint commissioner of the Maharashtra Anti-Terrorism Squad (ATS), was a respected, dedicated, and energetic officer who had successfully investigated several terrorist attacks, by both Muslim and Hindu extremists.[22] As ATS chief, he would have played a critical role in coordinating the Indian response to the raid. Karkare and three of his officers, responding to the railway station shooting, had moved through the terminus building from the rear as the terrorists fled; they climbed into a Qualis four-wheel-drive vehicle and pursued Kasab and Khan toward the Cama Hospital. In a lane near the hospital, the police spotted and fired on Kasab, but failed to notice Khan in the shadows. Khan returned fire, killing Karkare and two of his officers. The raiders dumped the bodies onto the roadway, seized the Qualis, and drove off toward South Mumbai. They fired at police outside a cinema, but then hit a roadblock set up by officers from the Gamdevi police station, on the coast road near Girgaum Chowpatty, one of Mumbai's most famous public beaches.

The police at the roadblock opened fire. In the ensuing gun battle Khan was killed and Kasab was captured when a heroic police constable, Tukaram Omble, charged him and seized the muzzle of his AK-47, taking a burst of fire in the chest at point-blank range but managing to keep hold of the rifle's barrel, thereby allowing other police to capture Kasab alive.[23] Omble died at the scene, and along with Commissioner Karkare was later awarded the Ashok Chakra, India's highest award for non-battlefield gallantry. Kasab, now wounded and in police custody, would be the only terrorist to survive the raid.[24]

### The Main Assault

It was 10:45 p.m., and the two assault pairs at the Taj Mahal had joined forces to attack the hotel. The four men charged through the front entrance, shooting staff at the reception desk, then split into pairs and attacked the hotel's two ground-floor restaurants, killing diners and throwing grenades into the basement. They began seizing hostages, focusing on British and American nationals, and herded them up to the nineteenth floor.

Despite the chaos, Taj Mahal staff managed to move about 250 people to the hotel's Chambers area, but terrified guests there soon began using cellphones to call and text their relatives, and in so doing they alerted the media. Indian and international television, Twitter, and Internet news sites soon reported that a large number of hotel guests were trapped, and named their hiding place. Within minutes, the LeT control room in Pakistan, monitoring the media, had passed this information to the assault team in the hotel, who immediately sent a search party to find them.[25] Also at about this time an Indian cabinet minister, trying to reassure the public, announced that India's elite Marine Commando (MARCO) counter-terrorism force was en route to the hotel and would arrive in two hours; this information, which the Karachi control room also passed to the raiders on the ground, alerted them that no response units were yet deployed and that they had a clear window of time to consolidate and harden their position.[26] The terrorists moved about the hotel, taking many hostages at gunpoint; hundreds of others were trapped in their rooms.

Hearing the gunfire, eight police officers arrived at the hotel just before midnight, but they soon realized they were too lightly armed to confront the terrorists—like most Indian police, they wore plastic-lined riot vests that would stop a hand-thrown rock but not a bullet, had vintage .303 bolt-action rifles with only a few rounds of ammunition, and carried wooden sticks known as *lathis*. Realizing they were seriously outgunned, the police backed off to wait for the MARCOs. The commandos were delayed by the need for coordination between India's central government and the Mumbai City and Maharashtra State authorities, a contentious process that took several hours, but they finally arrived at about 2:00 a.m. along with operators from the National Security Guard (NSG), a national-level counterterrorism unit of the Indian police. Two eight-man MARCO squads with an NSG team moved into the hotel, rescuing guests and engaging the terrorists in an intense firefight.[27] By 3:00 a.m. the hotel's historic dome had caught fire from a grenade blast, and a gun battle was raging on the upper floors as the flames spread. Fire trucks arrived, and firefighters attempted to deal with the blaze; they succeeded in res-cuing nearly two hundred hotel guests from their rooms using ladders, a heroic effort given that they were dealing with gunfire and grenades as well as smoke and flame. Again, the Karachi control room relayed media reports on the emergency response to the LeT assault teams, allowing them to stay one jump ahead of the Indian counterterrorism operators.[28]

The Taj Mahal Hotel is on the eastern waterfront of the heavily urbanized South Mumbai peninsula; less than a mile away on the western side of the peninsula, one more LeT pair was attacking the Oberoi Trident, another landmark luxury waterfront hotel. The assault was synchronized with the attack on the Taj Mahal and followed a similar tactical drill: the assault pair burst into the reception area, killed hotel employees at the main desk, then attacked diners in the hotel restaurant before moving to an upper floor, gathering hostages along the way. Disrupted by the loss of Commissioner Karkare and preoccupied by the simultaneous attack at the Taj Mahal, Indian security forces took more than four hours to respond. When the ATS and local police finally moved into the Oberoi compound at 2:25 a.m., they again found themselves outgunned by a well-prepared and forewarned terrorist pair, and had to pull back. At dawn the next morning, MARCO and NSG teams climbed the outside of the building via the fire escape to the top floor, then assaulted down through the hotel, trapping the terrorists in a room on the eighteenth floor. The LeT pair held out throughout that day, all the next night, and into the following afternoon (November 28) before finally being killed at around 3:00 p.m. as they tried to change locations. Meanwhile, police and firefighters had rescued many hotel guests.[29]

The third main target, the Jewish center at Nariman House, was in one of the most congested and densely populated parts of the Mumbai waterfront. Unlike the two high-rise hotels, the cultural center was a five-story house in a maze of narrow back alleys where there were extremely limited fields of fire and constricted access.[30] Also unlike the attackers at the two hotels, the LeT team at Nariman House entered and immediately seized hostages, then engaged in a classic hostage negotiation, holding their ground and awaiting the Indian response. Mumbai police and NSG established a cordon around the building and periodically exchanged gunfire with the terrorists, as well as intermittently trying to negotiate with them for the release of hostages, but again they lacked the firepower to attempt an attack on the house. At about midnight on November 27 the police managed to rescue nine hostages from the first floor of the house. By 8:00 a.m. on the twenty-eighth, however, intercepted communications suggested that the terrorists were killing their hostages, and NSG began an air assault, with operators fast-roping from helicopters onto the roof of the house. As in the hotel attacks, international and local media reported the NSG operation live on television, blogs, and Twitter, allowing the Karachi control room to alert the terrorists in the house in real-time. As a result, NSG took all day to clear the house in an extended room-to-room gun battle; by 9:00 p.m. the building was finally secure, with both terrorists killed. All the remaining hostages, including Israeli rabbi Gavriel Holtzberg and his pregnant wife, Rivka, were found dead: they had been horrifically tortured before being murdered.[31]

All this time, the Taj Mahal was still under siege, and there was little let-up in a series of intense firefights on the upper floors of the grand hotel and in the new high-rise tower next to the historic building. The LeT team set fires inside the building, partly to confuse the Indian responders and create cover, partly to increase the visual impact of the attacks from a media standpoint.[32] They may also have been trained to light fires to confuse thermal imaging equipment that might have been used to track their moves inside the building.[33] The terrorists took about 150 hostages and executed many, but dozens more were rescued by MARCO, fire-fighters, and NSG. After a false start, by 8:00 a.m. on November 29, Indian security forces were able to confirm that they had cleared the building.[34]

As the smoke cleared after sixty hours of destructive violence, the great city began to clean up the mess and analysts began piecing together what had happened. In all, 172 people were killed in the attacks, including 16 police, 27 hotel staff, 2 commandos, and 9 out of the 10 LeT terrorists, while another 304 were injured.[35] The vast majority of people killed and injured were civilians randomly caught up in the attacks, especially in the railway terminus, where the greatest carnage (52 dead and 108 wounded) took place among commuters trapped in a tight space, unable to escape.[36] Property damage from the raid was estimated at over US$18 million—not counting the broader cost to the Indian economy.[37]

### Infesting the Megacity

What do the Mumbai attacks tell us about the future spectrum of threats in coastal cities? Many excellent studies have analyzed the counter-terrorism lessons of the raid, but for our purposes it's worth focusing on aspects that relate to the urbanized, networked, littoral environment, where, as we've seen, most people will live in the future, and where most conflict will occur.

The first and clearest observation is that the raiders consciously exploited the urbanized coastal environment of Mumbai and Karachi. Karachi, a chaotic and unruly megacity of 21 million, is Pakistan's largest city and its busiest transportation hub. The city has experienced extremely rapid urbanization since Partition in 1947, when it grew rapidly with the influx of millions of Muslims from newly independent India, and again in the 1980s, when millions of refugees from Afghanistan and from Pakistan's tribal areas settled in periurban slums.[38] The port of Karachi handles 26 million tons of freight per annum, or 60 percent of the country's total shipping and cargo movement, giving the harbor and its approaches some of the heaviest coastal shipping traffic in the world.[39] The LeT raiders slipped out of Karachi under cover of this dense maritime traffic, infiltrated Indian territory in a fishing vessel among thousands of others, made their way into Mumbai by landing at a busy jetty in a coastal slum, and exploited the crowded, dense environment of the Mumbai waterfront to move without detection on foot and in public transport. Mumbai, a megacity of just over 20 million, is India's second-largest city, after Delhi, and is one of the most densely populated urban centers on the planet, with almost thirty thousand people per square kilometer.[40] Its urbanization has been largely organic and unplanned, resulting in a complex mix of different types of buildings—slums butting up against high-rise hotels, alleyways next to industrial facilities, and so on. The attackers skillfully exploited the complexity of this urban environment, using slums and alleys to cover their movement between targets.

The second major feature of the attack was that the attackers exploited networks of connectivity within and between the two coastal megacities of Karachi and Mumbai. As I mentioned earlier, it's possible that Captain Solanki of the *Kuber* didn't resist the terrorists because he thought they were smugglers, part of a broader network of contraband trading, drug smuggling, and human trafficking in the sea space around Mumbai, an illicit enterprise in which Solanki himself may have engaged in the past, and which—even if he wasn't personally involved—would have appeared to him as just part of the normal background environment. The locals who saw the team land might also have believed the terrorists were smugglers or illegal immigrants, while the manager on duty at the Leopold Café initially mistook them for backpackers, part of a busy traffic of low-budget tourists that flows through the area.[41] It's worth noting once again that dark networks—flows of people, money, goods, and information that lie outside the view of law enforcement and government authorities—are, in themselves, neither good nor bad, and their existence creates a venue for a wide range of beneficial, neutral, or (in this case) harmful activities. In this sense, any negative externalities of dark networks are effects of the *activities* of people in the network, not characteristics of the network itself.

Once they landed in Mumbai, the terrorists also exploited the connected, networked nature of the urban environment. They used Skype, cellphones, and satellite phones to connect with their handlers in Pakistan, who in turn monitored Twitter, news blogs, international and local satellite news, and cable television in real time, which allowed them to control the attacks and react as the Indian response developed.

The importance of the Karachi control node is obvious if we look at the role of Abu Dera Ismail Khan, the team leader, who died early in the operation, in a diversionary attack a long way from the main targets. If Khan had been running the operation in a classical military command-and-control manner, it would have made no sense for him to lead a secondary attack of this kind. His place would have been with the main team at the main objective: he would have given the job of leading the secondary attack to a trusted subordinate. That he was assigned to a diversionary objective—albeit one requiring considerable on-the-fly decision making—underlines the continuous and intimate control that the Karachi operations room exercised over the teams at the main objectives. Meanwhile, the assault pairs themselves seem to have operated autonomously, in a "flat" structure with no hierarchy among teams, each directly responsive to the command node in Karachi. The Mumbai attack was thus, in effect, directed by remote control, making the connectivity between the assault teams and the remote command center a critical element in the operation.

Likewise, the attack team's focus on foreigners seems to have been calculated by LeT controllers to maximize international attention, creating an extremely high level of news coverage—and resulting in an unusually large number of foreigners (including citizens of twenty-two countries) being killed.[42] This may have been, in part, the classic terrorist tactic of maximizing publicity, but it may also have been an operational requirement: since the raiders' command-and-control methodology relied on the Karachi operations room monitoring Twitter and Internet feeds in order to control the assault teams, the raiders needed to do something in order to create large-scale Twitter and Internet traffic, so as to generate a sufficient online signature to close the feedback loop with their command node.

The raiders mostly didn't target specific individuals—the killing of Commissioner Karkare, the Mumbai counterterrorist chief, seems to have been a pure accident, while the importance of each target group seems to have been determined either (in the case of the diversionary attacks) by effect on the city or (in the case of the main attacks) by its he attackers seem to have deliberately drawn out the oper- many days as possible, hardening and consolidating their n as they entered the main target sites, and preparing ge. Their goal seems to have been to maximize the raid's t and increase the effect of terror and urban dislocation bai down for as long as possible. The attacks on trans- portation and public health infrastructure (the taxis, railway station, and hospital) also seem calculated to maximize disruption within the urban flow of Mumbai and slow the Indian response.

This response was affected by problems in coordination among the city authorities of Mumbai (including local police, fire brigade, ambulance, and hospital services), the government of Maharashtra State, and the Indian central government in New Delhi. In order to use national-level assets such as the MARCO and NSG teams, the state government had to approve their deployment and agree to cede control over the incident sites to central government organizations, a process that took almost six hours to negotiate, delaying the national response; in the meantime, the local police were severely outgunned, while the Mumbai antiterrorism squad was reeling from the loss of its commander early in the raid.

The attacks didn't involve weapons of mass destruction or particularly high-tech equipment. As in most irregular conflicts, the raiders used small arms (rifles and pistols), improvised explosive devices, and grenades; they didn't even use rocket-propelled grenades. Small arms, however, because they involve intimate contact between attackers and victims, because their use implies the presence of an enemy on the spot, and because gun battles tend to last longer than bombings, can have a greater terror effect than a bombing or hostage situation. In an urban environment, where firefights tend to be fleeting and to occur at short ranges among small numbers of combatants, the terrorists' ability to operate in a distributed swarm of autonomous small teams, with low signature and high mobility (due to their light weapons and combat loads), was a key tactical advantage.

Likewise, the raiders used no unusually sophisticated or specialized communications devices: they employed commercially available phones and off-the-shelf GPS devices, and pulled much of their reconnaissance data from open-source, online tools such as Google Earth. They did, however, display an excellent standard of preparation and reconnaissance, and extremely good skills in sea movement, coastal infiltration, and small-boat handling, techniques that are obviously optimized for littoral environments. They clearly understood the urban-littoral dynamics of Mumbai—the systems logic of the way the city worked—and used this knowledge to their advantage. In this respect, assistance from state sponsors (or perhaps, nonstate sponsors who somehow managed to gain excellent access to military-grade equipment, training, intelligence, facilities, and weapons) was a key factor in the raid's success.

What does all this say about the future environment? First, I should make it clear that Mumbai represents only one kind of threat that will exist in the urban, networked littoral of the future; we'll take a detailed look at others later in this chapter. That said, Mumbai exemplifies the higher end of the threat spectrum, that of state proxies using irregular (sometimes called "asymmetric") methods to temporarily disrupt an urban target, rather than to control an urban population over a long period of time. Crime researchers John P. Sullivan and Adam Elkus describe this as an evolved twenty-first-century form of "urban siege":

> There are several methods that terrorists and criminal insurgents use to besiege cities from within—pure terror and systems disruption, although the two are often combined together. Both methods are sustained means of besieging a city with a campaign of protracted urban violence. Pure terror is a form of social systems disruption. It is a spasm of violence intended to demonstrate to the public that the authorities cannot help them, and that they are helpless against the

power of the gun. . . . While the success of the Mumbai terrorists came in large part from the tactical and operational inadequacy of Indian law enforcement response, it is easy to imagine a small group of terrorists creating multiple centers of disorder at the same time within a major American city in same manner. An equally terrifying scenario is a Beslan-type siege in school centers with multiple active shooters. Paramilitary terrorists of this kind would aim for maximum violence, target hardening, and area denial—capabilities that many SWAT units would be hard-pressed to counter.[43]

To my mind, Mumbai represents the current state of the art in urban littoral terrorism. The attack has served as the model for at least two planned copycat raids on major coastal cities in Southeast Asia and Europe, and its level of technical difficulty alone was enough to raise LeT's stature as a regional terrorist organization.[44] In this context it's worth noting that guerrillas and terrorists can gain strategic advantage just by demonstrating skill, daring, and tactical competence: the "style points" they acquire, and the shock value of showing they're a force to be reckoned with, can outweigh tactical failures.

But Mumbai was far from a tactical failure: on the contrary, the attack showed that a nonstate armed group can carry out an appallingly effective seaborne raid on a major coastal city, over a three-day period, in several dispersed locations—the type of operation traditionally associated with high-tier special operations forces such as the U.S. Navy SEALs or the Royal Marines' Special Boat Service. Indeed, Mumbai was a further demonstration of a long-standing trend, sometimes called the *democratization of technology*, in which nonstate armed groups are fielding highly lethal capabilities that were once the sole preserve of nation-states. As a combat-experienced officer with an understanding of urban riverine operations in Iraq said to me, the Mumbai terrorists' callous disregard for human life was deeply horrifying, but "any maritime special operator in the world would be proud to pull off such a complex operation."[45]

This was far from the first major seaborne terrorist attack—it wasn't even the first such attack in India. But the Mumbai raiders showed an extraordinary ability to exploit transnational littoral networks and both legitimate and illicit traffic patterns, inserting themselves into a coastal fishing fleet to cover their approach to the target. Their actions blurred the distinction between crime and war: both the Indian ship captain and local inhabitants initially mistook them for smugglers, and their opponents for much of the raid were police, not soldiers. They exploited Mumbai's complex patterns of coastal urbanization by landing from the sea close to the urban core but choosing landing places in slum settlements with limited government presence. Obviously enough, this approach wouldn't have worked without significant help from active or retired members of the Pakistani military, so Mumbai is rightly seen as a hybrid state/nonstate attack. Equally obviously, though, the attack could only have occurred in a highly networked, urban, littoral environment—precisely the environment that's becoming the global norm.

## II. Mogadishu: Things Fall Apart

Along with terrorism and proxy warfare, the urban, coastal, connected environment of the future will harbor more diffuse threats—what we might call "threats without enemies," which, by definition, aren't amenable to military or law enforcement responses.[46] These may arise not from the presence of armed groups per se but from complex interactions among criminal and military actors, domestic and international networks, city populations and governments, and the urban organism and its external environment.

Richard Norton's idea of the "feral city," quoted at the start of this chapter, is relevant here. A decade ago, in an influential article in the *Naval War College Review*, Norton defined a feral city as "a metropolis with a population of more than a million people, in a state the government of which has lost the ability to maintain the rule of law within the city's boundaries yet remains a functioning actor in the greater international system."[47] This kind of city, Norton points out, has no essential services or social safety net. Human security becomes a matter of individual initiative—conflict entrepreneurs and community militias emerge, Mad Max style. And yet feral cities don't just sink into utter chaos and collapse—they remain connected to international flows of people, information, and money. Nonstate groups step up to control key areas and functions, commerce continues (albeit with much corruption and violence), a black market economy flourishes, and massive levels of disease and pollution may be present, yet "even under these conditions, these cities continue to grow, and the majority of occupants do not voluntarily leave."[48] In urban metabolism terms, these are cities whose flows have overwhelmed the carrying capacity of their internal systems: the problem is not collapse (a lack of flow, as it were) but rather a superabundance of uncontrolled flows, and the toxic by-products arising from the city's failure to absorb and metabolize them.

Like the notion of urban metabolism, the idea of the feral city is drawn from a concept in biology. A feral animal is a domesticated one that has regressed to the wild, adapting to wilderness conditions and reacquiring (perhaps over generations) some characteristics of the original untamed species. The same thing happens with agricultural crops.[49] Feral populations may be coarser, rangier, and fiercer than their domesticated counterparts.[50] Norton applies this biological metaphor to cities that keep on functioning, after a fashion, even as they regress to the wild in the absence of government authority following a state collapse or during a war or natural disaster.

Feral animals and plants do actually infest cities during and after conflict or disaster and are prevalent on the fringes of larger built-up areas.[51] In Australian slang, the term *ferals* is also sometimes applied to humans who live in shanty settlements and reject the country's metropolitan culture. (Australia, like most developed countries, is heavily urbanized and, because of the inhospitable terrain and climate of its interior, it also has a very high degree of littoralization: 89 percent of Australia's population lives in cities and 82 percent lives within fifty miles of the sea.)[52] There's a radical, antiurban streak in "feral" subculture, and even though members may come from inner-city or middle-class areas, they favor a radical chic that makes a fetish of grassroots resistance to "the Man."[53]

A variant of this culture emerged in Britain during the August 2011 riots, in which marginalized city dwellers turned antiurban violence against the very cities where they lived. The destruction led *Daily Mail* columnist Richard Littlejohn to describe the rioters, who looted shops and vandalized symbols of authority and prosperity, as a "wolfpack of feral inner-city waifs and strays."[54] The notion of a lack of governability— the exact kind of thing Haussmann was trying to prevent in Paris, or the London authorities sought to address in their plan for the 2012 Olympics—is important here. It manifests in diffuse and apparently random patterns of crime and violence, and in self-marginalization by city dwellers who see themselves as victims of social injustice and economic exclusion, standing apart from the mainstream—in the city, but not of it—yet still maintain a high level of connectedness both with other members in their group and with the ebb and flow of the city itself.

The London riots also suggest that the idea of a peripheral settlement or population (which we've so far been using mainly in a spatial sense, meaning people or districts that are located on the edge of town) can be broadened to include people who are marginalized or excluded in an economic, political, or cultural sense, even if they live in the physical center of a city. In this reading, which is of course extremely familiar to anthropologists or urban sociologists, the "urban core" of a city isn't just the older, more central, downtown part of its built environment but also its economically, politically and culturally dominant terrain, the part of the city system that accumulates value at the expense of a periphery.[55] In fact, better-off populations in many countries have self-segregated, moving farther out of city centers to gated communities or simply to islands of prosperity in the suburbs, abandoning the city's center.[56] Urban peripheries, in this sense, aren't merely places on the physical outskirts of a city. Rather, they're areas that are dominated, marginalized, exploited, victimized, or excluded by the core—wherever they happen to be physically located. The "ferality" of the 2011 London rioters thus wasn't that of a core population attacking its own city but that of a marginalized population attacking a city it saw as someone else's.[57]

It's worth pointing out here that the conditions Norton describes can exist at multiple levels within an urban fractal pattern, meaning that one level of an urban system—a few districts within a city, a few neighborhoods within a district, a few blocks within a neighborhood, or a few houses within a street—can become feral even while the broader system remains within limits, or can slip out of equilibrium even as the higher-level system is getting more stable. Conversely, ferality can bleed from one level of an urban system into another, such as when a city's broader equilibrium is compromised by war or natural disaster, when a parent city or district loses the ability to integrate its component parts, when whole periurban districts effectively secede from the larger city (part of a broader process that some political geographers call "internal secession"), or when—as in the case of San Pedro Sula, discussed in Chapter 1—an urban metabolism loses the carrying capacity to process the by-products of the city's flows.[58]

The city or district may not collapse, and as we will see, it may be far from anarchic or ungoverned, but as it slips from state control and "goes feral," a series of overlapping threats emerges both for local residents and for the broader urban, national, and global systems that surround it.

Obviously enough, the very term *city* embodies peace, order, and tameness. English words that connote domesticity, peace, tranquility, development, and order, and which we use every day—words such as *politeness, civilization, citizen, civility, civilian, urbane,* and of course *police*—all derive from Latin and Greek words for the city (*polis, urbs, civis*). When Aristotle called man a political animal, he was referring to the predominantly urban habitat of our species: humans, he was arguing, are by their very nature "city-dwelling animals."[59] This idea of the city as the culmination of human development (literally, civilization) is so deeply embedded in our thinking that the notion of a feral city, moving backward in time and downward in social order, regressing to the warlike chaos of the wild—not a noncity but an *anticity*, a perversion of the natural way of things—can be deeply shocking.

This, I suspect, is what lies at the root of our modern fascination with world-ending societal collapse, a scenario beloved of survivalists and cinematographers. Think of the box-office success of movies such as *I Am Legend, Mad Max, World War Z,* or *28 Days Later*—or, indeed, the seductive appeal of any number of zombie apocalypse or dystopian sci-fi novels, comics, videogames, and television shows—all of which tap into a deep anxiety that underlies contemporary urbanized society. Urban theorists such as Stephen Graham argue that this anxiety is actually a direct result of the very processes of population growth, urbanization, and technological modernization that we're examining here, so attacks on a city's complex system-of-systems can be seen as a form of forced de-modernization.[60] Graham quotes the architecture critic Martin Pawley, who wrote that "fear of the dislocation of urban services on a massive scale" is now "endemic in the populations of all great cities."[61]

*The Battle of Mogadishu*

Richard Norton cited the Somali coastal city of Mogadishu as the only full-blown example of a feral city in existence when he was writing in 2003. Almost a decade later, my colleague Anna Prouse and I were fortunate enough to briefly visit Mogadishu, working on a field assessment for an NGO that provides reconstruction assistance in Somalia. By this time (in mid-2012) the country had been without a functioning government for more than twenty years, and the city was a byword for chaos, lawlessness, corruption, and violence.

But this wasn't the Mogadishu we saw. Far from it: on the surface, the city was a picture of prosperity. Many shops and houses were freshly painted, and signs on many street corners advertised auto parts, courses in business and English, banks, money changers and remittance services, cellphones, processed food, powdered milk, cigarettes, drinks, clothes, and shoes. The Bakara market in the center of town had a monetary exchange, where the Somali shilling—a currency that has survived without a state or a central bank for more than twenty years—floated freely on market rates that were set and updated twice daily. There were restaurants, hotels, and a gelato shop, and many intersections had busy produce markets. The coffee shops were crowded with men watching soccer on satellite television and good-naturedly arguing about scores and penalties. Traffic flowed freely, with occasional blue-uniformed, unarmed Somali National Police officers (male and female) controlling intersections. Besides motorcycles, scooters, and cars, there were horse-drawn carts sharing the roads with trucks loaded above the gunwales with bananas, charcoal, or firewood. Offshore, fishing boats and coastal freighters moved about the harbor, and near the docks several flocks of goats and sheep were awaiting export to cities around the Red Sea and farther afield. Power lines festooned telegraph poles along the roads, many with complex nests of telephone wires connecting them to surrounding buildings. Most Somalis on the street seemed to prefer cellphones, though, and many traders kept up a constant chatter on their mobiles. Mogadishu was a fully functioning city.

To be sure, after much time in Iraq, Afghanistan, and other garden spots, our standards of prosperity and order are somewhat elastic. (Anna, a civilian journalist by training, has eight years of continuous war zone experience in Iraq, working for the International Committee of the Red Cross, running a field hospital in Baghdad, then commanding the Italian provincial reconstruction team in Nasiriya; she tends to shrug off a little light mayhem as just part of an honest day's work.) And there were admittedly many signs of war and chaos: in the old part of town many houses remained ruined or pitted by bullets and shrapnel, and you could see the distinctive splash marks of RPG hits on many buildings. Refugees were camped in clusters of round, tarpaulin-covered, wood-framed huts in several parts of town, and (especially on the city's outskirts) civilians carried AK-47s casually slung over their shoulders or resting beside them as they worked. Weaving in and out of the traffic were "technicals" (pickup trucks that mount a heavy machine gun on the flatbed behind the driver's cab) crammed with Somali National Army troops in camouflage fatigues, armed police, or green-uniformed militia, and there were Soviet-made tanks and armored fighting vehicles on the roads out of town. On the fringes of the city there were signs of more recent fighting, with destroyed houses, downed trees, and the occasional shot-out vehicle or dead animal. Much of the country was still recovering from a deadly drought and famine that affected all of East Africa in 2010–11, and Shabaab militants still controlled a sizeable chunk of Somalia's territory and population, though they were fast losing ground.

Some government buildings in the central Villa Somalia compound were well maintained and luxuriously furnished, but others were much less salubrious: Anna and I sat in on a meeting between an NGO and a minister of the Transitional Federal Government in his well-furnished but darkened office, the only air-conditioned room in a large, mostly empty ministry building otherwise without water, furniture, or electrical power. This minister's family had fled Somalia in the early 1990s, and he'd lived most of his life in the United States; still, he unabashedly sought a bribe in return for helping the NGO's work by calling off members of his own ministry who were obstructing it. There was gunfire from time to time, Shabaab sent scouts and probing attacks into town on some nights, we moved mainly in South African–designed mine-resistant Casspir vehicles, and convoys belonging to AMISOM—the African Union Mission in Somalia, a peacekeeping force that had succeeded, against all expectations, in seizing Mogadishu from Shabaab over the past year— were occasionally ambushed. But it was nothing like the intensity of Iraq, Afghanistan, or even Pakistan: the conflict in Somalia in 2012 was a genuinely small war.

And Mogadishu was far from the dust-blown desert of popular imagination, with hopeless hordes of starving refugees, sinister gold-toothed warlords, and murderous militias battened like leeches onto the city's fly-infested corpse. That image, the dominant picture of Mogadishu in much of the Western world, crystallized in *Black Hawk Down*, Mark Bowden's graphic and intimately observed account of the bloody battle of Mogadishu on October 3–4, 1993, and in the 2002 Hollywood movie based on his book. Bowden's depiction of Mogadishu defined the city for a generation, creating a picture of the place in the public imagination (and in the minds of many military officers who read his book or studied accounts of the battle) that, in the rueful words of one Somali writer, would "inform all discourse on Mogadishu and Somalia from then on."[62]

There has been a debate in both popular and academic circles about whether Mogadishu in 2012 was improving and recovering from conflict or whether in fact the progress made since 2010 remained fragile and reversible. Some pointed to the city's growth and business activity as a sign of recovery. But many of the aspects I've described—functioning businesses, international connectedness, population growth, corruption, the presence of nonstate armed groups alongside state representatives, and so on—are accounted for in Richard Norton's concept of the feral city, so the city's vitality may have reflected not better governance or stability but rather just a robust and well-established ferality after two decades of conflict. Still, the city Anna and I saw in mid-2012 seemed to be very unlike the bleak, violent wasteland portrayed in *Black Hawk Down*.

*Black Hawk Down*, of course, is a work of narrative nonfiction. As such, the book describes Mogadishu through the eyes of the Rangers, SEALs, and Delta operators of Task Force (TF) Ranger as they flew into the heart of the city during the afternoon raid that triggered the battle. In the Rangers' eyes, Mogadishu was indeed "the world capital of things-gone-completely-to-hell. It was as if the city had been ravaged by some fatal urban disease. The few paved avenues were crumbling and littered with mountains of trash, debris, and the rusted hulks of burned-out vehicles . . . everything of value had been looted, right down to metal window frames, doorknobs, and hinges. At night, campfires glowed from third- and fourth-story windows of the old Polytechnic Institute. Every open space was clotted with the dense makeshift villages of the disinherited, round stick huts covered with layers of rags and shacks made of scavenged scraps of wood and patches of rusted tin. From above they looked like an advanced stage of some festering urban rot."[63]

The raid was intended as a quick, in-and-out snatch operation, lasting an hour at most. The mission was to seize two senior leaders of

Mohammed Hassan Farah Aidid's Somali National Alliance, including elders of the Habr Gidr, Aidid's segment of the influential Hawiye clan. A security force from the 3rd Battalion, U.S. 75th Ranger Regiment would lead the air assault, fast-roping into urban intersections to create a four-corner cordon around the target building, while Delta operators and SEALs would land on its roof and clear the building downward, floor by floor, to secure their captives. A ground convoy from the task force base at the Mogadishu airport, on the coast just outside town, would pick up the assault team and the detainees and return them to the base for questioning, under air cover from MH-60L Black Hawks and AH-6J Little Bird attack helicopters. The plan was based on a standardized mission template that the task force planners had developed over dozens of raids, and it had worked before. But this afternoon, in the dense urban maze around the Bakara market, things quickly unraveled.

From the moment the Rangers fast-roped into the ocher dust cloud their helicopters kicked up on the streets of Mogadishu, it was clear that there would be much more resistance than on previous raids: the target house was smack in the middle of the district that was the main stronghold for Aidid's Somali National Alliance militia, in one of the densest, busiest, and economically most important parts of the city, the so-called Black Sea. Though the assault force successfully cleared the house and seized the captives, both the assaulters and the ground convoy suffered many killed and wounded during the extraction, and they were forced to fight a series of running gun battles through the narrow streets of downtown Mogadishu that included several large ambushes and dozens of smaller ones. By 4:30 p.m., two Black Hawks of the U.S. Army's 160th Special Operations Aviation Regiment (160th SOAR) had been shot down in the city. TF Ranger became pinned down, unable to maneuver— "fixed," in military parlance—because of its need to secure the helicopter crash sites and to protect and extract its wounded.

Attacked from all sides by a self-organizing swarm of Somali National Alliance fighters and local citizens, who seemed able to concentrate and disperse at will and to predict the task force's moves faster than the Americans could react, TF Ranger was quickly surrounded. As night fell, the troops were trapped in a makeshift perimeter, bunkered in several houses near one of the Black Hawk crash sites, fighting for their lives. Just before dawn the next morning, an ad hoc relief column of Pakistani,

Malaysian, and U.S. troops under United Nations command, riding in tanks and armored personnel carriers, shot its way in and rescued them, but not before the stranded unit lost eighteen soldiers killed, seventy-three wounded, and one pilot captured. The UN relief force suffered two killed and nine wounded.

Several of the American dead were later dragged through the streets and publicly mutilated by the mob. This was a stinging humiliation for the world's most powerful military, the elite troops of a superpower that had just emerged victorious from the Cold War and the Gulf War, with expansive ambitions for what President George H. W. Bush had called a "new world order" defined by American primacy.[64] American losses were far less than those of the Somalis, however: militia sources later estimated that Aidid's militia lost 315 fighters killed and 812 wounded in the battle, while the International Committee of the Red Cross calculated that the battle cost somewhere between 1,500 and 3,000 Somali casualties, including many civilians.[65] Within weeks, President Clinton pulled American forces out, the United Nations drew down its involvement, and Somalia sank back into a pattern of chaotic violence that would last two more decades.

To the Americans, the dense coastal city of Mogadishu was an active, living participant in the battle: "It seemed like the whole city was shooting at them . . . Mogadishu was massing and closing in on them . . . the city was shredding them block by block . . . the whole fucking city was trying to kill them!"[66] These words resonate with what I (to a very slight degree, and others far more intensely) experienced during the urban counter-insurgency in Iraq: a powerful dread that seemed to seep out of the very buildings, roads, and other structures of the urban landscape itself. I remember one war game back in the United States in March 2008 when Lieutenant Colonel Joe L'Etoile, one of the most successful Marine battalion commanders of the war, was giving a brief on the way his unit had crushed Al Qaeda in the Zaidon area, west of Baghdad, the year before. He began talking about what it felt like to patrol the Iraqi streets, and I found myself breaking out in a cold sweat from the sudden inrush of memories. I turned, embarrassed, to leave and compose myself, only to see that at least half of the two hundred combat-experienced officers in the briefing room were sweating the same cold sweat; I quietly resumed my seat. The writer David Morris captured this feeling in his description of the city of Ramadi:

Even now when I try to recall what the city looks like, what comes to me is nothing more than a pocked stretch of boulevard surrounded on both sides by heaps of rubbled concrete, iron palings, trash. Swirls of dust playing over the blacktop. The smell of cordite. Everything still but a grizzled dog patrolling the ruins. It can be like this—high noon, not a soul around, no threat imminent—but you can feel the sheer sinister energy of the joint. As if even the streets want you dead. Driving through downtown Ramadi for the first time gave me an unshakable vision of mystery and death. Just staring at the rubble set my heart pounding with the knowledge of the lives lost per yard.[67]

In the case of Mogadishu, the Rangers had poked a hornet's nest in the Black Sea district: they had attacked the city itself, only to be chewed up and spat out, stunned and bloodied. In systems terms, this is pretty much exactly what happened on the day of the battle, which even today local civilians know as *maalintii rangers*, "the day of the Rangers," marking it as an unusually intense episode—even for a city that had already become habituated to enormous bloodshed during the civil war and would see at least two more pitched battles, in 2006 and 2011. TF Ranger's actions over the weeks before the battle had massively disrupted the city as a system: previous raids (in particular, an attack on a Mogadishu house by helicopters that fired Hellfire missiles, killing fifty-four people, including many noncombatants) had generated intense hatred of the Rangers and even greater hostility toward their helicopters. This contributed to the ferocity with which local fighters—Aidid's militia and armed civilians alike—responded after the two aircraft went down on October 3. The Americans had thrust a large force, with heavy weapons, many vehicles, and more than a dozen helicopters, into the core of the city. When they pushed hard into a key pressure point in the political, economic, and material flow of the urban organism, they jabbed the system in a place that hurt, and that system pushed back even harder.

Several days after the battle, as former ambassador Robert Oakley negotiated with Habr Gidr elders for the release of Mike Durant (the 160th SOAR pilot captured by Aidid's fighters), he made a revealing comment:

What will happen if a few weeks go by and Mr. Durant is not released? We'll decide that we have to rescue him, and whether we have the right place or the wrong place, there's going to be a fight with your people. The minute the guns start again, all restraint on the U.S. side goes. Just look at the stuff coming in here now. An aircraft carrier, tanks, gunships . . . the works. Once the fighting starts, all this pent-up anger is going to be released. This whole part of the city will be destroyed, men women, children, camels, cats, dogs, goats, donkeys, everything . . . That would be tragic for all of us, but that's what will happen.[68]

Ambassador Oakley was, in effect, warning the clan elders that if they did not release their prisoner, the Americans would kill the city. This tendency of military forces to kill cities—something political geographers call "urbicide"—is something to which we'll return at the end of this chapter. But first it's important to understand how TF Ranger's actions intersected with the metabolism of what clearly was already, by 1993, a feral city.

To understand this, it's useful to compare what occurred in Mogadishu in 1993 with what happened in Mumbai in 2008. In both cases, an external actor conducted a raid on a preidentified target; in both cases the raid drew a strong response from the targeted city. In Mumbai the LeT raiders moved dispersed in small teams, outmaneuvering the ponderous Indian response, and using low-tech weaponry, combined with high-tech situational awareness tools and a remote command-and-control node, to maintain the initiative, inflict severe damage, and achieve their political goal. In Mogadishu, on the other hand, it was the raiders who—despite their high-tech weaponry and helicopters—were outmaneuvered, became pinned down in the city by a swarm of small groups of local fighters, and lost the initiative. Lacking heavy armored vehicles, which would have allowed them to move through the urban environment without having either to leave the area or to shoot back and thus risk killing civilians, they were forced to apply heavy ground and airborne firepower in order to protect and extract themselves. Once they lost their mobility after the aircraft were downed, the raiders were forced to hold a static defensive position and to suffer and inflict very significant casualties. It was only the arrival of the armored relief column, with its hardened and protected mobility, that allowed TF Ranger to be safely extracted from the trap. In what was supposed to be a humanitarian operation to feed starving Somalis, such carnage was politically unacceptable at the strategic level, and the battle ultimately forced a U.S. withdrawal from Somalia. What was it that made the difference?

I've already mentioned how the LeT raiders at Mumbai nested within the urban metabolism of the two megacities—Karachi and Mumbai— that formed the launching pad and target for their raid. They slipped out of Karachi under cover of the harbor's dense maritime traffic, blended into the flow of local cargo and fishing fleets, then slipped into Mumbai by nesting within the illicit networks of smuggling, trade flow, and movement of people, exploiting the presence of informal settlements with little government presence (in effect, feral subdistricts) close to the urban core of the giant coastal city. Once ashore, the teams dispersed and blended into the flow of the city's densest area as they moved toward diversionary targets (taxis, the railway station, a café, a hospital) that had been carefully selected precisely to disrupt the city's flow, draw off Indian counterterrorism forces, and hamper an effective response, before they hit main targets that had been chosen for sustained local and international media effect.

This type of attack relies on understanding in great detail the urban metabolism and the associated material and nonmaterial flows that make a city function. This is probably why the LeT raiders and their sponsors put so much effort and time into detailed reconnaissance, building a picture of the city's physical and human terrain and of the urban metabolism of Mumbai and its surrounding coastal waters. In effect, the raiders had infested the city and were riding its internal systems, much as, say, a parasite infests and moves within the flow of a host's bloodstream.

In contrast, TF Ranger in Mogadishu had very little time (less than six weeks) to develop an understanding of the way the city worked—what we've called the *territorial logic* or *systems logic* of the city. Like LeT, the raiders came from the sea, maneuvering over the ocean in their helicopters before coming in low from the north to strike the target building. Unlike LeT, however, the Americans didn't nest in the city's natural flow: they deliberately ignored it. The task force commander, Major General William Garrison, knew the risks of going into Aidid's stronghold in the Black Sea neighborhood. Most of the United Nations forces in Mogadishu studiously avoided that area, including the Bakara market—the key economic terrain in the city, central to the Habr Gidr's control of Mogadishu's urban flow. By assaulting straight into the area, in broad daylight,

TF Ranger was directly challenging Aidid's power base and courting a strong counterpunch.

As Garrison had warned in a memo to Washington only a few weeks before the battle, "If we go into the vicinity of the Bakara Market, there's no question we'll win the firefight, but we might lose the war."[69] Apart from the obvious point that this was *not* a war but (in its original intent, at least) a humanitarian assistance operation, Garrison's memo makes it clear that he knew the risks involved. These risks arose not only from ignoring the spatial logic of the city (attacking the places where an enemy was strongest) or the temporal logic of the enemy network (selecting a place where Aidid's militia could respond quickly by massing combat power at short notice) but also from ignoring the city's metabolic flow—in particular, the daily qat cycle.

The leafy green qat plant is chewed as a stimulant across Somalia and the broader Horn of Africa and southwest Arabian region. Qat is very perishable and sours quickly, so over time a complex and informal but highly efficient system has evolved to ensure its timely distribution. The qat system involves a network of distributors and small traders in all major towns and cities and uses aircraft, boats, and trucks to link ports, airports, and distribution hubs with markets and small roadside stalls. This system puts the day's fresh crop on market stalls across the entire region by mid- to late morning every day, almost without fail. The plant contains an alkaloid compound called cathinone, which has ephedrine- or amphetamine-like qualities. True aficionados—most if not all of whom are men—crave Coca-Cola and other sweet drinks to accompany it. (This, incidentally, is partly why one of the few manufacturing facilities to survive in Somalia throughout the feral chaos of the last decade was a Coca-Cola bottling plant, financed by clan contributions, which opened in Mogadishu in 2004.)[70] By midafternoon the daily qat chew is in full swing across the region's towns and cities, with thousands of young, armed men engaged in argumentative conversation and agitated political discussion that often leads to fights and celebratory (or homicidal) gunfire. By early evening the buzz is over, the qat chewers have crashed, and the city goes quiet. But in the middle of the afternoon most military-age males in town are still violently high, making this perhaps not the best time to attack a nest of heavily armed qat-chewing militiamen.

The aviators of 160th SOAR are known as Night Stalkers because of their preference—like light infantry and special operations forces the world over—for fighting at night. Infrared and thermal imaging give modern forces of this kind a true nighttime edge and (combined today with real-time imagery from drones, satellites, and surveillance aircraft) can allow rapid and effective maneuver under pitch-black conditions. Indeed, the darker the night, the greater the advantage in strike operations of the sort in which TF Ranger specialized. Again, a midafternoon attack is hardly ideal for a force that's optimized to fight at night. That General Garrison chose to ignore these issues implies confidence rather than carelessness: as we've seen, he knew the risks but counted on his force's speed of movement and superior combat power, especially its helicopter support, to overcome them. His choice of an afternoon time frame was also almost certainly driven by the perceived need to strike a high-value target—a meeting of Aidid's two lieutenants and the Habr Gidr leaders, being held in the house that was attacked—before it disappeared. Indeed, this whole style of operations is known in the special ops business as "time-sensitive targeting," or TST, because of the paramount need for speed.

This highlights another key difference between Mogadishu and Mumbai: the Mumbai raiders were more or less agnostic as to the individual identity of those they killed. They focused on causing maximum disruption and shock to the city itself, and as described earlier, they killed civilians because of their group identity (their role in the city's emergency services, their presence at a key urban node, or their nationality) or their media value, rather than targeting particular individuals. In contrast, TF Ranger was going after specific individuals, so the organizing principle of the operation—time-sensitive targeting and individual identity—was completely different. For the LeT raiders the city itself was the target, while individuals were secondary; for TF Ranger the individuals were the target, and this—combined with confidence in their own airborne firepower and mobility—may have led them to discount the effect of their raid on the city as a system; when that system pushed back (and in particular when Aidid's militia unexpectedly succeeded in disabling their air assets), they quickly lost the initiative and got bogged down in an urban fight in which the locals had clear advantages. If the Mumbai raiders were like a parasite that infested the city and made it convulse, TF Ranger acted instead like a belligerent drunk in a bar brawl, poking someone in the eye and getting punched in return.

It's hard to confirm how many of the fighters who confronted TF Ranger in the battle of Mogadishu were members of Aidid's Somali National Alliance militia and how many were simply local armed civilians: militia affiliations in Somalia were, and are, loose and informal. In any case, the urban density and connectedness of Mogadishu were key factors in the locals' quick reaction against the raid. As we noted earlier, these days cellphone use is widespread among Somalis, but even in 1993, in the pre-cellphone area, the ability to pass word rapidly in downtown Mogadishu, using radios, runners, and signal fires, was a key local capability. The battle occurred in an area where the terrain and population were intimately familiar to the locals, distances were short, it was easy to move on foot, Aidid's core group could quickly draw on local allies for reinforcements, and there were multiple routes through the city to and from any given point. The locals could thus react flexibly to American moves—they could aggregate or disperse, their force could shrink or grow in size in response to the changing threat, and they could put ambushes or roadblocks in place ahead of the ground convoy.

Once Aidid's militia succeeded in downing the Black Hawks using specially modified RPGs, the Americans became pinned down, and they were forced to concentrate their firepower and air assets around the crash sites. When this happened, instead of exerting a general suppressive effect, TF Ranger was now focusing intense but localized combat power in a tightly limited area, and this relieved the pressure on fighters in other parts of the city, making it easier for them to maneuver with impunity and without detection. Local city dwellers—infuriated by the raids and humiliations of the past few weeks, motivated to repel the violent intrusion of the Americans, and hopped up on qat and Coke—quickly swarmed to the attack from all directions. TF Ranger was indeed in a fight against the whole city.

### Somali Swarm Tactics

On the other side of that fight, the Somali militia who faced off against Garrison's troops in the streets of Mogadishu had no formal military training, and many of its members were killed or exiled in the years of feral anarchy that followed. Mohammed Farah Aidid himself died, and his militia was broken up among various clan groups. So it's impossible to sit down and interview Aidid about his tactical reasoning on the day of the battle, or to directly observe his militia operating in the Mogadishu area. But we can do the next best thing: some units of today's Somali National Army (SNA) descend from the same clan militias that opposed TF Ranger, and even today these units fight the same way, with almost the same weapons. To the extent that these troops—whose military education consisted almost entirely of on-the-job training in battles among local clan militias in a feral city—represent the self-taught tactics that have proliferated across Somalia over the past twenty years, they can give us an inside view of the fast and deadly swarm tactics that TF Ranger experienced in 1993. They also highlight the differences between true, autonomous urban swarm tactics (as practiced in Somalia) and the superficially similar remote-control system used by the Mumbai raiders.

Thus in mid-2012 it was a distinct professional pleasure to see these troops in the field during an operation near Afgoye, a town about fifteen miles northwest of Mogadishu in the lower Shebelle River valley. Somali troops, with Ugandan and Burundian forces from AMISOM plus a small number of highly professional unarmed Western advisors, had captured the town from Shabaab a few days before Anna and I arrived, and they were busy consolidating their positions.

The SNA fighters talked me through the way they operated in the thickets and watercourses on the outskirts of Afgoye. The terrain here was fairly typical of this part of Somalia: an undulating camel-thorn scrub, broken by dry watercourses and the occasional road, farm plot, or cluster of houses, with visibility varying from a few yards to a few hundred feet. They explained how each squad operated with its technical (the gun-carrying truck I mentioned earlier, on which the Somali tactical system is centered) and how the different squads cooperated and coordinated their actions. What was most impressive was the speed and tactical skill with which these fighters—all ex-militia with little formal training—could move and fight.

These SNA troops had only one basic tactical unit (the mounted squad, comprising a technical carrying a heavy weapon and six to eight fighters with their equipment and supplies) and one tactical formation (the extended line). Their vehicles would move abreast through the bush, about one visual distance apart (a varying space, constantly changing so that each vehicle kept its neighbors just barely in view), and generally avoiding roads. In open terrain the formation would be extremely widely spread, and where visual ranges were shorter it would tighten up. In an urban environment the SNA troops would adopt a variation on this approach, moving whenever possible on several parallel streets at once, picking up their bearings at each intersection in order to stay roughly level with each other. In this way, they achieved the classic tactical goal of moving dispersed but fighting concentrated. Likewise, by expanding the size of their formation as far as the terrain and visibility would allow whenever they were out of actual contact with the enemy, they increased the likelihood that when they did make contact, the flanks of their formation would be wider than the enemy's position. Like a rugby team playing a running game, their entire approach—the tempo and flow of the way they moved and fought—was designed around creating and exploiting a series of these overlaps.

Because of the fluid nature of the fighting in the lower Shebelle River valley at this time, most combat actions were encounter battles—engagements where one or both sides are moving or temporarily halted (rather than dug-in in prepared defensive positions). When the SNA encountered a Shabaab group, the SNA vehicles that were first to meet the enemy would immediately halt and lay down heavy suppressive fire. The natural momentum of the advance would cause the other vehicles, not yet in contact with the enemy, to push forward a short distance, perhaps twenty-five or fifty yards, before they had time to react and turn in toward the firefight, putting them naturally in a flanking position. By the time the flanking vehicles did begin to react, there would be no need for radio communication, formal orders, or coordination—each vehicle would simply angle in toward the closest gunfire and, maintaining the extended line, sweep forward until it could see the enemy. This would naturally (again without orders) place these vehicles on the flanks or rear of the enemy, resulting in a quick and automatic encirclement, or near-encirclement, of the Shabaab position.

Once they could see the enemy, the troops in the back of each technical would dismount and form another extended line on foot about ten yards in front of their gun truck. The vehicle and the soldiers who had dismounted would then sweep forward together, the lightly equipped fighters jogging fast through the bush until they came under fire and were forced to take cover. Because of the technical's height, the muzzle of its weapon (often a Soviet- or Chinese-made 12.7 mm or 14.5 mm heavy machine gun) could be as high as nine or ten feet above the ground, and it could thus continue firing safely over the heads of the dismounted fighters. The squad leader would coordinate movement using voice commands. He would either fire the heavy weapon himself or stand next to the gunner on the flatbed of the technical, from where he could lean down and direct the driver through a window. Once the dismounted troops were engaged in a direct firefight, the gun truck's forward advance would stop, and it would lay down fire on the enemy position, allowing other vehicles and their dismounted troops to close in on it (again without orders, simply guided by the sound of the guns). These reinforcements would pile on until the enemy was destroyed or forced to break contact.

Now, this is an obvious point, but you should understand that I'm putting this into my words, not theirs, and that this is a neatened-up, theoretical description. Real fights are always messy and chaotic, and real fighters rarely do exactly what they're supposed to do under fire. And yet any leader of irregular cavalry or light infantry (or, indeed, any mounted constabulary officer) of the past century would recognize these simple tactics. Echoing the comment of the special operations officer on Mumbai, any professional soldier in the world would be proud to command troops with this kind of tactical initiative. Indeed, I found only one slight issue on which to fault the SNA tactics: the fact that the squad leader stayed in the vehicle while his troops dismounted to assault. Western tactics would call for the leader to dismount with the troops, carrying a radio to talk back to the vehicle and direct its fire, and leaving a trusted subordinate, as vehicle commander, to maneuver the gun truck.

But as soon as this thought entered my head, I realized I was looking at the Somali squad in completely the wrong way: I was misapplying the social and economic framework of a professional state-run military to an organization that had evolved from an irregular militia. In the Somali environment of fragmented, semianarchic clan organizations in which these tactics had emerged, the way someone became a squad leader in the first place was to own the technical (an extremely substantial piece of capital equipment). The squad leader became the squad leader precisely because it was his vehicle, so it would have been the height of stupidity for him to dismount and thereby cede control of the gun truck to someone else—let alone to leave someone behind him with a machine gun. He might not have remained the squad leader for long! Moreover, dismounted fighters are cheap and replaceable, but the vehicle is a precious investment that is decidedly not expendable. Seen from this perspective, the SNA's "mounted swarm" tactics have (like any tactical system) an economic, political, and social logic, as well as a military grammar.

It actually takes much longer to read these words than to execute a swarming maneuver of this kind. Because each vehicle and its fighters is a semiautonomous unit that needs no formal orders, because the momentum of the advance puts each vehicle in roughly the right position at any given moment, and because the overhead geometry of supporting fire from the vehicle avoids the need for complicated fire control orders, a swarm fight can be incredibly fast and smooth.

Each dismounted fighter and each vehicle commander need only remember five basic rules. These rules define how the group fights at every scale (the individual, the dismounted squad, the vehicle, and the group of vehicles) and they never change, regardless of the terrain, the tactical situation, or the size of the engagement. They are: "Maintain an extended line abreast," "Keep your neighbors just in sight, but no closer," "Move to the sound of the guns," "Dismount when you see the enemy," and "When you come under fire, stop and fire back."

This explains the speed and flexibility with which the fighters were able to react to TF Ranger's foray into the Black Sea: the swarm tactics I was observing in 2012 were directly descended from those used by Aidid's militia in 1993. In systems terms, this kind of autonomous, rule-based maneuver is the essence of a self-synchronizing swarm: like individual birds in a flock, each vehicle and its troops follow a few simple rules to maintain formation and react to the enemy, and like the overall flock, their formation constantly shifts and changes size and shape (without orders) in response to changes in the terrain and the tactical situation. The same rules that bring reinforcements to swell the size of the swarm when it hits a major obstacle also cause it to disperse when there is no imminent threat. In fact, the size, shape, and disposition of the tactical swarm are completely emergent properties of the rule-based swarm maneuver system itself, something that happens without conscious direction or formal control from a central commander.

This is why, in the battle for Afgoye just past, the Somali brigade commander had simply roamed about the battlefield, armed only with a pistol and carrying the short walking stick that's the symbol of age and authority across Somalia, and encouraging his troops: he had no need to run a centralized command post, since his fighters fought autonomously by rule, rather than following conscious, formally expressed orders. Rather, the commander's role was to read the battle, to know where his presence was most needed, and—critically—to think ahead, beyond the current fight, to the next engagement, and the next, and the next. He might also have brought with him, under his personal control, a commander's reserve of troops, vehicles, and ammunition with which to reinforce weak points or exploit success. A simple handheld radio, connecting him to his most trusted commanders, allowed him to tap into a continuous feed of chatter among those fighting the battle and thus maintain his situational awareness and decide where he needed to be. Strictly speaking, however, such a tactical system should work in complete radio silence, avoiding the need to expose plans to electronic eavesdropping and making the swarm formation relatively invulnerable to jamming or radio deception. Using these tactics, an experienced unit of this type (and remember, these fighters had, in some cases, ten years of nearly continuous irregular warfare under their belts) could—in theory at least—maneuver at a vastly faster tempo than a regular conventional force relying on orders.

At the unit level, an organization that operates like this doesn't have a command post that can be found and killed. Ever since J. F. C. Fuller's *Plan 1919*, modern maneuver tactics have centered not on fighting and defeating each and every enemy combat unit but rather on finding and destroying the enemy's command node. Writing at the bloody climax of World War I in 1918, Fuller argued that "the first method may be compared to a succession of slight wounds which will eventually cause [an enemy] to bleed to death; the second—a shot through the brain."[71] In a similar vein, Colonel John Warden's "five rings" model of targeting analysis for airpower seeks to achieve physical paralysis by finding and targeting key nodes (centers of gravity) in an enemy system.[72] But a fully decentralized swarm system like the one these Somali fighters employed *has* no brain, no central command node that can be killed. The swarm's command system is distributed, rule-based, emergent, and thus embedded in the system itself, not tied to any one person, vehicle, or physical location. This suggests the uncomfortable possibility that even if TF Ranger had succeeded in killing General Aidid, the loss of its commander would have had a negligible effect on his organization's ability to function.

The Somali approach is also a very different solution to the same problem that led Lashkar-e-Taiba to adopt its remote-node command model for the Mumbai attack: where LeT made its command node invulnerable by putting it in another country and relying on Internet and satellite connectivity to connect the operations room to the assault teams on the ground, the Somali militia made their command node invulnerable by not having one at all. When I asked the SNA soldiers how their tactics differed from those of Shabaab and the various local militias, they laughed. "They *are* us," they said with a shrug, pointing out that many of them—like many Shabaab fighters—had previously served with militias of one kind or another before joining the SNA.

### Long-Term Flows

As well as these swarm tactics (which we'll return to in Chapter 5), we've already noted the way that temporal rhythm and spatial logic affected the Mogadishu battle over the term of the city's daily flow cycle. But there is a lower-frequency cycle also, a longer-term metabolic flow that shapes the urban environment in a place such as Mogadishu. This is the pattern of population movement, urbanization, and littoralization, occurring over decades, and it was this pattern that gave the city its structure, both in 1993 and today. This is obvious if we note that—in common with other organisms—the history of an urban organism is physically recorded in its structure, just as scar tissue, a lost digit, a callus, or a growth in a biological organism is a permanent structural manifestation of that organism's past. Mogadishu today, like any other city or organism, embodies a physical record of its history.

The Somali writer Nuruddin Farah, writing in 1998, brilliantly captured the long-term flows that have shaped Mogadishu. "If Mogadishu occupies an ambiguous space in our minds and hearts," Farah wrote, "it is because ours is a land with an overwhelming majority of pastoralists, who are possessed of a deep urbophobia. Maybe this is why most Somalis do not seem unduly perturbed by the fate of the capital: a city broken into segments, each of them ruthlessly controlled by an alliance of militias."[73]

Farah identified several waves of urbanization and coastal settlement that over decades drew in population from the hinterland, expanded the city, changed its social and political character, and created accretions of new peripheral settlements around the older coastal core:

> Before independence, huge numbers of Somalis, who could best be described as semi-pastoralists, moved to Mogadishu; many of them joined the civil service, the army and the police. It was as if they were out to do away with the ancient cosmopolitan minority known as "Xamari," Xamar being the local name for the city. Within a short time, a second influx of people, this time more unequivocally pastoralist, arrived from far-flung corners to swell the ranks of the semi-pastoralists, by now city-dwellers. In this way, the demography of the city changed. Neither of these groups was welcomed by a third—those pastoralists who had always got their livelihood from the land on which Mogadishu was sited (natives, as it were, of the city). They were an influential sector of the population in the run-up to independence, throwing in their lot with the colonialists in the hope not only of recovering lost ground but of inheriting total political power. Once a much broader coalition of nationalists had taken control of the country, these "nativists" resorted to threats, suggesting that the recent migrants quit Mogadishu. "Flag independence" dawned in 1960 with widespread jubilation drowning the sound of these ominous threats. It was another thirty years before they were carried out.[74]

These tensions, which arose from long-term flows of population, goods, and money, and a struggle for control of economic resources and nodes within Mogadishu—including, particularly, the port and the livestock and trading markets—manifested themselves physically in a patchwork of informal urban settlements, and socially in a pattern of fragmented territorial control across the city, with each group dominating its own area and the clans coexisting in an uneasy, shifting pattern of temporary alliances of convenience.

Nuruddin Farah's analysis here echoes the Palestinian historian Hanna Batatu's comment on the urban-rural dynamic between Damascus and the rural hinterland of Syria, suggesting a widespread pattern of conflict between population groups that have traditionally dominated cities and the former peasants or rural dwellers arriving as migrants from the countryside. Batatu identifies this as a cyclical flow, "a phenomenon that repeats itself: rural people, driven by economic distress or lack of security, move into the main cities, settle in the outlying districts, enter before long into relations or forge common links with elements of the urban poor, who are themselves often earlier migrants from the countryside, and together they challenge the old established classes."[75]

Batatu's notion echoes an old and very influential idea that came out of the coastal cities of North Africa in the fourteenth century—a theory of the circulation of elites put forward by the great Tunisian scholar Ibn Khaldun. As Malise Ruthven points out, Khaldun's theory, sometimes called Khaldunian circulation, is based on the idea that "'leadership exists through superiority, and superiority only through *asabiyya*—social cohesion or group feeling. In desert conditions, the social solidarity of the tribe is vital to its survival. If and when the tribes decide to unite, their cohesion puts the city-folk at their mercy. Inspired by religion, they conquer the towns, which are incapable of defending themselves, and become the rulers until such time as, corrupted by luxury and the loss of their group cohesion, they are in turn replaced by a new nomadic dynasty."[76]

This same cyclic flow seems to have been present in Mogadishu's evolution. Indeed, Farah's and Batatu's analyses turn on its head one common interpretation of Somali history: namely, the idea that the intergroup competition, corruption, winner-take-all abuse of defeated opponents, and clan-based violence that Mogadishu experienced after the fall of the Barre regime in 1991 was primarily a *symptom* of state collapse. The popular notion is that this chaos emerged after Barre's rule fell apart under the pressure of war, drought, and economic collapse. On the contrary, in Farah's telling, it was the pattern of fragmented urbanization (producing marginalized garrison communities with patron-client connections to political leaders) and rapid population growth (with the resultant lack of resilience and carrying capacity in the city's metabolism) that produced the violence and instability that eventually destroyed the state. In this version of events, Mogadishu didn't become a feral city because the state collapsed; rather, the state collapsed because the city was *already* feral. Mogadishu's very structure created a political and social space for the city's own destruction at the hands of "a cast of borderline characters posing as city-folk leading armed communities of marginalised nomads. . . . The savageries visited on the city's residents [were] master-minded by urbophobics already installed in Mogadishu, which for hundreds of years has lain under the envious gaze of people who hated and feared it because they felt excluded from its power politics."[77]

I just used the term "garrison community" in reference to Mogadishu. This expression is widely used in the Caribbean, on the other side of the world from Somalia, to describe the informal systems of security and order that have emerged in marginalized urban settlements in Jamaica. One district of Kingston—the coastal slum known as Tivoli Gardens—exemplifies the threats and challenges of yet another part of the spectrum that will affect the urbanized, coastal, connected environment of the future.

## III.  Kingston: Garrison Communities and Nested Networks

*6:32 p.m., Monday May 24, 2010*
*U.S. Embassy, Kingston, Jamaica*

As the sun set on a long day, Isaiah Parnell, chargé d'affaires at the U.S. embassy in Kingston, sent an Immediate cable to Secretary of State Hillary Clinton in Washington, D.C., with copies to the Central Intelligence Agency, Drug Enforcement Administration, Department of Justice, Special Operations Command, Southern Command, chairman of the Joint Chiefs of Staff, and U.S. embassies in Ottawa and London. His cable read, in part:

> At midday on May 24 the Jamaican Defence Force (JDF) launched an all-out assault on the heavily-defended Tivoli Gardens "Garrison" stronghold controlled by Christopher "Dudas" Coke, the alleged overlord of the "Shower Posse" international crime syndicate who is wanted to face extradition to the USA on drugs and weapons trafficking charges. . . . The JDF fired mortars and then used bulldozers to break through heavy barricades which Coke's supporters had erected to block entry to the fortified enclave. As of 6:00 p.m. May 24, heavy fighting continued in Tivoli Gardens, and a fire was burning out of control in the adjacent Coronation Market. The JDF plans to continue operations through the night. Large numbers of women and children have fled the area. . . .

Elsewhere in the metropolitan area, armed gangs attacked police stations, overturned vehicles, and erected roadblocks. The Hannah Town
Jamaica Constabulary Force (JCF) station was destroyed by fire, and
police were pinned down by gunfire at their Denham Town station.
Armed gang members also surrounded and threatened to overrun
the central police compound and central lock-up. In response to the
escalating civil unrest, Prime Minister (PM) Bruce Golding declared a
limited state of emergency, which took effect at 6:00 p.m. May 23 and
is expected to last a month.[78]

We've already seen how the Mumbai raiders nested within licit flows and
illicit networks in the complex littoral of Karachi and Mumbai, and how
Somali militias nested in the maze of a feral city, using adaptive swarming
tactics to confront an American force that had confidently ignored the
spatial and temporal flow of Mogadishu. A different example of this
nested-network phenomenon—and one that illuminates another part
of the urban threat spectrum we have been describing—is the pattern of
criminal control within marginalized urban settlements such as Tivoli
Gardens. Local nonstate armed groups may gain control of these districts
and use their broader affiliations—both with offshore networks and with
leaders at the city or national level—to nest within larger networks for
protection.

As Parnell's Emergency Action Committee was meeting at the
embassy on the night of May 24, Kingston's waterfront was burning.
Dozens of small groups of fighters from Coke's Shower Posse and
from neighboring allied groups were swarming toward the scene of
the action—establishing barricades, ambushing police and military
vehicles, and creating blocking positions to deny the government
advance. Flatbed trucks belonging to Coke's construction company
(whose business was built on government contracts gained through his
relationships with city politicians) had hauled in building materials to
construct the barricades and fortified positions that were now under
attack by the government's own forces. Police stations, cars, and houses
were burning, and a heavy firefight between police, army troops, and
gang members with military-grade weapons (including AK-47 assault
rifles, machine guns, and .50-caliber heavy sniper rifles) was raging
throughout Tivoli Gardens and the surrounding settlements. Coke's

supporters had taken over the Kingston Public Hospital, violence had spilled into half a dozen districts across the city, and roads and airports were closed, cutting Kingston off from the outside world. Schools and businesses were shuttered and would stay closed for weeks. Kingston's hospitals were treating dozens of injured civilians, many of whom would later die from gunshot wounds. The Jamaican government was mortaring, bulldozing, and assaulting its own capital, and the city was pushing back.

According to the U.S. embassy cable, Kingston had become a war zone in the course of enforcing a United States extradition request against a single international drug trafficker. Coke's network operated in New York, Toronto, London, and farther afield. Parnell had sent copies of his cable to the CIA and DEA because United States agencies were intimately involved in this operation: as Parnell's team was composing the message, a Department of Homeland Security surveillance aircraft was flying over Tivoli Gardens, recording live video of the attack.[79] JDF major Wayne Robinson's master's thesis, completed in 2008 at the United States Marine Corps Command and Staff College at Quantico, Virginia, explored the application of American counterinsurgency tactics from Afghanistan to counter Jamaican organized crime: it became a key source for the JDF operation, which planners conceptualized as urban counterinsurgency.[80] DEA advisers, U.S. and Canadian Special Operations Forces, and U.S. surveillance drones had all helped prepare Jamaican forces for the operation or were supporting it in real time.[81]

This assistance came with strong international pressure on a Jamaican government that was extremely reluctant to comply with the American extradition request. Prime Minister Golding had already delayed action for more than nine months, claiming that the evidence against Coke had been obtained illegally through unauthorized U.S. surveillance of Coke's electronic communications. Golding, leader of the center-right Jamaican Labor Party (JLP), represented Tivoli Gardens in parliament and allegedly maintained a long-standing and close relationship with Coke and, before him, with his father and brother. The Shower Posse kept the peace, regulated criminal activity, and mobilized the district's residents to support the JLP in elections, making this a supersafe JLP constituency. In turn, JLP politicians such as Golding ensured that the district received lucrative government contracts and public services.

In the event, Christopher Coke escaped arrest during the invasion of his district, known as Operation Garden Parish, but the military occupation of Tivoli Gardens, under a national state of emergency, went on for weeks. It left parts of the city in ruins, disrupted Kingston's port, railway, and airport (all located close to Tivoli Gardens and all—especially the port—influenced by Coke's network), led to more than five hundred arrests, displaced thousands of local inhabitants, killed at least seventy-three civilians and six police and military personnel, and injured many more.[82] The upheaval cost Golding his position and contributed to the JLP's landslide December 2011 election defeat at the hands of its archrival, the left-wing People's National Party (PNP). Christopher Coke was eventually captured a month after the start of Operation Garden Parish. Police found him hiding in the trunk of a car while attempting to flee the area, which had been cordoned off and subjected to weeks of strict curfews, searches, and police and military saturation patrols. Coke was extradited under heavy guard, tried in New York on weapons and drugs charges, found guilty, and on June 8, 2012, sentenced in federal court to twenty-three years in jail.[83]

But to frame this series of events solely as a law enforcement action to arrest an international drug trafficker is entirely to misunderstand what happened in Tivoli Gardens throughout the summer of 2010. Likewise, to characterize the Shower Posse solely as the U.S. embassy cable did—as an "international criminal syndicate"—is to describe only a small part of the group's role. The Shower Posse was (and is) both local and transnational, a nonstate armed group that nests within a marginalized and poor but tightly knit local community in Kingston, yet is connected both to the Jamaican government and to a far broader international network. It was and is as much a communitarian militia, social welfare organization, grassroots political mobilization tool, dispute resolution and mediation mechanism, and local informal justice enforcement system as it is an extortion racket or a transnational drug trafficking organization. Drug trafficking doesn't define what an organization like Coke's group *is*; it's just one of the things the group *does*. To grasp this deeper background, we first have to understand the origins of Tivoli Gardens and the other garrison districts of Kingston.

## What Goes Around Comes Around

In the words of one of Coke's henchmen at his subsequent trial, *garrison district* is the Jamaican term for an urban or periurban "neighborhood whose members are armed by the leader of the community, and also a neighborhood that is loyal to and affiliated with one of the major Jamaican political parties . . . in the case of Tivoli Gardens, the Jamaica Labour Party (JLP)."[84] Tivoli Gardens is the oldest of Kingston's garrisons, and its history shows how Jamaican clientelism, political populism, gang violence, and international connectedness have shaped (indeed, in large measure created) the very urban landscape and flow of the city, and have in turn been influenced by that landscape.

As it turns out, 2010 wasn't the first time police had brought in bulldozers to demolish dwellings or fought a pitched gun battle for control over this area. Indeed, that was exactly how Tivoli Gardens was created in the first place. In October 1963, only fourteen months after Jamaica gained its independence from the United Kingdom, the newly elected JLP government brought in JCF officers and bulldozers to forcibly evict squatters and PNP gunmen from a poverty-stricken, strategically located, PNP-dominated slum known at that time as Back o' Wall. Against significant armed opposition and public unrest, the JLP demolished the slum, expelled its residents, then proceeded to build modern housing on the site and install its own supporters (who were given free accommodation and government benefits), creating a bastion that allowed the JLP to mobilize the community and dominate the area thereafter. The government called the new district, built on the ruins of the old Back o' Wall slum, Tivoli Gardens.[85]

The struggle between the two political parties, along with the armed gangs of enforcers they sponsored and the government benefits and public goods they channeled to their supporters among the marginalized poor, shaped the urban landscape of Kingston over subsequent decades. When in office, each party reinforced its power by giving its supporters free housing and social services, and in the process creating residential bastions on strategic pieces of urban terrain. Each party used evictions, forced residential cleansing, denial of public services, government-sponsored gang violence, intimidation by a politicized police force, and outright demolition of entire garrisons to punish the other party's supporters. Elections, by the 1970s, had become violent turf battles in which whole neighbor-hoods voted en bloc and fought each other with rifles in the streets. They were fighting quite literally for survival, since the losers' districts might be physically demolished. This pattern empowered nonstate armed groups. By 1972, Tivoli Gardens had in effect been subjected to military conquest by the JLP: it was a JLP-only district, purged of PNP supporters and run by a local system in which JLP politicians distributed state largesse in return for votes at election time, residents had become a dependent and captive constituency, and local gangs—led by Christopher Coke's father, among others—kept the peace and enforced the rules.[86] Tivoli was the first of the garrison districts.

The symbiotic relationship between political leaders and their armed partisans—each influencing the other, each limiting the other's options, and each demanding support from the other—literally created the city's physical landscape. In essence, the two political parties were playing an extreme urban-planning version of tic-tac-toe, each party placing strategic garrison communities in key locations when it could, to dominate popu-lations and block the other's access, and each erasing the other's garrisons when feasible. This process created and destroyed whole settlements, determined the location of major infrastructure projects such as markets, highways, and the airport, and shaped the flow of Kingston's urban metabolism. As in Mogadishu, the political struggle, expressed in com-petition for residential space and urban services, defined the very land-scape of the city. It transformed poor neighborhoods, creating a mosaic of politically homogenous, gang-controlled, party-sponsored garrisons, each competing for government resources and criminal income, each beholden to (and making demands on) a political patron, and all engaged in a per-petual violent struggle for political and economic advantage. If Moga-dishu was a feral city—in Nuruddin Farah's phrase, "a city broken into segments, each of them ruthlessly controlled by an alliance of militias"—then Kingston had evolved into something that could scarcely be called a city at all: from a distance, it might look like a single contiguous stretch of urban terrain, but in fact it was a balkanized patchwork of entrenched strongholds perpetually at war with each other.

Within each stronghold the formal institutions of the Jamaican state were almost entirely absent, but nonstate armed groups (initially licensed by the dominant political party, but increasingly independent over time) exercised informal governance responsibilities, including law and order. The gang leader in each area, known as a "don," maintained a group of armed followers or "shooters" who acted as enforcers, kept down petty crime, and enforced a strict normative system of punishment and reward upon the population. The don acted as a mediator and resolver of disputes, liaised with police and city authorities to manage violence and crime, and became an intermediary for the distribution of government handouts—jobs, housing, welfare benefits, contracts—to the population.

Christopher Charles and Orville Beckford of the University of the West Indies did field research on informal governance systems in the garrison districts in 2010 and 2011. They found that the dons and their shooters enforced an informal but highly structured system of governance: "Society abhors a governance vacuum. People will replicate police when the police are inadequate. Governments have reduced public spending in the inner city [while] criminal dons have replaced the state as the major patrons of residents and replicated state services including an informal justice system."[87] Charles and Beckford observed the dons trying cases and resolving disputes, while the shooters meted out punishment to shore up the don's authority and maintain order. In one incident, a man was shot in the leg for kicking a pregnant woman. In other cases, the don issued a public warning to two women who created a public disturbance by fighting each other. People who assaulted others or abused their spouses were beaten by the shooters. The harshest punishment—death—was reserved for police informers, renegade shooters, and people who refused to repay money they had borrowed from the don. An older woman acted as a political enforcer, ensuring strict party allegiance to the JLP—those suspected of switching party allegiance were expelled from the community.[88] All these cases tended to cement the authority of the local strongman, who in turn maintained close ties with a member of the Jamaican political establishment.

While some people in these communities accepted the system only through fear of violence, most did so willingly "because of the perception that this is swift justice, because of conformity pressures, and because of the influence of group solidarity and communal identity."[89] The don of each garrison district enforced this system (which was, in fact, locally known as "the System").[90] It applied not only to the ordinary population but also—indeed, especially—to shooters, members of the nonstate armed group that enforced the system. This was crucial, because it created predictability and order by demonstrating that nobody was above the rules and by establishing criteria for fairness that were beyond the don's personal whims.

Charles and Beckford give one striking example of this internal justice system, associated with the extortion racketeering that is the dons' main source of income. In Eastern St. Andrew district, one shooter tried to shake down a popular and respected shopkeeper who had helped many people in the community with loans and other assistance. The shopkeeper refused to pay protection money, counting on his popularity and the local don's policy that gangs don't target entrepreneurs who help the community. The shopkeeper's refusal to pay infuriated the shooter, who killed him. As soon as the don heard of the killing, he sent the rest of his posse to find the renegade shooter—they chased him through the streets, shot him dead, and burned down a relative's house. As Charles and Beckford point out, maintenance of the system demands public and impartial enforcement of the rules, while the don needs to keep his own people in line because of the armed threat they pose to his own authority: "Renegade shooters have to be dealt with not only swiftly but also severely. Lesser action would signal that the don is 'soft' and that his informal authority can be successfully challenged. The shooters, as the line staff in the security structure of the garrison, have to be closely monitored and controlled, because they have the firepower to act in concert to oust the don."[91]

This element of nonstate control of population groups is not unique to Kingston. Indeed, in Chapter 3 I'm going to argue that the Kingston garrison constituencies represent just one example of an extremely widespread mechanism that I call "competitive control." But for now, it's enough to note that the garrison districts, while lying outside formal government control, are far from ungoverned or anarchic. On the contrary: just as we've seen in the case of Mogadishu (and as leading Africa analyst Ken Menkhaus noted in a 2007 article), these districts are *intensively* governed—just not by the government.[92]

### Long-Duration Patterns

As in Mogadishu and Mumbai, longer-term processes of population growth, urbanization, and coastal migration lay beneath Kingston's surface problems. As the capital of the British colony of Jamaica, Kingston exercised a magnetic pull on the island's population that intensified as the city's economy developed and the rural population grew in the early twentieth century. By the Second World War, Kingston was experiencing rapid population growth and urbanization, as displaced rural poor and immigrants in search of a better life crowded into coastal slums—often places of extreme squalor—in Kingston's urban core, while better-off Jamaicans moved to the city's suburbs. As noted earlier, marginalization, economic inequality, and exclusion of the population in these areas rendered them periurban, in the sense that they were on the periphery of the city's politico-economic core, even though their physical location was close to the city's center. Middle-class enclaves emerged in the northern and eastern parts of Kingston, while newer, poorer districts, "teeming with rural migrants, unemployed workers and destitute itinerants," clustered in the city's western areas.[93] By the early 1940s, residential segregation was a fact of urban life in Kingston.[94]

In urban systems terms, Kingston's carrying capacity—the ability of the urban organism to absorb, transform, and disperse the by-products of this massive influx of people—was simply inadequate to the demand. There was neither the urban infrastructure, the social or government services, nor the economic basis to absorb the flow of population or to support the rapid growth in size and spatial sprawl of the port city. As Jamaica's political and economic hub, and as the location of its main seaport and (initially) its only international airport, Kingston was the country's gateway to the outside world. Immediately after independence, the creation of the garrison communities cemented the dependent position of the marginalized urban poor and redrew the city's landscape into a patchwork of competing fiefdoms. This blocked the city's flow and made it next to impossible for successive Jamaican governments or city administrators to develop urban systems able to handle ongoing population growth, rapid urbanization, and increasing international connectedness. This international connectedness was a key element of the problem and the ultimate trigger for the Tivoli Gardens fighting of 2010.

As Professor Desmond Arias has pointed out in a series of well-argued articles on criminal governance in Jamaica, gangs in the garrison neighborhoods were initially creatures of the political parties.[95] But they also maintained extensive criminal activities, focused on cocaine and marijuana trafficking, extortion, and weapons smuggling. As people emigrated from Jamaica to the United Kingdom, Canada, and the United States, gangs in their home districts would force them to remit some of their earnings to the local don, threatening to hurt family members still in Jamaica if they didn't pay protection.[96] As conditions in the garrisons became even more dangerous and bleak, prompting a surge in Jamaican emigration in the 1970s and 1980s, these forced remittance networks grew and became a source of funding for the gangs that was independent of their political patrons. The dons' connectedness to the Jamaican diaspora—and to the transnational protection racket it enabled them to run—began to free them from dependence on local politicians, changing the power balance in ways that increased the garrison districts' autonomy and empowered the gangs that ran them.[97]

In the 1980s, the booming international cocaine trade dramatically empowered the gangs, whose existing networks allowed them to take advantage of Jamaica's strategic position as a staging point for Colombian cocaine trafficking into the United States and Canada. Christopher Coke's father, Lester, benefited from this influx of cash and influence, which, like the transnational extortion racket that preceded it, was ideally suited to exploit the gangs' connectivity to the Jamaican diaspora. The diaspora networks, already closely connected to garrison district gangs in Jamaica, became a ready-made channel for drug trafficking and for the enforcement and expansion of the networks' turf. This process bolstered the new status of garrison posses: they had evolved from being tools of the political parties, dependent on patronage, into semiautonomous transnational nonstate actors. Their international networks also allowed them to bring in heavy weaponry, further freeing them from dependence on local politicians.[98]

This crowded, urban, coastal, connected environment was the world in which Christopher Coke ascended to the powerful position of don in Tivoli Gardens after his father's death in 1992. A witness at Coke's trial described his role as head of the Shower Posse:

> Posse members who relocated to the United States from Jamaica were obligated to contribute a portion of their illegal gains back to Jamaica to support the gang. Contributions could be made in the form of cash, goods such as clothing or appliances, or firearms. Relatives of these US based Shower Posse members who remained in Jamaica were at

risk of physical harm by members of the gang if these contributions were not forthcoming. . . . As the area leader, Coke, like his father and brother, provided certain services to the community. For example, he assigned paid work to members of the community arising out of government contracts that he obtained—such as contracts to clean streets, fix roads or engage in other construction projects. For these projects, Coke would deduct from the salaries paid a portion of funds as a contribution to the "System"—essentially a required payment to the gang, which the witness said was used to purchase guns and ammunition and also to provide assistance to the members of the community. Coke also provided funds to individuals on an as needed basis—generally for food, medical care, school supplies or other necessities. He also held what was known as "treats," which are community events where various artistes would perform for the community, for free, and at which necessities would be handed out to community members, such as school supplies, packages of food and holiday gifts. During the time that Coke was in control of Tivoli Gardens, he, like [his father], imposed a strict code of conduct upon members of the community, which he personally enforced. Residents of Tivoli Gardens and surrounding areas such Denham Town did not report crimes or acts of violence to the Jamaican Constabulary Force. Instead, residents of Tivoli Gardens reported such incidents to Coke directly, the witness said. Coke would listen to both parties and make a determination about who was right and who was wrong, then directing the Shooters or other senior members of the gang to impose a penalty.[99]

When the United States government began to push for Coke's extradition on narcotics and firearms charges, the scene was set for the confrontation of May and June 2010, which, as described already, turned parts of the city into a war zone. Indeed, given the fragmentation of Jamaican sovereignty—the fact that the gang enclaves operated as autonomous mini-states, outside government control, and beyond the reach of the Jamaican judiciary—the operation to clear Tivoli Gardens and capture Coke had a lot more in common with warfare than with ordinary law enforcement. The distinction between war and crime, and between domestic and international affairs, had effectively disappeared in Kingston, just as it had in Mumbai.

*Transnational Conflict Ecosystems*

Kingston represents a third major part of the threat spectrum that will confront future cities. The Mumbai example embodies the high-end threat of terrorism or state-sponsored proxy warfare, with a fully external actor disrupting and convulsing a megacity by infesting its internal flows; Mogadishu symbolizes the low-end threat of urban ferality, with fully internal actors—the populations of excluded and marginalized districts— forcing parts of a city to de-modernize and regress, collapsing the state, then fighting over what remains. Tivoli Gardens, on the other hand, exemplifies a hybrid internal/external pattern in which governments and nonstate armed groups develop a symbiotic relationship that both creates and destroys the physical city and generates a transnational version of a traditional protection racket.

As in the other cases, an urban metabolism approach helps us interpret the violence of Tivoli Gardens, and garrison districts like it, as a side effect of the patterns of rapid coastal urbanization, population growth, and rural-to-urban migration that affected Jamaica in the run-up to independence and in the half century since—the same patterns will affect the entire globe in the next generation. The inability of Kingston's economic, governance, and social service systems to handle the influx of population helped create marginalized periurban slums whose residents were excluded and unemployed yet politically influential. The urban organism lacked the ability to metabolize the byproducts of these inflows, and there was insufficient carrying capacity in the system for the city to handle these byproducts. As political parties competed for the allegiance of these populations, gang warfare and conflict over residential space in Kingston created and destroyed neighborhoods, changing the very landscape of the city.

What I find interesting and distinctive about Tivoli Gardens is not that it was a slum area that fell under the control of a nonstate armed group linked to political elites. There are literally dozens of examples of this kind of district, in virtually every rapidly urbanizing city on the planet. No, what's interesting here is the way that the Shower Posse outgrew its masters, and that this happened through a sort of unconscious, unplanned, organic process of evolution. The posse built a normative system to control inhabitants in Tivoli Gardens, but in doing so, it became part of a pattern of escalating violence that traumatized Jamaica in the 1960s and 1970s. People fled this violence (taking advantage of the fact that they lived close to Kingston's port and airport, which were next to the garrison and which connected Jamaica to the outside world) and thus contributed to a flow of Jamaican emigrants to North America and Europe. This—entirely accidentally, as far as I can tell—created a dark network of external connections between Jamaicans abroad and the Shower Posse at home, and the posse was entrepreneurial and opportunistic enough to see this network's potential as the basis for a transnational protection racket. Once the drug economy boomed in the eighties, the posse was able to reverse the flow of its external network, so that instead of siphoning money inward from the diaspora, the network now enabled a two-way flow—drugs flowed out, money and weapons in. Shower Posse gangs (and others originating from Kingston's garrison districts) emerged among the Jamaican diaspora in Toronto, New York, and London, thus spreading patterns of violence and crime, which had originated in Kingston's lack of urban capacity, to cities across the world.

Once the Shower Posse established itself as an international drug trafficking network, it freed itself from its original dependence on the JLP, allowing it to become a semiautonomous power center within Kingston. Again, this seems to have happened entirely unconsciously, through a process of evolution. At the same time that the posse kicked free of the control of its erstwhile political masters, both of the major Jamaican political parties were making efforts to clean up election violence, reduce urban organized crime, and professionalize and depoliticize the police. These efforts further alienated groups such as the Shower Posse from their former sponsors. At the same time, the negative externalities of the gangs' offshore drug trafficking and racketeering businesses brought American, Canadian, and British law enforcement down on the Jamaican government, pressuring the government to move against the gangs. Despite the still-close political relationships between Christopher Coke and JLP leaders at the city and national levels, this pressure was ultimately enough to force the Jamaican government to move against him.

When it did, Coke's influence through the normative system he'd created in his district ("the System," which Charles and Beckford observed at first hand) allowed him to mobilize people to resist the government incursion, rally local gang allies to support him, and centralize weapons, ammunition, and building materials to turn Tivoli Gardens into an urban fortress. It took a full-scale military effort, lasting weeks and leaving many dead and injured, to clear Tivoli Gardens and arrest Coke. Yet the underlying patterns of urban exclusion, social marginalization, and residential garrisons in Kingston remained in place after the military crackdown ended, meaning that the potential for future conflicts of this kind remains.

Fascinating as this example of urban conflict may be in its own right, there seems to be a broader implication here: as the planet urbanizes, as populations centralize in coastal cities, and as increasing international connectivity enables globalized communication and population movement, this kind of local/transnational, criminal/military hybrid threat—which John P. Sullivan has insightfully labeled criminal insurgency, "a global form of neo-feudalism linked together by cyberspace, globalization, and a series of concrete ungoverned zones"—may affect vastly more cities on the planet than it already does.[100]

## IV.  Hybrid, Irregular, and Nested

The three examples we've explored here offer several insights into the future of conflict at the city level, and it's worth quickly noting them before we move on.

### Same Threats, Different Environment

Taken as a whole, an obvious characteristic of the future threat seems to be that it will be irregular. Military analysts use the term *irregular warfare* to describe conflicts that involve nonstate armed groups: combatants who don't belong to the regular armed forces of nation-states. More broadly, the term *irregular methods* (sometimes *asymmetric methods*) describes techniques such as terrorism, guerrilla warfare, subversion, and cyberwarfare, which typically avoid direct confrontation with the military power of governments. Instead, like the Somali militias engaging TF Ranger in Mogadishu, these methods pit a nonstate armed group's comparative advantages of stealth, small size, distributed command and control, and local knowledge against conventional militaries, which, though large and powerful, tend to bog down in complex terrain such as cities, jungles, or mountains.

As we noted in Chapter 1, state-on-state conflict has always been relatively rare, and it is getting rarer. At the same time, irregular warfare has historically been and will probably continue to be the main form of organized violence across the planet.[101] We can therefore expect that nonstate armed groups will keep choosing irregular methods to confront nation-states. A renewed U.S. focus on conventional threats as the wars in Iraq and Afghanistan wind down would only reinforce this tendency, since America's unprecedented military supremacy means that no enemy in its right mind would choose to fight the United States conventionally, and this pushes all potential adversaries—state or nonstate—in the direction of irregular methods. Meanwhile, operations involving nonstate groups—from humanitarian assistance and disaster relief to peacekeeping, evacuation, military assistance, and (somewhat less often) counterinsurgency and stabilization operations—are happening just as often as in the past. This means that conventional militaries, police forces, aid agencies, and NGOs will keep coming into frequent contact with nonstate armed groups.[102]

Proxy groups sponsored by foreign states (such as the LeT terrorists in Mumbai) will also adopt irregular methods. In particular, governments that acquire nuclear weapons, which allow them to deter conventional attacks, may be emboldened to use proxy warfare against an opponent. This might well be the case if Iran acquires a nuclear weapon, and it has certainly already occurred with North Korea and with Pakistan, the alleged sponsor of the Mumbai attack. As a recent study pointed out:

> After becoming an overt nuclear power, Pakistan has become emboldened to prosecute conflict at the lower end of the spectrum, confident that nuclear weapons minimize the likelihood of an Indian military reaction. In the wake of nuclearization, substate conflict expanded dramatically. In 2001, the Pakistani operation [during the Kargil crisis] was enabled by the protective nuclear umbrella ensuring that India's conventional response would be constrained. Similarly, groups that were previously limited to the Kashmir theater expanded into the Indian hinterland following the 1998 nuclear tests.[103]

All this suggests that the most prevalent future security threats will come from nonstate armed groups, or irregular actors, and from state and nonstate groups using irregular methods. This isn't new: it's the environment that will be different, not the threat.

The typical environment for irregular conflict in the past has been a remote, rural one—mountains, forests and jungles, villages and farms. Examples of urban guerrilla warfare do exist, including the battle of the Casbah in Algeria in 1957, the battle of Grozny during the First Chechen War, the battles of Jenin and Nablus during the Second Palestinian Intifada (all of which are described below), and of course the fighting in Baghdad and other Iraqi cities that I mentioned earlier. But as a proportion of the whole, irregular warfare has historically been much less common in cities than in rural districts.[104]

Since irregular combatants don't have the combat power to stand up to government forces in a direct fight, they tend to hide, and thus to rely on cover and concealment. The concealment and protection afforded by complex environments help them avoid detection by security forces, letting them move freely and fight only when and where they choose. For this reason, guerrillas, bandits, and pirates have always flourished in areas where cover was good and government presence was weak. For most of human history, this meant remote, forested, mountainous areas such as the Afghan mountains discussed in the preface. But with the unprecedented level of global urbanization, this pattern is changing, prompting a major shift in the character of conflict. In the future environment of overcrowded, undergoverned, urban, coastal areas—combined with increasingly excellent remote surveillance capabilities (including drones, satellites, and signals intelligence) in remote rural areas—the cover is going to be in the cities.

One implication of this is that nonstate armed groups—because of heavier urbanization and greater connectedness—will be increasingly able to draw on the technical skills of urban populations whose access to and familiarity with advanced technologies greatly enhance their military potential. At the low end of the scale, these might include weapons systems and dual-use technologies (such as TV remote controls repurposed as triggers for roadside bombs, or industrial solvents repurposed as chemical weapons—both actual examples from Iraq). At a higher level, urban populations can access factories and workshops (as in Libya in 2011, when technically skilled but militarily inexperienced rebels used workshops around Benghazi to build and modify weapons and vehicles).

Or—like the Syrian rebels, who built a homemade armored vehicle that used a videogame controller to manipulate a remotely mounted machine gun, and linked external cameras to a flat-screen TV to help the driver see without gaps in the armor—urban populations can turn consumer entertainment gadgets into military systems.[105] This is the high end of the scale, and these are obviously high-tech examples, but such systems need not be high-tech to be effective: the same Syrian rebels also built medieval-looking catapults, trebuchets, and slingshots using ordinary urban materials, then used them to launch highly effective homemade bombs and rockets over the rooftops of Aleppo.[106]

## Hybrid Threats

I discuss all these examples in more detail in Chapter 4, but for now the main point is that they highlight the second major characteristic of the future threat: namely, that it will be a *hybrid* in which different threat categories increasingly merge.

The future threat won't be neatly divisible into the categories we use today (state versus nonstate, domestic versus foreign, or war versus crime). As the Mumbai, Mogadishu, and Kingston examples illustrate, future threats will be hybrid: that is, they'll include irregular actors and methods, but also state actors that use irregulars as their weapon of choice or adopt asymmetric methods to minimize detection and avoid retaliation. Neither the concept nor the reality of hybrid conflict is new—writers such as Frank Hoffman, T. X. Hammes, and Erin Simpson have all examined hybrid warfare in detail. At the same time, Pakistan's use of the Taliban, LeT, and the Haqqani network, Iran's use of Hezbollah and the Quds Force, or the sponsorship of insurgencies and terrorist groups by regimes such as Muammar Gadhafi's Libya, Saddam Hussein's Iraq, and the Soviet Union, go back over many decades.

In the future, though, we're likely to see many of the methods of proxy or nonstate conflict being used under conditions of interstate war as well. Even though wars between nation-states might theoretically be considered "conventional," so much of the world's population is going to be living in coastal cities that all future conflict, including state-on-state conflict, will be pushed in an irregular direction—toward small-unit hit-and-run attacks, ambushes, use of snipers, bombings, and other tactics traditionally used by nonstate actors. This is because, as we've already seen in Mogadishu and Mumbai, urban environments tend to disaggregate and break up military forces. They break battles up, too—into a large number of small combat actions that are dispersed and fragmented, rather than a single large-scale engagement. For example, the second battle of Fallujah, during the Iraq War, included 13,500 American, Iraqi, and British troops, opposed by somewhere between 2,000 and 4,000 insurgents, for a total of roughly 17,500 combatants. But the battle didn't take the form of a single large combat action: rather, it was fought over forty-seven days between November 7 and December 23, 2004, across the entire city of Fallujah and its periurban districts, and was made up of hundreds of small and medium-sized firefights distributed over a wide area, each involving a relatively small number of fighters on each side.[107]

This disaggregating effect of urban environments is a key reason why even state-on-state conflict in the future will exhibit many irregular characteristics—especially if a state adversary adopts irregular methods. This would very obviously be true in the hypothetical case of a war with Iran, given Iran's use of proxies and irregular forces across its region and beyond. Even the most stereotypically conventional scenarios—say, a war on the Korean Peninsula—wouldn't remain conventional for long. The North Korean military, for example, would almost inevitably be defeated in a conventional fight, and could be expected to resort to guerrilla and irregular methods (as well as using its weapons of mass destruction) almost immediately. Even if North Korea collapsed without a major conflict, in such a hypothetical scenario the need for stabilization and humanitarian operations would be immense and protracted.

And in the even more far-fetched hypothetical case of war with China—a conflict sometimes seen as primarily a maritime, sea-air battle—the fighting would in fact almost certainly take an irregular, urban, coastal turn. As we saw in the last chapter, China is more than 51 percent urbanized and its urban centers are clustered along its coastline. Chinese officers literally wrote the book on irregular tactics (the 1998 classic *Unrestricted Warfare*, by Senior Colonels Qiao Liang and Wang Xiangsui of the People's Liberation Army).[108] Chinese officers have also, undoubtedly, been watching U.S. debates over air-sea battle, military funding, and protracted conflict, and noting the difficulties that

Americans (like any other military force in history) have experienced in large-scale, long-duration stabilization and counterinsurgency operations in places such as Afghanistan and Iraq. Unless they're stupid—and the evidence suggests the opposite—Chinese war planners would be considering a strategy of drawing an adversary into a protracted struggle, to soak invading forces up in the urbanized littoral. This may well be a major adjunct to any anti-access, area denial, or maritime combat strategy they might adopt. All this suggests that even a future hypothetical war with China—as unintended as that may be—would actually *not* be the purely conventional force-on-force scenario some have seemed to suggest, but would quickly devolve into the mother of all messy, irregular fights in a complex, urban, coastal environment.

In more general terms, the environment for future conflict is clearly shifting. The four megatrends of population growth, urbanization, littoralization, and connectedness suggest that conflict is increasingly likely to occur in coastal cities, in underdeveloped regions of the Middle East, Africa, Latin America, and Asia, and in highly networked, connected settings. Adversaries are likely to be nonstate armed groups (whether criminal or military) or to adopt asymmetric methods, and even the most conventional hypothetical war scenarios turn out, when closely examined, to involve very significant irregular aspects.

The military implications are obvious, if difficult to act upon in today's fiscal environment. There's a clear and continuing need for Marines, for amphibious units and naval supply ships, for platforms that allow operations in littoral and riverine environments, and for capabilities that enable expeditionary logistics in urbanized coastal environments. Rotary-wing or tilt-rotor aircraft, and precise and discriminating weapons systems, will also be needed. There's also a clear need to structure ground forces so that they can rapidly aggregate or disaggregate forces and fires, enabling them to operate in a distributed, small-unit mode while still being able to concentrate quickly to mass their effect against a major target. Combat engineers, construction engineers, civil affairs units, intelligence systems that can make sense of the clutter of urban areas, pre-conflict sensing systems such as geospatial tools that allow early warning of conflict and instability, and constabulary and coast guard capabilities are also likely to be important. The ability to operate for a long period in a city without drawing heavily on that city's water, fuel, electricity, or food supply will be important as well, with very significant implications for expeditionary logistics. I go into detail on all these issues, and other military aspects of the problem, in the Appendix.

The implications for civil government are equally obvious—expanding social services, city administration, and rule of law into periurban areas is clearly important, as are investments in infrastructure to guarantee supplies of fuel, electricity, food and water. Less obvious but equally important are investments in governance and infrastructure in rural areas, as well as efforts to mitigate the effects of rural environmental degradation, which can cause unchecked and rapid urban migration. Given the prevalence and increasing capability of criminal networks, police will need a creative combination of community policing, constabulary work, criminal investigation, and special branch (police intelligence) work. And local city managers, district-level officials, social workers, emergency services, and ministry representatives may need to operate in higher-threat governance environments in which they face opposition.

The implications for businesses, civil society, and the public go well beyond the rather narrowly scoped conflict-related considerations I've just described. As mentioned in Chapter 1, the environmental shifts I've described are, in essence, a "theory of everything" in the sense that the megatrends identified here will affect every aspect of life on the planet in the next few decades, not just conflict. McKinsey's Urban World program and the IBM Smarter Cities project are two examples, among many, of holistic attempts by private industry and civil society to consider the future of the city, and thereby to anticipate and address the full range of future issues that cities will confront.[109] Using the urban metabolism and city-as-system approaches I described earlier may allow planners to identify emergent patterns in a complex urban flow, make sense of the system logic of a city, understand the relationships among complex problems that may appear unrelated on the surface, and thus to design tailored interventions. As I discuss in Chapter 5, such interventions must involve a co-design element in order to be effective. They would need to begin in a consciously experimental way, seeking to reveal the interactions between different parts of systems, but would rapidly increase in effectiveness as each intervention generates new data that enhances the next.

## Beyond Military Urbicide

Another insight is that military operations have immense destructive effects on cities, so military "solutions" to problems in future urbanized environments may be no solution at all.

It's a hard fact of life that armies kill cities. We've already seen how Ambassador Oakley, negotiating after the battle of Mogadishu, warned Somali leaders that large-scale military intervention in their city would inevitably kill it. The destruction sustained by Tivoli Gardens during Operation Garden Parish was on a far smaller scale, yet the engagement of the JDF inevitably brought far greater disruption, death, and damage than previous police-led operations had done. Even in Baghdad in 2007, in an operation designed to save rather than destroy the city, we made people safe but only, to use Steve Eames's phrase, by "putting the city on life support."

We could think of classical examples such as the battles of Stalingrad in 1942, Warsaw in 1944, or Berlin in 1945, all of which inflicted immense and enduring damage on the cities involved. More recently, in irregular conflicts, Marines in Hue City during the 1968 Tet offensive in Vietnam engaged in heavy urban fighting, while the Russian army more or less flattened the city of Grozny during the First Chechen War of 1994–96.[110] The Russians—after losing many troops during their failed New Year's Eve assault of December 31, 1994—spent most of January 1995 shelling, mortaring, and bombing the city before moving in to systematically destroy it block by block.[111] The U.S. Marine Corps in Iraq, during the two battles of Fallujah in April and November 2004, took extraordinary measures to avoid this kind of wholesale destruction, yet the city still suffered immense damage and dislocation.

The ethics of military proportionality and protection of noncombatant civilians become extremely important in conflicts involving nonstate armed groups in urban terrain. In the Palestinian Territories, for example, the Israel Defense Forces (IDF) have used armored bulldozers and heavy artillery in towns including Jenin and Gaza, and Israel has been criticized for its policy of punitively destroying the houses of suicide bombers (which IDF spokesmen argue is an important deterrent) and for demolishing Palestinian homes it claims have been built illegally.[112] Yet in the extremely densely populated, heavily urbanized Palestinian Territories, even "normal" IDF combat maneuvers can involve massive damage to the fabric of a city, as the Israeli architect Eyal Weizman pointed out in May 2006 in his description of the battle of Nablus four years earlier:

> During the battle soldiers moved within the city across hundreds of metres of "overground tunnels" carved out through a dense and contiguous urban structure. Although several thousand soldiers and Palestinian guerrillas were manoeuvring simultaneously in the city, they were so "saturated" into the urban fabric that very few would have been visible from the air. Furthermore, they used none of the city's streets, roads, alleys or courtyards, or any of the external doors, internal stairwells and windows, but moved horizontally through walls and vertically through holes blasted in ceilings and floors. This form of movement, described by the military as "infestation," seeks to redefine inside as outside, and domestic interiors as thoroughfares. The IDF's strategy of "walking through walls" involves a conception of the city as not just the site but also the very medium of warfare—a flexible, almost liquid medium that is forever contingent and in flux.[113]

This IDF tactic of moving within the actual fabric of the city's buildings, burrowing into the concrete and brick of the urban environment itself, takes notions of infestation, nesting, and property destruction to an entirely new level. An Israeli commander interviewed by Weizman described his unit as moving "like a worm that eats its way forward, emerging at points and then disappearing." Weizman also quotes a Palestinian mother on the effect of such tactics on the local civilian population:

> Imagine it—you're sitting in your living-room, which you know so well; this is the room where the family watches television together after the evening meal, and suddenly that wall disappears with a deafening roar, the room fills with dust and debris, and through the wall pours one soldier after the other, screaming orders. You have no idea if they're after you, if they've come to take over your home, or if your house just lies on their route to somewhere else. The children are screaming, panicking. Is it possible to even begin to imagine the horror experienced

by a five-year-old child as four, six, eight, 12 soldiers, their faces painted black, sub-machine-guns pointed everywhere, antennas protruding from their backpacks, making them look like giant alien bugs, blast their way through that wall?[114]

John P. Sullivan, to whom I'm greatly indebted for these insights, quotes Weizman at length in his writings on what he, like others including Stephen Graham, calls "military urbanism"—the response to urbanized threats that turns cities into fortresses and populations into denizens of occupied territory. This has the extremely negative side effect of shutting down a city's flow, or even physically destroying the city itself, in order to save it from an external threat, as in the famous words of a U.S. Army major in Vietnam, who said of the 1968 battle of Ben Tre, "It became necessary to destroy the town to save it."[115]

Lest we imagine that such actions are a thing of the past, we should remember that in the wars in Iraq and Afghanistan, military urbicide— the "deliberate destruction of the urban fabric"—has at times been a United States policy also, albeit on a smaller scale than that of Grozny or the Palestinian Territories. Mark Owen, in *No Easy Day*, his account of the raid that killed Osama bin Laden, describes an operation against an Iraqi insurgent weapons facilitator in Baghdad in 2005, in which his team was unable to subdue the target and ended up using cannon fire from an armored vehicle, plus a thermobaric demolition charge, to destroy an entire two-story home in a densely populated Baghdad neighborhood.[116] Dozens of similar operations took place in 2006, 2007, and 2008, leaving significant damage across the city.

More recently, in early 2011 Paula Broadwell drew controversy when she approvingly reported the total destruction of the village of Tarok Kolache in Arghandab district of Afghanistan's Kandahar province. The village had been occupied by Taliban fighters and laced with improvised explosive devices that caused numerous U.S. casualties; as a consequence, rather than engage in the difficult and dangerous task of clearing the village, on October 6, 2010, the U.S. Army approved the use of heavy artillery and aircraft to destroy the village, dropping just under fifty thousand pounds of ordnance on the area and totally leveling it. Although the operation allegedly caused no civilian casualties, and the same unit followed up with a massive reconstruction program that commanders expected to take up the entire remainder of their combat tour in the area, the notion that an American counterinsurgency force in 2010 would literally destroy a village in order to save it led to intense criticism.[117]

If we want to move beyond military urbanism and urbicide, we need to think much more creatively about ways to secure urban environments. As I've suggested, focusing on cities as systems, exploring ways to expand the carrying capacity and improve the flow of the urban metabolism, may be important preventive measures. But—as discussed in Chapter 1— historical patterns of intervention suggest that military forces will still be dragged into these environments on a regular basis, responding to problems (as in Tivoli Gardens) that have spiraled beyond the capacity of civilian government to handle them.

Governments such as that of the United States that draw sharp distinctions between warfare and law enforcement and between domestic and overseas legal authorities will experience great difficulty, and may find it impossible to act with the same agility as irregular actors who can move among these artificial categories at will. Capabilities that combine policing, administration, and emergency services, backed up with military-style capabilities so that police can deal with well-armed adversaries—capabilities traditionally associated with constabulary, *gendarmerie, carabinieri*, or coast guard forces—may be more effective against these hybrid threats than civil police forces alone, and less destructive than unleashing the military.

*Nested Networks*

Another implication from this discussion of the future threat is that it will be *nested*—threat networks will be embedded in a complex urban littoral environment, illicit activities will nest within licit systems and processes, and local threats will nest within networks at the regional and global level.

In the extremely complex, coastal, urban, and connected environment I've outlined, threat actors (like the terrorists in Mumbai, the Somali militias, or the Jamaican organized crime posses in Kingston) will be able to nest, avoiding detection, by remaining beneath the clutter of dense urban development and overpopulation. Because of the connectedness among threat networks, periurban communities, and city systems, it will be virtually impossible to target a dark network without also harming the community within which it nests. This will deter some governments from acting, while making it harder (as we've just seen in the case of Israel in Nablus and the United States in Tarok Kolache) for those who do act to justify their actions.

As well as nesting in the urban environment itself, threats can nest within international and national systems, including international transportation networks, financial networks such as the remittance industry, and even humanitarian assistance systems. In Mogadishu, for example, there's evidence of connectivity among Somali piracy syndicates, organized crime networks in Europe, and the Shabaab insurgency. Clans and criminal networks in Mogadishu, or in Somali coastal cities including Kismaayo and Haraadhere, draw little distinction between their military and political activities, on one hand, and their business activities (both legitimate and criminal), on the other. Conflict entrepreneurs—such as the clan traders who set up refugee camps around Mogadishu in 2008 to divert humanitarian assistance into the black market or to their business partners in Shabaab—operate on a continuum from legitimate business through illicit activity, outright crime, terrorism, and insurgency.[118]

Because threat networks often nest within essential licit flows, it can be virtually impossible to shut them down. For example, as the investigative journalist Matt Potter showed, drawing from official and academic sources as well as local eyewitness accounts, some (though, of course, by no means all) of the same air charter companies that operate humanitarian assistance flights into drought-stricken or conflict-affected areas such as the Horn of Africa also smuggle weapons, drugs, and other contraband. Humanitarian aid workers and NGOs are perfectly well aware of this, but neither they nor the governments involved in relief efforts can shut down these trafficking flows, since it would mean an end to the movement of humanitarian assistance cargo.[119]

### Beyond Counterinsurgency and Counterterrorism

A final, very obvious point is that counterterrorism and counterinsurgency (dominant discourses of the past few years) are clearly only part of the solution here—and to only part of the problem. Neither of these approaches would have allowed us to fully understand, let alone deal with, any of the three cases discussed in this chapter.

I've written elsewhere in detail on the intellectual history of counter-insurgency, and on various critiques of the theory.[120] For now, though, it's enough to note that there is solid evidence that counterinsurgency, or COIN, can work if done properly, with sufficient resources, for long enough.[121] But it's also clear that COIN is not the answer to every question. Likewise, counterterrorism (ranging from the comprehensive "global war on terrorism" of President George W. Bush's administration to President Obama's unrestrained drone warfare) can help to temporarily suppress a particular type of threat, but it can't do much about the broad and complex range of challenges we're about to face. In fact, any theory of conflict that's organized around dealing with a single type of enemy is unlikely to be very helpful in a conflict environment that includes multiple overlapping threats and challenges.

Instead, to deal with complex future conflicts, we're going to need something more like a unified field theory: an approach that is framed around the common features of all types of threats (rather than optimized for the particular characteristics of any one type of threat) and considers the environment in toto as a single unified system. We'll need to acknowl-edge that many security challenges in the future environment will be "threats without enemies," which, by definition, are just not amenable to military solutions. And we'll need to recognize that even when there's an identifiable adversary—usually, but not always, a nonstate armed group—there are still no *purely* military solutions to many of the challenges we will encounter, meaning that disciplines such as law enforcement, urban planning, city administration, systems design, public health, and inter-national development are likely to play a key part in any future theory of conflict.

The unified field theory that best fits the currently known facts is what I call the "theory of competitive control." This is the notion that nonstate armed groups, of many kinds, draw their strength and freedom of action primarily from their ability to manipulate and mobilize popula-tions, and that they do this using a spectrum of methods from coercion to persuasion, by creating a normative system that makes people feel safe through the predictability and order that it generates. This theory has been part of many people's thinking about insurgency and civil war for a long time. But the cases we've examined in this chapter suggest that it applies to any nonstate armed group that preys on a population. It applies to insurgents, terrorists, drug cartels, street gangs, organized crime syndicates, pirates, and warlords, and it provides useful explanations and insights for law enforcement, civil war, and diffuse social conflict—not just for insurgency. I will suggest that we treat this theory (until another theory emerges that better fits the available facts) as a working model for dealing with future threats. The next chapter explores the theory of competitive control in detail.

# 3

## The Theory of Competitive Control

Development in my area was slow until a huge migration of people especially from the northeast of Brazil, in the late 70's came to Rocinha. Then some major building took place in many areas of the favela. The drug gangs came into power around this same time and instituted rules in the favela. Since the government and police never came here anyways, the drug guys took control of the neighborhoods and set the rules, no stealing, raping or killing inside the favela. I am not sure on the exact details because I was a kid. . . . The drug gang bought hearts and minds by aiding some of the poorest residents by providing food and necessities. Also many in the drug gang were "cria" or from the favela. Interesting dynamic it is and far more complicated than I can explain here. The drug gang became the parallel power and filled the role of the government. The gang built community centers and had simple roads paved. If you live in the community what would you think? After years of being neglected and shunned by the government, who do you turn to? The gang filled that role. I wouldn't say people were happy about it, but they accepted it. What else could they do?

*—Life in Rocinha*, 2012

### I. The Fish Trap

*5:20 a.m., April 15, 1999*
*Mushu Island, East Sepik Province, Papua New Guinea*

The camp is quiet in the dawn. I've just rolled out of my mosquito net by the buttress roots of the enormous jungle tree my signalers are using as an antenna mast for our high-frequency radio, the only link for over a thousand miles back to our headquarters in northern Australia. Most of my soldiers are still sleeping, but a few have been up for hours, fishing in the inlet with spears and traps, which they and our local partners made the day before. We're in our third week of survival training with our sister unit, 2nd Battalion of the Pacific Islands Regiment, on an island off the north coast of New Guinea.[1] And I'm looking closely at the fishing trap as I rub the sleep out of my eyes.

Many societies in Australasia and the Pacific, like most others throughout the world, seem to have independently invented the fishing trap some time in the late Mesolithic period of prehistory.[2] One traditional type is woven from narrow strands of bamboo, reeds, or grass, to form a cylinder that is closed at one end, with a conical opening at the other that lets fish enter but stops them from backing out. This is a standard type of trap in New Guinea, and as well as being a beautifully intricate work of traditional art, a trap like this is a highly effective hunting tool. With the right bait, placed with a good understanding of tides, currents, fish behavior, and movement patterns, it can produce at least one catch every day. The trap I'm looking at is only a few hours old, but it has already caught four coral trout from the inlet.

Fish traps look ephemeral, but their flimsiness is a deliberate deception: the strands, individually weak, form a resilient network. Indeed, the flimsier the trap looks, the less the fish notice it—on their way in, hungry for bait, they brush nonchalantly past the very spikes that will later imprison them. The trap's strength is its structure.

Insurgents make fish traps, as do militias, gangs, warlords, mass social movements, religions (Jesus, for instance, called his apostles to be "fishers of men") and, of course, governments.[3] Like real fish traps, these metaphorical traps are woven of many strands—persuasive, administrative, and coercive. Though each of the strands may be brittle, their combined effect creates a control structure that's easy and attractive for people to enter, but then locks them into a system of persuasion and coercion: a set of incentives and disincentives from which they find it extremely difficult to break out.

We've already looked at the megatrends that are transforming the planet and will shape the conflict environment of the next generation. We've explored concepts such as urban metabolism, carrying capacity, cities as biological systems, feral cities, dark networks, and the ways in which nonstate armed groups interact with populations and governments in these complex urban systems. In Chapter 2, we looked at three examples—Mumbai, Mogadishu, and Kingston—that cover the spectrum of threats that exist now and which will be even more widespread in the urban, littoral, networked environment of future conflict. In each of these examples, the interaction between a nonstate armed group and a local population prompted a series of events in an urban microhabitat, while networked connectivity gave these events a far broader effect.

In this chapter, I want to drill down to that hyperlocal level, to look at the intimate interaction between nonstate groups and populations. My goal here is to understand the way that nonstate armed groups try to control populations, and the way those populations manipulate them in return. A secondary objective is to begin the search for a paradigm that goes beyond the confines of classical counterinsurgency theory, and I start by examining the relationship between armed groups and populations from the point of view of the armed actor, before looking at the same relationship from the standpoint of the unarmed or noncombatant civilian. In essence, this chapter looks at how nonstate armed groups of all types (and the states with which they compete, coexist or partner) seek to control populations—the kind of complex two-way interaction that's highlighted in the quote that began this chapter, from a resident in an urban slum in Brazil.[4] And the fish trap is, it turns out, a very useful analogy for the network of incentive structures they use to do so.

## II. Insurgent Control Systems in Afghanistan

It's useful to begin with a description of how a real-life control system operates, and the war in Afghanistan has unfortunately provided many opportunities to observe such systems in action. It's also helpful to start with a nonurban example, since this lets us look at processes of control in a simpler society and a less cluttered environment, without initially having to account for the complex impact of urbanization, littoralization, and networked connectivity. In addition, this example helps to demonstrate that patterns of competitive control are independent of terrain or type of group—indeed, they may be universal.

So, let's imagine a village elder in Kandahar province in 2011.[5] He may have a dispute with a neighboring village over orchard land, grazing rights, or water for irrigation. Such disputes are common in Afghanistan, where population displacement, agricultural disruption, and changed settlement patterns have eroded community consensus about land ownership. Decades of conflict, in a society where 44 percent of the population is under fifteen years old, have meant that disorder is all most Afghans know.[6] Written records of land ownership either never existed or have been destroyed. The fall of the monarchy in 1973, the brutal Communist land reform program in 1973–78, the Soviet-Afghan war of 1978–89, the civil war of the 1990s, the 2001 invasion, and since then the Taliban insurgency have all contributed to population movement and displacement that magnifies this chaos.

Traditionally, a dispute such as this would have been solved through negotiation among elders, by calling a mediator from another district, through a *jirga* (a tribal assembly), or, less often, through the government courts. Elders would have been familiar with the *nirkh*, the customary table of punishments and payments used to settle disputes; some would specialize in this area of traditional justice. If two parties to a dispute couldn't agree on a common *nirkh*, they might use that of another village or tribe.[7] But today the elders in many parts of Afghanistan are gone— dead, exiled, cowed, or in hiding—or perhaps co-opted by the insurgents, by local warlords or corrupt officials. Fake "elders," who specialize in negotiating with foreigners, travel from district to district, giving villages a front man who looks the part and can extract money, contracts and concessions from international troops or aid agencies, while the real elders hang back or hide. The government has little permanent presence in this district, and there's no reliable or legitimate government court system. How can our hypothetical elder resolve his dispute?

Well, he can turn to the Taliban. Over the years, the insurgents have evolved a resilient set of local guerrilla governance institutions. They've appointed a governor for each local area, part of a shadow provincial and district government cadre (sometimes also known as the "district commission") that includes a financial comptroller, a military commander, and a *qazi*—a religious judge. Dispute resolution and mediation are the traditional functions of religious leaders in Afghan society, and before the Russian war respected mullahs or *maulawis* often mediated exactly this sort of conflict.[8] Likewise, law and order have always been the Taliban's primary concerns—indeed, the movement got its start during the Soviet-Afghan War in the 1980s, when madrassa students and their teachers from districts west of Kandahar City took up arms in reaction to the perceived un-Islamic behavior of other mujahideen, and fought the Soviets in "Taliban fronts."

As Dr. Carter Malkasian—one of our generation's greatest analysts of insurgency, and a courageous participant-observer of conflict on the ground—has noted in the case of Helmand province, religious leaders had a resilient, mobile, and dense network before the war. Mullahs traditionally moved from village to village every few years, maintaining close communication with other clerics in distant villages.[9] As a result, being less tied to the interests of any one village or group of elders, they had an independence of action, a less parochial outlook, and a widespread and well-organized social, political, and economic network that allowed them to mediate local disputes and to assume a leadership role during the upheavals of conflict. By tapping into this religious network, co-opting local mullahs, the Taliban were able to multiply and enhance their influence. This is not, of course, unique to Islam or to Afghanistan—I saw the same thing happen with Greek Orthodox priests when I was a peacekeeper in Cyprus in 1997 and with Catholic clergy during the violence in East Timor in 1999.[10] But in Afghanistan, because of the weakness of secular state institutions, this pattern has taken a particularly powerful form.

After the Soviets pulled out in 1989, many members of the original Taliban fronts returned quietly to their madrassas, while non-Taliban mujahideen commanders quickly seized urban centers, expropriated economic resources (especially land), and built militias to secure their supporters and prey on road traffic and market activity. These petty racketeers, dignifying themselves as "regional commanders," soon became local warlords. In the early 1990s many of them made deals with the post-Soviet government of President Najibullah, which allowed them de facto autonomy over a patchwork of fiefdoms across the country, in all the areas that Najibullah's government felt itself too weak to control directly.[11]

Around Kandahar, these warlords so abused the population that the Taliban came out of retirement and fought back—some Taliban leaders, such as Mullah Abdul Salam Zaaef, have claimed they did this on behalf of the community, though others assert that the Taliban were acting in their own interest.[12] Taliban groups served as a public law-and-order force. They gained support from local communities by freeing the population from the warlords' predation: applying rough vigilante justice, trying abusers in ad hoc Islamic courts and publicly executing them, expelling the militias, and ending the warlords' system of institutionalized highway robbery with its shakedowns and checkpoints. As Anand Gopal noted in 2010, Kandahar, the original home of the Taliban, fell into chaos as mujahideen commanders from the seven major factions that had fought the Soviets "carved up the province for themselves. By 1994, tales of rape and plunder became widespread, prompting Taliban commanders, who had been sitting aside during this civil war, to rise up against these warlords. Taliban leaders saw their role as restorative (rescuing jihad from the hands of rapacious commanders who were using it for their own ends) and judicial (halting the conflict-fueled breakdown of society by installing their interpretation of Islamic law)."[13]

In this way, the Taliban gained a reputation for austere incorruptibility, and for a harsh and conservative fairness. They also fulfilled society's traditional expectations of religious elders by resolving and mediating disputes, thereby enhancing their own credibility and prestige. Most important, they established a pattern of predictability, order, and consistency. Over the years, many Afghans have told me that it was this sense of order, and the way that it made people feel safe after the chaos of the anti-Soviet war and the predations of the warlords, that accounted in large measure for people's initial support for the Taliban.

The Taliban expanded the area under their control as they took over fiefdom after warlord fiefdom, and they gradually evolved into a regional government. They were aided in this by the civil war that broke out in Afghanistan among rival mujahideen factions after the fall of the Soviet Union in 1991 cut off the flow of assistance to President Najibullah's regime. After the Najibullah government collapsed a year later, fighting between influential regional commanders and warring factions destroyed much of what remained of the country. With no unified opposition, and supported by people who sought relief from the unpredictable brutality of the civil war, the Taliban rapidly gained ground. By the end of September 1996 they had captured Kabul, where their first act—on the very day the city fell—was to torture, castrate, and then hang ex-president Najibullah and his brother in a traffic circle in downtown Kabul.

Thus, in its origin, the Taliban was as much an armed social justice and law enforcement movement—albeit in many ways a ferociously violent and noxious one—as a religious faction. It was certainly not a classical insurgency: far from seeking to overthrow a dominant government, the movement represented an attempt to create order and governance in a chaotic, predatory ecosystem where *nobody* was in charge. In a society that had been undergoing an unstable and involuntary transition to modernity since the early 1960s and had been subjected to intense violence during that time in the name of progressive causes—land reform, women's rights, universal education, industrialized agriculture, secularization, and so on—it's hardly surprising that many people's search for relief from the chaos led them to look back to the certainty of traditional systems and conservative authority structures rather than forward to the creation of a modern democratic nation-state. In the chaotic conditions of the 1990s, there was little practical alternative anyway—there was no normality or stability to restore. Likewise, in its original form the Taliban wasn't a proxy for Pakistani ambitions in Afghanistan. Support from Pakistani intelligence came later, as the movement began to expand beyond its birthplace around Kandahar and the Pakistanis saw an opportunity to displace Indian and pro-Soviet influence in the rest of Afghanistan. Although Pakistani support helped the Taliban grow and prosper, most Afghans agree that the movement was not created so much as exploited by Pakistan.

Today, the Taliban justice system draws on the movement's reputation for harsh predictability and consistency: it attracts people with the promise of fair dispute resolution, just and enforceable mediation, and the prevention and punishment of crime and corruption. One locally famous example occurred in Wardak province in November 2009:

> Local people said they supported the Taliban because the police never tackled the criminal gangs smuggling drugs, running prostitutes and kidnapping local businessmen. In Wardak, a Taliban-controlled province south of the capital, the insurgents last month seized four men involved in kidnapping the son of a wealthy Kabul tea merchant. The kidnappers told their victim to pretend he was their nephew if they met anyone on the way to their safe house in a remote area. But Taliban soldiers at a checkpoint noticed his expensive shoes, jeans and leather jacket, and arrested the gang. Four bodies were then left swinging from a tree in Maidan Shah, the provincial capital. A note pinned to one read: "The same fate awaits others who choose to kidnap for a living."

The Taliban caught the kidnappers, tortured them and executed them in public. The tea merchant donated $US200,000 to the Taliban as a gift for his son's release. The story quickly spread through the districts around Highway One. "It proves the Taliban have no problem with ordinary Afghans—they only have a problem with those Afghans who work in high government positions, who run crime in this city," said Karimullah, 40, who owns a shop selling flour, oil and rice.[14]

Note that it wasn't simply the punishment of crime that mattered here. The Taliban publicly announced a set of rules, as laid down by Mullah Omar (who has banned kidnapping for ransom), and then arrested, tried, and executed a gang who had broken these rules. Via placards on the executed kidnappers' bodies, they sent a message of consistency, predictability, and order, by which they distinguished themselves from corrupt officials. The locals clearly understood this—as Karimullah's comment shows, they got the point.

In contrast, Afghans whom I asked (during fieldwork in December 2009, the year of the Wardak kidnapping) about their perceptions of the national police or the government court system, just laughed and said that government courts take months to resolve the smallest dispute, cost thousands of dollars in bribes, and render judgments that always favor the most influential power brokers, who can simply ignore the judgment anyway if they don't like it.[15] By contrast, the Taliban come from the local area, so they understand the issues people are dealing with. Their justice is free of charge, judgments are rendered quickly (sometimes in as little as half an hour), and unlike the Afghan National Police, who are often seen as corrupt and in the pay of local elites, people expect that the local Taliban underground cell will consistently enforce the court's judgment. "Many people don't like the Taliban," a businessman from Kandahar told me, "but at least you know what you're getting: they're consistent and fair. You know what to expect from them."[16]

Predictability is the basis for secure dispute resolution and thus for social stability—something that's deeply attractive to a population buffeted by decades of instability and desperately worried about the future. Indeed, Taliban courts seem to spend a lot of effort on what we might call civil or commercial, rather than criminal, law: they issue birth certificates, mediate divorces and resolve inheritance disputes, and have been known to issue land title deeds, perhaps recognizing that this is one of the few ways in which a community can gain a recognizable, enforceable, and secure claim to its property. As the Peruvian economist Hernando de Soto showed in *The Mystery of Capital*, his study of property ownership in poor societies, secure title to assets is often one of the strongest desires of poverty-stricken populations, whose possessions are normally unregistered and unrecognized by the state.[17] Acquiring title to their land can transform people's feelings of security and well-being—in de Soto's home country of Peru, Shining Path guerrillas gained significant popular support early in the conflict by taking local people's side in land reform issues of this kind.

But the attractiveness of Taliban dispute resolution is the bait in a fish trap. When the Taliban court has reached a verdict, both parties to the dispute are obliged to sign, or make their mark, on a court record held by the local underground cell. This record allows enforceability, but it also puts those who sign it at the mercy of the Taliban. By recognizing the Taliban court's authority to resolve disputes, our hypothetical elder has literally signed onto their broader agenda. The local Taliban have his name and signature on their court document, and at any time they can make a claim on his allegiance or blackmail him by threatening to expose his involvement to the authorities.

Moreover, suppose the Taliban court rules in the elder's favor. He's now becoming locked into a system of incentives controlled by the Taliban. He holds his land title or has access to grazing land or irrigation water on the basis of their authority. He must now acknowledge that authority in other matters, or else he'll simply be undermining his own claim to the valuable disputed asset that he now holds on the authority of the Taliban. If the Taliban come to his village seeking to recruit men as part-time guerrillas in the local area, or asking for money, or seeking information on government activity, this elder will find it impossible to refuse them, whatever his private view of their cause. At the same time, he has of course technically broken the law by turning to the Taliban to have his dispute resolved, and thus is further alienated from the police and the government. As long as the Taliban court's judgment is fair and consistently enforced, he has no incentive to oppose the Taliban and every incentive to support them, regardless of his view of their ideology.

As Professor Stathis Kalyvas pointed out in his groundbreaking 2006 study, *The Logic of Violence in Civil War*, we tend to intuitively assume that insurgents become strong in a particular area because people support their cause or agree with their ideology, but actually the exact opposite is the case. Kalyvas showed in a comprehensive series of case studies that armed groups in civil war don't become strong because people support their ideology; on the contrary, people start supporting a given group's ideology in places where that group is *already* strong. Kalyvas argued that as conflicts continue, people increasingly collaborate with whatever actor controls their area, "because political actors who enjoy substantial territorial control can protect civilians who live in that territory—both from their rivals and themselves—giving survival-oriented civilians a strong incentive to cooperate with them, irrespective of their true or initial preferences."[18] In other words, people support armed groups in places where those groups are already strong enough to impose an incentive structure (or system of control) that provides predictability, order, safety and stability. Support follows strength, not vice versa. This is a critically important observation, to which we'll return shortly.[19]

In the meantime, however, we can note that even if the government improves its service delivery in this particular elder's area, reduces corruption, does a better job of law enforcement, and creates a more consistent local presence in his area—key objectives of counterinsurgency theory, and exactly what we were trying to achieve across Afghanistan for much of the past several years—this may not help. At this point, having availed himself of the Taliban justice system, the elder's claim to a valuable disputed asset depends on the guerrillas' authority, and that makes it extremely difficult for him to support the government or go against the insurgents, whatever his feelings about the state. The elder in this context is a fish in the trap: he's locked into an incentive structure that is easy and attractive to get into, but hard and painful, if not impossible, to escape. This example, then, shows a real-world competitive control system in action. The next section unpacks the theoretical basis for such a system, and as we shall see, it has broad applicability beyond insurgency.

## III. The Theory of Competitive Control

The pattern in which nonstate armed groups create predictability and order as a way of generating popular support, and build incentive systems to corral target populations, is not unique to Afghanistan. Indeed, it's a near-universal phenomenon, present in insurgencies but also in many other social systems. It is, in fact, utterly characteristic of the relationship between local populations and nonstate armed groups of all types, and is thus an excellent place to begin our search for a set of ideas beyond classical counterinsurgency that may more fully explain the patterns of conflict we see around us.

Before we discuss the theory, I should make a brief comment on terminology. Throughout this book, I use the term "nonstate armed group" to refer to any group that includes armed individuals who apply violence but who aren't members of the regular armed forces of a nation-state. I draw this formulation in part from Charles Callwell's late-nineteenth-century definition of small wars, and I prefer it to the more common terms "nonstate actor" and "illegal armed group."[20] Nonstate armed groups can include urban street gangs, communitarian or sectarian militias, insurgents, bandits, pirates, armed smugglers or drug traffickers, violent organized criminal networks, vigilantes and armed public defender groups, terrorist organizations, warlord armies, and certain paramilitary forces.[21] The term encompasses both combatants and individuals (for example, facilitators, covert operatives, or political cadres) who don't personally carry arms or use violence but who belong to groups that do. Terrorists, insurgents, and militants—such as the LeT raiders in Mumbai—who are sponsored but not directly employed by a nation-state form a special subcategory of irregular proxies or state-surrogate groups.

The basis for the control systems applied by nonstate armed groups of all kinds, including the Taliban approach described above, is what I call the theory of competitive control. We can formally express this theory as follows:

> *In irregular conflicts (that is, in conflicts where at least one combatant is a nonstate armed group), the local armed actor that a given population perceives as best able to establish a predictable, consistent, wide-spectrum normative system of control is most likely to dominate that population and its residential area.*

Simply put, the idea is that populations respond to a predictable, ordered, normative system that tells them exactly what they need to do, and not do, in order to be safe. We've already seen this system in operation at the hands of criminal groups in the "System" of Jamaican garrison communities, in the actions of clan militias in Somalia, and in the operations of Taliban courts in Afghanistan. The feeling of safety that this predictability creates, in a chaotic and dangerous environment, trumps everything. As a result, even people who would otherwise dislike an armed group (such as the people of Wardak in the kidnapping example, or the people of Mogadishu or Tivoli Gardens in Chapter 2) end up supporting a group because of the order it creates.

Besides explaining one possible mechanism for the support-follows-strength pattern that Stathis Kalyvas observed, this theory suggests a behavioral explanation for the way in which armed groups of all kinds (insurgents and criminals alike) control populations. It also suggests that group behaviors, such as the rule-based Somali swarming tactics I mentioned in Chapter 2, may be emergent phenomena at the level of the population group (rather than rational or conscious choices by the individual), implying that traditional counterinsurgency notions, including "hearts and minds" (the belief that populations can be swayed if their conscious choices are influenced), may need a rethink. Changing the rule set and incentives that define emergent behaviors may be a better option, if indeed such change is possible, rather than attempting to influence conscious choices. Likewise, it may be that there's a window of opportunity during which such changes can work, but that after this window closes, a population may be locked into an incentive structure that is extremely difficult to shift.[22]

### Sucking the Population In

The Afghan example is just one illustration of an underground control structure (a form of illicit social control, sometimes referred to in classical counterinsurgency theory as a "parallel hierarchy" or "guerrilla government"). Of course, insurgents aren't the only ones who use systems like this, and nonstate armed groups don't simply wait until a genuine dispute emerges, then resolve it to gain popular support. On the contrary, they deliberately create disputes, promoting insecurity or fear, precisely in order to pose as saviors and thereby win local allegiance. The very problems that a group inflicts on a community can thus translate into community support. The group itself is the disease it purports to cure.

This way of looking at illicit control structures is far from a new idea. As early as June 1927, the Employers' Association of Chicago coined the term *racketeering* to describe a form of social control in which a criminal entrepreneur's organization gains support from populations (local businesses, residents, or labor unions) by promising to protect them from the very problem of violent crime that the criminal organization itself creates, thereby locking them into a structure that alienates them from the state, while creating incentives for continued support and silence. This is exactly what we saw in Tivoli Gardens, or in the Afghan case just mentioned.[23] Insurgents in this sense behave much like gangsters: "In a situation [in 1920s Chicago] where the legal system offered little security, organized crime provided regulatory and mediation services—what some have come to call 'licensing.'"[24] In Afghanistan the overlap between crime, insurgency, tribal or business patronage networks, and government itself is often so extensive that the same individuals play roles in multiple hierarchies.

Analysts looking at underground Communist parties in the 1930s described similar methods of social control by clandestine political movements. Revolutionary cells would absorb and mobilize recruits, blood them in violent street confrontations with rival groups, groom them through a series of increasingly illicit actions, lead them progressively into an ever-greater level of illegality and alienation from society, and thus make it harder for them to betray or leave the movement lest they be punished by the government whose laws they had broken.[25] The RAND analyst Philip Selznick wrote in 1951 that in a revolutionary organization, "the emphasis on illegal work creates a conspiratorial atmosphere; this has the dual consequence of disintegrating normal moral principles, thereby reducing inhibitions that might hamper manipulability, and of increasing the dangers (real or imagined) of leaving the organization."[26] Selznick described this process as one of "absorption," in which an individual is gradually brought further and further into the control system of the underground movement. In our analogy, this is akin to being drawn into the trap.

As part of this process, armed groups often deliberately make local populations or new recruits complicit in acts of violence, as a way to alienate them from the government or other communities, so that they have no choice but to support the dominant group in their area. A 2004 study of former child soldiers in Uganda, for example, found that many new recruits were forced to kill innocent people—in some cases other recruits or even members of their own families—as part of the induction process.[27] Compelling children to commit acts that society condemns and the law forbids not only desensitized the children to extreme violence but also separated them from society, bonded them to the insurgent group, and made them feel they could never go back. Some groups cut or otherwise scarred the faces of children who had killed in this way, marking them for life so that they could never go home. Similar rituals are, of course, well known as part of the initiation processes of gangs, organized crime families, and terrorists. Gang tattoos, in this sense, fulfill the same social marking function as the face scarring inflicted on the African child soldiers. In the gangs of San Pedro Sula, discussed in Chapter 1, killing a member of a rival gang or being "jumped in" (beaten by the group for a ritually significant length of time—thirteen seconds for MS13, eighteen seconds for Calle 18, and so on) also became important steps in the induction process.

Diego Gambetta, in his fascinating study of criminal communication, *Codes of the Underworld*, notes similar initiation behaviors among mafia families, prison gangs, insurgents, and drug trafficking organizations. Gambetta points out that mafia novices are usually required to kill someone as part of their induction process, as a test of loyalty. "The mafia usually does not kill anyone purely for the sake of a test—it optimizes by 'whacking' someone who was meant to be whacked anyway *and* at the same time trying out the determination and bona fides of the novice. The Aryan Brotherhood in prison adopted the same test: to gain membership, candidates 'had to kill whomever the Brotherhood targeted.'" Gambetta also described cases in which recruits were asked to commit atrocious crimes purely as tests. In youth gangs in Colombia, for example, "it is not uncommon for new gang members to be asked to murder innocent friends or members of their own family, which pushes the test to the extreme."[28] As we've seen, though, for many nonstate armed groups, such violence is more than a test of loyalty—it's a way of separating a new recruit from outside society.

An even starker example of this same technique was the way that nationalist militias in the Balkans in the 1990s forced local people to kill their neighbors. Militias would round up people from another religion or ethnicity, then assemble residents from their own group and force them, sometimes at gunpoint, to massacre their neighbors.[29] In 1992 in the northeastern Bosnian town of Brčko, for example, Serb militias rounded up Bosniac Muslim men, women, and children and forced local Serbs—these people's neighbors, who had known them their whole lives—to kill them, right then and there, in the street. According to eyewitness testimony, given in 1993, the process of ethnic cleansing in Brčko began on May 2, 1992 with the arrival of Serbian "special units" including a group we will return to later, Arkan's Tigers:

> In these first couple of days several hundreds of innocent [Bosniac] civilians were killed in the following locations: in the local police station, behind Posavina Hotel, in the town's trades center and near the Brka river. Furthermore, people were taken from their houses and killed on their own threshold, yard or on a street. Those Serbs who did not assent to those crimes were executed without any mercy. There are many examples how Brčko Serbs were forced to kill their Muslim neighbors in order to preserve their own lives.[30]

This happened in dozens of places in 1992–93 and had the effect of forcing the population to become complicit in mass murder and ethnic cleansing in their own villages.[31] After the killing, militia leaders would tell people they now had no choice but to join the movement, because they could never reconcile with the families whose relatives they had killed. My soldiers and I saw the horrendous effects of the same thing in East Timor in 1999, as militias forced local people to kill members of their own communities before forcibly marching them across the border into West Timor, thereby assuring themselves that the expelled population could never return.[32] Likewise, Shining Path guerrillas in Peru gathered villagers and forced them to stone local government representatives and prominent villagers to death. This made the villagers complicit in illegal, violent, collective action—cutting them off from the state and putting them at the mercy of the movement.[33] All these examples represent extreme, and extremely effective, forms of coercion within an overall system of control over the population.

In a similar vein, in a December 1964 lecture at the U.S. Naval War College, the classical counterinsurgency theorist Bernard Fall had this to say about insurgent control:

Any sound revolutionary warfare operator (the French underground, the Norwegian underground, or any other anti-Nazi European underground) most of the time used small-war tactics—not to destroy the German army, of which they were thoroughly incapable, but to establish *a competitive system of control over the population*. Of course, in order to do this, here and there they had to kill some of the occupying forces and attack some of the military targets. But above all they had to kill their own people who collaborated with the enemy.[34] [Italics added]

Fall was talking of the coercive end of a spectrum of incentives—the application of lethal force against those who collaborate with an insurgent's rivals. Any sensible guerrilla, terrorist, or organized criminal network will of course attack soft targets (the unarmed civilian population that supports a government) in preference to attacking the government itself. Besides being a less risky target than the police or the military, the civilian population is more numerous and easily accessible than are government installations and officials.

But Fall's point here is larger than simply a comment on the mechanics of violence. Note his language: a *competitive system of control*. Fall never developed his concept fully—he was killed in February 1967 while accompanying a U.S. Marine Corps patrol near Hue, South Vietnam. But his later writings give a series of examples of this idea of competitive control—an idea that's not spatial ("insurgent-controlled" or "contested" areas) or structural ("networks" and "movements") but rather functional. It implies the presence of a range of incentives and disincentives, all of which are used to generate control over population groups—the individual strands of a networked system of control that attracts and then corrals a population, much as a fish trap cages fish. It also implies a competition among several actors who are all trying to control the population in a violent and contested environment.

### Normative Systems

I find it helpful to locate Fall's "system of competitive control" within the broader theoretical discourse of normative systems. The notion of normative systems is long established in sociology and legal theory and, increasingly, in computer science, where developers have found it useful in agent-based modeling (where researchers assign behavioral rules to computer-generated "bots" and then watch how they behave in complex systems).[35]

For our purposes, we can define a normative system as *a set of rules that is correlated with a set of consequences.*[36] In essence, it's a system of norms (behavioral rules) that is paired with a set of sanctions (costs and punishments for breaking those rules). This system of norms and sanctions defines the boundaries of permissible behavior for a population. It makes the behavioral space inside its boundaries a safe zone for those who follow its rules, while the space that lies outside the boundaries becomes deeply unsafe. Implicit in this idea is the notion of an actor (an "owner" or proponent of the normative system) who sets the rules, bestows benefits for following them, and inflicts punishments for breaking them, and is thereby able to control a population. According to this theory, the owner of a normative system becomes the dominant actor in a given area (or over a given population) precisely to the extent to which people in that area or population abide by its rules. This applies equally to a wide range of actors: the don of a Jamaican district enforcing his "System," the leader of a Somali militia, a Taliban court dispensing justice, and a Honduran gang enforcing an extortion racket are all applying variants of the same norms-based approach.

This actor may be a government or a nonstate group; it may be benevolent or malevolent, legally recognized or illicit, formal or informal. But two characteristics must always be present: the actor must always be *armed* (that is, it must have the capacity to inflict violence as part of its spectrum of sanctions) and it must always be a *group* (some form of collective entity), not just an individual. An unarmed actor lacks the capacity both to enforce its own normative system and to resist predation from other armed actors in the violent ecosystem we've just described. And enforcing a normative system is fundamentally a group activity, since it involves regulating people's behavior over a wide area of time and space, a task that lies beyond the capacity of any one individual (as we saw in the Tivoli Gardens example in Chapter 2).

In an environment with only one dominant actor possessing a monopoly on the use of armed violence, we would expect to see an extremely high degree of control over a population or area. This, indeed, is demonstrably the case in areas that are fully controlled by governments. But in the examples we've been examining in this book—insurgencies, urban street gangs, informal periurban settlements beyond the direct reach of the state, diasporas subjected to a protection racket by gangs who dominate their town of origin, and so on—we are looking not at *uncontested* control but rather at a pattern of contested space and at a competition for control among several actors. Each actor tries to create a normative system of competitive control, and the better it does this, the more likely it is to dominate the contested space. Thus we are talking here of competition among organized, armed groups seeking to control populations through normative systems—a construct that applies equally well to insurgency and crime, to state and nonstate actors, and indeed to the actions of states and those of governments.

Within the behavioral space bounded by its rule set, an actor can apply a spectrum of means ranging from persuasion through administration to coercion. At the persuasive end of this spectrum are arguments and inducements to support the dominant rule set. These include propaganda, political and ideological mobilization, social pressure, and identity manipulation. But as we've seen, often the most persuasive element is the feeling of security, predictability, order and cohesion (closely related to Ibn Khaldun's idea of *asabiyya*, discussed in the Mogadishu example) that comes with adherence to a dominant actor's norms. In the middle of the spectrum, administrative tools—justice systems, mediation and dispute resolution mechanisms, essential services, social and economic institutions—make it easier for people to follow the rules, and give them tangible benefits for doing so. At the coercive end of the spectrum are punishments that impose costs on people who break the rules. These include punitive violence—up to and including death—as well as expropriation (fines, penalties, or seizure of assets), expulsion and exile, or imprisonment.

Max Weber, of course, famously defined the state as a political organization that "upholds a claim to a monopoly of the legitimate use of physical force in the enforcement of its order."[37] We might reformulate this, in the context of our discussion of competitive control, to say that a government is a political organization that has successfully outcompeted its rivals across the full coercion-persuasion spectrum, allowing it to establish an uncontested normative system over a given population or territory.

The coercive end of the spectrum is critical, because it supports and enables the rest of the system: the persuasive and administrative parts of a normative system work (as Weber noted) only because they rest on the ultimate sanction of force, which a dominant actor can apply against those who break its rules. From the insurgent standpoint, Mao Zedong explained this fundamental truth in 1938:

> Every Communist must grasp the truth, "Political power grows out of the barrel of a gun." Our principle is that the Party commands the gun, and the gun must never be allowed to command the Party. Yet, [by] having guns, we can create Party organizations ... We can also create cadres, create schools, create culture, create mass movements. Everything in Yenan has been created by having guns. All things grow out of the barrel of a gun.[38]

Clearly, however, the resilience of an armed group also depends on the capabilities it can bring to bear across the full spectrum of a competitive control system. As we'll see shortly, groups that can only apply coercion may achieve temporary dominance over a population. But their control will be brittle, lacking resilience, because it depends on fear alone—in normative systems terms, it covers only a narrow band of the persuasion-coercion spectrum. A purely coercive actor can cast a spell of fear over a population, but as soon as this spell is broken, the population will turn on its tormentor with incredible speed and violence. By contrast, a group that applies a range of coercive, administrative, and persuasive means has a much stronger and more resilient control system. Such a group can respond to a setback in one part of the spectrum by increasing its efforts in another, and can therefore maintain greater and more flexible control over time.

As we saw in the Afghan example with which we began, the creation of safe behavioral space, as part of a wide-spectrum normative system, has an attraction effect on an at-risk population, who tend to flock to it, drawn by the persuasive inducements and administrative benefits of the system, as well as by the fear of what may happen to them in the unsafe space outside it. This, I suspect, is one of the primary mechanisms for the support-follows-strength pattern that Stathis Kalyvas observed. Once in the system, however, people are corralled and prevented from leaving by the threat of coercion. We might call this the "fish trap effect," since it induces people to enter a system which they then find extremely difficult and painful to leave. Thus, Fall's "competitive system of control" can be seen as just one type of normative system, and its application to insurgencies as but one example among many, in which state and nonstate armed groups of all kinds compete to control population groups. To illustrate this in a way that might be closer to home for many readers, let's consider the everyday example of road rules in a large city.

### Rules of the Road as a Normative System

Think about the last time you drove your car in a large urban area. You may have been driving to work, or going into the city for a meeting or to go shopping. As you got behind the steering wheel of your car and drove onto the road, you entered a violent, dangerous, and unpredictable environment—across the United States in 2010, for example, roughly 33,000 people died in road traffic accidents; someone was killed on average every sixteen minutes.[39] What makes you willing to commit yourself and your family to such a risky activity on a daily basis? Among other things, it seems to me, one reason is that the rules of the road give you a degree of order and predictability, and this sense of predictability gives you the confidence to function in a dangerous environment (with, perhaps, little conscious perception of risk).

This is because, thanks to the rules, the driving environment—though it's undoubtedly dangerous—is far from chaotic. There's a designated side of the road on which all vehicles have to drive. There's an approved speed limit. There are road signs, in a standardized format, that warn of hazards and prompt certain key behaviors—braking, yielding, or stopping. There are traffic lights that regulate intersections, and lines marked on the road that ensure each vehicle keeps within its own lane. There are television, radio, and billboard advertisements that publicize these rules, seeking to persuade motorists of the benefits of following them, and warning of the consequences (death and injury, speeding fines, loss of license) that follow from breaking the rules.

And sitting behind this system, underpinning it though often not directly visible, is a government, with a traffic authority or transportation department that sets the rules, a police force or highway patrol that enforces them, a court system that tries those who violate the rules, a system of fines and penalties, and, ultimately, a prison system. People follow the rules (norms) for a variety of reasons—because they fear the punishments (sanctions) that correlate with breaking the rules, because they're persuaded of the risks of speeding or driving drunk, because they fear public opinion (the embarrassment of having to catch the bus because of a suspended license, or a spouse's disapproval because of speeding fines), or because they value the ease and convenience of efficient road transport that would be impossible without rules to tame the chaos. Even in a less formal system of road traffic control, where some of these visual cues and formal traffic control measures (signs, lane markings, and so on) may be missing, the cooperative behavior of motorists moving on a busy road is underpinned by the presumed or actual presence of an enforcer, in the form of police or a locally dominant group.

What we're describing here is of course a normative system, one that's owned by the government, enforced by the police, and seeks to control the population of road users within a given territory. This normative system embodies rules and sanctions that create a safe area of behavioral space within which people can go about their business with a basic expectation of safety, and indeed without a great deal of conscious thought. This barely noticed system of control, however, rests ultimately on the power of an armed actor—the police—and on the coercive sanction of the courts and the correctional system.

It seems to me that this is probably what Joseph Conrad meant in his novel *Heart of Darkness* when he described the ordinary citizen as living within a control system of which he or she is barely aware, with the police at one end of the spectrum and public opinion at the other. Kurtz, the novel's antihero, finds himself wielding immense power, alone and unsupervised, in a jungle outpost:

> He had taken a high seat amongst the devils of the land—I mean literally. You can't understand. How could you? With solid pavement under your feet, surrounded by kind neighbours ready to cheer you or to fall on you, stepping delicately between the butcher and the policeman, in the holy terror of scandal and gallows and lunatic asylums—how can you imagine what particular region of the first

ages a man's untrammelled feet may take him into by the way of solitude—utter solitude without a policeman—by the way of silence—
utter silence, where no warning voice of a kind neighbour can be heard
whispering of public opinion?[40]

*Heart of Darkness* is, of course, fiction. But most analysts agree that it
closely parallels Conrad's real-world experience as captain of a river
steamer, the *Roi des Belges*, in the Congo in the 1890s.[41] In an earlier piece,
written soon after his return from Africa, Conrad made a similar point:

> Few men realize that their life, the very essence of their character, their
> capabilities and their audacities, are only the expression of their belief
> in the safety of their surroundings. The courage, the composure, the
> confidence; the emotions and principles; every great and every insig-
> nificant thought belongs not to the individual but to the crowd: to the
> crowd that believes blindly in the irresistible force of its institutions
> and of its morals, in the power of its police and of its opinion.[42]

And here lies another critically important point: as Conrad understood,
it's the *predictability* inherent in the existence of rules, publicly known
and consistently enforced, not the *content* of the rules themselves, far less
the *popularity* of a given government, that creates the feeling of safety that
allows a normative system to function. Predictability, not popularity, is
the key: you don't need to like the police or agree with the speed limit for
the road rules to make you feel safe.

As long as people have a well-founded expectation that the police will
consistently enforce the rules—that those who break the rules will be
punished, while those who obey have nothing to fear—then the government's popularity or otherwise is completely irrelevant. We saw this in
Tivoli Gardens, where many people supported the local don because of
the perception of predictable security that the System generated, while
the don had a strong incentive to be consistent, fair, and predictable in
enforcing his rule. The same set of incentives is at work in the Taliban
court system described earlier. More broadly, in the kinds of normative
systems that Bernard Fall, Stathis Kalyvas, and Joseph Conrad describe,
people don't have to support a group's ideology in order to follow its rules.
They do so because of the predictability the normative system creates,

whether they like its owner or not, or indeed whether they're even fully aware of the system or not.

## Al Qaeda in Iraq: Brutal and Brittle

We noted earlier that a group that establishes a wider range of capabilities, covering more of the spectrum from persuasion to coercion, will be stronger and more resilient. This is worth exploring in some detail, by comparing narrow-spectrum to wide-spectrum groups.

Al Qaeda in Iraq (AQI) is a good example of a narrow-spectrum group that mainly applied coercion. Early in the Iraq war, AQI cells moved into Sunni neighborhoods and established control over the population through acts of terror. They applied restrictive rules—banning smoking or the playing of music, prohibiting any kind of cooperation with the government of Iraq or the occupation forces, enforcing the strictest imaginable codes of Islamic dress and behavior upon both men and women, forbidding people from listening to tapes of moderate imams' speeches, seizing control over economic activity in the district, and so on—and punished anyone who broke these rules in a brutally harsh, violent, and public manner. Thus, although they did establish a normative system (rules and sanctions) they focused their efforts entirely at the coercive, violent end of the spectrum.

It wasn't uncommon, for example, in towns such as Ramadi and Tal Afar, for the bodies of local civilians to turn up in the street with the two first fingers of the right hand cut off (a punishment for smoking); for non-AQI religious leaders to be assassinated; for the children of tribal leaders who opposed AQI to be tortured to death, their broken little bodies sent back to their families as a message; or for acid to be thrown in women's faces as a punishment for wearing their veils pushed back too far.[43] In farming areas, AQI developed the habit of leaving the decapitated heads, or other body parts, of their victims in fruit boxes to be found by their families.[44]

AQI cells were thus cruelly capable and effective at the coercive end of the spectrum, but almost totally lacking in administrative and persuasive capabilities (as well as basic humanity). AQI attempted nothing like formal governance, nor did it ever even try to provide any significant administrative services—it gave no tangible benefits to its supporters and provided no essential support or humanitarian assistance to the Sunni population. Its message to the population was, in essence, "Follow our rules, or we'll kill you." (In this, AQI differed greatly from Shi'a militia groups such as Jaysh al-Mahdi or the Badr Organization, both of which—though also extremely violent—put a great deal of effort into winning support through social, economic, and humanitarian programs.)

This is not to say that AQI's approach to violence was unsophisticated. On the contrary, the group cleverly established domination over the community through fear and through a carefully engineered cycle of sectarian violence, intimidation, and revenge. The cycle worked as follows. Having established a base in a Sunni-majority neighborhood and enforced their code of silence and fear on that community to give themselves a secure base of operations, members of an AQI cell would set out to provoke a neighboring Shi'a community. They would kidnap Shi'a children, especially young boys, brutally torture them to death, and then dump the bodies in their families' streets, or would attack Shi'a social and religious institutions, seeking to throw the blame on the Sunni community. These atrocities in turn would prompt retaliatory attacks by the Shi'a population against Sunni districts. Perhaps the most prominent example of this was AQI's bombing of the Samarra mosque, one of the holiest shrines in Shi'a Islam, on February 22, 2006. This attack prompted a tsunami of retaliatory bloodletting by Shi'a groups, targeting Sunnis across Iraq. At the local level, AQI launched dozens of attacks against Shi'a districts from bases in Sunni-majority areas, including a notorious and bloody series of market bombings in 2006–7, which prompted Shi'a retaliation against Sunni neighborhoods.

This approach worked for AQI at first. Members of the Sunni community, attacked by Shi'ite vigilantes and hounded by representatives of the Shi'a-dominated Iraqi state (especially the Iraqi National Police, some units of which became notorious for extrajudicial killings of Sunni men and boys), felt they had nowhere to turn.[45] Many began to see AQI as the only thing standing between them and oblivion at the hands of the Shi'a, an ironic turn of events since (like a gangster in a protection racket) AQI posed as the protector of the Sunnis—pretending to be the solution to a problem that AQI itself was creating and exploiting.

After the death of its first *emir*, Abu Musab al-Zarqawi, on June 7, 2006, AQI's new leadership began a limited attempt to translate its terror into broader political support, through the establishment of the Islamic Emirate of Iraq and the Mujahideen Shura Council. But AQI's approach was still fundamentally one of intimidation and fear, an approach that relied heavily on coercive means with little attempt at building administrative capability or persuasive activity. Thus, while AQI did indeed establish a normative system that was capable of controlling the population, its capabilities all lay at the coercive end of the spectrum, and its control was therefore brittle. AQI could offer its supporters nothing positive, and its violence and brutality against the population, along with its disregard of community leaders' authority, its intolerance of traditional forms of Islam, and the fact that its leadership was largely urban or non-Iraqi, was building a groundswell of hatred against AQI within rural and periurban Sunni communities. The only thing that kept these communities from turning against AQI was the pall of fear the terrorists had cast over the population, and the expectation that anyone who opposed AQI would die a slow, horrible, and publicly humiliating death.[46]

The so-called Awakening, the uprising against AQI from within the Sunni community that began in 2006 under a group of leaders that included Sheikh Sattar of the Albu Risha, was by no means the community's first attempt to throw off these parasites. On the contrary, the 2006 Awakening was at least their fifth uprising.[47] What made all the difference in 2006 was the U.S. troop surge. It wasn't enough for the local community to hate AQI: to rise up successfully, local civilians also had to believe they would survive the attempt. On every previous occasion, community leaders who went up against AQI had been slaughtered. In 2006–7, the extra troop presence of the surge meant that for the first time, the coalition could hold and defend population centers on a permanent basis, support the Sunnis when they turned against the terrorists, and protect people against retaliation. The partnership between U.S. troops and the local community—arising in part from counterinsurgency tactics that emphasized protecting the people where they slept—gave the community the confidence to rise up again, and this time they succeeded. Within a matter of weeks AQI was destroyed, its control was swept away, and its cadres were mercilessly killed by the very population they had terrorized.[48]

Thus, AQI is an excellent example of the brittleness that can result from too narrow a spectrum of capabilities. AQI established a terrifyingly effective ascendancy over the Sunni population, but because this dominance was based entirely on fear and coercion, it had no resilience. As soon as the surge created a minimal assurance for people that they would survive the attempt to turn against AQI, and as soon as coalition forces in Anbar demonstrated that they could kill or capture members of AQI cells, the myth of AQI's invincibility was shattered and the people turned on AQI in a flash and swept it away. And because the terrorist group had little to offer but fear and intimidation, it had no way to counteract or bounce back from its loss of control.

We might note in passing that trying to control a population solely through persuasive or administrative means, relying on these parts of the spectrum only and excluding coercion, is equally doomed to failure. Making a population like you, through administrative benefits and persuasive "hearts and minds" programs—an approach taken by some coalition contingents in both Iraq and Afghanistan—may initially appear to work. But at some point a competing armed group will turn up, put a gun to community leaders' heads, and ask, "Who do you support now?" At that point, coercion trumps persuasion. More broadly, the field evidence that has emerged from many recent conflicts, as well as from patterns of organized crime and gang activity, suggests that a wider spectrum of control measures generally tends to overpower a narrow set of measures, whether these are primarily coercive or persuasive.

### Living the Hezbollah Lifestyle

In contrast to AQI, the example par excellence of a wide-spectrum group is Lebanese Hezbollah. Hezbollah brings to bear an extremely broad range of capabilities across the full spectrum of a well-developed normative system. The resilience and staying power that this generates can be seen most clearly in the events of 2006, which was a watershed year in Lebanon, as in Iraq.

Hezbollah (the name means "Party of God") was established after the 1982 Israeli invasion of Lebanon, with the goal of protecting the Shi'a community, resisting Israeli military occupation, and fighting Israel's allies in the Phalangist militia and the South Lebanese Army (SLA). The organization began as a small militia that received training from the Iranian Revolutionary Guard Corps, funding from Iran, and political support from Syria as well as from the Lebanese Shi'a community. Over time, however, Hezbollah has expanded and diversified into a wide-spectrum social and political movement that not only includes a capable military wing but also maintains regional and district administrative councils, law enforcement organizations, dispute resolution and mediation systems, employment programs, health clinics, schools, labor representation, a reconstruction organization, charity programs, a mass political party with elected representatives in the Lebanese parliament and at the local and regional levels, a series of local radio stations and print publications, the satellite television channel Al-Manar, and a significant Internet presence. Hezbollah is, in effect, a counterstate within the territory of Lebanon. This counterstate fields an extraordinarily effective "fish trap" system of incentives and disincentives that fully encapsulate its target population: you can live your whole life within the Hezbollah lifestyle and almost never need to engage with the outside environment.

Hezbollah's strength derives from its ability to create a full-spectrum normative system that dissuades people from opposing its agenda, gives them tangible administrative and economic benefits in return for support, and persuades them to participate in its program. The system rests on three pillars—Hezbollah's capable terrorist and military organizations (giving it coercive and intimidatory power); its social and administrative programs, which benefit Lebanon's urban poor and marginalized communities of all religious groups; and its noncoercive political and propaganda capabilities.

The organization's nonmilitary capabilities proved critically important during the 2006 July War (also known as the Second Lebanon War) between Israel and Hezbollah. During the thirty-four days of formal hostilities, the IDF launched extensive air raids across Lebanon and conducted a heavy artillery bombardment of the south. This caused severe damage to Lebanese government and civilian infrastructure, destroyed thousands of houses, and killed roughly one thousand civilians and two hundred Hezbollah fighters. Israel also mounted a ground invasion of Lebanon and imposed a naval and air blockade that continued for almost three months. Israeli attacks, according to some reports, left more than a million cluster bomblets scattered across residential areas of Lebanon, and flattened villages and buildings across the south.[49] In the twenty square miles of Beirut's southern suburbs, more than half a million inhabitants—most of whom were Shi'a—lost their homes.[50] Hezbollah's postwar role in reconstruction and repair of this urban damage helped consolidate its political position within Lebanon, making it arguably stronger after the war than it had been before the conflict.[51] As the British journalist Robert Fisk reported in the immediate aftermath of the war, Hezbollah "trumped both the UN army and the Lebanese government by pouring hundreds of millions of dollars—most of it almost certainly from Iran—into the wreckage of southern Lebanon and Beirut's destroyed southern suburbs. Its massive new reconstruction effort—free of charge to all those Lebanese whose homes were destroyed or damaged in Israel's ferocious five-week assault on the country—has won the loyalty of even the most disaffected members of the Shia community in Lebanon."[52]

This reconstruction effort was directed by Jihad al-Binaa ("Construction Jihad") the reconstruction and humanitarian assistance arm of Hezbollah. The leader of Construction Jihad is Kassem Allaik, a civil engineer partly educated in the United States. The organization was bombed out of its headquarters in Beirut's southern suburbs during the war.[53] But within a day of the cease-fire, Construction Jihad sent assessment teams out into the destroyed suburbs of Beirut and across southern Lebanon to survey the damage from the Israeli bombardment. As Roula Khalaf reported a few weeks after the conflict:

> Today, Construction Jihad's makeshift premises in a south Beirut branch of the Mahdi school, the organization's education association, is a hive of activity. Between pictures of Hezbollah leaders holding children, and the party's yellow flags, a large map of the area is plastered on the wall, dividing neighbourhoods into small numbered zones. Engineers huddle along the length of a table strewn with forms detailing damage to individual properties from the conflict between Israel and Hezbollah. Since the ceasefire two weeks ago, Construction Jihad has moved into high gear, dispatching agents to areas affected by the conflict to measure the damage—they estimate 15,000 properties were destroyed or damaged—and send the forms back to this central office. This information is entered into computers, before people are paid compensation from the party itself, or assisted with reconstruction. Construction Jihad is part of a social network, including schools,

hospitals, and a banking institution, that was critical to Hezbollah's ability to fight Israeli troops during the occupation of Lebanon in the 1980s and 1990s.[54]

From a purely military standpoint, many analysts consider that Hezbollah performed well in the 2006 ground war.[55] In an example of the "style points" phenomenon that I mentioned in the case of Mumbai, Hezbollah achieved military credibility simply because, despite Israel's best efforts, the organization succeeded in launching thousands of rockets against northern Israel throughout the war, surprising both Israeli and international analysts with the sophistication of its capabilities and its ability to stockpile munitions.[56] The Israeli government's Winograd Commission subsequently acknowledged several problems in the IDF's execution of the war, and General Daniel Halutz, the IDF chief of staff, was forced to resign as a result. Nevertheless, Israeli air superiority (aided by intelligence and precision munitions from the United States) meant that the final military outcome was at least a draw, if not a clear-cut defeat for Hezbollah. But the *political* outcome of the war left Hezbollah considerably strengthened in Lebanon, largely because the organization leveraged its nonmilitary capabilities (those residing in the persuasive and administrative parts of the spectrum, such as Construction Jihad) to bounce back quickly from its military losses.

*Evolving Traditionalists*

The Afghan Taliban lie somewhere between the two extremes of AQI and Hezbollah, though their recent performance puts them much closer to the Hezbollah end of the scale than to AQI. At the same time, the history of the Taliban's relationship with the population also illustrates how groups can evolve over time. We've already noted how the Taliban got its start as a vigilante law-and-order movement opposing the depredations of the warlords after the Soviets left Afghanistan. We've also examined the relatively effective Taliban local governance presence today in many contested districts of Afghanistan, and the way that Taliban local cells use governance, dispute resolution, mediation, and essential services to mobilize and manipulate populations in these areas.

It's worth noting, however, that the Taliban's local governance performance today, as an insurgency, is markedly different from—and, in fact, significantly better than—its performance as the actual government during the five-year Taliban regime between September 1996 and 2001. During its period in government, the Taliban moved its capital from Kabul to Kandahar and ignored central ministries, international relations, economic development, and the broader functions of the state, focusing instead on issuing religious edicts and preventing un-Islamic behavior.

The following Taliban edict, issued nine weeks after the movement seized Kabul, became a key document in the history of the Taliban's approach to governance. It established the set of behavioral norms to be enforced by the Taliban religious police, the Directorate for Enjoining Good and Forbidding Evil (Amr bil Maroof wa Nahi Anil Munkar). The edict was one of the first public declarations of the normative system that the Taliban imposed on Afghans under its control. It's worth quoting in full, as it represents a catalog of the issues in which the regime was interested, and defines the boundaries of safe and unsafe behavior for the population:

**Islamic State of Afghanistan**
General Presidency of Amr Bil Marof Wa Nai Az Munkir
Administration Department
To: The received letter from the Cultural and Social Affairs Department of General Presidency of Islamic State of Afghanistan No. 6240 dated 26.09.1375 [December 16, 1996] states that:
The rules and regulations of Amr Bil Marof Wa Nai Az Munkir are to be distributed via your office to all whom it may concern for implementation.

1. **To prevent sedition and uncovered females**: No drivers are allowed to pick up females who are using Iranian burqa. In the case of violation the driver will be imprisoned. If such kinds of female are observed in the street, their houses will be found and their husbands punished. If the women use stimulating and attractive clothes and there is no close male relative with them, the drivers should not pick them up.

2. **To prevent music**: To be broadcast by the public information resources. In shops, hotels, vehicles and rickshaws cassettes and music are prohibited. This matter

should be monitored within five days. If any music cassette is found in a shop, the shopkeeper should be imprisoned and the shop locked. If five people guarantee, the shop could be opened and the criminal released later. If a cassette is found in a vehicle, the vehicle and the driver will be imprisoned. If five people guarantee, the vehicle will be released and the criminal released later.

3. **To prevent beard shaving and cutting**: To be broadcast by the public information resources. After one and a half months if any one is observed who has shaved and/or cut his beard, he should be arrested and imprisoned until his beard gets bushy.

4. **To prevent not praying and [to] order gathering [for] prayer at the bazaar**: To be broadcast by the public information resources that the prayers should be done on their due times in all districts. The exact prayer time will be announced by the Amr Bil Marof Wa Nai Az Munkir department. Fifteen minutes prior to prayer time the front of the mosque, where the water facilities and amenities are available, should be blocked and transportation should be strictly prohibited and all people are obliged to go to the mosque. At the prayer time this matter should be monitored. If young people are seen in the shops they will be immediately imprisoned. If five people guarantee, the person should be released, otherwise the criminal will be imprisoned for ten days.

5. **To prevent keeping pigeons and playing with birds**: To be broadcast by the public information resources that within ten days this habit/hobby should stop. After ten days this matter should be monitored and the pigeons and any other [pet] birds should be killed.

6. **To eradicate the use of addiction and its users**: Addicts should be imprisoned and investigation made to find the supplier and the shop. The shop should be locked and both criminals (the owner and the user) should be imprisoned and punished.

7. **To prevent kite flying**: First should be broadcast by the public information resources advising the people of its useless consequences such as betting, death of children and their deprivation from education. The kite shops in the city should be abolished.

8. **To prevent idolatry**: To be broadcast by the public information resources that in vehicles, shops, room, hotels and any other places pictures/portraits should be abolished. The monitors should tear up all pictures in the above places. This matter should be announced to all transport representatives. The vehicle will be stopped if any idol is found in the vehicle.

9. **To prevent gambling**: In collaboration with the security police the main centres should be found and the gamblers imprisoned for one month.

10. **To prevent British and American hairstyles**: To be broadcast by the public information resources that people with long hair should be arrested and taken to the Amr Bil Marof Wa Nai Az Munkir department to shave their hair. The criminal has to pay the barber.

11. **To prevent interest charges on loans, charges on changing small denomination notes and charges on money orders**: All money exchangers should be informed that the above three types of exchanging money are prohibited in Islam. In the case of violation the criminal will be imprisoned for a long time.

12. **To prevent washing clothes by young ladies along the water streams in the city**: It should be announced in all mosques and the matter should monitored. Violator ladies should be picked up with respectful Islamic manner, taken to their houses and their husbands severely punished.

13. **To prevent music and dances in wedding parties**: To be broadcast by the public information resources that the above two things should be prevented. In the case of violation the head of the family will be arrested and punished.

14. **To prevent the playing of music drums**: First the prohibition of this action to be announced to the people. If anybody does this then the religious elders can decide about it.

15. **To prevent sewing ladies' cloth and taking female body measures by tailors**: If women or fashion magazines are seen in the shop the tailor should be imprisoned.

16. **To prevent sorcery**: All the related books should be burnt and the magician should be imprisoned until his repentance.

The above issues are stated and you are requested, according to your job responsibilities, to implement and inform your related organizations and units.

Regards,

Mawlavi Enayatullah Baligh

Deputy Minister

General Presidency of Amr Bil Marof Wa Nai Az Munkir[57]

This edict is the basis for the often-quoted claim that the Taliban banned music, kite flying, long hair, and so on. All these things are certainly covered in the decree, but it's worth noting that the edict's deeper purpose is to regulate an entire set of behaviors and social relationships (especially between the sexes) and thereby establish a normative system with which the movement could control the population. The decree lays down the boundaries of acceptable behavior so that, by implication, behavior that falls within the rules will not be punished. It gives a population, terrorized by years of violent chaos, a clear understanding of *how to be safe*—something that's reassuring and comforting, irrespective of the content of the rules themselves. Note that in many cases husbands or heads of households are to be punished for infractions on the part of female family members, rather than the women themselves—a measure that effectively delegates enforcement of these rules to male heads of households, relieving the Taliban of part of the burden of enforcement, making men complicit in the ownership of the rule set, and thus reducing the Taliban's transaction costs in enforcing the rules. It also provides a measure of protection to women, guaranteeing that family members (rather than outsiders or strangers) will stand as an intermediary between the women and the

Taliban state. Likewise, in articles 2 and 4, the community is given an enforcement role via the stipulation that rule breakers can be released or spared from punishment "if five people guarantee."

This rule setting and enforcement system was one of two major Taliban governance behaviors; the other was creating a monopoly of force. The religious police operated alongside the Taliban's security police, whose primary role was to disarm the population so as to establish a monopoly of force for the Taliban regime. As the Afghan writer Nushin Arbabzadah points out, when the Taliban captured Kabul, they didn't "make use of their unspoken [customary] right to pillage and loot. They searched the conquered populations' homes, but only to confiscate weapons and so ensure a monopoly of violence for their state. The Taliban were exceedingly ignorant—which made them cruel—but there's no doubt that they saw jihad as a means to establish a state rather than legitimacy to pillage a conquered territory. Building a state was of utmost importance to the Taliban because without it the sharia law could not be enforced.... With the Taliban, rural Afghans came to power, ruling over the more sophisticated urban populations."[58]

Arbabzadah's comment here echoes that of Nuruddin Farah in Chapter 2 on what happened in Mogadishu when the urbophobic "country cousins" captured the city and controlled its population. In Kabul, the rural Taliban government's behavior between 1996 and 2001 showed a similar disdain for the urban population and a distrust of the capital's cosmopolitan and worldly traditions—they dropped most of the traditions of Afghan courtesy and moved their capital out of Kabul and back to Kandahar, in part to avoid the polluting effect of governing from the ancient royal capital.[59] Their primary goal was to impose behavioral control over the urban population and establish a monopoly of force, not to govern the city or develop its institutions or economy.

It's instructive to contrast the Taliban-as-government of 2001 with the Taliban-as-insurgent of 2011. A decade of conflict has changed the movement's approach, forcing it to focus much more on local-level administrative and governance activities, designed to put in place a Hezbollah-like spectrum of coercive, administrative, and persuasive tools to control and mobilize the population. These include the mobile court system, as we've seen; a public safety structure at the village level that seeks to prevent and punish crime; an ombudsman or accountability committee that investigates accusations of corruption or abuse by the Taliban itself; a system of provincial, local, and district shadow governors; a published code of conduct (*layeha*) that states the rules and obligations incumbent on Taliban commanders; a taxation system; an economic and agricultural policy; a series of small-business assistance programs; and even infrastructure projects. Vajid Mojdeh, a former Taliban foreign ministry official who monitors the movement, argued in 2010 that the Taliban "have totally changed. They've totally put behind them their international agenda of spreading Islamist revolution and now are just focused on Afghanistan. . . . There's a new generation. They are familiar with computers. They communicate with text messages. They're in favor of education." Unlike the Taliban of the 1990s, he said, "they are no longer all illiterates."[60] Mojdeh pointed to changes in the Taliban policy on education for women, inoculations, and school curricula. He's not an impartial observer, of course, but this still suggests a significant evolution in the Taliban's approach over time. The intent—to establish a predictable rule set and thus control the population—doesn't seem to have changed, but the methods have expanded to fill almost the entire spectrum of competitive control, from persuasion to coercion.

### State Versus Nonstate Normative Systems

Insurgents such as AQI, the Taliban, and Hezbollah are not, of course, the only actors who are trying to corral, control, or manipulate a population: governments do exactly the same thing, using rather similar methods. In this context, governments can be considered as owners or proponents of a wide-spectrum normative system.

This also is a critical point, because it means that populations are confronted not with one system of control but with several—the insurgent's, the government's, and the systems of social control that occur naturally within the population itself, based on locality, kinship or economic ties. Indeed, in a real-world situation the members of any given population may confront several actors, all of whom are trying to control them— multiple different insurgent groups, competing government officials, foreign occupation forces, organized crime networks, and governments of neighboring countries. The way populations deal with and exploit this situation is discussed in detail in the next section. For the moment, all we need to note is that in order to understand which of the possible options a population is likely to choose, we must understand both the initial attractiveness of each option and the strength of the incentive spectrum that locks the population in once the choice is made.

But comparing the strength of state systems of control with those of insurgents, tribes, gangs, smuggling networks, and so on is extremely difficult if we think in terms of organizational structure, since state and nonstate systems are so structurally different. For example, although populations in rural societies usually meet the state only in the person of police officers, district officials, and tax collectors, modern states have relatively elaborate bureaucratic, legal, military, and administrative structures. These involve many employees, buildings, and facilities, organized into a large, obvious, permanent footprint that includes everything from mobile police patrols, roving courts, and itinerant officials through district administrative centers, government branch offices, checkpoints, provincial offices, and so on, right up to the ministries themselves at the level of the central state.

By contrast, nonstate armed groups tend to lack such a permanent and obvious structure—they often deliberately seek invisibility, in fact—and although they may field a comprehensive shadow governance system, this is neither overt nor necessarily large-scale. Such a system usually works in a nonobvious "underground" manner that makes it hard to observe and even harder to compare with competing structures. The well-developed, overt structure that Hezbollah has created is a rare exception in this context: the vast majority of nonstate armed groups have nothing of the kind.

For example, we might look at an Afghan district and count the number of school buildings, state-employed teachers, and children attending school as a means of gauging the strength of the Afghan education ministry in that area. These are all relatively obvious and easy to count, especially the number of school buildings, one reason why this is such a popular measure of performance for aid agencies and governments providing assistance in Afghanistan. There are problems with this metric, by the way—it measures inputs (expenditure on education) rather than outcomes (how many teachers and students in schools) or impact (changes in literacy levels or the effectiveness of programs). But at least the number of schools is an observable though partial *negative measure* of government presence, since if there are no schools in an area, there's clearly little influence by the government education ministry.

But measuring the strength of a nonstate armed group in this structural way is deeply problematic. The Taliban don't build school buildings. Nor do they establish many of the other obvious statelike bureaucratic or administrative structures that governments create. Even their intimidation may not be obvious—in 2009, after killing a few teachers and burning schools to send a message, Taliban in some parts of Afghanistan began letting children go to school unhindered, so that if we were to try to gauge Taliban influence over the school system in these areas through the number of teachers or students being killed or school buildings being burned, there would be nothing to see. And yet, of course, nobody in these districts had the slightest doubt as to who was in control—some I talked to even said that they were grateful to the Taliban for "allowing" their children's education.[61] Likewise, according to U.S. officers in a district in eastern Afghanistan, the Taliban didn't interfere with school attendance but did dictate the curriculum: at a school in the village of Chawni, "the Taliban recently posted a letter on the wall detailing the curriculum that was to be taught. 'So here they get money from the government, books from the government, and they think it's perfectly legitimate to teach what the Taliban tells them.'"[62]

How then can we compare the strength of a nonstate armed group to that of the state—an essential activity, if we want to understand which actor is becoming dominant in the competition for control? As Bernard Fall suggests, we need a functional model rather than a structural one, and we need to think in terms of competitive systems of control. Joel S. Migdal suggested just such an approach in his 1988 study, *Strong Societies and Weak States*.[63] Migdal argued that you could understand state effectiveness by measuring capability across four clusters (or subsystems) of government activity—"the capacities to *penetrate* society, *regulate* social relationships, *extract* resources, and *appropriate* or use resources in determined ways."[64] The distinguished analyst and Afghanistan-watcher William Maley applied Migdal's model in his history of state collapse in Afghanistan, *The Afghanistan Wars*, demonstrating its applicability to both state and insurgent capabilities.[65]

This functional approach lets us compare the strengths of various incentives and control systems. Though they don't own and operate school buildings, the Taliban do run underground indoctrination programs. They *penetrate* the school system and attempt to *regulate* the behavior of people in it, so that their ideas are reflected in the school curriculum and individual teachers are pushing the insurgent line in the classroom, and they try to intimidate teachers and students, using threatening text messages on cell phones or threatening notes on school buildings or the houses of teachers. They *extract* resources from the school system through extortion or by taxing teachers, parents, and local businesses, and they *appropriate* those resources to their own programs.

To summarize, it's worth referring back to the systems of competitive control we observed in the previous chapter—in particular, the "System" in Tivoli Gardens, Kingston. Like the Taliban system of local courts, the informal justice system in garrison communities creates a mechanism for dispute resolution, mediation, and enforcement that makes populations feel safe, creates order, and generates predictability. At the persuasive end of the spectrum, the parties and community events sponsored by the gang, the political participation of the community in the JLP's electoral process, and the subjective feelings of respect, affection, and prestige that built up over time created a resilient, wide-spectrum system of competitive control for Christopher Coke's group. In the administrative part of the spectrum, the ability to access government contracts, social services, housing, health care, and food supplies provides incentives for the population to support the posse, while locking them into dependence on the gang's largesse. And at the coercive end of the spectrum, the gang controlling each garrison has the demonstrated capacity to kill informers, fight off rivals, and punish those who transgress its rules. It also polices its own members in order to maintain internal discipline and external predictability. Thus, at the hyperlocal level, we see exactly the same pattern of competitive control at work in the gang environment of Kingston as we saw in the Taliban, Hezbollah, and AQI. This, along with the mafia, street gang, prison gang, and drug trafficking network examples mentioned earlier, suggests that the mechanism of competitive control isn't restricted to insurgency or civil war but is rather a universal aspect of the way in which nonstate actors control population groups.

There's one very obvious difference, however, between what the Shower Posse achieved in Tivoli Gardens and what the Taliban has attempted to establish in Afghanistan, and this is the transnational network—initially an international protection racket, then a drug trafficking organization—that the Shower Posse created by exploiting the urban, networked, littoral environment in which it operated. In particular, as local levels of violence spiked in the 1970s and people escaped to the United States, Canada, and Great Britain, these emigrants created urban networks that connected the Kingston garrisons to cities across the planet. As they remitted money back to the gang to ensure protection for their families still in Jamaica, members of the diaspora created the basis for a transnational system of competitive control. This has also been seen with Hezbollah and with insurgencies such as the Tamil Tigers, both of which exploited large diaspora populations to generate international support networks, and with Kenyan and Nigerian organized crime, as well as with the Russian, Italian, and Albanian mafias, Latin American *narcos* and street gangs, and Chinese snakeheads (people smugglers) and Triads (transnational organized crime networks). As coastal urbanization and connectedness increase, transnational networks of this kind, tapping into the flows of urban connectivity between home populations and diasporas, will increasingly be able to create transnational systems of competitive control that mimic the functions of the state and compete with governments. Indeed, they'll be even better able to compete with national governments, which will be tied to one particular territory and limited by national sovereignty and international law, while transnational networks will be increasingly able to skip between jurisdictions at will, avoiding governments whenever the pressure on them gets too great.

Before we move on to look at the elements of this international connectivity, however, we must first examine the other side of the coin—the way that populations attempt to manipulate and control armed groups.

## IV. Population Survival Strategies

*March 19, 2008*
*Office of the Independent Directorate of Local Government, Kabul*

Mullah Abdul Salaam Alizai sat at the head of the long teak-veneer table in the conference room of a run-down Afghan government office in Kabul. He was a big man in every sense—big-boned, haughty, with a magnificent scented black beard and a black turban, dressed in tradi-tional garb right down to his curly-toed slippers, every inch a tribal chief. His gaze casually took in, assessed, dominated, and dismissed the room. Only a few weeks before, he had been a pro-Taliban commander in his home district of Musa Qala, in the northern part of Helmand province in Afghanistan's southwest.

As a leader of the Alizai, the dominant Pashtun tribe in Musa Qala district, Mullah Salaam had allied with the Taliban and had been a mil-itary commander during the Taliban regime of 1996–2001. The Taliban appointed him governor of Uruzgan province, and he later served as governor of Kajaki district in Helmand. After the coalition invasion of 2001, Sher Muhammad Akhundzada, the newly appointed governor of Helmand province, imprisoned Mullah Salaam for several months: although (or rather, because) Sher Muhammad was also an Alizai, his rivalry with Salaam was intense and personal. Sher Muhammad and Abdul Salaam hailed from competing subtribes, and while Salaam was pro-Taliban, Sher Muhammad was one of the former mujahideen com-manders we've already discussed, who sought to divide Afghanistan among themselves after the defeat of the Soviets, and then fought each other and the Taliban during the civil war of the 1990s.

After his release from Sher Muhammad's prison, Mullah Salaam returned to his compound at Shah Karez, eight miles east of Musa Qala, and became a member of the tribal council. On the surface, he had recon-ciled with the new government—he even served for a time as head of Sher Muhammad's bodyguard—but in February 2007 he switched sides. The British Army had moved into Helmand in force in July 2006, bringing intense fighting to Musa Qala, interfering with poppy cultivation and other agriculture, and causing major disruption to licit and illicit business. By late 2006, realizing they were overstretched, the British had agreed to a cease-fire under which both they and the Taliban would withdraw from Musa Qala district center, leaving it under the protection of the tribal council.

After biding their time and gathering their forces through the winter, in the spring of 2007 the Taliban broke the truce and moved in to seize the town. Salaam sided with the Taliban, leading his Alizai fighters in support of the insurgents as they took the rest of the district. But after a few months Salaam changed sides once again. He'd become disillusioned when, in his words, Taliban leaders had "shown lack of respect for the tribal council." After secret negotiations with British officers and with Michael Semple, an Irish diplomat who was later expelled from Afghanistan by the Karzai government for making direct contact with Taliban leaders, Salaam switched sides once more to support the government in late 2007. Since his latest change of sides, his efforts to rally the local population in support of the government and against the Taliban had earned him appointment as Musa Qala district governor—which was why he was in Kabul now, looking for concrete rewards in the form of weapons, money, protection, and contracts for people in his district.

Now Mullah Salaam surveyed the room confidently, gazing around at the eleven elders from his district (mostly Pashtuns, with one Hazara) who had made the long journey to Kabul to show their solidarity with him, along with a collection of officials of the Independent Directorate of Local Government (IDLG), the part of the Afghan government that is (in theory at least) responsible for district and local administration. Mullah Salaam and his elders had come to put their case for support to the IDLG leadership. Headed by Jalani Popal, President Karzai's cousin, IDLG was working to bring essential services and government presence to local populations across the country, creating local governance centers and appointing district governors, in order to solidify President Karzai's control over the Afghan countryside. This effort was codified two years later as the District Delivery Program, which Popal described at the 2010 London Conference (displaying his, or perhaps his speechwriter's, superb mastery of international development terminology) as aiming "to establish or improve the visibility of the Government by holistically engaging the governance system at the district level to ensure that the basic level public services are available directly to communities."[66] More concisely, an official from Nangarhar province described the program to me as "the re-elect Karzai campaign."[67]

I was at the table as a visiting official from Washington, D.C., along with a small field team. We were conducting a theaterwide campaign assessment for the U.S. secretary of state, traveling to different parts of the conflict area, talking to local populations and key officials, trying to get a feel for the state of the war and, more important, the reach and effectiveness of the Afghan government. Things didn't look good, to say the least. At this time NATO's campaign plan included a governance line of operation, which declared that the coalition's governance objective was "to extend the reach of the Afghan government."[68] The problem with such a strategy of government extension was that it lacked a comparable governance reform element. If your strategy is to extend the reach of a government that is corrupt, abusive, ineffective, and alienates the people, then the better you execute that strategy, the worse things are going to get—which is exactly what was happening.

Then, as now, the problem in Afghanistan wasn't fundamentally a military one: the Taliban, for all their ferocious reputation, were no match for NATO in military terms, and they'd been solidly defeated several times over in campaigns around the country since 2001. But because there was no viable, effective, nonabusive government to replace them—or, putting it in competitive control theory terms, because the Afghan government couldn't muster a wide-spectrum normative system to compete with that of the Taliban—the insurgency always returned, because it did things that the people needed and that the government either could not or would not do. Active sanctuary in Pakistan—including advisers, money, weapons, training support, and protection from U.S. interference—certainly helped, but ultimately even Pakistani support wouldn't have allowed the insurgency to continually recover from its military losses had the insurgents not also had a robust normative system that could outcompete the government's. Like Hezbollah in Lebanon, the Taliban could and did bounce back from a series of military defeats by using capabilities in the other parts of the persuasion-coercion spectrum.

Now Mullah Salaam began his pitch, with his elders looking on but remaining silent, acting as living props who indicated, by their mere presence, the district governor's influence and prestige. Their role was to demonstrate allegiance to him, while he in turn would act as an intermediary, using their support to prove his influence, and so garner resources from the government that he would in turn distribute to them. Mullah Salaam had come over to the government side a few weeks before, he said, along with all the elders from his district, because he wanted the best for his people. He explained that he needed to protect his district and its population from all comers—the Taliban, the government, the drug traffickers, the British currently occupying his area, everyone. To do this, he needed resources that would be under his personal control. He was happy the British had driven off the Taliban, and he was happy that he had been appointed district governor, but he needed either a permanent garrison to take care of his district or weapons to arm his own fighters. He wanted to establish his own local police (*arbakai*) to secure his district. And he needed contracts—reconstruction contracts, aid projects, transportation and supply contracts—to bring wealth to his people. He and the elders would see to it that any assistance was fairly distributed, he promised.

After half an hour of inconclusive discussion, as we stood to leave, he grabbed my hand tightly. "Give me American troops to protect my district," he said. "If I can't have Americans, I want my own weapons back so I can protect my people myself." Explaining that I was just a low-level diplomat with no influence over the military, I asked what would happen if neither of those options was possible. "If I can't have my own weapons, I'll accept the Afghan Army in my district, and if I can't have the army, then I'll accept the Afghan Police—but only as a last resort." I asked why his own government should trust him with new weapons when he'd been so recently aligned with the Taliban. Didn't he still have his own weapons? Had he really switched sides so completely? Since when did the Alizai take orders from Kabul, anyway?

He smiled at me, perhaps marveling at my idiotic naïveté.

"I wasn't with the Taliban before, and I'm not with the government now. I'm just trying to take care of my people. Before, I thought we were better off with the Taliban. Now I think we're better off with the government, but that could change."

Clearly, terms such as *pro-Taliban* or *pro-government* are meaningless as a description of a local leader such as Abdul Salaam Alizai. For one thing, these terms represent not fixed and unchanging inherent identities that predict a person's behavior but rather labels that can be acquired and discarded at will. For another, these labels—while they might make sense in the externally imposed construct (what anthropologists might call the etic framework) of counterinsurgency theory—are virtually irrelevant at the local level, where every elder furthers his own interests and those of his group, and partners with whatever outsider he needs to—Taliban, government, or other—in order to advance those interests. A change of sides didn't indicate a change of loyalty, for each local leader's loyalty was only ever to himself and his primary group. Anything else was just window dressing.

Just consider Mullah Salaam's personal history: he was originally a Taliban military leader, and then a provincial and district governor for the Taliban regime. Next he was a prisoner of, then an ally of, then head of the bodyguard for, the new regime's governor, who happened to be his tribal relative and personal rival. Then he fought with the Taliban to throw that governor, and the British, out of his district, and after that he turned against the Taliban once more, welcomed the British back, and became district governor himself. Now he wanted a payoff from the government for his "loyalty," when it should be abundantly clear that Salaam's loyalty was to nobody but himself, his subtribe, and his subdistrict. As far as he was concerned, the dominant feature of any external intervener—Taliban, British, Kabul government, American, anyone—was precisely that it *was* an external actor, to be allied with or opposed on a pragmatic basis, only to the extent that such an alliance served his or his district's local interest and furthered his ability to defeat his tribal and economic rivals.

A few months after this meeting, after the Taliban had targeted him twice for assassination, Mullah Salaam found himself in an open dispute with the British Army once more. As Jerome Starkey reported:

A former Taliban commander who swapped sides last year has accused his British allies of jeopardising security and undermining his authority in a row that has plunged their relations to an all time low. Mullah Salam was made governor of Musa Qala, Helmand, after British, American and Afghan forces retook the town in December. His defection was the catalyst for the operation. But the British fear his warlord ways are hampering their efforts to win over local people, and driving them back into the hands of the insurgents. Mullah Salam says British soldiers are wrecking his attempts to bring security by releasing people he arrests and underfunding his war chest—which he claims is for buying off insurgent commanders. . . . The top British diplomat at the headquarters, Dr Richard Jones, said: "He likes to feather his own nest." . . . Lieutenant-Colonel Ed Freely, who commands the Royal Irish troops training Afghanistan's army, said: "He appears less interested in governing his people than reinforcing his own personal position of power." . . . The British believe he taxed his own villagers more than a ton of opium at the end of the poppy harvest. They also suspect his militia of stealing land, money and motorbikes, and beating people who can't pay. Mullah Salam denies the allegations. "If I see anyone in my militia doing these things I will shoot him," he said, revealing his own brand of Taliban-style justice.[69]

Even by the baroque standards of Afghan tribal leaders, Mullah Salaam has a reputation for eccentricity and drama. But—as we've seen—his words and actions in this case were utterly typical of the behavior of local leaders in environments such as insurgencies, civil wars, and failed states, in feral cities such as Mogadishu, in marginalized urban settlements such as the Kingston garrison communities, or in periurban slums such as those of Mumbai.

We often (consciously or otherwise) tend to regard such marginalized and excluded populations as passive, supine recipients of government intervention and international assistance, or as victims of groups (such as an insurgents, gangs, or criminal networks) that governments regard as illegitimate. We think of the population as lacking in agency, simply a beneficiary or victim of the actions of others—like a silent-movie heroine tied to a railway track, helplessly awaiting rescue.

As Mullah Salaam's case shows, nothing could be further from the truth: not only are noncombatant civilians in these environments extremely active and highly influential, but they are in many cases masters of manipulation and experts in leveraging the presence of rich, ignorant, gullible outsiders in order to get what they need, outsmart their rivals, and survive another day. Indeed, any community leader who is still alive and in a position of authority today in Afghanistan, after thirty years of war (or in Tivoli Gardens, after sixty years of gang domination, or in Mogadishu, after twenty years of state collapse) is, through natural selection alone, almost certainly an expert in manipulating and balancing external interveners and local armed groups. For this reason, to examine the relationships between nonstate armed groups and populations solely through the lens of the normative systems that armed groups create is to miss at least half of the interaction that generates competitive control.

### Domination, Resistance, and Manipulation

The great Professor James C. Scott of Yale University, writing in 1976, described subsistence farmers in Southeast Asia in the following terms: "There are districts in which the position of the rural population is that of a man standing permanently up to the neck in water, so that even a ripple is sufficient to drown him."[70] Scott, the father of an entire genre of political ethnography sometimes known as "resistance studies" or "subaltern studies," explains that peasant populations—precisely because they live on the subsistence margin, where the downside risk of failure is so much greater than the upside potential for success—tend to be extremely risk-averse. One year's crop failure can push a peasant family below the starvation threshold, forcing family members to sell capital assets (such as land or livestock) to survive, reducing them to supplicant status in a village, or forcing them off the land entirely, so they never recover their independence. For this reason, over generations, marginalized populations have become experts at fine calculations of risk and tend always to minimize risk, maximize predictability, and limit the influence of outsiders such as governments. They value predictability, even at the expense of overall profit, and have developed what Scott calls a "safety-first principle" that embodies a series of "classical techniques for avoiding undue risks often at the cost of a reduction in average return."[71]

Scott cites as an example of this risk-aversion behavior peasants' resistance to government interventions designed to improve their lot; another is their reluctance to embrace agricultural innovations such as higher-yield but less reliable strains of rice.[72] He argues convincingly that this behavior isn't limited to Southeast Asia but can be seen in precapitalist or subsistence farming populations across the planet; in his later work he examines marginalized and excluded urban and periurban populations and shows that a similar calculus of risk-minimizing resistance permeates the behavior of urban as well as rural groups.[73] Scott argues that populations on the margin typically prefer the kinds of patron-client relationships that we observed in Tivoli Gardens—predictable arrangements whereby better-off members of a community sponsor its weaker members—even though such relationships are often exploitative, involving long-term dependency and what Jamaican commentators such as Obika Gray call "benefits politics."[74]

Like Scott, Karl D. Jackson, in his classic study of traditional authority and religion during the Darul Islam insurgency in West Java in the 1960s, showed similar patterns of patron-client relations in village and periurban populations in Indonesia.[75] My own fieldwork with the same population in the same area almost thirty years later showed that these patterns can be remarkably persistent once established: once locked into an incentive system, it can be extraordinarily difficult for a population to break out of established behavior patterns of this kind.

In the presence of an insurgency, criminal network, or gang conflict—bringing the risk of violence, death, and major property damage into the equation—the downside risk of miscalculation becomes dramatically higher, but so do the potential upside benefits. Aid agencies, police, military forces with emergency funds, and government and nongovernment "experts" of all kinds (most of whom are entirely ignorant of local conditions but have vast amounts of money, little time, and less accountability) flood into a local area, looking for allies and creating enormous opportunities for profit and benefit. Local elites (such as Mullah Salaam, as we have seen) can see outsiders as a source of revenue and influence as well as of risk.

Moreover, since outside military or law enforcement interveners often bring with them heavy weaponry and enormous coercive firepower, well beyond anything that the local community can muster, they can radically alter the local balance of power among competing armed actors and can therefore become a game-changing resource for any local player who can successfully manipulate them into destroying his or her enemies. Any coalition soldier who has worked in Afghanistan or Iraq, or indeed any inner-city police officer or counternarcotics agent, can give dozens of examples of populations trying to use the police or military as a tool to smash local rivals, reporting their local adversaries as "insurgents," "criminals," "terrorists," or "militia" to persuade security forces to target them, or settling scores by informing on each other.

Like Scott's marginalized peasants and periurban populations, communities in a high-risk environment such as an insurgency, a garrison neighborhood, or a slum that's experiencing high levels of violent crime become expert at navigating a complex and ever-changing set of choices, always seeking to maintain safety, minimize risk, maximize profit from external interveners, improve their position vis-à-vis local rivals, and resist or exploit external control. Indeed, one reason effective normative systems attract support from such populations is that—as Stathis Kalyvas showed, and as the Taliban decree I quoted earlier illustrates—normative systems create predictability and order, reducing transaction costs for populations and minimizing the risk of a potentially fatal miscalculation. My own observations in places as variable as Pakistani refugee camps, port cities in New Guinea and Indonesia, East Timorese coastal towns, Sri Lankan displaced persons' camps, and cities such as Mogadishu, Kandahar, Tripoli, and Baghdad suggest that population survival strategies in these environments fall into seven basic categories: fleeing, passivity, autarky, hedging, swinging, commitment, and self-arming. Let's briefly examine each in turn.

*Fleeing*—an extreme response to chaotic violence—occurs when populations react to the danger of their situation simply by leaving an area. For unencapsulated nomads or tribal pastoralists (such as the Bedu of Iraq, the Kuchi of Afghanistan, or Somali clans), fleeing to avoid government influence or escape violence is an entire way of life: as I've noted elsewhere, desert tribes run when mountain tribes would fight.[76] Pastoralists' wealth is mobile, residing in their flocks, and thus movement away from threat is a natural response. But for agriculturalists or, even more so, urban dwellers, fleeing an area is an extreme step. Their wealth is in the land, in their business, or in their residence, and moving away may mean that they can never come back and that local rivals will seize their property. Thus, whole families rarely leave a violence-affected area—but individuals may emigrate, move to the city, or move to another district. The flows of rural-to-urban migration that we noted in Chapter 1, along with the patterns of emigration and diaspora formation in the Somalia and Jamaica examples in Chapter 2, clearly illustrate this tendency.

*Passivity* occurs in populations that have been traumatized by extreme violence or where local elites have been killed or driven off by conflict. This approach manifests itself in an extreme reluctance to take any kind of action or to accept responsibility for any decision whatsoever. Some neighborhoods (*muhallas*) in Baghdad in 2007 exemplified this survival strategy. These areas were subjected to atrocious sectarian violence and were left largely to their own devices in 2005–6. As a result, community leaders in these *muhallas* were highly reluctant to take any initiative in rebuilding or securing their communities: the carnage of the preceding year, on top of decades of Ba'athist oppression, had taught them that the most dangerous thing they could possibly do was to take responsibility for their own actions. Indeed, the people left in charge of these neighborhoods after the intense violence of 2005–6 were often the *least* decisive leaders—the active players had been weeded out, or had exposed themselves by taking the initiative to protect their communities and had been killed, often in ways that traumatized the community or were specifically designed (by groups such as AQI) to discourage such independence.[77] Those who survived sought to hide behind the excuse that the coalition or the insurgents had forced them to take a particular action. This strategy of appearing helpless, while clearly well adapted to minimizing downside risk, was ineffective in generating benefits or support from the government or the coalition. Over time, some communities moved past this approach to a hedging or swinging strategy, but others— often the most marginalized and traumatized periurban communities— never did.[78]

*Autarky*, in this context, is an extreme from of armed neutrality, a strategy of self-sufficient independence that denies allegiance to anyone or anything outside the local level. It's sometimes expressed as a "plague on all your houses" attitude toward the government and nonstate armed groups alike, or—more subtly—in the kinds of independence-maximizing strategies we saw in the case of Mullah Salaam or the Somali clans. If fleeing is the default strategy of desert nomads, then armed neutrality is the natural strategy of mountain people. The behavior of the Waygal Valley elders before and during the battle of Wanat (described in the introduction) typifies the behavior of mountain populations, who for terrain reasons can't flee the encroachment of government or external armed actors, are tied to particular pieces of land, and must therefore stand and fight to resist outside influence. Autarky, as a strategy, can be effective in minimizing risk (through the deterrent effect of armed neutrality) and generating benefits for a local population. It needn't be purely defensive, and may manifest itself in externally aggressive behavior aimed at deterring interference. In particular, the ability to raid or prey on other local groups or passing travelers—especially for populations who sit astride key flows in an urban metabolism, as do the Kenyan gangs discussed in Chapter 1, or who control a major port or airport, as does the Shower Posse—can force outsiders to buy off an autarkic group, or allow a marginalized group to maintain its autonomy.

*Hedging*, one of the commonest survival strategies in conditions of competitive control, consists in simultaneously supporting all sides. Like a bettor laying an across-the-board bet on a horse race, or a corporation giving campaign donations to both parties in an election, a population that adopts a hedging strategy seeks to minimize risk by paying off all sides—while maximizing the potential for benefits by ensuring it supports the winner, whoever that may be. This strategy is popular precisely because it simultaneously lowers risk and heightens the prospect of profit. But, like cheating on a mafia don, it can be risky if one particular armed actor discovers the population has been supporting another, and so it is often conducted subtly. For example, some Afghan families have one son fighting with the Taliban and one in the Afghan Army—not because their loyalties are confused but as an insurance policy against a victory by either side. They can support each side as needed but can also maintain plausible deniability. Similarly, urban populations who pay protection money to a local gang but also pay off the police are adopting a hedging strategy—but they can always claim that the money was extorted by force. In this context, playing the victim and deemphasizing autonomy can be a useful tactic to support a hedging strategy.

*Swinging*, like hedging, consists of supporting all sides in a conflict, but unlike hedging (which involves simultaneously but covertly supporting each side), a swinging strategy involves periodic, carefully timed switching of sides. A population engaged in a swinging strategy supports only one side at any given moment but shifts its allegiance as the local balance of power changes. If hedging is like sleeping around, swinging is like serial monogamy. The population's goal is to back the strongest local side at any given moment, changing sides when one group becomes more dominant, changing back when the situation shifts, and strategically throwing their own influence into the balance in order to ensure a result that benefits a local leader or group. Mullah Salaam's behavior, described in detail above, exemplifies such a swinging strategy, along with a strong tendency toward autarky. Like hedging, swinging is popular since it minimizes subjective risk while maximizing opportunities to extract benefits and concessions from all sides. But it too is a dangerous game, since it depends on correctly predicting changes in the relative strength of armed actors: populations have to learn to switch sides at just the right moment to avoid being caught on the losing side. We might also note that populations tend to factor into their risk calculus the degree of violence an armed group is likely to inflict as punishment for changing sides. Violence trumps benefits in this context: if an insurgent or street gang is going to kill you for switching sides but the police or army is likely to try to win you back with benefits, then you'll default to supporting the gang, since the downside risks of opposing it are greater. This is precisely why, as we saw in Chapter 2, Jamaican gangs reserved their harshest punishments for those who informed to the police or changed political allegiance. It's also why, in our discussion of normative systems, we noted that the strength of a normative system—however well developed its persuasive and administrative elements might be—ultimately rests on the coercive capabilities of its enforcer.

*Commitment* involves picking one side or actor and depending on that side for protection and support. Populations that adopt this strategy have effectively nailed their colors to the mast and are therefore accepting a very high degree of downside risk. For obvious reasons, such a strategy is not a popular one. It tends to be chosen by populations, such as the Tivoli Gardens residents in Chapter 2, who are so enmeshed in a resilient, full-spectrum normative system of control that it becomes effectively impossible for them to change sides. Such switching may even become literally unthinkable for the population if the proponent of the normative system can muster sufficiently persuasive discourse-framing propaganda capabilities. In the most developed cases, the population may internalize the ruling group's ideology to the point where it eventually becomes seen as axiomatic, or as common sense rather than as an ideology at all, and where the population ceases to realize that it has any choice in the matter—the sort of situation Antonio Gramsci called "ideological hegemony."[79] Of course, while few nonstate armed groups ever get to this level, 100 percent commitment is the goal of any normative system, at least in theory. In practice, it takes enormous effort and intrusive presence in a population's residential area to generate such commitment. The one exception to this is the case of ethnic or religious minority populations, or people with a public or family track record of supporting a given side—Assyrian Christians in Iraq, Hazaras in Afghanistan, Alawites and some Christians in Syria, regime supporters in Libya—who have no chance of successfully switching sides in a conflict and thus no choice but to commit.

*Self-arming*—the final strategic option for a population at risk—involves taking an active, armed role in the conflict, coming off the sidelines to become involved in the armed struggle for control, and shedding any pretense of noncombatant status. It differs from commitment in that, rather than choosing an existing armed group and offering that

A mine-resistant ambush protected vehicle (MRAP), a few minutes before the ambush in Dara-i Nur District, Afghanistan, September 10, 2009. Photo: David Kilcullen.

Hindu Kush, Afghanistan—the remote landlocked mountain environment has become the default for many western militaries, diplomats, and development agencies since 2001. Photo: David Kilcullen.

Forward operating base (FOB) of French *Chasseurs Alpins* in the mountains of Afghanistan, December 2009. Photo: David Kilcullen.

American and Iraqi troops securing an area south of Baghdad, 2007. The Iraq War saw intense urban fighting, but mainly in U.S./Iraqi operational areas. Photo: David Kilcullen.

Coastal megacity—a Mumbai slum. Note the mix of high-rise and shanty settlements and the satellite dish in the center of the photograph. Photo: Gordon Dixon.

Feral city—African Union peacekeepers drive past shops and power lines on the streets of Mogadishu, June 2012. Photo: David Kilcullen.

Competitive control—Somali clan militia at a checkpoint on the outskirts of Mogadishu, June 2012. Photo: David Kilcullen.

Competitive control—a Somali building destroyed by militants as punishment for its owners' failure to pay insurgent taxes. Photo: David Kilcullen.

Competitive control—African Union troops with weapons, radios ,and ammunition captured from al-Shabaab during the battle of Afgoye, June 2012. Photo: David Kilcullen.

The feral city—flourishing shops and markets in a Mogadishu street, 2012. Photo: David Kilcullen.

The Libyan uprising—apartments in the coastal city of Misurata. Note the satellite antennas and the heavy weapons on "technicals" in the foreground. Photo: Anna Prouse.

Urban overstretch—flimsy dwellings on stilts in a riverside slum in Dhaka, Bangladesh.
Photo: Niels Van Gijn.

"Informal governance—rooftop water systems and satellite antennas in the favela of
La Rocinha, Brazil. Photo: Linda Epstein.

Co-design—residents in a district in Monrovia, Liberia, building a map to illustrate patterns of crime, commerce, and violence, August 2012. Photo: Matt McNabb.

Co-design—women in a Liberian district gather data on community confidence and threat perceptions, August 2012. Photo: Matt McNabb.

group its support in exchange for protection, a population that adopts this strategy gives up its civil status, arming itself instead. For populations under extremely severe threat, this may be an attractive strategy, because whatever else it may do, it reduces the subjective perception of risk by making the population less of a soft target. Such a strategy may deter an armed group altogether, or (more likely) may make the population that adopts it less likely to suffer predation than some other, less well armed, population group in the same area. This attitude—"we may as well go down fighting"—probably lay behind the thinking of at least some of the Iraqi tribal leaders who joined the Anbar Awakening in 2006–7 in Iraq, and it clearly underpinned the thinking of tribal groups who raised their own *arbakai* in Afghanistan, participated in the Village Stability Operations program, or joined the anti-Taliban, antigovernment *qiyam* uprising in many districts in eastern Afghanistan in 2012–13.

### Conclusions: Urban Competitive Control

As I mentioned at the start of this chapter, techniques that we might label as "fishing traps," which attract populations and then lock them into a network of incentives to prevent them from escaping, are common to insurgencies, criminal organizations, mass movements, and other state and nonstate groups, as well as governments. In the context of violent conflict, however, the most relevant subset of these techniques is the group of methods I've described, using the theory of normative systems, as *competitive control*. These systems of competitive control apply a range of capabilities across a spectrum from persuasion through administration to coercion, and they are designed by armed actors—owners or proponents of the system—as a means to corral, control, manipulate, and mobilize populations. As we've seen, a wide-spectrum system of control tends to outcompete a narrow-spectrum one, because its proponent can always bounce back from a defeat in one part of the spectrum by compensating with capabilities from another.

The initial examples we examined were from relatively simple rural settings in Afghanistan. Exactly the same types of behaviors and patterns of interaction are evident in the urban examples we looked at in previous chapters, and in the urban Iraqi examples discussed in this chapter. As we've also just noted, the interaction between armed groups and populations is not a one-way process: populations employ many strategies to manipulate and manage armed actors, seeking to minimize risk, maximize predictability, and limit encroachments upon their autonomy. Again, this pattern of behavior isn't unique to insurgencies but is applicable to all forms of nonstate armed group that seek to control a population, and (in a functional sense) to states as well. It is thus potentially a useful explanatory tool as we examine the interplay between populations, nonstate armed groups, and governments in the marginalized urban and periurban environments that are becoming increasingly common across the planet.

Where urban environments of the future will differ from these examples, however, is in the vastly increased local and transnational connectivity they can access, and thus in the ability of nonstate armed groups or state sponsors in marginalized areas in one part of the world to manipulate and mobilize populations on the other side of the globe, and vice versa. The next chapter looks at the broader connectivity and networking issue, and seeks to locate this theoretical discussion in some practical observations of current conflict in connected cities.

# 4

## Conflict in Connected Cities

[We] are engaged in a social netwar. The information age of the
late 20th Century has enabled activists to work together globally
while maintaining local autonomy. The power of this movement
arises from its structure; namely, a decentralized network capable
of instant communication, collaboration, coordination and action (C3A). The implications of this movement are profound and
amount to what has been called an "'associational revolution' among
nonstate actors that may prove as significant as the rise of the nation
state."

—Christopher Burnett, 2000

*April 2011*
*Yefren, Jabal al-Gharbi District, Libya*

It's a cool night in western Libya. The uprising against Muammar Gaddafi
is eight weeks old and intensifying by the day. Guerrillas are maneuvering
in the outskirts of Yefren, a town about fifty miles from the Mediterranean coast, southwest of Tripoli. Yefren district is home to about
180,000 people, mainly ethnic Berbers, and the whole area has been in
open rebellion since mid-February. Now regime troops and loyalist militias have besieged the city, bringing up heavy ordnance to bombard the
town center, seeking to cow its people into submission. Sifaw Twawa and
his group of fighters are stalled on the edge of the city, armed only with
AK-47s, facing off at close range against a Soviet-made Grad 122 mm
multiple-barrel rocket launcher.[1]

Twawa's cell phone rings. Two friends are on the line, via a Skype conference call. Nureddin Ashammakhi is in Finland, where he heads
a research team developing biomaterials technology, and Khalid

Hatashe, a medical doctor, is in the United Kingdom. The Qaddafi regime trained Hatashe on Grads during his compulsory military service. He explains that Twawa's *katiba*—brigade—is well short of the Grad's minimum range: at this distance, any rockets fired would shoot past them. Hatashe adds that the launcher can be triggered from several hundred feet away using an electric cable, so the enemy may not be in or near the launch vehicle. Twawa's men successfully attack the Grad— all because two civilians briefed their leader, over Skype, in a battlefield a continent away.[2]

This account is part of an impressive body of reporting by the technology writer John Pollock, produced in 2011 during months of courageous work on the frontlines of conflict in Tunisia, Egypt, and Libya.[3] Pollock's writing focuses on social media, youth mobilization, and digital connectivity in the Arab Awakening, a wave of anti-authoritarian uprisings that began in late 2010 in Tunisia, spread to Egypt, Libya, Bahrain, Yemen, and Syria, destabilized Morocco, Jordan, and Lebanon, and is continuing to transform the political landscape of the Middle East and coastal North Africa. The Arab uprisings brought down governments in Tunisia, Egypt, and Yemen, led to a violent crackdown against democracy protestors in Bahrain, prompted the overthrow of the Gaddafi regime in Libya, and triggered a bloody civil war in Syria. These uprisings are the most prominent recent illustration of the way that increased connectedness is affecting urbanized conflict.

This chapter focuses on one aspect of this broader pattern of connectedness, namely, the rapidly expanding electronic connectivity that has been enabled by improved access to electricity, lower-cost mobile technology, and recent changes in the way the Internet is organized.[4] This democratization of connectivity, which is closely connected to the patterns of population growth and coastal urbanization we've been examining, is part of the broader democratization of technology that we've already discussed. It enables alliances between online activists who operate in a contested global information space and nonstate armed groups who compete for control on the streets of marginalized urban and periurban communities. The aim of this chapter is to round out our discussion on urban metabolism, feral cities, and the range of urban threats in Chapter 2, and on the theory of competitive control in

Chapter 3, with a look at how enhanced connectivity is transforming the way people fight in cities.

In his account of Sifaw Twawa's engagement at Yefren, Pollock is describing an important feature of conflict in this highly connected environment: the rise of remote warfare, and of what we might call *virtual theaters*. Before turning to the Arab uprisings, therefore, it's worth examining these aspects in a little more detail.

## I.  Remote Warfare and Virtual Theaters

The military term *theater of war* means "the area of air, land and water that is, or may become, directly involved in the conduct" of a conflict.[5] A theater of war can include theaters of operations—subareas containing forces that "conduct or support specific combat operations" and are normally thought of as "geographically separate and focused on different enemy forces."[6] Traditionally, theaters are thus discrete areas of geographical space, within which all the participants in a given conflict are physically located. This is an important legal construct, as well as a strategic and operational one: governments typically designate specific geographical areas as "war zones," apply more or less restrictive laws of armed conflict to these zones, and assert certain legal protections for military forces and populations in such areas, while excluding other populations and territories (for example, the home populations of countries engaged in expeditionary wars overseas). In this way, a theater of war, like the rule set in a system of competitive control, defines an area of dangerous space, marks it off from safe territory, and establishes a set of sanctions that applies on one side of the boundary but not the other. The theater construct thus helps define *spaces of normality*. It's part of a global normative system (international law) that divides physical space into a realm of war, where the laws and customs of war apply, and a realm of peace, where norms of civil society, domestic law and civil protections apply.[7]

The key phrases in the official definition of a theater of war are "directly involved" and "conduct or support": if everyone involved in conducting or supporting combat action in a given war is located within a definable geographical space (say, the European Theater of Operations or the South-West Pacific Area during World War II, or the Korean Theater of Operations during the Korean War), then it makes sense to bound that war in a geographical manner. But this is rarely so in contemporary conflict, and in the highly connected environment of the future it will be even more unusual.

We've already discussed how the traditional notion of a "littoral area" has expanded to the broader idea of a "littoral influence zone," taking account of the reach of modern weapons and mobility platforms such as cruise missiles or extended-range ship-borne helicopters, which can extend littoral warfare well beyond coastlines themselves. But in a general sense, modern long-range communications and globally networked connectivity, and the addition of cyberspace to the traditional land, air, and sea domains of the littoral zone, have already undermined the spatial conception of war zones, creating virtual theaters—conflict spaces that draw in populations and forces with no geographical connection to the conflict, and which may be located anywhere on the planet.

In 2003, the Australian Army noted this emerging reality in its future operational concept, *Complex Warfighting*, which argued that "virtual theatres arise from globalised communications systems, allowing distributed command and control over vast distances. These systems, many of which are commercially available, benefit our enemies as well as us. . . . During the Afghan war in 2002, CIA operatives in Langley, Virginia, flew Predator remotely piloted aircraft, armed with Hellfire missiles, against Taliban targets. By the traditional definition, Virginia is not part of the Afghan theatre. But with globalised communications, an operator in Langley can participate in operations as effectively as can a soldier in Kabul. Langley is thus 'virtually' in theatre."[8]

In the decade of war since these words were written, the remote warfare capabilities of the United States (and many other states, not all of which are friendly to U.S. interests) have expanded dramatically. Nonstate armed groups can also access dramatically improved connectivity, giving them off-the-shelf capabilities for remote warfare, so virtual theaters are now the norm. Drone warfare is perhaps the foremost example of this "new normal."

### Kill Shots and Soccer Games

The 432nd Wing of the United States Air Force flies most of the U.S. military's fleet of Predator and Reaper drones. The wing's six squadrons are at Creech Air Force Base, Indian Springs—a town in the high desert of Nevada, about fifty miles outside Las Vegas, on the edge of an old atomic test range. Forward-deployed teams launch, recover, and maintain the aircraft from airstrips close to their targets, but the Reapers and Predators are flown remotely—and their targets are chosen and killed—by operators at Creech.

One of these operators, Major Erik Jacobson, said in 2012 that "the interesting thing about what our operations are at Creech is that we supported the war in Iraq *from* Creech . . . to know that you had a direct impact on battles and ops on the ground just from being stateside . . . you're executing a combat mission and then you drive home and you're at your kid's soccer game."[9] Note Jacobson's language here: "we supported the war," "direct impact on battles," "executing a combat mission." He is exactly restating the textbook definition of a theater of war. Yet Jacobson's physical location is on the other side of the planet from the war, the city where he lives is at peace, and he (along with the rest of its population) is subject to U.S. domestic law. He's in a virtual theater, not a physical one.

Other remotely piloted aircraft are controlled from bases in suburban neighborhoods, such as Hancock Field in upstate New York. As the *New York Times* reported in July 2012:

> From his computer console here in the Syracuse suburbs, [Colonel] D. Scott Brenton remotely flies a Reaper drone that beams back hundreds of hours of live video of insurgents, his intended targets, going about their daily lives 7,000 miles away in Afghanistan. Sometimes he and his team watch the same family compound for weeks. . . . When the call comes for him to fire a missile and kill a militant—and only, Colonel Brenton said, when the women and children are not around—the hair on the back of his neck stands up, just as it did when he used to line up targets in his F-16 fighter jet . . . Colonel Brenton acknowledges the peculiar new disconnect of fighting a telewar with a joystick and a throttle from his padded seat in American suburbia.[10]

Clearly, the pilots and crew who operate these aircraft, target the Taliban, and support ground troops in Afghanistan are not (in any spatial sense) *located* in the Afghan theater of operations, and neither are they in physical danger. It's also worth noting that what's new about remotely piloted aircraft is not so much the airframes and weapons (most of which are commercial off-the-shelf systems, or readily available technologies used in piloted aircraft for years) but rather, the communications systems that allow them to be controlled from the other side of the planet—along with the Internet, communications networks, and GPS navigation satellites that support these globalized systems. In other words, it's not the aircraft themselves, but rather their access to globally networked connectivity that lets these crews take a direct and lethal role in the conflict, makes them an intimate (though geographically disconnected) part of the operation, and thus puts them *virtually* in theater.

This has huge implications, and not only for the psychological welfare of the participants in this videogame-like conflict or for the human rights of their targets. Legally, how are we to conceive of cities such as Indian Springs, Nevada, or Syracuse, New York? These cities—deemed to be outside any war zone, with populations living under United States domestic law—are, through the emergence of virtual theaters, directly engaged in conflict overseas, whether the people who live there realize it or not. If Taliban militants managed to insert an assault team to raid these cities, in a variant of what Lashkar-e-Taiba did in Mumbai, would that action be illegal? During the Second World War, the Allies conducted hundreds of strategic air raids against German bomber airfields that were thousands of miles away from the front lines, many of which happened to kill civilians in nearby urban areas. Might an insurgent (or an enemy nation-state) argue that an attack on Indian Springs or Syracuse would be exactly equivalent to one of these air raids?

The United States government has repeatedly asserted, and the U.S. Supreme Court has upheld, the legal position that America is in a state of war with al Qaeda and related terrorist groups.[11] If we consider it a legitimate act of war for a Predator to strike a target in, say, a city in Pakistan, killing militants in the houses where they live, but also potentially injuring or killing noncombatant civilians, is it legitimate for those same Pakistani militants to strike the city where that Predator's pilot lives? If it's legitimate to kill a militant attending a wedding in the tribal areas, is it also legitimate to kill a Predator pilot at his kid's soccer game in Indian Springs? The U.S. government considers Predator crews combatants, and awards them medals for their service; are they and their families, then, and the bases and communities where they live, legitimate targets, like the German bomber airbases of World War II? Do ordinary Americans living in these towns realize the implications, and would they have a different attitude about "overseas contingency operations"—the latest euphemism for the permanent, globalized war on terrorism established after 9/11—if they did? The answer to these questions is far from clear, let alone widely agreed. Much of the debate on so-called drone operations (drones are actually fully autonomous robotic platforms, whereas Predators and Reapers are remotely piloted aircraft that need to be controlled, moment to moment, by a human operator) has focused on questions of ethics and targeting—but the enormous conceptual and practical implications of remote warfare are yet to be fully explored.

These aren't academic questions: as I've just shown, any enemy who can read English can download the details of drone operations from the *New York Times* website and therefore almost certainly realized long ago that the suburbs of Syracuse, the crews who live there, and their families are much softer targets than the armored vehicles or special forces patrols those Predators support, and on whose operations U.S. ground forces rely. Any enemy suffering continual losses at the hands of remotely piloted aircraft would be stupid *not* to try to strike the aircraft's controllers. In fact, something like this has already happened: Hakimullah Mehsud, head of the Pakistani Taliban, launched a suicide attacker against New York City in May 2010, in what he claimed were legitimate acts of war in retaliation for Predator strikes against his followers in the tribal areas of Pakistan— strikes that were controlled from the United States.[12] One might suggest that the only reason such attacks don't occur every week is that most populations targeted by Predators simply lack the means to strike back at intercontinental distances. In part, this is because (as Akbar Ahmed points out in *The Thistle and the Drone*, his excellent study of the effects of drone warfare on traditional populations in Pakistan, Yemen, and Somalia) over the last decade these have been tribal groups in remote, marginalized, landlocked communities, such as the mountains of the Afghanistan-Pakistan border.[13] But in this, as in other areas, we need to get our heads out of the mountains: as we've seen, settlement patterns are changing as the planet urbanizes, and populations in coastal, connected cities, plugged into global networks, have many more counterstrike options open to them.

Such counterstrikes need not be physical. In one 2009 example, Iranian-backed insurgents in Iraq used Skygrabber, a "$26 piece of off-the-shelf software" made by the Russian company SkySoftware, "to intercept live video feeds from Predator drones, potentially providing the insurgents with information they need to evade or monitor U.S. military operations."[14] The insurgents simply pointed satellite television dishes at the sky, then used them to intercept video from the satellite uplink that connects the aircraft to their controllers back at bases such as Creech, exploiting the fact that the uplinks were (at that time) unencrypted. U.S. troops discovered the problem when they detained a Shi'a fighter whose laptop turned out to contain intercepted drone video feeds.[15] Other detainees had similar pirated video on their laptops, "leading some officials to conclude that militant groups trained and funded by Iran were regularly intercepting feeds . . . the military found 'days and days and hours and hours of proof' that the feeds were being intercepted and shared with multiple extremist groups."[16] In effect, the insurgents had hacked the drone control system, a far easier way to deal with the threat than to try to shoot down the actual aircraft.

Like the Lashkar-e-Taiba raiders' use of Twitter as a command network at Mumbai, this incident illustrates that—alongside the democratization of lethality that now lets individuals access weapon systems that were once only available to nation-states—we're seeing a democratization of digital connectivity that lets individuals access very long-range communication and control systems (including encrypted systems) on the open market, giving them remote warfare capabilities that are starting to rival those of governments. Indeed, both these trends are part of a broader pattern that we have called the *democratization of technology*. This is affecting all aspects of human life and, at least in relation to warfare, is breaking down classical distinctions between governments and individuals, between zones of war and zones of peace, between civilians and combatants, and therefore between traditional concepts such as "war" and "crime" or "domestic" and "international."

In another incident in mid-2011, a virus carrying a so-called key-logger payload, which records every keystroke a computer user makes, infected computers at Creech and other Predator bases. Air Force security officers were unsure if the virus was just a random piece of malware that had somehow found its way onto the system or if it was part of a deliberate cyberattack.[17] This highlights another very major recent shift in remote warfare capabilities: the entry of the United States into the business of offensive cyberwarfare.

*"Olympic Games" and Offensive Cyberwarfare*

In June 2012, David Sanger published *Confront and Conceal*, a description of the Obama administration's covert and remote warfare programs that drew on a series of revelations by administration officials that were startlingly indiscreet, to say the least. The book included a well-sourced account of Operation Olympic Games, a joint U.S.-Israeli cyberoperation that combined virtual and physical attacks—using cyberweapons, including the Stuxnet worm (and, possibly, the related DuQu and Flame worms), to attack physical structures and infrastructure in Iran's nuclear weapons program.[18] Sanger claimed that the operation had begun under President George W. Bush and that President Obama had dramatically accelerated and expanded it.[19] U.S. government sources later confirmed Sanger's account in interviews with the *New York Times*.[20]

Later the same year, U.S. defense secretary and former CIA director Leon Panetta cautioned of the threat of cyberwarfare, warning "that the United States was facing the possibility of a 'cyber–Pearl Harbor' and was increasingly vulnerable to foreign computer hackers who could dismantle the nation's power grid, transportation system, financial networks and government."[21] Panetta's statement was met with derision from online activists and cybersecurity professionals, who accused the United States of hypocrisy, given its own use of offensive cyberweapons in Olympic Games. Mikko Hyppönen, the cybersecurity expert who exposed Stuxnet and Flame, wrote in an enraged blog post:

> It's quite clear that real-world cris[e]s in the future are very likely to have cyber components as well. If we look for offensive cyber attacks that have been linked back to a known government, we mostly find attacks that have been launched *by* [the] United States, not *against* them. So far, antivirus companies have found five different malware attacks linked to operation *"Olympic Games"* run by US and Israel. When New York Times ran the story linking US Government and the Obama administration to these attacks, White House started an investigation on who had leaked the information. Note that they never denied the story. They just wanted to know who leaked it. As United States is doing offensive cyber attacks against other countries, certainly

other countries feel that they are free to do the same. Unfortunately the United States has the most to lose from attacks like these.[22]

Hyppönen highlights an obvious risk here: using a conventional kinetic weapon (say, a bomb or missile) generally destroys it. But using a cyberweapon is equivalent to sharing it—the code, and thus the capability, residing in the weapon is now loose in the virtual ecosystem, where it can be picked up, studied, and reused by the intended target, or anyone else.

As Thomas Rid has suggested, this is a particular problem because the current U.S. focus on offensive cyberwarfare isn't matched by an equivalent effort on defensive cybersecurity, despite the rhetoric of Secretary Panetta and others. "At present," Rid argues,

> the United States government is one of the most aggressive actors when it comes to offensive cyber operations, excluding commercial espionage. The administration has anonymously admitted that it designed Stuxnet (codenamed Olympic Games), a large-scale and protracted sabotage campaign against Iran's nuclear enrichment facility in Natanz that was unprecedented in scale and sophistication. Close expert observers assume that America also designed Flame, [an] operation against several Middle Eastern targets mostly in the energy sector. The same goes for Gauss [which was] designed to steal information from Lebanese financial institutions . . . The Obama administration seems to have decided to prioritize such high-end offensive operations. Indeed, the Pentagon's bolstered Cyber Command seems designed primarily for such purposes.[23]

What enables all these capabilities, both for drone warfare and cyberwar, is a dramatic rise over the past decade and a half in networked digital connectivity, part of the megatrend of enhanced connectedness that we've already identified as one of the main influences shaping future conflict. Through the democratization of technology, such connectivity is also, of course, available to nonstate armed groups, local regimes, civil society, and individual citizens—especially those in urbanized, connected societies. With this as prologue, let's look at the impact of that networked connectivity on the Arab Awakening.

## II. The Arab Awakening

John Pollock's reporting, with that of technology writers such as Quinn Norton and Julian Dibbell and war correspondents including Martin Chulov, C. J. Chivers, Robert Worth, Dexter Filkins, and the late Anthony Shadid, doesn't just illuminate the rise of remote warfare among nonstate groups. It also helps highlight an important shift that occurred over the course of the Arab Awakening in 2011–12: the evolution from an alliance of online activists and street protestors during the Tunisian uprising through network-enabled urban revolution in Egypt to connectivity-enhanced insurgency in Libya and something approaching full-scale social netwar in Syria. This shift has seen evolving complexity, increasing lethality, and rising global engagement over the course of the uprisings, along with increasingly effective regime countermeasures and active and sophisticated repression from governments.

I should note at the outset that this section doesn't attempt a comprehensive discussion of these uprisings, or of the Arab Awakening as a whole. Complete accounts of the Libyan war or the Egyptian revolution alone would be full-length books in their own right, while the Syrian civil war is still going on as I write, its outcome very much in doubt. So all this section does is to examine how networked connectivity affected these conflicts, and the predominantly urban, coastal environment in which they occurred, seeking to illuminate some possible aspects of future conflict in similar environments.

Throughout the entire region affected by the Arab Awakening, motivated, mobilized, and connected populations (most of which are urbanized and coastal) are opposing disrupted, disorganized governments that initially were on the defensive but now are pushing back hard, and all this is happening within a globally contested information space. As Pollock notes, this unrest is taking place against the backdrop of trends we have examined already. The "elderly regimes of the Middle East and North Africa are unwilling to leave the stage, yet unable to satisfy the political and economic demands of a demographic youth bulge," he argues. "Around two thirds of the region's population is under 30, and youth unemployment stands at 24 percent. Inevitably, the rapidly changing landscape of media technology, from satellite TV and cell phones to YouTube and Facebook, is adding a new dynamic to the calculus of power between the generations."[24]

## Tunisia: Taks, Ultras, and Anons

Online activists played a key role in Tunisia's Jasmine Revolution. "Takrizards" or "Taks" (members of Takriz, a hacker group founded in the late 1990s) had long been active opponents of the authoritarian regime of President Zine el-Abidine Ben Ali, who had denounced them repeatedly since 2000 and sought to block their online presence. Many had been driven into exile, from where they collaborated closely with Taks still in Tunisia. They'd become increasingly innovative users of mobile communications technology, "'geo-bombing' the presidential palace by adding videos of human rights testimony that appear in the YouTube layer of Google Earth and Google Maps, and charting Tunisia's prisons" as well as hosting satirical anti-regime chat forums, and using Mumble (a voice-over-Internet-protocol communications application which they considered more secure than Skype) to coordinate protests and anti-regime activities.[25]

In the half century before the revolution, Tunisia had experienced rapid growth, its populace more than doubling from 4.2 million in 1960 to 10.7 million in 2010, with a high rate of coastal urbanization. As more and more Tunisians moved to coastal cities, they gained access to the Internet and global media, and acquired email addresses, Facebook accounts, smartphones, and digital cameras. Throughout the last decade of Ben Ali's dictatorship, the expansion of electronic access for urban dwellers in Tunisia was especially fast-paced, and Takriz surfed this wave of increasing connectivity to propagate its anti-regime messages. And as rural-to-urban migration continued apace, many urban Tunisians retained close ties to their villages of origin, maintaining human networks that allowed information to circulate quickly by telephone and word of mouth among urban, periurban, and rural communities. Newer, virtual social networks thus meshed with preexisting, trusted human networks, generating synergies between activists in the real and virtual worlds when the uprising came.

Similarly, since the late 1990s, the Takrizards had evolved from merely mocking the regime online: they'd taken their protest action into the real world, forming a street-level alliance with disaffected youth in Tunisia's cities. As well as the youth bulge, urbanization, and high youth unemployment mentioned above, Tunisia (as we saw in Chapter 1) has an extremely high level of urban littoralization, second only to Libya in the region, with 70 percent of its population concentrated in coastal cities.[26] Soccer fans in these cities—especially disaffected young men who joined tight-knit, highly motivated, violent groups of militant fans known as "Ultras"—became central to the opposition movement. Since the early 2000s, Takriz had hosted a Web forum where Ultras from different teams could interact and discuss their street battles with the regime's police. This forum helped build relationships and collaborative alliances among fans of different teams—urban youth tribes who normally would have spurned each other as enemies—so that over several years "a distinctive North African style of Ultra—one with more political character—spread quickly among Tunisia's soccer-mad youth and then to fans in Egypt, Algeria, Libya and Morocco. When the revolution began, the Ultras would come out to play a very different game. They were transformed into a quick-reaction force of bloody-minded rioters."[27]

It's important not to romanticize the Ultras here: radical soccer fans have a long history of involvement in ethnic cleansing, urban violence, radicalism, and street conflict, and historically have been just as willing to back authoritarian causes as to support liberal ones. In the Balkan Wars of the 1990s, for example, one of the most violent Serb paramilitary groups, Arkan's Tigers—the group that led the Brčko ethnic massacres I described in Chapter 3—was recruited primarily from urban soccer fans and led by Zeljko Raznatovic, a former street criminal and gangster who became an Ultra mobilizer and head of the Red Star Belgrade supporters' club.[28] Several groups of Ultras also engaged in violent action in Croatia, Bosnia, and Kosovo.[29] Likewise, in East Timor in 1999–2000, some of the most violent militias were recruited from urban soccer fans and marginalized teenage street youth, and their sponsors (often members of the urban political establishment or rogue members of Indonesia's security forces) used them as proxies in mass killings and expulsions in Timorese coastal towns including Dili, Batugade, and Suai.[30]

The role of Ultras as a politically biddable, readily mobilized, self-organized, street-savvy, battle-hardened *corps d'élite* in urban conflict has been underexamined but would clearly repay deeper academic interest. One of the world's pioneering researchers in this field, James Dorsey, has written extensively on the role of Ultras in European, Southeast Asian, and Middle Eastern politics. As Dorsey points out, Ultras—by virtue of the militarization and fortification of soccer stadiums (the "military urbanism") that they confront, and the pitched battles against police, security forces, and other fan groups that their urban tribal lifestyle involves—have become increasingly radicalized and militarily experienced. "With elaborate displays of fireworks, flares, smoke guns, loud chanting, and jumping up and down during matches," Dorsey writes, the Ultras form a hard-core supporter element for their team, seeking to intimidate opposing fans and rally their own, and this brings them into constant conflict with the police.[31] Most ultras are young working-class men "who embrace a culture of confrontation—against opposing teams, against the state, and against expressions of weakness in society at large."[32] For many years, Ultras in Tunisia, Egypt, Libya, and other parts of the Middle East engaged in stadium battles against police and other fans on a weekly basis. Indeed, their actions can be seen as a struggle (like that of gangs in San Pedro Sula or Kingston, Jamaica) for control over key urban terrain—in this case, soccer stadiums—in what Dorsey describes as "a zero-sum game for control of a venue they saw as their own."[33] Regimes across the region saw these urban youth tribes as a challenge to their monopoly on the use of force. "In the name of public safety they turned football pitches into virtual fortresses, ringed by black steel and armed security personnel. The ultras, for their part, radicalized in response to the militarization of the stadium."[34] As Dorsey points out, however, they did not always view their own actions as political:

> "We steer clear of politics. Competition in Egypt is on the soccer pitch. We break the rules and regulations when we think they are wrong. You don't change things in Egypt talking about politics. We're not political, the government knows that and that is why it has to deal with us," said one Egyptian ultra in 2010, after his group overran a police barricade erected to prevent it from bringing flares, fireworks and banners into a stadium.[35]

Despite their initial lack of political consciousness, Dorsey's description shows these organizations (including the Tunisian Ultras) for what they are: nonstate armed groups that engage in exactly the kind of competitive control behavior we discussed in Chapter 3. They seek to control not only urban populations (soccer fans, opposition supporters, and local inhabitants) but also physical and economic terrain (stadiums, social venues, and rallies) in the cities where they operate. They compete for control against other fan groups and against the police, security services, and other representatives of the state, and they apply a spectrum of coercive, administrative and persuasive tools in order to do so. They're also, of course, a primarily urban and periurban phenomenon, since major sporting events tend to occur in cities and towns, though Ultras—like other urban nonstate armed groups—often live in marginalized areas that are physically or functionally on the periphery of the urban core. Likewise, access to mobile communications technology, especially cellphones, text messaging, or Twitter feeds, gives soccer fans a degree of connectivity that lets them self-synchronize their activity, and such connectivity (via Wi-Fi or cellphone network coverage) is also usually much greater in urban than in rural areas.

We should note here, of course, that the vast majority of soccer fans (like fans of any other team sport) aren't particularly violent, and there's nothing necessarily disruptive about most supporters' behavior. The Ultras are a small, hard-core, organized, violent minority within a much larger and more diverse movement—an urban vanguard, as it were. Their tight cohesion, self-synchronizing swarming behavior, willingness to engage in violence, and battle-hardened tactical competence in the scrappy business of street fighting combine to give this radical subset of fans a great deal of latent military strength. In particular, Ultras—who battle the cops every weekend anyway, just in the normal course of events—have little fear of, and much familiarity with, police riot control tactics, and this turned out to be a key adaptive trait when the uprisings came. When online activists such as the Taks managed to unify the disparate Ultra groups in Tunisia via the Internet, and thus helped raise the fans' political and anti-regime consciousness, they were creating an alliance with an urban tribal force. This alliance had enormous military potential for conflict in cities—but its power rested on the twin pillars of *electronic connectivity* (which connected Taks with Ultras and broke down barriers among rival Ultra groups) and *virtual-human network overlap* (the meshing of real-world and cyber relationships), which allowed online networks connecting city-dwelling activists to map onto human networks that connected Tunisian cities with rural towns and villages.

*The Uprising*

In December 2010, Tunisians' long-simmering opposition to the Ben Ali dictatorship boiled over into open violence. The immediate trigger was the self-immolation of Mohamed Bouazizi—a fruit vendor in the central Tunisian town of Sidi Bouzid who, on December 17, 2010, doused himself in paint thinner and struck a match in protest against police corruption and harassment—but the reaction to Bouazizi's act drew on a deep reservoir of frustration and resistance that had been fed over many years by a cycle of protests and violent regime repression.[36] While Bouazizi lay in critical condition in a hospital burn unit, protests broke out almost immediately in several Tunisian towns, then rapidly escalated, spread, and became more violent in response to regime brutality against demonstrators.[37] This included targeting the funerals of activists killed by police. (As we'll see in Egypt, Libya, and Syria, regime targeting of protestors' funerals created a self-replenishing cycle of violence: when protests led to regime repression and deaths, demonstrators who gathered to mourn these deaths were themselves targeted, leading to more protests, more deaths, more funerals, more attacks on funerals, and so on.)

By January 2011, after two weeks of violence, several Tunisian cities were in open revolt, workers were on strike, businesses were closed, foreigners had fled the country, and urban elites were joining the protests. Street demonstrations had reached the capital, Tunis—a coastal city of just over 1 million inhabitants, with roughly 2.5 million people (almost a quarter of Tunisia's total population) in its greater metropolitan area, and by virtue of its size and political importance the decisive terrain of the uprising. At this point, the Takrizard-Ultra alliance came into its own: online groups produced and disseminated anti-regime information, helped mobilize and organize protestors, and provided situational awareness for opponents of the regime. Simultaneously, the connectivity between urban Tunisians and relatives in their rural villages of origin allowed awareness of the uprising to spread rapidly—initially from the countryside into Tunis and later, as the revolution took hold, from the capital back to smaller towns and villages. The Ultras, for their part, formed the hard core of the mass protests. Their experience in urban fighting against police gave them a self-confidence and tactical skill that made them less fearful of the regime, and their confidence was infectious. They set the example and reassured other demonstrators, who might otherwise have wavered, by showing it was possible to fight the regime and survive.

In the virtual world, online activists such as Slim Amamou, one of Tunisia's most prominent regime opponents, used their access to mobile connectivity to help rally these broad-based street protests against the regime.[38] This wasn't a "Twitter revolution"—Twitter was not well known in Tunisia (where, "pre-revolution, only around 200 active tweeters existed out of around 2,000 with registered accounts")[39] and Twitter feeds weren't a key part of the protestors' arsenal. But resistance groups did make extensive use of Facebook, which had an unusually high subscribership in Tunisia and was one of the few social networking sites that the regime didn't block.[40] After an unsuccessful attempt to block Facebook that collapsed after sixteen days of online protests back in 2008, the regime had instead decided to set up fake "phishing" sites that mimicked Facebook and drew dissident users to reveal their login details, so that security forces could track their movements.[41] Despite this harassment there were 1.97 million Tunisian Facebook users by early 2011, representing "over half of all Tunisians online, and almost a fifth of the total population."[42]

In late 2010, the synergy between virtual and real-world activism escalated into revolution. As John Pollock described it:

On December 27, thousands rallied in Tunis. The next day Ben Ali sacked the governors of Sidi Bouzid and two other provinces [and] threatened to punish the protestors. On December 30, a protestor shot by police six days earlier died. Lawyers gathered around the country to protest the government and were attacked and beaten. On January 2, the hacking group Anonymous began targeting government websites with distributed denial-of-service attacks in what it called Operation Tunisia. As the academic year started, student protests flared. A flash mob gathered on the tracks of a Tunis metro and stood, covering their mouths, eloquently silent. On January 4, Bouazizi died of his burns. The next day, 5,000 people attended his funeral. January 6 brought the regime's response to the Anonymous attacks: several activists were arrested. . . . Cyber-activist Slim Amamou was also arrested, and he used the location-based social network Foursquare to reveal that he was being held in the Ministry of the Interior. . . . The next day, 95 percent of Tunisia's lawyers went on strike. The day after, the teachers joined in. The following day, the massacres began.

Over five grisly days starting on January 8, dozens of people were killed in protests, mostly in towns like Kasserine and Thala in the poor interior. There were credible reports of snipers at work. These deaths would turn the protests into outright revolution. One graphic and deeply distressing video was highly influential: it shows Kasserine's hospital in chaos, desperate attempts to treat the injured, and a horrifying image of a dead young man with his brains spilling out. "It was really critical," [said a Takriz activist]. "That video made the second half of the revolution." Posted and reposted hundreds of times on YouTube, Facebook, and elsewhere, it set off a wave of revulsion across North Africa and the Middle East. The regime had cut Internet service to Sidi Bouzid [so] Takriz smuggled a CD of the video over the Algerian border and streamed it via MegaUpload. [Takrizards] saw the video and found it enraging. Takriz then forwarded it to Al Jazeera.[43]

The role of Anonymous in this process illustrates the fact that, beyond enabling the Tak-Ultra alliance we have discussed, networked connectivity allowed international groups to play a part in the revolution in real time—something not seen, at least not to the same extent, in any previous uprising. Quinn Norton's reporting on Anonymous, in a seminal series of articles she wrote for *Wired* magazine in 2012, shows that Tunisia was a new departure for the "anons," as participants in the hacker group are known. Norton points out that anons' activism in support of WikiLeaks and its founder, Julian Assange, during 2010—activism that was virtually leaderless, an online variant of the swarming behavior discussed in Chapter 2, or perhaps an emergent characteristic of what Norton calls the "hive mind" of the Internet—led directly to the hacker group's involvement in the Tunisian uprising:

[In December 2010, Ben Ali] began blocking web access to Wikileaks cables that pertained to his and other Arab nations. A few anons formed a new channel called #optunisia on IRC [Internet Relay Chat] and started talking about what they could do ... Over the next couple of weeks the small group brought down the website of the Tunisian stock exchange and defaced various sites of the Tunisian government.

It also passed media and news reports about the Tunisian uprising in and out of the country. It distributed a "care package" containing details about how to work around privacy restrictions in Tunisia, including a Firefox script to help locals avoid government spying while they used Facebook. Some who supported #optunisia were themselves Tunisians, including Slim Amamou, an outspoken blogger. After Amamou was arrested on January 6, 2011, the anons on the #optunisia IRC channel barely slept as they waited for word. But eight days later, the regime fell, and Amamou was appointed a minister in the new government. We'll never know how important Anonymous was for Tunisia, but Tunisia changed everything for Anonymous. OpTunisia was the first of what became the Freedom Ops, which focused largely on other Middle Eastern countries during the Arab Spring but spread much farther. For the first time, Anonymous had gotten on the winning side of a real fight, and it liked the feeling.[44]

Within twenty-four hours, Anonymous had taken down several of the Tunisian government's websites, including not only that of the stock exchange but also those of the Foreign Ministry, the Ministry of Industry, the Ministry of Commerce, the presidential palace, the electoral commission, and the central government Web portal.[45] Although the attacks likely had little or no direct effect on Tunisian security forces' ability to suppress the revolution, they demonstrated strong international support for the uprising and thus probably both encouraged anti-government protestors (online and on the street) and undermined regime officials' and supporters' morale. This contributed to a cascading loss of cohesion within the government and security services, ending in the fall of Ben Ali's regime as the dictator fled to exile in Saudi Arabia on January 14, 2011.

Along with WikiLeaks and Anonymous, other nonstate groups were closely involved in the contested information space of the uprising. Activists living in Europe who were members of *Nawaat* (a Tunisian diaspora-based collective blog that functioned as an online democracy forum) played a critical role in getting news out of Tunisia when the regime attempted to censor and block information about the uprising, while global groups such as the Open Net Initiative and WikiLeaks provided support from abroad, and anti-secrecy sites such as Cryptome carried leaked information relating to the uprising.[46] Thus access to networked connectivity, which enabled an urban street-level alliance of online activists with Ultras and demonstrators in Tunisia, also enabled collaboration among individuals and organizations across the planet. This same pattern would be repeated in the next major uprising of the Arab Awakening, which was already beginning to break out in Egypt.

### Egypt: Network-Enabled Revolution

Many features of the Tunisian uprising—the role of hard-core soccer fans as shock troops of a broad-based protest movement, the self-selected engagement of international and local activists, the synergy between online activism and street protest, and the mass mobilization of a frustrated citizenry in response to crackdowns against an initially smaller radical group—also emerged in the Egyptian revolution. Indeed, the Egyptian uprising itself resulted in part from an extremely high level of networked connectivity across the entire densely populated, heavily urbanized coastal strip of North Africa that stretches from Tunisia in the west through Libya to Egypt—a zone that, as we've noted, experienced rapid coastal urbanization during the generation prior to the uprisings, making Tunisia, Libya, and Egypt three of the most heavily connected, urban, littoralized countries in the entire Mediterranean basin.[47]

Egypt, like Tunisia, had experienced extremely fast population growth and coastal urbanization in the generation prior to the uprising—indeed, between 2006 and 2012 alone, Egypt's population grew by fully 18 percent, to reach 83 million people within the country, along with another 8 million in the diaspora, and just over 9 million people in the greater metropolitan area of Cairo, the capital city.[48] Unlike Tunisia, however, until 2011 Egypt had enjoyed an unusually high and unfettered degree of network connectivity: unlike many other authoritarian regimes in the region, the Egyptian government "never built or required sophisticated technical infrastructures of censorship. (Of course, the country has hardly been a paradise of free expression: the state security forces have vigorously suppressed dissent through surveillance, arbitrary detentions and relentless intimidation of writers and editors.)"[49] Partly because of its relatively liberal telecommunications policy, "Egypt became a hub for internet and mobile network investment, home to a thriving and competitive communications sector that pioneered free dial-up services, achieved impressive rates of access and use, and offered speedy wireless and broadband networks at relatively low prices. Indeed, Egypt is today one of the major crossing points for the underwater fibre-optic cables that interconnect the regions of the globe."[50]

Popular uprisings against the regime of President Hosni Mubarak began on January 25, 2011. Egyptian activists, both secular and religious, had followed the Tunisian uprisings closely on Internet forums and via radio, Twitter, newspapers, and electronic media including Al Jazeera satellite television. Tunisian and Egyptian democracy activists had coordinated and shared tactics and lessons learned over several years, and studied methods of nonviolent revolution together, in online forums and face-to-face seminars.[51] Egyptians reacted to the news of Ben Ali's fall on January 14, 2011, with immediate calls for the ouster of Mubarak: that evening, protestors rushed to the "heavily guarded Tunisian embassy in Zamalek, one of Cairo's most affluent residential districts . . . 'We are next, we are next, Ben Ali tell Mubarak he is next,' the protestors chanted."[52]

On January 25, eleven days after Ben Ali's fall from power, Egyptian pro-democracy groups organized a national day of protest, in which massive rallies of peaceful demonstrators called for democratic freedoms similar to those just won by Tunisians. The day of protest was sponsored by a loose alliance that included secular democracy organizations, liberal and leftist groups, and the youth wing of the Muslim Brotherhood, and it was timed to coincide with Egypt's National Police Day.[53] As in Tunisia, brutality against the early demonstrators led to an escalation of the protests, which rapidly turned into a series of violent uprisings in Egypt's major cities, including Alexandria, Cairo, and Port Said.

On January 28, in response to protestors' defeat of the police during the battle for the Qasr al-Nil bridge (discussed below), President Mubarak disabled the Internet across Egypt, blocking access to the Web in most cities throughout the country, and suspended cellphone networks in many urban centers. This was possible "because Egypt permitted only three wireless carriers to operate, and required all Internet service providers (ISPs) to funnel their traffic through a handful of international links. Confronted with mass demonstrations and fearful about a populace able to organize itself, the government had to order fewer than a dozen companies to shut down their networks and disconnect their routers from the global internet" in order to suspend Internet and cellphone services in a matter of minutes.[54] This action was designed to hamper protest organizers, who were using Facebook, Twitter, and cellphone text messages to coordinate their action. But it backfired, encouraging demonstrators by showing that their protests had rattled the regime, and angering many Egyptians who had stayed neutral to that point. By blocking their access to international media and communications, the regime gave them a personal grievance against the government and a personal connection with the protestors.

Many people subsequently joined the demonstrations, including the "days of rage," a series of mass protests in major cities on successive Fridays, which turned violent as security forces and pro-regime activists attacked demonstrators. Striking workers in Egypt's textile industry and on the Suez Canal formed a key urban center of resistance to the regime. The focal point that emerged through the unrest was Tahrir Square, a huge open space strategically located in the urban core of Cairo that was permanently occupied by an enormous number of protestors (up to a million people at the revolution's peak) and was encircled and besieged by regime supporters and security forces. Besides Tahrir Square, however, street fighting, rioting, and mass anti-regime protests spread across most urbanized areas in coastal Egypt during the uprising, and it was this broad-based urban unrest—as much as events in Tahrir Square itself—that resulted in Mubarak's stepping down as president on February 11, 2011.

As in Tunisia, highly connected, marginalized youth in Egypt's coastal cities played a central role in the revolution. Along with labor unions and the youth arm of the Muslim Brotherhood, the main organization involved in the 2011 uprising was the April 6 Movement, a secular pro-democracy group formed in response to brutal police repression of demonstrations in Mahalla, a city in the Nile River delta, on April 6, 2008. April 6 had spent years consciously copying the techniques used in "color revolutions" in Europe and the Middle East and seeking assistance from international online activist groups:

> The first thing the April 6 leaders did was study. They started with the Academy of Change, an Arabic online group promoting nonviolent civil disobedience. Its inspiration was Optor, a youth movement

cofounded by a Serbian revolutionary, Ivan Marovic, which helped overthrow Yugoslavia's Slobodan Miloševic in 2000 by means of a "Bulldozer Revolution" that was remarkably peaceful: only two people died. Marovic later cofounded the Center for Applied Non-Violent Action and Strategies (Canvas), which has since trained activists from more than 50 countries. In the summer of 2009, April 6 sent an activist named Mohammed Adel to train with Canvas in Serbia. He returned with a book about peaceful tactics and a computer game called *A Force More Powerful*, which lets people play with scenarios for regime change. Taking advantage of the game's Creative Commons license, April 6 members wrote an Egyptian version. "We used it to help train our activists," says [the group's founder, Ahmed] Maher.[55]

When the uprising broke out on January 25, the already connected and tech-savvy Egyptian protestors were able to draw on immediate international support from groups like Anonymous, which had rolled directly from its #OpTunisia "Freedom Op" into #OpEgypt. "Anonymous started to set up lifeline internet connections and target government servers [with distributed denial-of-service attacks] just as they had in Tunisia. Three days later, Mubarak turned off the Internet. Anonymous was aghast, both at this display of existential threat to the net as a way of political expression, and [at] their impotence in the case of a nation just taken offline."[56]

But other groups were already stepping into the breach. Peter Fein, a Chicago-based member of Telecomix, an online hacker/activist collective that describes itself as an "ad-hocracy" that engages in "guerrilla information warfare," worked twenty-hour days during the uprising, creating tools to help Egyptian protestors fight back against the Web blackout:

> The Internet was being cut off, and telephones were cut off and communication across the country got much more difficult. Suez was completely cut off. And so this kind of created a need for internal communication—not for people to be able to talk on Facebook or Twitter to the world, but amongst themselves . . . so there were a number of tools, mesh technology and so on—that we tried to help people figure out. I had several hours of chats with guys on the ground [to determine] what they needed. A lot of the time they don't have

the technical knowledge of what they actually need, they just want to be able to communicate without being wiretapped . . . so we'll send them [the secure web browser] Tor or something. Towards the end they were just asking us how they could hold [Tahrir] Square—it's difficult and necessary to communicate across an area that large and packed and we helped them. [We sent them] instructions on how to set up a wireless mesh network [a way of creating a communication network] often using mobile phones' Bluetooth technology or two-way radio [microphones]. One of the things we started working on is a how-to, a set of instructions, to build two-way radios, walkie-talkies . . . with hardware that people already have and the best thing we came up with is if you take a normal clock radio, smash it apart and cross a couple of wires and you can get them to communicate with each other. They have a two-kilometre range.[57]

It's worth noting that there are two essential prerequisites for a Bluetooth mesh-network or radio net of this kind: first, the population must have a base level of technical knowledge and access to electricity and electronic componentry, and second, there must be a sufficient residential density that members of the network are close enough to each other (about a mile at most) to receive short-range radio signals. Both these requirements, of course, imply an urban or periurban rather than rural environment.

Hacktivists such as Anonymous and Telecomix weren't the only international groups to rally in support when Mubarak blocked the Internet: for-profit companies joined in, too. Google engineers took only two days to build "a system that enabled protestors in Egypt to send tweets even though the Internet in their country had been shut down. 'Like many people', they blogged, 'we've been glued to the news unfolding in Egypt and thinking of what we can do to help people on the ground. Over the weekend we came up with the idea of a speak-to-tweet service—the ability for anyone to tweet using just a voice connection.' They worked with a small team of engineers from Twitter and SayNow (a company Google [had] recently acquired) to build the system. It provides three international phone numbers and anyone can tweet by leaving a voicemail."[58]

Google's involvement went back several months before the revolution. In mid-2010 Google marketing executive Wael Ghonim had created an online anti-regime Facebook group, We Are All Khaled Said, named for an Egyptian youth publicly beaten to death by police in June 2010. Working closely with the April 6 Movement and the National Association for Change—a broad-based opposition group led by Mohamed ElBaradei, the Vienna-based former head of the International Atomic Energy Agency, and a prominent Egyptian secular pro-democracy politician—Ghonim publicized the injustice and cruelty of Khaled Said's death and filled the Facebook site with images, news clips, and videos of police brutality, along with pro-democracy messages. The group "eventually attracted hundreds of thousands of users, building their allegiance through exercises in online democratic participation."[59] The April 6 Movement then used We Are All Khaled Said as a forum to announce and organize the January 25 protest that sparked the uprising.

As in Tunisia, the Internet, radio, and television propaganda battle between Mubarak's regime and pro-democracy activists in cyberspace and on the airwaves was only one part of a multidimensional fight—the "air war" counterpart, as it were, to a "ground war" that played out simultaneously on the streets of Egypt's cities. Online activists relied on a broader set of Internet-based tools than had the Tunisian groups, using Facebook to organize and announce protests and demonstrations, Twitter to coordinate them, and YouTube videos to capture and disseminate the results to mass media outlets and international supporters. Again, however, as in Tunisia, an intense escalatory synergy developed when real-world trusted human networks, based on residential and family loyalties and local allegiances, meshed with virtual social networks. Street fights created the raw material for the propaganda battle, while media messaging reinforced the political impact of events on the street.

*The Ultras in the Urban Ground War*

Again, Ultras played a key role in the ground component of the uprising. Soccer fans from rival teams joined forces to oppose the regime during several critical street battles, including the two most important urban engagements of the revolution: the fight for the Qasr al-Nil bridge on January 28, 2011, and the "Battle of the Camels" in Tahrir Square on February 2, 2011. In Egypt, as in Tunisia, Ultras formed the hard core of the street protests, and took the battle to police and security forces in a way that rallied and motivated other protestors.

Qasr al-Nil is an imposing colonial-era road bridge, four lanes wide, that spans the Nile in central Cairo. It's an important chokepoint, covering the western approaches to Tahrir Square from the Gezira district, which includes the Opera Square and the Mokhtar al-Tetsh Stadium, a major soccer venue and the original home of the al-Ahly soccer club. On the first Day of Rage on Friday, January 28, 2011, tens of thousands of protestors, organized by April 6 and other activist movements, motivated by the arrival from Vienna of Mohamed ElBaradei, and spearheaded by Ultras from al-Ahly who had temporarily united with fans from their archrival club, Zamalek, tried to march from Gezira to join fellow protestors in Tahrir Square. The march began peacefully, with the demonstrators singing the Egyptian national anthem, but turned deadly when they reached the bridge.[60] Blocking the bridge's eastern end were more than a thousand riot police with armored vehicles, mobile barriers, batons, and shields. They attacked the marchers with tear gas, rubber bullets, "an unidentified, burning red liquid" (probably pepper spray), and water cannons.[61] The protestors made it about a third of the way across the bridge before being forced back to the Opera Square, where police repeatedly attacked them with tear gas; after a period of confusion they fought back hard, with the Ultras in the vanguard. The battle raged all afternoon, the crowd repeatedly surging forward, chanting anti-Mubarak slogans and trying to breach the police line, only to be thrown back by police baton-charges under a barrage of tear gas, rubber bullets, and high-pressure water sprays.

Dozens of demonstrators were seriously injured or killed, but the Ultras, along with an ad hoc group of young men who aggregated around them as the battle wore on, continued to spearhead the fight. The Ultras and the self-selected group who had rallied to them played a critical role in motivating the broader crowd on several occasions: at one point, "when the bursts from the tear gas launchers quickened, the protestors retreated, until the young men at the front told them to come back."[62] As the crowd advanced in great depth on the narrow four-lane frontage of the bridge, a simple rotation system developed in a self-synchronized way: "the people who were injured would go to the back and other people would replace them . . . we just kept rotating."[63]

By 5:30 p.m. the demonstrators had seized the bridge and pushed the riot police back, overrunning several armored vehicles, destroying mobile police posts, throwing hastily erected metal police barriers into the Nile, and capturing and wounding several police officers. In the late afternoon the riot police counterattacked in strength, recaptured the bridge, and penned the demonstrators next to a nearby park, using an aggressive counter-riot technique known as "kettling," in which rioters are encircled and attacked in order to inflict casualties, allow the arrest of ringleaders, and cow them. Many demonstrators were hurt, but the Ultras fought back once more—by the middle of the evening they had broken the encirclement, retaken the bridge, and pushed through to join other protestors at Tahrir Square. As burned-out police vehicles smoldered in the streets, a strong smell of tear gas lingered, the headquarters of Mubarak's ruling party burned late into the night, the police retreated and—foreshadowing what was to come—military armored vehicles began to close in on Tahrir Square for the first time.[64]

The political effect of the bridge battle, amplified by online and media reporting—in particular, the extensive camera-phone and digital video footage of the violence that was captured by people in the crowd and by observers from rooftop vantage points around the bridge and subsequently posted on YouTube—was immense. Indeed, it was this surge of handheld cellphone video footage, and the subsequent negative press, that caused the regime to shut off the Internet. As Kareem Fahim reported from Cairo on the evening of the battle:

> The long struggle for the bridge set the tone for the momentous events throughout the country on Friday. Egyptians slowly shed their fear of President Hosni Mubarak's police state and confronted its power, a few halting steps at a time. The protestors came from every social class and included even wealthy Egyptians, who are often dismissed as apolitical, or too comfortable to mobilize. For some of them in the crowd on Friday, the brutality of the security forces was a revelation. "Dogs!" they yelled at the riot police, as they saw bloodied protestors dragged away. "These people are Egyptians!"[65]

This day of street fighting came to be seen by external observers as "perhaps the most pivotal battle of the revolution."[66] Likewise, Ahmed Maher, founder of the April 6 Movement and organizer of the January 25 protest that sparked the revolution, regarded the fight for Qasr al-Nil bridge as a turning point. He saw January 28 as "a very important day . . . in the morning, it was a demonstration, in the evening, it was a revolution."[67] The government's most public counterattack against that revolution was only a few days away—and again the Ultras were to play a key role as the hard core of the anti-regime protest.

As the uprising developed, President Mubarak hadn't restricted his response to the use of regular police and military forces. Just as Egyptian protestors had learned from the experience of their Tunisian colleagues, Mubarak's regime seems to have observed the experience of Ben Ali's government in Tunisia, responding to the initial protests with the "rapid implementation of a strategy of survival."[68] Before banning the Internet and blocking cellphones, Mubarak created what he called an "Electronic Army" to put out pro-regime messages on the Internet and social media. He also used group text messages via the mobile phone network in an attempt to rally supporters to head out into the streets and counter the protestors' message; when this failed, he opened jails to release hundreds of violent criminals into major urban centers, probably as a way of intimidating the demonstrators. The regime also organized an informal street militia of its own, a pro-government equivalent of the Ultras. These irregulars formed, in effect, a state-proxy armed group that was sponsored by pro-Mubarak business people and officials and drawn from pro-regime bureaucrats, plainclothes police, party activists and members of Mubarak's ruling National Democratic Party.[69] It also included people who were paid to participate and brought in by buses from periurban areas outside the city.[70] Six days after the Qasr al-Nil bridge battle, this group launched its attack on Tahrir Square.

At 2:30 p.m. on the afternoon of Wednesday, February 2, thousands of pro-regime irregulars charged the square, entering in cohesive columns from several side streets, and armed with rocks, clubs, firebombs, improvised explosives, pistols, shotguns, and rifles. Some observers noted plainclothes and uniformed police, who seemed to be playing a coordinating role, among the attackers. The militia pelted the protestors with rocks and attacked them with clubs and sticks. Other Mubarak supporters rained firebombs, bottles, bricks, chunks of concrete, and rocks down onto the protestors, from rooftops and a highway overpass.[71] Then, in a move reminiscent of a cavalry charge, a column of pro-regime irregulars, mounted on horses and camels, burst onto the square and galloped into the packed crowds of pro-democracy protestors, riding people down and hitting them from horseback with sticks, whips, and clubs.

At first the protestors tried nonviolent resistance, but by 3:30 p.m. they began to retaliate, with the hard core by this time comprising Ultras from the al-Ahly and Zamalek clubs, along with the radicalized young men who had coalesced around them during the Qasr al-Nil fight and—a new element—the youth wing of the Muslim Brotherhood. Other protestors swarmed to join the battle or to provide nonviolent support. The hard-core protestors formed a combat wing that fought to protect the thousands of peaceful demonstrators still on the square. They pulled several Mubarak supporters down from horseback, kicking and punching them; threw rocks and pavers in retaliation; formed a defensive cordon around the noncombatant demonstrators; and turned the lower level of the local subway station into an ad hoc prison where they held pro-regime militia fighters under guard.[72] The battle quickly broke up into a general mêlée, with dozens of fights going on simultaneously all over the square: "The two sides pummeled each other with chunks of concrete and bottles at each of the six entrances to the sprawling plaza, where the 10,000 anti-Mubarak protestors tried to fend off the more than 3,000 attackers who besieged them. Some on the pro-government side waved machetes, while the square's defenders filled the air with a ringing battlefield din by banging metal fences with sticks."[73]

In a continuous fight that raged through the night and into the next morning, somewhere between 600 and 1,500 people were injured, and many were killed, especially when "heavy gunfire broke out after 10 p.m. while the opposing factions traded Molotov cocktails from one rooftop to another, setting small fires that continued to burn but did not spread."[74] After initially standing back from armed confrontation with the regime, the Brotherhood had reversed its position after the battle for the Qasr al-Nil bridge, calling for all able-bodied young men to join the protest on Tahrir Square. Now the Brotherhood and the Ultras cooperated in an ad hoc alliance against their attackers.

As an underground network that had been illegal in Egypt for a generation, the Brotherhood didn't have a lot of experience operating in the open street, but what it did have was an organized and disciplined cadre structure. Now the Brotherhood organized the protestors into teams and helped plan their defense against the regime attacks, breaking pavement up into chunks to be thrown, building barricades, and organizing a defensive line.

> "The youth of the Muslim Brotherhood played a really big role," [April 6 Movement founder Abdul] Maher said. "But actually so did the soccer fans [who] are always used to having confrontations with police at the stadiums," he said. Soldiers of the Egyptian military . . . stood watching from behind the iron gates of the Egyptian Museum as the war of stone missiles and improvised bombs continued for 14 hours until about four in the morning. Then, unable to break the protestors' discipline or determination, the Mubarak forces resorted to guns, shooting 45 and killing 2. . . . The soldiers—perhaps following orders to prevent excessive bloodshed, perhaps acting on their own—finally intervened. They fired their machine guns into the ground and into the air, several witnesses said, scattering the Mubarak forces and leaving the protestors in unmolested control of the square, and by extension, the streets.[75]

By the morning of February 3, as the sun rose over the chaos and the smoke and tear gas began to clear, it was clear that Egypt's political landscape had changed forever: the regime could no longer count on the support of the military. Army troops had refused to fire on their own citizens: in fact, they had intervened to protect *anti*-regime protestors on the square and to disperse the *pro*-regime irregulars. For their part, the police—though generally loyal to the regime—had been defeated in the field in two successive major engagements. In terms of competitive control theory, the protestors (especially the Ultras) had shown sufficient capability at the coercive end of the spectrum to defeat the police in a straight fight, and because the police could no longer rely on the military (the ultimate coercive sanction on which the government's entire normative system rested) the regime as a whole was now being outcompeted, leaving the protestors in control of the cities.

Reflecting this change in the relative balance of power, no security vacuum emerged when the police were forced to withdraw from many districts in Cairo—local citizens' committees and neighborhood watch groups, most of which opposed the regime even if they hadn't taken a direct hand in the uprising, immediately seized control. Other cities—notably Alexandria (hometown of Khaled Said), Mansoura, Suez, Port Said, and many smaller towns—were in uproar, with regime control completely breaking down in Alexandria, and Mansoura declared a "war zone" and evacuated by police. A week later, after continued mass demonstrations in Tahrir Square, and amid rumors of an impending military coup, President Mubarak stepped down in disgrace, handing control to the Supreme Council of the Armed Forces (SCAF), whose leaders immediately promised major concessions and a transition to full democracy.

Mubarak's departure was, of course, by no means the end of the Egyptian revolution. Violent mass demonstrations, as well as online and street-level activism, continued throughout 2011 and 2012 and into 2013, under both SCAF and the elected Muslim Brotherhood government of Mohammed Morsi. And Ultras from several clubs were involved in deadly stadium riots and urban unrest. But the first days of the uprising showed a clear evolution beyond the techniques used in Tunisia—both on the part of pro-democracy protestors and by the regime and its supporters—into a form of network-enabled urban revolution.

The regime's attempts to oppose this revolution online (by suspending the Internet and cellphone networks, and through the Electronic Army) and on the ground (with riot police and pro-regime militia) backfired spectacularly, only helping to mobilize the mass of the Egyptian people and drawing in an ad hoc network of international supporters such as Anonymous and Telecomix. Ultimately, the uprising involved, as we've seen, components of both an "air war" (online and media) and a "ground war" (street and urban fighting), enabled by access to the Internet and cellphones, and by the alliance of real-world groups such as the Ultras and the Brotherhood with online activists, mass movements such as April 6, and social media groupings including We Are All Khaled Said. All these elements, which depended for their success on a sufficient density of tech-savvy population with access to communications technology, electricity, and the Internet, were artifacts of the predominantly urban, highly networked environment, in which the revolution took place.

If Egypt's revolution was in some ways a larger, more intense version of the Tunisian uprising, then what was about to happen in Libya was to be something else entirely. President Mubarak's quick climb-down and the restraint shown by Egypt's powerful army stopped the uprising from escalating into insurgency. In Libya, events were to take a sharply different turn.

### "A Savage Rampage": Network-Enabled Insurgency in Libya

On February 15, 2011, four days after Mubarak resigned, and just over a month after the fall of Ben Ali, protests began in the eastern Libyan city of Benghazi.

Since mid-January, responding to events in Tunisia and Egypt, President Gaddafi had been cracking down on activists and tightening security in towns across Libya, including Benghazi—Libya's second-largest city and capital of the eastern region, known as Cyrenaica.[76] Gaddafi had flown weapons and mercenaries into desert oases in southern Cyrenaica and into Libya's southwestern region of Fezzan in a series of cargo flights from the Republic of Belarus, whose president, Aleksandr Lukashenko, was one of his few allies.[77] He'd given a speech decrying the protests, saying that the fall of the Tunisian regime "pained him" and claiming that WikiLeaks and foreign ambassadors had "led protestors astray."[78] He would later call the Libyan protestors "greasy rats," blame their actions on hallucinogenic drugs in their Nescafé, call for them to be shot without trial, and attribute the uprising to forces as diverse as al Qaeda and America.[79]

Libya, as noted, has the highest level of coastal urbanization in the Mediterranean, with fully 85 percent of its people living in urban areas on coastlines. Indeed, just two coastal cities—Benghazi (with 1.1 million people) and Tripoli, the capital (with 1.55 million)—together account for almost half of Libya's total population of 5.6 million.[80] This is a huge level of urban concentration, even for coastal North Africa. Like towns in Tunisia and Egypt, Libyan cities had experienced rapid population growth in the decade before the uprising, and though overall per capita income was higher and education levels better in Libya than in either Tunisia or Egypt, urban youth unemployment was still significant, there were ominous inequalities and injustices among various population groups, and the average age of the population (twenty-four years old) reflected a similar urban youth bulge.[81]

Beside these general sources of unrest, there was a strong interregional dynamic: Libya's economy depends on petroleum exports, and much of the oil and gas that drives these exports comes from Cyrenaica. Yet throughout his forty-two-year rule, Gaddafi (who came from Sirte, in Libya's western region of Tripolitania) had favored communities in and around Tripoli. The regime neglected Cyrenaica, allowing Benghazi's infrastructure to decay and—in the view of many residents—denying the city its due political influence.[82] This was particularly galling for Cyrenaicans because King Idris as-Senussi, Libya's Cyrenaica-born monarch whom Gaddafi had overthrown in a coup in 1969, had treated Benghazi and Tripoli as coequal centers, dividing his time between the two cities. As a consequence, cities in eastern Libya saw frequent unrest and protests throughout the Gaddafi regime, with periodic demonstrations and violence against officials and security forces, and a major uprising in 1996 that the secret police (the Mukhabarat al-Jamahiriya) suppressed with great bloodshed. Beside this tradition of unrest, eastern Libya had excellent connectivity with Egypt, and there was a history of events in Egypt influencing conditions in Cyrenaica. After Mubarak's fall, it was thus only a matter of days before unrest began to affect Libya.

On February 15, several hundred demonstrators gathered in front of the Revolutionary Committee (local government) center in Benghazi, then marched to police headquarters to protest the detention of Fatih Terbil, a lawyer representing the families of more than a thousand detainees killed by the secret police in Abu Salim jail, Tripoli, after the 1996 uprising. As in Tunisia and Egypt the protests began peacefully, but when police attacked the demonstrators, killing twenty-four, the National Conference for the Libyan Opposition (an umbrella group like those in Tunisia and Egypt) called for a Day of Rage on February 17. Mass demonstrations broke out that day—sponsored both by pro-democracy activists and by regime supporters mobilized to drown out the protest—and rapidly turned deadly as security forces fired tear gas, rubber bullets, water cannons, and ball ammunition into the crowds. Dozens were killed. Numerous observers reported mercenaries and Mukhabarat in plain clothes roaming Tripoli in unmarked cars, committing drive-by shootings against any group of more than three people on the street in an effort to dissuade protestors from gathering.[83] As in Tunisia, the regime attacked protestors' funerals, and this heavy-handed brutality created such an immense popular backlash that the number of demonstrators swelled dramatically, with many violently confronting police in towns across the country. [84]

On February 21, after a week of rioting, rebels in Benghazi announced the formation of a provisional government, the National Transitional Council. The council sought recognition from the international community, reinstated the royal tricolor of independent Libya to replace

Gaddafi's plain green revolutionary banner, and declared its intention to overthrow the regime, by force if necessary. This prompted the immediate resignation of Libya's entire mission at the United Nations in New York and the defection of Libyan ambassadors to China, India, Indonesia, and Poland.[85] Mustafa Abdul Jalil, the former justice minister, defected to become head of the National Transitional Council and called for an end to the regime. A former interior minister and several army generals later joined the rebels. The same day, two Libyan air force pilots defected to Malta with their Mirage fighters, in protest at being ordered to bomb demonstrators on the streets of Benghazi, while French workers from an offshore oil platform near Benghazi fled by helicopter, also to Malta.[86]

Like the French oil workers, most of the 1.5 million expatriates in Libya (many employed in the economically critical oil and gas sector) were "scrambling for the border, or waiting from help from their governments. Several passenger ferries [were] waiting in the choppy waters off the coast of Benghazi for any evacuation order," and the harbors of Brega and Benghazi were crowded with refugees.[87] Convoys of expatriate workers headed along the coast road for the Egyptian and Algerian borders, and international companies pulled workers out and closed facilities. The regime's control was unraveling fast.

Though the uprising centered on Benghazi and other eastern cities, towns in Tripolitania—including Zintan, Yefren, Misurata, and Tripoli itself—were also experiencing unrest, with police stations on fire and violent battles in the streets. Far from remaining peaceful or taking the path of civil disobedience as in Tunisia and Egypt, the Libyan uprising was fast evolving into a military struggle—a proto-insurgency. Resistance groups were forming on their own initiative, seizing weapons from the regime, arming themselves, allying with military and police defectors, capturing and holding territory, and establishing local neighborhood watch groups to administer the areas they had liberated from regime control.[88] This was classic competitive control behavior, with numerous groups struggling for dominance over the same key terrain—almost exclusively the coastal cities, the routes between them, and people living in those areas. The competition had a hard coercive edge: there was much brutality and little quarter given on all sides.

Libyans were now using the expression *intifadat al-Libya* (Libyan uprising) to describe the revolt, implying an armed insurgency, alongside the generic term *at-thawra* (the revolution), which protestors had used in Egypt and Tunisia. Insurgent groups were forming simultaneously alongside the continuing mass civil unrest in Libya's cities—a civilian pro-democracy movement and a diverse armed resistance were thus emerging in parallel. The death toll had passed one thousand, with thousands more wounded, and police, troops, and mercenaries were firing into crowds in Tripoli and other cities, killing dozens every day. It was clear that this was going to be different from, and far more intense than, the revolutions in Tunisia and Egypt. The protests were more violent, the protestors were better armed, and President Gaddafi—spooked by the rapid collapse of regimes to his east and west—was showing a great deal of fight. Besides rallying supporters to stifle protests and having the security forces, including the army, immediately escalate to lethal force against the demonstrators, Gaddafi's regime had created an Electronic Army in a similar vein to Egypt's, but with a much more active strategy of hacking, spoofing, and breaking up anti-regime networks, as well as using phishing techniques to identify the locations of online regime opponents, who would then be arrested or killed. Gaddafi quickly imposed a near-total media and Internet blackout on the country, cutting off web access as early as February 18, making it extremely difficult for outsiders and Libyans alike to understand what was happening, but also having the unintended effect of blinding his own Electronic Army, undermining his own awareness of the insurgents' "air war."

As in Egypt, when the Libyan regime blocked international news media, social media networks stepped into the breach, enabled by the fact that virtually all the fighting was in urban centers, which initially had good cellphone coverage. Besides passing information to the outside world—mainly cellphone videos and photographs smuggled out to Al Jazeera television and rebroadcast into Libya—social media networks emerged as remote command-and-control nodes that played a practical coordination and logistics role. Social media, in this sense, besides the "air war" function of popular mobilization as in Tunisia and Egypt, also performed a command function like that of the Mumbai raiders' Karachi control room, though in this case the command system was distributed through multiple networks and remote platforms, rather than concentrated in a single node. Twitter was used "to transmit information on medical requirements, essential telephone numbers and the satellite frequencies of Al Jazeera—which [was] continuously being disrupted . . . Social networking sites have supplied the most graphic images of the crackdowns on protestors, but also broadcast messages from hospitals looking for blood, rallied demonstrators and provided international dial-up numbers for those whose internet has been blocked. Libyan activists also asked Egyptians to send their SIM cards across the border so they could communicate without being bugged."[89]

John Pollock, in a brilliant piece of contemporaneous reporting on the uprising, highlighted the ways in which social media and online tools began to fulfill these practical military functions. We've already looked at his account of the engagement outside Yefren in which Sifaw Twawa's team destroyed the Grad launcher with help from virtual advisers over Skype, an example of something closely approaching nonstate remote warfare. He also describes how activists in Benghazi reacted to the regime's downing of the Internet on February 18: "Internet and cell-phone access was cut or unreliable for the duration, and people used whatever limited connections they could. In Benghazi, [a citizen journalist named] Mohammed 'Mo' Nabbous realized he had the knowledge and the equipment, from an ISP business he had owned, to lash together a satellite Internet uplink. With supporters shielding his body from potential snipers, Nabbous set up dishes, and nine live webcams, for his online TV channel Libya Alhurra ('Libya the Free'), running 24/7 on Livestream."[90]

Nabbous gave interviews to international media, created the nucleus of what later became the Rebel Media Center, and inspired international supporters much as activists in Tunisia and Egypt had done. "Nabbous had only enough bandwidth to broadcast," says Pollock, "so volunteers [in Europe and elsewhere in the Middle East] stepped forward to capture and upload video. Livestream took an active role, too: it archived backups several times a day, dedicated a security team to guard against hackers, and waived its fees. Others ran Facebook groups or monitored Twitter, pasting tweets and links into the chat box."[91] A self-organizing corps of volunteers, many of whom had never met a Libyan or been to Libya, thus became critical to the Libyan intifada.

As well as getting the message out, these volunteers provided training in first aid, taught Libyans how to communicate securely via Skype and email, and gave intelligence support to the rebels by passing updates on regime actions and weapons sightings. Steen Kirby, a high school student in the American state of Georgia, was one such volunteer: "As well as identifying weaponry, Kirby pulled together a group through Twitter to quickly produce English and Arabic guides to using an AK47, building makeshift Grad artillery shelters, and handling mines and unexploded ordnance, as well as detailed medical handbooks for use in the field. These remotely crowd-sourced documents were produced in a matter of days, then shared with freedom fighters in Tripoli, Misurata, and the Nafusa Mountains."[92] The American broadcaster Andy Carvin, of National Public Radio, used Twitter to crowd-source weapons technical intelligence: it took his Twitter followers only thirty-nine minutes to correctly identify an unusual parachute-equipped bomb seen lying on the docks during fighting in Misurata—it turned out to be a Syrian-made variant of the Chinese Type 84 air-scatterable mine, which regime forces were dropping from helicopters over the city and harbor. Carvin's effort to identify the mine was permanently recorded on the social networking site Storify.com—this was the Type 84's first known use in war.[93]

As the conflict progressed, international supporters—including hacktivists in Europe and the United States, and Anonymous via its latest Freedom Op, #OpLibya—helped coordinate humanitarian aid, disseminated information on displaced persons and logistics needs, and organized operations to smuggle Western journalists, supplies, and activists into Libya. Many of these—including Christopher Stevens, the future U.S. ambassador to Libya (later killed in the September 2012 Benghazi terrorist attacks)—landed at night from boats on the Mediterranean coast.[94] The fact that Libya's population is spread out along the country's 1,100-mile coastline made it virtually impossible for the regime to block access to rebel-held areas from the sea, and this allowed the rebels to move people and supplies around, giving them access to seaborne support and the ability to maneuver, especially once NATO's blockade began, denying sea space to the regime. Along with the Mediterranean sanctuary, the virtual networks of international support represented a complete logistical, informational, and command-and-control hinterland for the uprising, providing instant strategic depth as the movement gathered momentum. They later remotely organized medical supplies, aid convoys, and an entire hospital ship that came in under fire to dock at the port of Misurata during the siege of the city.

The "air war" in Libya was thus far from merely an Egypt- or Tunisia-style propaganda battle: it was becoming the command-and-control backbone for the uprising, helping synchronize and coordinate the combat power of a diverse group of nonstate actors. This allowed a diverse movement of small groups, spread across several coastal cities, to act in a unified manner against the regime, making this a true case of network-enabled insurgency. Access to sea-based resupply and to globalized electronic connectivity for these urban populations in Libya's coastal cities was creating a virtual theater that mobilized nonstate supporters of the uprising from all over the world.

### The Electronic Levée en Masse

In this sense, Libya was one of the earliest and clearest examples of what Audrey Kurth Cronin calls the electronic levée en masse. In 2006, she argued that digital connectivity was changing the process of mass mobilization in warfare, enabling "a mass networked mobilization that emerges from cyberspace with a direct impact on physical reality. Individually accessible, ordinary networked communications such as personal computers, DVDs, videotapes, and cell phones are altering the nature of human social interaction, thus also affecting the shape and outcome of domestic and international conflict."[95]

In a prescient article, written five years before the Arab uprisings, Cronin pointed out that "modern" warfare—state-based, industrialized total war involving massive national mobilization—dates from the American and French Revolutions at the end of the eighteenth century, and from the turmoil of the Napoleonic Wars that followed. This was a period of mass movements, democratic uprisings, and urban insurgencies against authoritarian regimes, with strong similarities to the Arab uprisings we're examining here. The hallmark of modern warfare, in Cronin's analysis, was "a fundamental shift from dynastic warfare between kings to mass participation of the populace in national warfare."[96] Enabling this shift was a capability—pioneered by French revolutionary leaders in 1793, exploited by Napoleon in his conquests across Europe, and later copied by others to compete with him—to mobilize, manipulate, and control an enormous population. This capability (known as the levée en masse) rested on a rapid expansion and democratization of communications technology:

an analog equivalent of the democratization of digital connectivity that we're experiencing today. As Cronin argued, "the French populace was reached, radicalized, educated, and organized so as to save the revolution and participate in its wars. It is no accident that the rise of mass warfare coincided with a huge explosion in the means of communication, particularly a dramatic growth in the number of common publications such as journals, newspapers, pamphlets, and other short-lived forms of literature. No popular mobilization could have succeeded in the absence of dramatically expanding popular communications."[97]

Cronin rightly predicted the profound implications of this shift, pointing to "a democratization of communications, an increase in public access, a sharp reduction in cost, a growth in frequency, and an exploitation of images to construct a mobilizing narrative" as key new elements.[98] All these elements were apparent in the Arab uprisings of 2011. Beyond its political mobilizing effect, however, as we've observed in several examples already, this enhanced connectivity is enabling an ongoing diffusion—a democratization and decentralization—of military coordination, logistics, and intelligence functions that were traditionally centralized and state-owned. This allows nonstate armed groups of all kinds, as well as noncombatant civilians, to establish distributed, remotely based command and control systems. These in turn can support self-synchronized swarming tactics (as in Mumbai or Mogadishu). Lacking a centralized "brain," these systems are invulnerable to attacks from conventional armed forces.

The process of diffusion, enabled by globalized connectivity, is thus allowing civil society and nonstate groups to play the same game of remote warfare that developed states are playing, albeit with very different tools. It puts a sharp point on Marshall McLuhan's 1970 prediction that "World War III is a guerrilla information war, with no division between military and civilian participation"[99]—and, we might add, no division between domestic and international space, meaning that activists (such as Stephanie Lamy, who supported the uprising from Paris, or Steen Kirby in his high school in Georgia) were virtually in theater in Libya, much as Predator pilots are virtually in theater in Afghanistan. Increased connectivity has placed this electronic levée en masse capability directly into the hands of the ordinary citizen—provided, of course, that he or she lives in a place with access to electricity, cellphone service, and the Internet, or among a population with the technical know-how to reestablish such connectivity if interrupted (in other words, probably in a major city). In Libya's cities, the levée en masse had allowed the intifada by this time to escalate to full-scale, urban, networked insurgency, with rebels seizing several cities across the country.

### "Open the Arsenals"

The first and largest of these was Benghazi. The first Western journalist to reach the city, Martin Chulov of the *Guardian*, found scenes of utter carnage and chaos when he arrived on February 22. Chulov reported that (just as in Tunisia, and later in Syria) the regime's control had begun to collapse when soldiers fired on mourners at a funeral close to the main military base. "The people were leading a funeral march past the big roundabout and people from inside the base opened fire," one protestor told Chulov. "They went home, gathered themselves and came back. This is what happened."[100]

What happened was a full-scale urban battle. Seizing earthmoving equipment from nearby construction sites, and armed with AK-47s and RPGs captured from security forces during the past week's fighting, enraged protestors mounted a direct assault on the base, using bulldozers to create breaches in the perimeter walls, through which they streamed into the compound. Other protestors, alerted by social media, cellphone calls, or text messages, grabbed weapons and moved to the sound of the guns, joining the battle in a continuous flow of ad hoc reinforcements coming in from all directions. Regime troops set up a Soviet-made 23 mm anti-aircraft gun in ground defense mode and poured hundreds of explosive shells into the crowd of attackers, killing many, but to no avail—people were soon inside the base, seizing weapons, setting fire to the barracks, and slaughtering troops and police in a frenzy of retaliatory bloodletting. They soon moved on to the Mukhabarat headquarters, killing many secret police on the spot, arresting some, and beating others to death; a few members of the Mukhabarat tried—usually unsuccessfully— to save their skins by defecting.

In the ground war, the Ultras were playing their familiar role as hard-core shock troops of the street protests, but this time many other groups of young men, organized by tribe or district, were swarming to join the intifada. There was also a regional twist, with Benghazi soccer fans avenging themselves for years of abuse at the hands of the regime. Gaddafi had tried to associate himself with Libyan soccer, despite little real interest in sports. He emblazoned quotes from his Green Book on stadiums across the country, "including the notion that both weapons and sports belong to the people. He appointed his son [Al-Saadi] head of the Libyan Football Federation. Al-Saadi placed himself in the starting lineup of the Ahly club of Tripoli and pursued a stormy rivalry with the Ahly club of Benghazi."[101] In 2000, Al-Saadi blatantly rigged several soccer matches to favor his own team; when Benghazi officials protested, he imprisoned them, relegated Benghazi to the Libyan league's second division, and burned the club's headquarters to the ground.[102] This mirrored, on the sports field, the injustice Cyrenaicans felt in political and economic life. A decade later, it was payback time: as in Tunisia and Egypt, Ultras became the vanguard of the street fighting, and contributed to several of the ad hoc militias that emerged as the uprising continued.[103]

As mentioned earlier, the presence of black African mercenaries working for the regime, hundreds of whom had been flown into an air base outside the city over the preceding two weeks, provided a further, racially tinged source of irritation for the rebels. Gaddafi had always thought and spoken of himself as an African (not solely Arab) leader and supported revolutionaries across the continent, but many Libyans from the heavily populated, predominantly Arab coastal areas found this offensive, looking to the Arab world for their identity.[104] Many mercenaries were found dead inside the barracks when the fighting ended, and others were arrested. Gaddafi's "use of mercenaries appears to have tipped the hand of many protestors and [defecting] armed forces. 'That is why we turned against the government,' said Air Force major Rajib Feytouni. 'That and the fact that there was an order to use planes to attack the people.'"[105] By the time Chulov arrived two days after the fall of the base, the city was firmly in rebel hands:

> Residents who would not have dared to approach the town's main military base without an invitation were doing victory laps around it in their cars. Every barrack block inside had been torched and looted. . . . All day defecting troops and officers were lugging in thousands of pounds of ammunition to a courtyard inside the secret police

headquarters on Benghazi's waterfront. By the day's end an arsenal that could easily supply an army brigade was piled up. There were plastic explosives, rockets, machine guns and even the anti-aircraft weapon that was used to mow down demonstrators as they assaulted the military base on Sunday. Evidence of the carnage it caused was clear on the walls of nearby buildings and in the mortuaries. . . . This was a savage rampage on both sides, a blood and guts revolution, fuelled by decades of repression, neglect and rage. Neighbourhood Watch–like groups, all armed with AK-47s, manned checkpoints in and out of all the towns. But every military and police post for 360 miles had been abandoned. The scattering of the police was leading to claims of victory and the feeling of triumphalism among many of the city's young people.[106]

But Gaddafi had no plans to accept the loss of Benghazi (and with it, control over 25 percent of Libya's population and much of its oil revenue): he began to gather forces, including tanks, outside the city for a counterattack. This was no surprise for the rebels. A twenty-four-year-old student told Martin Chulov: "If [Gaddafi] feels he is cornered he will come for us. Those roads you came in on may be clear, but you did not see who is hiding over the hills?"[107] Gaddafi's intent wasn't just to recapture Benghazi. He also planned to make an example of the city, to cow the rest of Libya's population and teach Cyrenaicans a lesson in brutality they would never forget. This counterattack—or, more accurately, its effect on international opinion via social media—would be the turning point of the war.

Within days of the liberation of Benghazi, the intifada had spread across the country. All of Cyrenaica was lost to the regime, the important harbor cities of Ra's Lanuf and Brega had fallen to the uprising, western towns such as az-Zawiya were in revolt, and Berber-majority cities including Yefren, Zintan, and Jadu were in rebel hands. By February 25 the uprising was in full swing in Tripoli itself, with violence in many urban districts, regime gunmen in unmarked cars shooting protestors, corpses and burned-out vehicles littering the streets, and unarmed demonstrations giving way to street battles with rifles, RPGs, and grenades. President Gaddafi appeared in Green Square to taunt the protestors and threatened to "open the arsenals."[108] In reality, the dictator had bunkered down in his compound at Bab al-Azizya, emerging only occasionally to make bizarrely unrealistic speeches to a group of Western journalists held under tight regime control in Tripoli. More military officers and some whole units had defected, and intense fighting had broken out in Misurata, Libya's third-largest city and business capital, a hundred miles east of Tripoli along the coast road. Libya's diplomats at the UN in Geneva and envoys in France, Australia and Bangladesh had defected, and now claimed to represent the rebels. Perhaps the most important defection was that of the entire Libyan delegation to the Arab League, members of whom—like other defectors—called for international intervention to prevent a humanitarian catastrophe.[109]

This defection, alongside Gaddafi's loss of control over at least half the country, encouraged the Arab League and the United Nations to support military intervention, while the United States and others froze Libya's financial assets and the International Criminal Court announced it would investigate the regime's crimes.[110] These diplomatic moves eventually resulted in the adoption of Security Council Resolution 1973 on March 17, 2011. The resolution, under Chapter 7 of the UN charter—the authority that allows the United Nations to conduct armed, coercive peace enforcement operations, rather than "blue helmet"–style peacekeeping— called for an immediate cease-fire and authorized the international community to establish a no-fly zone and use "all means necessary short of foreign occupation" to protect civilians.[111] This, along with pressure from Australia, France, Great Britain, and the United States, cleared the way for intervention by NATO.

Two days later, Gaddafi's troops moved on Benghazi. After protesting the UN resolution as a "crusader" and "colonial" intrusion into Libya's sovereignty, Gaddafi declared a cease-fire and claimed he was halting his troops, who had been making steady progress toward Benghazi in a series of bloody battles in towns along the coast road. But then on the morning of March 19, his forces began bombarding Benghazi and moved into the outskirts of the city from the west, with armor and infantry columns supported by air strikes.

Western media and NGOs had set themselves up in the city over the previous month but now fled in large numbers toward the Egyptian border, as did many Benghazi residents, who rightly expected a bloodbath when the assault reached the city center. One member of the rebel council, who returned from the diaspora when the uprising began, told me that she stood at the entrance to the rebel headquarters, in tears, as the foreigners left. Many had become her friends over past weeks and were reluctant to go; several asked her, "What can we do to help you?" Fully expecting to die, knowing that the departure of foreign observers would give the regime space for unrestrained vengeance once the city fell, she told them: "Tell our story. Tell what happened here, so people will know that someone dared to stand up to Gaddafi."[112] For her, it felt like the end of the world.

The world didn't end, at least not that day: the regime's assault never reached the city center. While the armored columns were still on the city's outskirts, NATO intervened with massive air strikes, launching more than a hundred Tomahawk cruise missiles from ships offshore, and sending strike aircraft to attack Libyan army units, Gaddafi's compound in Tripoli, air defense systems and other regime installations. The NATO operation was a classic example of evolved, light-footprint littoral warfare in an urbanized environment. It used a mix of amphibious ships, submarines, and aircraft carriers in the Mediterranean, a sea blockade, Predators operating overhead, land-based aircraft flying from Europe and the Middle East, sea-based attack helicopters from ships offshore, and a limited ground presence in Libya's coastal cities. NATO ground forces kept an extremely low profile during the operation, inserting only a very small number—a few dozen at most—of special forces operators, military advisors, intelligence personnel, search-and-rescue personnel, and joint attack controllers (specialists in directing air and naval strikes) from several NATO and Arab countries.[113] Ultimately, over 222 days, NATO and allied aircraft from fifteen countries flew 9,600 strike missions against more than six thousand targets.[114]

These strikes helped the rebels push back and ultimately defeat the Gaddafi regime. This took months, with many ups and downs—towns such as Brega and Ajdabiya changed hands several times, there was a long and brutal siege in Misurata, and fighting in the Nafusa Mountains (around towns including Yefren) seesawed back and forth for many weeks. The fighting consisted almost entirely of battles to control coastal cities and petroleum infrastructure, and of fighting on the coastal highway and the inland connecting roads between these cities and port facilities. The intervention wasn't without its problems—NATO forces bombed rebel columns in error on at least one occasion, and accidentally struck a critical trans-Sahara water pipeline on another.[115] But NATO air support changed the balance of the conflict within days, relieving the rebels of pressure from Gaddafi's tanks and aircraft, leveling the military balance between the regime and the rebel fighters, and allowing them to gradually expand their initial footholds.

By mid-June, the rebels had significantly improved their position; by August 28, after a three-pronged offensive from the east, west, and south, they'd captured Tripoli, declared an end to Gaddafi's regime, and formed an interim government that was recognized by the United Nations on September 16. Gaddafi retreated to the town of Bani Walid, which, along with his home city of Sirte, continued to hold out for several months. During this time the regime launched several counterattacks, and Gaddafi continued to taunt NATO and the rebels on radio and television, even as his family and supporters fled to Niger, Algeria, and Tunisia. The stronghold of Sirte finally fell, after an intense urban battle, on October 17, 2011—eight months after the first protests in Benghazi. Three days later, on the morning of October 20, Gaddafi was captured on the outskirts of Sirte as he tried to flee the city. The man who had called the rebels "rats" was found skulking in a drain under the roadway, seeking refuge after NATO missiles disabled his fifty-car convoy, and rebels encircled and attacked his escort as they tried to continue on foot. Groups of rebel fighters, mounted on weapon-carrying technicals and using similar self-synchronizing swarm tactics to those of the Somali fighters I described in Chapter 2, flocked toward the scene from as far away as Tripoli and Misurata. They were drawn by cellphone calls and text messages from fighters who had been alerted to Gaddafi's presence by members of his escort whom they'd captured in the firefight, and were now frantically searching the area for the dictator they called "Callsign One."[116]

They found him within an hour. Grainy cellphone video showing Gaddafi as a blood-covered captive, begging the mob for his life—before being beaten, hauled onto the hood of a Toyota technical while jubilant fighters photographed him with cellphones, then killed (off-camera) and his half-naked body dragged through the street—was uploaded in real time. The video reached al Jazeera and YouTube only forty minutes after the dictator's death; within another ninety minutes, it was being shown on all major international cable and satellite news channels and carried on Twitter, Internet news sites, and radio stations.[117] Thus, in the uprising's final moments, it was globalized digital connectivity that gave a fleeting incident on the coast road outside Sirte an instantaneous national, then global, political impact.

Faced with incontrovertible evidence of Gaddafi's humiliating demise, the regime's resistance collapsed within hours. Further videos followed, showing Gaddafi's body, with that of his son Mutassim, lying uncovered for four more days. "Hundreds of ordinary Libyans queued up outside a refrigerated meat store in Misurata, where the dead dictator was being stored as a trophy. A guard allowed small groups into the room to celebrate next to Gaddafi's body. They posed for photos, flashing victory signs, and burst into jubilant cries of 'God is great.'"[118] The transitional government declared victory, and NATO called an end to military operations on October 31, 2011.

### Benghazi: Urban-Networked Intifada

As I said earlier, this isn't the place for a full description of the Libyan civil war. But several aspects of the uprising were relevant to our look at the future environment. Firstly, virtually all the fighting in Libya was urban and coastal. In part, this was an artifact of Libya's geography, with a narrow, relatively fertile, urbanized coastal strip backing onto the largely unpopulated Libyan Desert (which, at about 425,000 square miles, covers most of the country); the vast majority of Libya's population is sandwiched between the Mediterranean to the north and the Sahara to the south. But it's also clear that urban discontent—especially in Benghazi—was the mainspring of the intifada.

Benghazi, in fact, is an excellent illustration of the way in which population growth, urban sprawl, and rural-to-urban migration can stress a city's metabolism, leaving it with insufficient capacity to process the toxic by-products of urban overstretch. Along with the economic marginalization of populations within Benghazi, the political marginalization of Benghazi within Libya contributed significantly to the violence of the uprising when it came.

As a focus of Italian power during the colonial period, and a coequal city with Tripoli under the monarchy in the 1950s and 1960s, Benghazi has impressive art deco and midcentury modern buildings, open squares, wonderful beaches, an important harbor, and a historic claim to greatness. But the city is run-down after decades of official neglect, unplanned urbanization, and rapid population growth. Outside the urban core, streets are muddy and filled with rotting trash, and only the main roads are paved.[119] The city has one sewage treatment plant, built more than four decades ago. "Waste is just flushed into the ground or the sea, and when the water table rises in winter, the streets become open cesspools."[120] The anger this generated among Benghazi residents is clear from media interviews conducted during and after the uprising:

> "Why do we have to live like this?" says Rafiq Marrakis, a professor of architecture and urban planning at Benghazi's Garyounis University, Libya's oldest. . . . "There's no planning, no infrastructure, no society. Gaddafi has billions and billions in banks all over the world. But he's left us here with nothing." "There is a severe, chronic housing shortage," he continues. "Young people can't own their own homes, can't get married, can't start their lives." . . . And what social welfare projects the regime did undertake, such as a medical center with the pompously literal name "One Thousand Two Hundred Bed Hospital" became white elephants. "They've been building it for more than 40 years and it still isn't finished," says Marrakis.[121]

The Libyan government had in fact made enormous efforts to improve Benghazi's water supply through the Great Manmade River Project of the 1980s, which brought underground water from the Nubian Sandstone Aquifer in the Libyan desert to towns such as Tripoli, Benghazi, and Sirte via a network of trans-Sahara water pipelines.[122] But other systems within the city's infrastructure (including governance, housing, public sanitation, and traffic flow) had been neglected. This lack of capacity made it hard for the city to cope with an inflow of population and housing growth over several decades, and ultimately "became one of the major reasons why Benghazi turned against the government."[123]

As the regime relaxed some restrictions on contact with the outside world and grew more integrated into the international community after giving up its nuclear program in 2003, people in Benghazi became better connected with Libyans in the diaspora and with other populations in the Mediterranean basin and the broader Arab world. This was not always a positive thing: many young men from Benghazi went to Iraq to fight the coalition after 2003, for example, contributing to a radicalization of the city's youth. Al Qaeda documents captured in Iraq in 2006 showed that the two cities of Benghazi and Derna (the next town to the east along the Cyrenaican coast road) together accounted for almost 85 percent of Libyan foreign fighters entering Iraq.[124] More broadly, satellite television and the Internet showed Libyans how the rest of the world lived, making people realize how badly "they were being shortchanged. The example of the rapid development of the Persian Gulf countries, particularly the Emirati city-state of Dubai . . . was particularly galling."[125] Libyans could suddenly see how people in the Emirates—with a harsher climate, a smaller population, and a similar degree of coastal urbanization—had prospered under their government's policies. They could look around and see their own city falling apart. "[Then] young people get YouTube and see how one of Gaddafi's sons spent a million dollars to have Beyoncé perform at his party."[126]

Oil revenues drove Libya's economic development over the second half of the twentieth century. Funded by oil money, government policies—including free education and public health—lowered maternal and infant mortality (thereby contributing to an urban youth bulge) and created a literate population. Libya recorded the highest literacy rate in the Arab world in 2006, and the UN Human Development Index (which assesses standard of living, social security, health care, and other development factors) ranked Libya at the top of all African countries in 2007.[127] But in the same year, the country was struggling with overall unemployment of 20.7 percent, and far higher youth unemployment—largely because Libya's education system simply didn't generate graduates with skills the country's labor market actually needed.[128] Thus the economically vital oil sector depended on foreign labor, while Libyan high school and college graduates tended instead to seek jobs in the government bureaucracy, which was already full of older Libyans and therefore couldn't absorb them all.[129] And because the bureaucracy's main function was as a jobs program for otherwise unqualified Libyans, ministries became bloated, inefficient, and unresponsive. They enforced unnecessarily complex regulations and processes in an attempt to justify high staffing levels and create opportunities for corruption and rent-seeking, and officials demanded bribes to supplement their meager salaries. In this sense, the problem in Libya's cities wasn't so much a lack of governance as a surfeit of inefficient and predatory bureaucracy.

All this, combined with a lack of economic opportunity for young people, meant that Libya's cities—especially Benghazi, because of its marginalization by the central government—gradually filled with educated, politically aware, unemployed, radicalized, alienated youth, with little opportunity to improve their lives within the existing system. There was massive resentment against foreign workers, the government in Tripoli, the repressive police and Mukhabarat, and local bureaucrats. When the Arab Awakening began, "although unemployment was not the only source of the grievances that led to the 2011 uprising, Libya's chronic youth unemployment problem was a major reason behind the instability."[130]

When the intifada did break out, the Libyan army failed to play the restraining role that the military had played in Egypt.[131] The regime's hyperviolent response turned an uprising that began in a similar way to Tunisia's and Egypt's—with peaceful pro-democracy demonstrations and street riots by unarmed protestors—into full-scale civil war. The army's inability to exercise a mitigating influence resulted from the fact that Gaddafi had deliberately kept the national army weak, creating local militias personally loyal to himself, as well as a network of secret police informers and a strong armed police presence in all major cities and towns. The core of the Libyan regular army consisted of four mixed armor-infantry brigades, mostly drawn from tribes loyal to the Gaddafi family, and in some cases commanded by Gaddafi family members (including Al-Saadi, who led the special forces, and Khamis, who commanded the feared 32nd Brigade, one of three well-armed "regime protection units" similar to Saddam Hussein's Special Revolutionary Guard in Iraq).[132] The proliferation of militias, armed police, and mercenaries working for the regime meant that the army, while perhaps first among equals, didn't have a monopoly on the use of force, and thus lacked the coercive edge it needed to effectively compete with the other groups. Dozens of officers defected to the rebellion, a few units switched sides, and upward of 130 soldiers were executed for refusing to fire on their own people, but the army as an institution remained loyal to the regime for most of the uprising.[133]

For their part, the rebels lacked military experience, but what they did have was an urbanized population with good functional knowledge of technology. Libya didn't have a gun culture like that of, say, the tribal areas of Pakistan, Somalia, or Yemen.[134] Most anti-regime fighters, except for military defectors, had little background in weapons or tactics for urban fighting. They were unemployed youth, shopkeepers, teachers, mechanics, bus drivers, civil servants, sports fans, and so on—and one of the main tasks of rebel leaders was to train these city dwellers and forge them into a unified force.[135] They never truly achieved this: by the end of the war there were dozens of local autonomous guerrilla groups fighting the regime, collaborating loosely (at best) with the rebel council. Weapons were scarce, and here the skills of the urban population came into their own: workshops sprang up in liberated areas, with vehicles and weapons being modified or made from scratch. Rebel mechanics welded helicopter rocket pods onto trucks, rigged vehicles with home-made armor plating, and mounted anti-tank guns, heavy machine guns, and anti-aircraft cannon onto pickup trucks to create Somali-style technicals. They dismantled and reused damaged and captured regime weapons and vehicles, and modified mines and RPGs with high explosives for use against urban strongpoints.[136] Access to urban industrial facilities and an urban population with basic technical skills was essential to this effort.

Weapons weren't the only kind of technology the rebels were able to repurpose. A network of rebel supporters evaded the regime's attempts to block the Internet and cellphones by smuggling Thuraya satellite phones, thumb drives, and CD-ROMs of geospatial, humanitarian, and intelligence information into and out of the country. During the siege of Misurata in summer 2011, for example, fighters used Google Earth data on CD-ROMs, in combination with iPhone compass apps, to adjust rocket fire in the city's streets. "After a rocket was fired, a spotter confirmed the hit, reporting that it had landed, for example, '30 yards from the restaurant.' They then calculated the precise distance on Google Earth and used the compass, along with angle and distance tables, to make adjustments."[137] Others—including children—used Google Maps and smartphones to mark regime sniper positions, which NATO strike planes then engaged from aircraft carriers offshore. In this sense, the same factors that helped create the rebellion—a connected, tech-savvy, radicalized, underemployed youth population in Libya's crowded, marginalized, and overstressed cities—also helped the rebels strike hard at the regime when the time came.

The proximate trigger for the uprising, of course, was Libyans' awareness of successful revolutions in Tunisia and Egypt. Thus the Libyan revolution can be seen in part as a spillover from these uprisings, enabled by digital connectivity across the region. After the end of the Libyan war, another spillover occurred: many mercenaries recruited by Gaddafi, who had fought hard for the regime and lost, returned to their countries of origin. As well as fighters from Niger, Burkina Faso, and Chad, these included Tuareg fighters from Mali, some of whom had lived in Libya ever since a failed uprising against the Malian government in the 1960s.[138] Up to five thousand more Tuaregs were recruited by the regime in February 2011, many joining at recruiting centers in several Malian cities.[139] Once the regime fell, these fighters moved back into northern Mali, where they sparked a resurgence of the Tuareg separatist insurrection. This, combined with an al Qaeda–linked radical movement and a military coup in February 2012, triggered the collapse of Mali's democratic government and prompted yet another military intervention in Africa, this time led by France, in early 2013.

The other major impact of the war in Libya is still being felt, across the eastern Mediterranean, in Syria.

## Social Netwar: Syria 2011–13

As mentioned earlier, the war in Syria is going on as I write, and its outcome—after two years of fighting, a million refugees crowded into squalid camps in neighboring countries, millions of displaced persons within Syria, and eighty thousand killed and counting—remains in doubt. Syria represents a huge escalation in violence, scale, and scope over previous uprisings in the Arab Awakening, as far beyond the conflict in Libya as Libya was beyond the uprisings in Tunisia and Egypt. To do justice to the Syrian uprising would require a full-length study, and I don't propose to discuss it in detail here—only to highlight aspects that are directly relevant to our examination of future conflict environments.

The Syrian war began, like the other uprisings, as a series of peaceful protests. These first broke out in the southern city of Daraa on March 15, 2011, a few days before NATO began its intervention in Libya. Daraa was experiencing significant stress: decades of neglect and mismanaged resources contributed to an unprecedented and severe drought, and there had been am influx of population into the city's outlying districts over the past few months.[140] Syria has lost half its available water supply over the past decade, in part because of mismanagement and urban growth, in part because of changing weather and rainfall patterns. As a result, water is rationed in all of Syria's cities, the water system in most towns is operating right at the limit of its capacity, and disturbances in water supply can have immediate destabilizing effects.[141] As noted in Chapter 1, water supply is one of the most challenging aspects of urban governance, and the influx of a large number of displaced people, seeking water, into a city already rationing its water supply represents one of the most severe possible stresses on a city's metabolism. In Syria's case, this was an added burden on top of the demands of roughly 1.5 million Iraqi refugees, many of whom moved to the Sayyida Zeinab neighborhood south of Damascus as the Iraq war worsened after 2004. "Although political repression may have fuelled a steady undercurrent of dissent over the last few decades, the regime's failure to put in place economic measures to alleviate the effects of drought was a critical driver in propelling such massive mobilizations of dissent . . . Syrian cities [served] as junctures where the grievances of displaced rural migrants and disenfranchised urban residents meet and come to question the very nature and distribution of power."[142]

The immediate trigger for the protests was the arrest and beating of three teenage boys, inspired by protesters in Tunisia, Egypt, Libya, and elsewhere, who tagged a building with anti-regime graffiti. Several hundred people rallied to demand the boys' release, and the protests turned violent after security forces fired on the crowd.[143] Riot police killed more than four hundred protestors, particularly targeting mourners at protestors' funerals, in the first three months of clashes in Daraa alone. They attempted to seal off Daraa from the outside world, but as in the other uprisings, thousands of demonstrators across the country subsequently took to the streets, and the demonstrations quickly spread to towns across Syria in March and April 2011. Activists used cellphones and social media to connect with each other and with international supporters, and human networks linked urban dwellers in Damascus and Aleppo (Syria's two largest cities) to people in rural areas experiencing unrest. By early May, hundreds had been killed or detained in massive riots, and the army had deployed tanks and thousands of troops in Homs and Daraa to suppress what was now morphing into an armed uprising.[144]

Pro-regime militias, known in Syria as *shabiha*, "ghosts," committed massacres in several towns, and secret police arrested (and in many cases tortured, killed, or "disappeared") dissidents across the country as the conflict escalated in May and June.[145] The *shabiha*, in a pattern that mirrors the other examples we have explored, were drawn largely from gangs of marginalized street youth, criminal networks, and organized thugs who operated in poor, marginalized "garrison districts" in Syrian cities and often had close patron-client relationships with regime officials. As the uprising escalated, the *shabiha* became a key irregular auxiliary force, which the regime regularly employed in order to intimidate the population.[146]

Learning from the experience of the Egyptian and Libyan regimes, the Syrian government under President Bashar al-Assad quickly offered a series of compromises and concessions, but none of these offers to relax regime restrictions and introduce limited democratic freedoms was enough to appease the protestors. Assad initially left the Internet and phone networks up and quickly mobilized an Iranian-supported Electronic Army to harass activists, hack opposition websites, and undermine anti-regime cohesion by spreading confusing messages.[147] More sophisticated than the government in Egypt, the Syrian regime had created an extremely effective system of wiretapping, cellphone interception, and Internet surveillance, and so the security forces' instinct at first was to allow unrestricted use of these tools as a way of gathering information on the protestors. When protestors began using cellphones to post updates on Twitter, however, and using cellphone cameras to gather and broadcast images of regime brutality, this caught the security services by surprise, forcing a rethink.[148]

Over the preceding decade, there'd been an explosion in digital connectivity and information access in Syria. Hafez al-Assad, Syria's dictator from 1971 until his death in 2000, had enforced extremely tight restrictions on information and connectivity—allowing no international media, satellite television, cellphones, or Internet access whatsoever.[149] However, his son and successor, Bashar al-Assad, was something of a computer geek, taking an active role as the head of the Syrian Computer Society after his brother Basel died in 1994. On his accession as president in 2000, Bashar al-Assad initially made efforts to modernize Syria, tolerating a limited amount of political dissent during a short-lived period known as the Damascus Spring, and opening up electronic connectivity to ordinary Syrians, to include satellite and cable television, cellphone networks, and open Internet access.[150]

Despite occasional crackdowns—the regime banned YouTube, for example, in April 2007 after the site uploaded a clip of President Assad's wife, Asma, with her underwear exposed in a gust of wind[151]—Syrians generally had excellent access to digital connectivity, and Internet penetration and cellphone usage rates in Syria were vastly higher than in any other country affected by the Arab Awakening. According to World Bank data, between 2002 and 2012, Syrian cellphone usage rates "shot up by 2,347 percent (by contrast, they increased by 83 percent in the US during the same time period). This was almost double that of similarly repressive environments in Egypt and Tunisia at the time. What is perhaps even more incredible is Syria's Internet penetration growth rates, which shot up by 883 percent, greater than Egypt, Libya, and Tunisia (for comparison, Internet penetration only increased by 27 percent in the US during the same time period)."[152]

But by June 4, 2011, the regime was forced to suspend Internet access in an attempt to stanch the flow of damaging images and video clips documenting regime brutality, which were being posted on the Internet and broadcast on satellite television. Another reason for the ban on land-based Internet may have been that this enabled the regime's security services to detect who was still using satellite-based Internet in the country, and thus to locate and target dissidents and guerrilla groups.[153] As in the other uprisings, when the regime banned the Internet, Syrians improvised mesh networks, smuggled videos out to Lebanon to be uploaded there, and jury-rigged their own satellite uplinks (a traditional pastime—under Hafez al-Assad's ban, the Syrian army had run a lucrative side business in black market sales of satellite dishes so that people could access banned satellite television channels).[154] At the same time, international activists (including Anonymous, once again, with #OpSyria) and a network of diaspora supporters and social media networks stepped into the breach.

By July, cities across the country—including Damascus, Aleppo, Daraa, Idlib, Homs, and Hama, together representing almost 40 percent of Syria's population of just under 21 million—were experiencing violent unrest. Protestors were arming themselves, guerrilla groups were forming, and the regime had lost control of many outlying towns and cities. As in

Libya, a civilian democracy movement was emerging in parallel with a diverse armed resistance that included jihadist groups, secular nationalists, ethnic separatists, military defectors, and tribal groups. On the ground in Syria, leaders of armed groups rapidly marginalized and overshadowed the unarmed pro-democracy movement as the violence spread, emphasizing the importance (which we noted in the last chapter) of coercive means as the underlying enabler for competitive control over populations: armed groups could always outcompete unarmed groups at the coercive end of the spectrum of control, and thus rapidly became dominant on the ground.

At the same time, liberated areas formed district and neighborhood councils to administer their areas and provide essential services once the regime had withdrawn. Relations between the armed resistance and these local administrative councils were often complex and fractious, with armed groups trying to co-opt or intimidate the councils, and civilians trying to manipulate armed groups to further their own interests and minimize risk. The situation stabilized somewhat after September 25, when military defectors (many of whom were Sunni officers of the Syrian army) formally announced an armed insurrection against the regime and formed the Free Syrian Army. A week later, on October 2, civilian opposition groups formed the Syrian National Council, similar to Libya's National Transition Council, and sought to impose order on a chaotic set of military and political actors opposing the regime. In this effort, the rebel movement was (consciously or unconsciously) acting to create the kind of wide-spectrum competitive control system that we discussed in Chapter 3, adding persuasive and administrative capabilities to their existing coercive capabilities in order to give them more resiliency and a stronger capacity to control territory and population.

Unlike in Libya, however, there has so far been no NATO intervention in Syria, so the regime has enjoyed virtually uncontested control of the sea and air throughout the conflict, and (apart from some shoulder-launched anti-aircraft missiles and light anti-aircraft guns) the rebels haven't been able to challenge the regime in these domains at all. For this reason, and because Syria is much less littoralized than the other countries we've examined, the fighting in Syria has been just as urban, but much less coastal, than in Libya, Tunisia, or Egypt. Weapons and humanitarian supplies, instead of being smuggled in via sea as in Libya, must come in overland.

For example, Libyan supporters of the Free Syrian Army, some of the most active international supporters of the uprising, have to send shipments by ship or cargo plane from Libya via a circuitous route to Qatar, then by air into Turkey, then into Syria by truck across rebel-controlled border crossings, such as Bab al-Hawa in northwestern Syria.[155] Attempts by international supporters to encourage the rebels to capture and thus unlock part of Syria's Mediterranean coastline, so as to open up a direct sea-based supply route, have failed to date, and the regime continues to control the ports and coastal areas.[156]

As well as sectarian tension between Syria's pro-regime Alawite and Shiite minorities (which account for about 15 percent of Syria's population and dominate the mountainous areas overlooking Syria's coastline) and the Sunni majority (75 percent of the population, mostly centered further inland), a strong urban-rural dynamic had emerged by late 2011. The regime held Damascus and other major urban centers but was increasingly ceding control of Syria's rural hinterland, and many smaller towns, to the rebellion. In part, this reflected small-town opposition to the regime that was brought on by a feeling of neglect and relative deprivation (as with Benghazi residents in Libya), but unlike in Libya and Egypt, the major fault line in Syria emerged between rural and small-town residents, who felt marginalized at the expense of Damascus, and big-city populations, some of whom were pro-regime for economic and political reasons or were part of the same Alawite minority as President al-Assad. Syria is thus, in many ways, a war of the peripheral and marginalized against the dominant center, a fact that's reflected in the spatial pattern of the violence, with the regime holding urban cores and major public areas and the rebels operating in city outskirts, periurban areas, some marginalized big-city districts, and rural zones.

Underlying these tensions, however, were dynamics similar to those we've observed in other examples: cities under stress, marginalized urban and periurban populations, high youth unemployment, and lack of carrying capacity in a society experiencing significant population growth and urbanization but limited economic expansion over the past generation. The strongest areas of opposition to the regime were Syria's poorer, more radical Sunni areas (the so-called "poor, pious and rural").[157] These included districts such as al-Ghuta in Damascus, Baba Amr in Homs, and Bustan al-Basha in Aleppo, places where some of the largest initial anti-regime protests broke out, and where the demonstrations first became militarized. There was also extremely strong anti-regime activity in cities with high levels of poverty, including Daraa and Homs, and in drought-affected urban districts in cities such as Deir ez-Zor that had experienced water shortages before the uprising.

The regime's economic policies—including economic liberalization under President Bashar al-Assad in the early 2000s—had benefited only a small minority of the Syrian population. This created income inequalities and a perception of favoritism, unfairness, and social injustice, and it spurred in many Syrians a sense of relative deprivation. Businessmen and urban elites closely connected with the government, along with merchants in Damascus and Aleppo, were the prime beneficiaries of the government's economic policies, and these populations tended to support the regime (as did recently arrived Iraqi refugees, who depended on government handouts). By early 2011, however, the rest of Syria's population was experiencing a falling standard of living, declines in government subsidies for food and fuel, water shortages, and extremely high youth unemployment brought on by a massive youth bulge.[158] This economically and politically marginalized population tended to be heavily anti-regime, and it included Syria's large population of Palestinian refugees, many of whom had been in the country since 1948, living in periurban refugee camps such as Yarmouk and in the poorer districts of major cities.

As the conflict escalated through 2011–12 with battles in Aleppo and Damascus, increasing numbers of combatants, atrocities on both sides, and a series of failed cease-fire attempts, most of the fighting centered in urban areas (as in the other examples we have looked at), but there was very little coastal fighting, probably because the dominant population groups in coastal areas (Alawites and Shiites) tended to support the regime, and Syria's largest cities, Aleppo and Damascus, weren't on coastlines. In mid-August, there was some littoral maneuver and coastal shelling by regime forces, including ships offshore, as the regime used gunboats and tanks in an effort to maintain control of the Sunni-majority port city of Latakia, but in the absence of international intervention, government forces quickly regained control of the city, cementing their dominance over Syria's coastline.[159]

As we noted in Chapter 2, the Free Syrian Army and other groups developed a suite of "do-it-yourself" weapons, drawing on the technical skills of Syria's urbanized population and access to industrial facilities. These weapons included low-tech but effective slingshots, catapults, and trebuchets used to lob homemade bombs and shells over the rooftops of urban areas such as Aleppo, as well as prefabricated launch stands to allow individual rockets to be fired electrically.[160] At the high-tech end of the scale, fighters built an armored vehicle around a car chassis, including a remotely controlled machine gun operated by the driver using a Game Boy videogame console, externally mounted video cameras, and a flat-screen TV.[161] The Free Syrian Army repurposed a factory in Aleppo that had previously manufactured iron and steel into a mortar bomb production line, and produced grenades, bombs, shells, and rockets in similar factories. As in Libya, they mounted heavy machine guns and anti-aircraft weapons on pickup trucks to create technicals, manufactured improvised mortars and rocket launchers, and fitted improvised armor to cars to create makeshift tanks.[162] They produced homemade explosives, pipe bombs, and missiles, and created rifle-launched grenades that could be fired over rooftops from street to street in urban areas. As in the other conflicts we've studied, the rebels relied on a technically skilled and capable urban population, plus access to urban areas that contained workshops and industrial facilities, to enable this kind of homegrown DIY warfare.

In 1998, a group of RAND researchers led by John Arquilla, David Ronfeldt, Melissa Fuller, and Graham Fuller identified the potential for what they called "social netwar," arguing that

> the information revolution is favoring and strengthening network forms of organization, while simultaneously making life difficult for old hierarchical forms. The rise of networks—especially "all-channel" networks, in which every node is connected to every other node— means that power is migrating to non-state actors, who are able to organize into sprawling multi-organizational networks more readily than traditional, hierarchical, state actors can. This means that conflicts will increasingly be waged by "networks," perhaps more than by "hier- archies." It also means that whoever masters the network form stands to gain major advantages.[163]

All the examples I have cited from Syria tend to suggest that although the war is far from over, it's showing many similarities to the other Arab

Spring conflicts we've examined in this chapter. In particular, enhanced digital connectivity—along with urbanization, the democratization of both weapons technology and communications technology, and the emergence of virtual theaters made possible by social networks and the Internet—seems to be enabling something approaching full-scale social netwar in Syria.

## III. Networked Connectivity and Urban Conflict

One morning in Baghdad in early 2006, I was in a meeting with members of the Iraqi prime minister's national security council. U.S. vice president Dick Cheney had visited Iraq in mid-December 2005, and one of the Iraqi security advisers was unhappy about a press conference he had given. "Your vice president comes here, he sits with us," the official said, "and he says, 'Don't worry, we'll stand with you, we won't leave Iraq till you're ready, we're with you.' Then he flies to Paris, he gives a press conference, and he says, 'Don't worry, we're leaving Iraq, we'll have our troops out of there in a year.' Do you think we don't have satellite TV? Do you think we can't speak French? If you tell us one thing, and you tell other people something else, do you think we won't find out? How stupid do think we are?"[164]

The same thing these Iraqi officials complained of is affecting regimes across the region today, but even more so. A report by the International Crisis Group in July 2011, for example, quoted a Syrian regime insider as saying: "They [the regime] believe that some of the methods used in the early 1980s still apply. Today, every Syrian with a mobile phone can turn himself into a live satellite television broadcaster. How can we resort to such means when we are facing 24 million satellite televisions in our midst?"[165] The explosion in electronic connectivity—not just satellite television, but also Internet, cellphones, and social media—that we've discussed in this chapter is merely one aspect of the broader megatrend of enhanced connectedness, which will affect how most people on the planet will be living within the next generation. The Iraq war—with the kind of connectivity this Iraqi official described, with its urban fighting, and with its technically skilled population able to repurpose garage door openers, TV remote controls, cellphones, and satellite dishes as weapons of war—was just a mild foretaste of what conflict will be like in the connected cities of the future. The Arab uprisings, particularly the Libyan and Syrian civil wars, are another, and remote warfare capabilities (drones and cyberweapons, but also crowd-sourced logistics and intelligence and the involvement of global networks in local conflicts) are yet another.

Hafez al-Assad denied his population virtually all access to digital media, but when his son Bashar reversed the policy in 2000 there was an explosion of connectivity in Syria, at an even faster pace than in the rest of the world. When Muammar Gaddafi opened up to the outside world in 2003, Libyans experienced a similar sudden increase in situational awareness that transformed ordinary people's understanding—people in Benghazi could suddenly see how they were being shortchanged, people in Syria could see what was going on in the rest of the Arab world, and when the uprisings in Tunisia and Egypt succeeded, it was only a matter of time before Libyans rose up as well. The same connectivity enabled the Syrian uprising and is creating pathways that now allow Libyan groups to provide material and political support to Syrians as they fight their own regime.

Closer to home, in 2011–12 the Occupy movement, beginning in downtown Manhattan's Zuccotti Park, spread across cities in the United States and into many other urban areas of the developed world. Like the Arab movements, Occupy was a diverse and unorganized collection of different factions with a largely urban and online support base. Unlike pro-democracy activists in the Arab uprisings, the Occupy protestors were never able to develop a unified agenda or a practical program, nor did they effectively mesh human support networks with virtual support networks (except in major cities). The Occupy movement thus never became more than a fringe political grouping with extremely limited influence, at best, on mainstream politics. In part this was because countries such as the United States already have democratic electoral processes—or, in competitive control theory terms, well-developed persuasive and administrative means—that can absorb and relieve this kind of mass popular discontent. In part, however, it was because the movement never turned violent—thanks to the nonviolent intent of the Occupy organizers, but even more so to the professionalism and restraint generally shown by police and security services. The Arab uprisings started off peacefully, too, in every single case: it was lethal regime reactions to initial protests, carried out by politicized security services, that turned these peaceful demonstrations into violent riots and then into armed uprisings.

There was another factor, too, one that relates directly to electronic connectivity. In Tunisia, Egypt, Libya, and Syria, when governments shut down the Internet and cellphones in response to the protests, they gave ordinary people a personal grievance (denial of access to the connectivity they had come to count on) that brought them onto the streets in large numbers. Far from stifling the protests, cutting off connectivity spread the outrage—it suddenly gave the mainstream population a reason to support anti-regime movements, which until that time had been fringe activists with little wider appeal. It made every citizen feel a sense of repression directly in his or her own life, and thus broadened the opposition to the regime dramatically—sometimes, as we saw in the case of Egypt, literally overnight. In the United States, in virtually every case, Internet and cellphone systems stayed up. In one incident, however, authorities did disable the cellphone system, with remarkably similar results to what was observed in Egypt.

The place was San Francisco, California. On August 11, 2011, Occupy protestors tried to mount a demonstration against the Bay Area Regional Transit (BART) authority, with demonstrations on BART platforms and on trains across the San Francisco metropolitan area, to protest a shooting by BART police in July. BART officials responded by blocking cellphone services. "They turned off electricity to cellular towers in four stations from 4 p.m. to 7 p.m. . . . after BART learned that protesters planned to use mobile devices to coordinate a demonstration on train platforms."[166] The backlash was immediate. Online protests broke out against BART from Anonymous and a collection of online democracy and civil liberties groups. The Electronic Freedom Foundation likened BART to the Egyptian regime, claiming on its website, "BART officials are showing themselves to be of a mind with the former president of Egypt, Hosni Mubarak."[167] Michael Risher, a staff attorney for the American Civil Liberties Union, said: "All over the world, people are using mobile devices to protest oppressive regimes, and governments are shutting down cell phone towers and the Internet to stop them. It's outrageous that in San Francisco, BART is doing the same thing."[168] Although the planned demonstration was disrupted, the cellphone blockage gave ordinary commuters a shared grievance with the protestors and led to a series of even larger protests and an escalating online campaign against BART (under the punning Twitter hashtag #MuBARTek) that involved denial-of-service attacks, leaking of sensitive information, and cyberintrusions designed to shut down BART's computer system.[169] Protestors gathered for demonstrations that grew over time until BART was effectively "under siege—in cyberspace and underground . . . working round the clock to fend off a disparate group of hackers who penetrated the agency's Web sites [and] released sensitive information, in retaliation for the shutdown of the cellphone and wireless services."[170]

The San Francisco protests never escalated beyond peaceful demonstrations, primarily because there wasn't the violence against protestors (by police or security services) that occurred in the other examples we've looked at, and as a result the escalatory cycle of tit-for-tat protest and violent repression never got off the ground. The BART police should count themselves lucky, too, that there were no San Francisco Ultras. But as politically inaccurate as it might have been for the protestors to label an American city's transit system as a Middle Eastern dictatorship, the functional parallels with Egypt are actually quite clear: blocking access to connectivity was *in itself* a sufficient grievance to bring many people over to the side of the protestors, who otherwise might have remained a marginal fringe group. Just as in Tunisia, Egypt, Libya, and Syria, people rapidly came to rely on digital connectivity, counting on it and taking it for granted, and any disruption in that connectivity was seen as a major infringement on their rights. This was clearly puzzling to the BART spokesman, Linton Johnson: "The protest never materialized, but the action provoked outrage. The next day, Mr. Johnson was dismissive of complaints. 'It is an amenity,' he said. 'We survived for years without cellphone service,' he continued, but now people are 'complaining that we turned it off for three hours?'"[171] Well, actually, yes: one effect of the democratization of technology, including weapons technology, that has emerged through the radically increased electronic connectivity of the past decade is that people have come to see systems such as cellphones, Wi-Fi, the Internet, and satellite television as theirs by right. Information access and information flow, especially in urbanized areas, have become almost as basic to urban dwellers' existence and to the metabolism of cities as flows of water, food, fuel, or shelter, and this has happened in a historically short time.

In all the examples we've looked at in this chapter, virtual or electronic connectivity wasn't enough, on its own, to spread or sustain an uprising. There had to be a virtual-to-real overlap. In the case of the Arab uprisings, this can be seen in the air-war/ground-war dynamic of online activists working with soccer fans and street-level demonstrators, providing a virtual hinterland for protestors, rioters, and eventually full-scale guerrilla war. It was seen in the way that remote warfare capabilities became available to urban street fighters who could now run remote command-and-control nodes as in Mumbai, crowd-source intelligence and logistics, and synchronize urban swarm tactics, as in Mogadishu—but with much greater precision. In the case of Libya, access to a long open coastline gave the rebels enormous opportunities for littoral maneuver and resupply. Combined with the improvised weapons and communications systems that urbanized populations proved able to pull together, and the competitive control behavior of both civilians and guerrillas in liberated areas, these capabilities add up to a significant shift in the way that conflict in connected, coastal cities is likely to occur in the future. And we've not yet seen the full effect of this shift. As John Pollock points out:

> The world's nodes and networks are multiplying and growing denser: a third of the world's population is online, and 45 percent of those people are under 25. Cell-phone penetration in the developing world reached 79 percent in 2011. Cisco estimates that by 2015, more people in sub-Saharan Africa, South and Southeast Asia, and the Middle East will have mobile Internet access than have electricity at home. Across much of the world, this new information power sits uncomfortably upon archaic layers of corrupt or inefficient governance.[172]

Chapter 5 draws together the implications of this shift, along with insights from the previous chapters, to explore the ways in which communities, cities, companies, and governments can respond to the challenge of conflict in connected cities.

# 5

# Crowded, Complex, and Coastal

Unless we imagine that such urban transformations are less gigantic than these linear projections indicate, and unless we hope that we are witnessing a retreat toward middle-rank towns, these great cities will essentially be no more than juxtapositions of flimsy houses without street maintenance, police, or hospitals, surrounding a few wealthy neighborhoods turned into bunkers and guarded by mercenaries. Mafias will control immense zones outside the law (this is already the case) in Rio, Lagos, Kinshasa, and Manila. Formerly rural people, with a few members of the privileged classes, will be the primary organizers of new social and political movements demanding very concrete changes in people's lives. It is on them, and no longer on the workers, that the great economic, cultural, political and military upheavals of the future will depend. They will be the engines of history.

—Jacques Attali, 2006

## I. The New Normal

I began this book by describing an incident that happened in early autumn 2009, in a remote Afghan valley, where watching a patrol fight its way out of the mountains helped crystallize some questions in my mind about the applicability of classical counterinsurgency theory to modern conflict. Four years later, the war in Afghanistan continues, but the outlines of a new environment are already emerging across the planet. This chapter summarizes the key elements of that environment, draws together the main ideas we've been exploring about the problems that will confront tomorrow's cities, and considers how we might choose to respond to them.

As we've just seen, one face of the new complex of urban problems is playing out in Syria today. As I write, rebels are fighting from house to house and block to block in several cities, while vast refugee settlements are congealing around the edges of towns in Turkey, Lebanon, and Jordan. Online activists of every ideological bent, in a dozen countries, are supporting the uprising; cyberguerrillas of the Free Syrian Army are blocking regime websites, running propaganda on YouTube, and using Twitter for command-and-control. Fighters are using cellphones, global positioning systems, and satellite receivers to enable their urban swarm, and they're building do-it-yourself weapons in the workshops of what has been called the first "maker war."[1] Food, weapons, ammunition, medicines, and communications gear are flowing into Syria via overlapping networks—official and private, overt and dark, licit and illicit—that all use the same interconnected global transportation, financial, and communications systems. Flows of money, information, and fighters follow the same pathways. Meanwhile, Bashar al-Assad's Electronic Army has hacked the websites and Twitter feeds of a string of human rights NGOs and the U.S. secretary of state and is phishing for rebel supporters online.[2] A "siege mentality has taken hold" in government-controlled coastal cities, while a huge influx of displaced regime supporters puts these towns under further stress.[3] The Syrian army has fired Scud missiles against its own cities, and people fear the regime is using nerve gas to stifle the uprising.[4] Overhead, drones—flown remotely, by crews who drive home to their families after work through suburban America—are monitoring the fighting, and the CIA is reportedly considering Predator strikes against al Qaeda–aligned militants fighting alongside the rebels. The CIA story, first reported by Ken Dilanian and Brian Bennett of the *Los Angeles Times*, is on Twitter, Facebook, and news blogs in minutes; in less than an hour it's on satellite channels across the globe—including Press TV (the official Iranian outlet), which predictably calls the plan "a dangerous escalation."[5] It's not reported in Syria, though, because the regime has Iranian software that lets it scramble satellite feeds; word has it the Iranians got the software from China.[6]

At the same time, halfway across Asia and at the other end of the violence spectrum, we can see another face of the new normal, in the world's fastest-growing megacity—Dhaka, capital of Bangladesh, which is also experiencing severe unrest. A general strike and bombings on the streets stopped the city in its tracks in early 2013, as opposition parties protested a government crackdown, which itself was prompted by violent riots a few weeks before. The riots were triggered by death sentences given to opposition leaders a few months before that, in government-run trials that the opposition argued were politically motivated.[7] Like Daraa and Benghazi, where the Syrian and Libyan civil wars began, Dhaka is an urban ecosystem under extreme stress, operating right at the edge of its capacity. Urban economic growth—combined with poverty, soil salinity, water contamination, and land-use conflict in the countryside—has brought a massive flow of rural people into the city.[8] Dhaka is growing at an incredible rate: a woman born in Dhaka in 1950 would have been a toddler in a midsized town of roughly 400,000 people; by her fiftieth birthday the place was a megacity of 12 million. Today, Dhaka's population is almost 15 million—nearly a 38-fold expansion in a single lifetime.[9] This breakneck growth puts immense strain on governance: fire, ambulance, and health services are overstretched, local government is plagued by corruption and inefficiency, and the police have ceded whole districts to gangs and organized crime. Unplanned industrialization has given Dhaka the unenviable title of "least livable city on the planet," according to an annual survey of 140 world cities.[10] Hundreds of unregulated brick kilns on the city's outskirts pump out toxic smoke as they produce the construction materials that feed Dhaka's urbanization—a process that's creating vast, polluted, overcrowded, marginalized shantytowns that lack water, sanitation, lighting, and even footpaths.[11] Since 1971, when "Dhaka became the capital of an independent country, the pressure on it has been enormous, [resulting in] the growth of slums on any available vacant land."[12] Government responses have sometimes been heavy-handed—as in 2007, when authorities razed squatter settlements and expelled inhabitants by force—and this is closely connected with the unrest.[13]

And then, of course, there's this:

> Take one of the most unplanned urban centres in the world, wedge it between four flood-prone rivers in the most densely packed nation in Asia, then squeeze it between the Himalaya mountain range and a body of water that not only generates violent cyclones and the occasional tsunami, but also creeps further inland every year, washing away farmland, tainting drinking water, submerging fertile deltas, and displacing villagers as it approaches—and there you have it: Dhaka.[14]

Like 80 percent of cities on the planet, Dhaka is in a littoral zone. The vast majority of its people live less than forty-two feet above sea level, making the city extremely vulnerable to coastal flooding. Floods in 1998 put 60 percent of Dhaka's districts underwater, killed more than a thousand people, and caused more than US$4 billion in damage.[15] You don't need to believe in human-caused climate change to recognize that this is a problem. Even if you assume no climate change effects whatsoever, the city will become steadily more vulnerable over time, as more people move to low-lying areas in the next generation. If, on the other hand, Bangladesh experiences any sea level rise, the effects will be catastrophic—five feet of rise would put 16 percent of the country's land area and upwards of 22 million people underwater, prompt massive refugee movement, and leave vast areas of cropland too salty to farm.[16] It doesn't take much to generate five feet of water—during Hurricane Sandy in November 2012, for example, lower Manhattan experienced a storm surge almost twice that height, while Hurricane Katrina generated a storm surge more than five times as high in Mississippi.[17]

As the evening rush hour gets under way on Dhaka's waterfront, across the world the sun is rising through the smoke haze over La Rocinha, in the South Zone of Rio de Janeiro. La Rocinha is the largest *favela* in Brazil, a crowded hillside slum less than a mile from the sea, with a population of 350,000 people. Before it became a shantytown in the 1930s, the area was a farming community (*rocinha* means "little farm"), growing vegetables and flowers for Rio's markets. Today those commodities have to be trucked in from farms further out, adding to the city's legendary traffic flow. La Rocinha was occupied in 2011 by Brazilian special operations police and military police trying to control crime and drug trafficking in Rio—yet another coastal megacity that has grown rapidly in the last decade and today has a population of more than 12 million. Despite being economically marginalized and politically excluded, people in La Rocinha are highly connected: cellphones are common, most houses have satellite dishes and TV antennas, Internet usage is high, many bloggers and citizen journalists are active in the neighborhood, and there are local community radio and TV stations.[18] As there's no work in the actual *favela*, the vast majority of people in the district who do have jobs go to work in Rio, meaning that the district is very connected—as a source of labor—to the economic life of the city. Today it's occupied by the 28th

Pacification Police Unit, which has deployed seven hundred paramilitary police in nine fortified patrol bases throughout La Rocinha, along with a hundred surveillance cameras that monitor movement. Patrols roam the narrow streets on foot and by motorcycle, working the areas between outposts and checkpoints, in an operational pattern that looks a lot like a police-led version of urban counterinsurgency, Baghdad style. Pacification of the *favela* has driven violent crime underground, but it feels— to at least some residents—little short of military occupation and urban warfare against the poor.[19]

On the other side of the Atlantic from Rio, it's midday on Africa's west coast, in the flooded ruins of Makoko, part of the Lagos waterfront. Makoko is (or rather, was) a famous 120-year-old shantytown built on stilts over a lagoon, and until recently it was home to 250,000 people. The government demolished it with only seventy-two hours' warning, against strong community opposition, in August 2012. Violent clashes broke out with residents as the authorities began cutting down homes with chainsaws.[20] Nigeria's government is trying to "unclog the city and spur economic growth," and clearing waterfront slums—where families have lived for generations, albeit without written title to their houses—is part of this effort.[21] "Built on a swamp, Lagos is fighting for survival. Ceaseless migration is strangling it. City fathers foresee the doubling of the population to 40m within a few decades, which would make it the most populous city in the world."[22] But in the attempt to renew the city, it's the people of urban, coastal, marginalized districts that suffer most. Around the time that Makoko was being demolished, up the coast from Lagos, the cities of Conakry, Freetown, and Dakar (capitals of Guinea, Sierra Leone, and Senegal, respectively) were suffering a huge cholera epidemic. It was caused by the lethal combination of nonexistent sewage systems, lack of clean water, overstretched public health services, heavy rains, and coastal floods that inundated waterfront slums, spreading disease across their parent cities. The connectedness among cities along the West African coast quickly helped spread the epidemic across the region.[23]

I could continue this coastal tour at length, but the overall point is clear: the same patterns exist in littoral cities across the entire developing world. As well as occurring simultaneously in different cities, these problems—from poverty and social unrest to gang warfare, organized crime, insurgency, terrorism, and even out-and-out civil war—can coexist in one city at the same time. Feral cities are emerging in some countries, and feral districts have arisen in many cities. Acute violence exacerbates deeper, chronic issues, making every other problem worse and harder to get at. In the words of Mike Davis, the world is becoming a "planet of slums," with "more than 200,000 slums on earth, ranging in population from a few hundred to more than a million people" and the emergence of "'megaslums' . . . when shantytowns and squatter communities merge in continuous belts of informal housing and poverty, usually on the urban periphery."[24] The periurban world is also, as we've seen, highly connected: as of early 2013, more than six billion people across the planet own cell-phones (that is, about two billion more than have access to clean water or toilets)—and problems in one place can rapidly escalate and spread to others.[25]

This, then, is the suite of problems—framed by the megatrends of population growth, urbanization, littoralization, and connectedness—that will define the environment for future conflict, and for every other aspect of life, in the next generation. How do we react to this? How should we think about the coming environment, how can we prepare for it, and what can we do about it?

That depends on what the word *we* means in that sentence. In cities under stress, there's no inclusive "we," no single unified society, but rather a complex shifting ecosystem of players cohabiting in segregated communities with competing interests, clashing cultures, and differing perspectives. Are we Baron Haussmann, trying to manicure an urban jungle, or Victor Hugo, lamenting the loss of people's autonomy? Are we the Jamaican constabulary, or the population who get their law and order from the gang dons of the Kingston garrison communities? Are we the community organizations trying to mitigate violence in San Pedro Sula, the businesses making clothes in its outskirts, or the workforce in those factories? Or are we the American public, buying clothes and cocaine, both of which stage through Honduras on their journey to the U.S. market, supporting the deportation of Honduran gang members (and thus both funding and fueling San Pedro Sula's astronomical murder rate), while tut-tutting as if we had nothing to do with it? Are we the entrepreneurs who run businesses (licit, illicit, or both) from La Rocinha, or the police working to pacify the place? Are we the Western militaries, diplomatic services, and aid agencies wondering how to operate in this environment if, God forbid, we find ourselves dragged into it? The examples discussed in previous chapters suggest insights for several of these groups, and the rest of this final chapter outlines some of these insights—not as definitive conclusions, but as tentative hypotheses that will need a lot of further testing. Before examining specific insights, though, it makes sense to put forward some overall observations.

## II.  "Bending the Curve"

The first, most obvious insight is that whatever the future of conflict may be, most of the time it won't be much like Afghanistan. Given the historical patterns I mentioned in Chapter 1, we'll probably see strong *operational continuity* (frequent irregular and unconventional warfare, stabilization operations, humanitarian assistance, and disaster relief, with rare but dangerous instances of state-on-state conflict). But we'll also see a sharp *environmental discontinuity*: the future environment (crowded, coastal, urban, connected) will be so different from Afghanistan (remote, landlocked, rural) that we'll have to consciously reconsider much of what we think we know about twenty-first-century conflict.

How, for example, will drones and satellites operate over urbanized spaces where we can see any house from the outside—but not know who lives in it, or what's moving in the sewer systems underneath it, or in the covered laneways that link it with other houses under the urban canopy? The capacity to intercept, tag, track and locate specific cellphone and Internet users from a drone already exists, but distinguishing signal from background noise in a densely connected, heavily trafficked piece of digital space is a hugely daunting challenge. How will special operators or strike aircraft engage targets in the same tenement or shack system as thousands of innocent bystanders? These people won't long remain bystanders if we go in hard after a target and disrupt their lives in the process. How will heavy armored vehicles maneuver in streets that are three feet wide? How will battalions and brigades do population-centric counterinsurgency in cities so gigantic they could soak up a whole army and hardly notice? How will expeditionary logistics function, in cities that can barely feed or water themselves or supply their own energy needs, let alone fill logistics contracts to support an external military force? How will offensive cyberoperations help against virtual swarms of hackers when disrupting an urban population's electronic connectivity turns out to be one of the most provocative things you can possibly do? All these things will demand hard and wide-ranging thought. (Some detailed ideas on these issues, and others, are in the Appendix.)

Don't get me wrong: the counterinsurgency era is far from over, much as people might want it to be—historical patterns suggest that Western countries will almost certainly do large-scale counterinsurgency again, probably sometime in the next decade or two, whether we want to or not. So it's absolutely imperative that military forces retain the lessons and skills they've learned in those conflicts, yet simultaneously figure out how to do such operations in the megaslums of tomorrow—a tall order indeed. Mountain warfare, with its extreme demands on troops and equipment, is also far from a thing of the past: mountain campaigns will most certainly happen again. Specialist mountain troops (such as France's outstanding Chasseurs Alpins, who so distinguished themselves in Afghanistan), light infantry (such as the American 10th Mountain Division), and airborne (parachute) or air assault (helicopter-borne) forces will remain essential because of their ability to infest a landscape, move quickly across broken and complex terrain, engage with a population, and get right up close and personal with a determined enemy. As the world gets ever more littoral, Marines will, if anything, become even more the force of choice for the complex expeditionary operations in which they specialize.

But as a proportion of the whole, wars in remote, mountainous, land-locked places such as Afghanistan will get rarer by comparison to urban littoral conflicts, simply because wars happen where people live, and people will be overwhelmingly concentrated in coastal cities. We may be doing the same kinds of operations as today, but the places where we'll be doing them will be radically different. Versatility and adaptability—being able to work in the widest possible variety of environments, perform the widest possible range of missions, and transition rapidly and smoothly between terrain and mission types—will therefore be much more important than optimizing for any one scenario. Terms such as *full-spectrum*, *versatile*, and *adaptable* are often used as a way to avoid making hard choices about capability trade-offs: by optimizing for everything we optimize for nothing. But, as Chapter 1 showed, even though we can't predict specific future conflicts (akin to predicting the weather), we can make informed judgments based on projections about the future conditions and circumstances under which these conflicts will take place (under-standing the climate). That future conflict climate, as we have seen, will be coastal, networked, and overwhelmingly urban—so we need to orient ourselves toward, rather than optimizing solely for, conflict in connected cities.

This leads to my second overall observation, which is that security thinkers need to start treating the city as a unit of analysis in its own right. Dominant theories of international relations take the nation-state as their basic building block. Western governments talk of "national security"; there are "country teams" in our embassies and "country desks" in our diplomatic services, intelligence organizations, and aid agencies. This national-level shorthand ("Indonesia," "Pakistan," "Nigeria," "India," "China") lumps together huge and diverse areas of enormous countries as if they were single, indivisible units and flattens out the crucially impor-tant variations among population groups within them. Yet Jakarta and Merauke, Karachi and Quetta, Lagos and Kano, Mumbai and Hyder-abad, or Shanghai and Urumqi could hardly be more different from each other, and each of these cities contains dozens of distinct population groups who also differ dramatically. We need to bring our analysis down to the city and subcity level, understanding communities and cities as systems in their own right (perhaps, via the flow-modeling approach I've described in this book, treating cities as biological or natural systems). We need to understand how a city's subsystems and subdistricts fit together as well as how that city nests within and interacts with regional and trans-national flows and networks. Much of the work to enable this approach has already been done in the urban studies, ecology, systems engineering, political geography, and architecture communities—it's partly a matter of taking models that already exist in other disciplines, bringing them into the national security field, building on them, plugging in new var-iables, and looking closely and creatively at the results. In this respect, the political science community may perhaps be able to help, applying recent research on modern and medieval city-states as an organizing framework—doing for coastal cities what Antonio Giustozzi did for Afghanistan's city-states in his magnificent study of Afghan warlord state-building, *Empires of Mud*.[26]

A related insight is the need to conceive of a city as flow and process, rather than just place, with violence shaping and creating the landscape, not just happening in it. This jumps out at me from the Tivoli Gardens example we looked at in Chapter 2. The military traditionally treats urban terrain as a "special environment," which makes sense at the tactical level, where combat engagements are so fleeting (seconds and minutes, to hours or days at most) that the landscape is effectively a constant. Having been brought up this way, until I studied Kingston through the lens of competitive control theory, looking at it in terms of long-term conflict between Jamaican political parties and their client gangs, I naively thought of a city as just a piece of real estate—a fixed backdrop against which the action happened. I understood how dramatic an effect urban terrain could have on conflict; what I didn't fully grasp was that this could work the other way—that processes of conflict and competitive control at the street level could literally *create* the physical terrain of an urban area, demolishing entire districts in one place, creating new districts in another, determining the locations of key pieces of urban infrastructure, and defining the spatial relationships between parts of the city. And physical terrain (initially formed by conflict) can then channel and define how subsequent conflict occurs, so the urban organism both reflects and perpetuates the conflicts that created it.[27] Having once had this insight (which I'm sure is entirely obvious to many people but just hadn't quite struck me before), I can never see cities the same way again. An urban area, as it exists in any one instant, is now to me just a snapshot of a dynamic disequilibrium. Like a still image from a video clip, it's in midflow, and it seems permanent only if you ignore what's happening on either side of the freeze-frame you happen to be looking at in any one moment. Flow, not space, is what defines urban areas: the mathematics of cities is calculus, not geometry.

But if cities are in a state of dynamic disequilibrium, this calls into question policy makers' emphasis on stability as a goal. Planners talk about stabilizing a country, returning to normality. The military has a whole doctrine called "stability operations," NATO has a school for "stability policing," aid agencies do "stabilization programming," the World Bank and the IMF issue "stabilization loans," and political scientists talk of "status quo powers" and "hegemonic stability theory."[28] But at the city level, none of this makes much sense—there is no status quo, no "normal" to which to return, no stable environment to police. Think about Dhaka, exploding from 400,000 to 15 million, or Lagos, growing from 3 to 20 million, or Mumbai from 2.9 to 23 million, all in the same time frame.[29]

These aren't stable systems; even if you could somehow temporarily get every city function under control, the frantic pace of growth would rapidly overtake the temporary illusion of stability. In fact, that's exactly what has occurred in many cities, where planners have repeatedly devised solutions to problems as they exist at one particular moment, only to find these solutions overtaken by events before they can be implemented. In maneuver theory terms, rapid dynamic change has gotten inside planners' and political leaders' decision cycles: they repeatedly develop policies that *would have been* adequate for a set of circumstances that no longer exists. Rather than focusing on stability (a systems characteristic that just isn't present in the urban ecosystems we're examining here), we might be better off focusing on resiliency—helping actors in the system become better able to resist shocks, bounce back from setbacks, and adapt to dynamic change. Instead of trying to hold back the tide, we should be helping people learn to swim.

Another insight that arises from this line of thinking is that the territorial logic of any given city—the way things work, how the place flows, what drives what, what matters and what doesn't—will be totally opaque to outsiders, at least at first. Taking the time to observe a city for long enough to sense the flow and to see the rhythms of its metabolism turns out to be critical in understanding it. (Think about how thoroughly Lashkar-e-Taiba scoped Mumbai before the 2008 attacks, studying the city and its flow for more than a year, and compare that to Task Force Ranger in Mogadishu.) A one-time analysis, however detailed, doesn't say much about a city's flow. Big data can sometimes help, since advances in cloud computing and data mining now make it possible to produce dynamic visualizations of flow patterns. Analysts can track millions upon millions of data points (traffic patterns, say, or cellphone usage, or pedestrian movement, or prices in markets, or Internet hits, or bank transactions, or numbers and types of cars in parking lots)—things that dozens of businesses across the world analyze every day for marketing purposes—to understand how a city works. But how do we do that in enormous megaslums that are constantly growing and morphing and which don't have the spatial frameworks (down to street names and building addresses, for example) that allow geo-referenced data to mean something?

Obviously enough, we go in on the ground, and we engage directly with the people who live there. Caerus field teams under Matt McNabb and Richard Tyson have done exactly this in Liberia and Nigeria over the past two years, working with marginalized urban communities to help them create maps of their own environment and thus give them a voice in negotiations on land use, infrastructure, crime, and public safety. These teams have found that in these poorly serviced and barely governed periurban settlements, basic spatial relationships and flows are highly contested, which makes them extremely hard (and sometimes very dangerous) to map. This underlines another basic insight, namely, that self-aware ignorance—a constant realization that outsiders *don't* understand how things work, and therefore need to experiment, test hypotheses, start off small, and seek local context—is a crucially important mental discipline if we want to be effective. If a city is a continuous dynamic flow, then it's also a continuous natural experiment, and taking a consciously experimental approach will be key.

Less obviously, though, the same city that baffles outsiders may be completely opaque to locals. It's clear enough that strangers coming in—the proverbial white guys with clipboards, patting the locals on the head, telling them to "stand aside, there's a good little fellow, while we fix your problem"—have often done vastly more harm than good. You could think of UNICEF's disastrous intervention in water supply in Bangladesh, which, at a conservative estimate, left twenty million people with chronic arsenic poisoning.[30] Or the well-meaning efforts of Western movie stars handing out mosquito nets, putting local net manufacturers out of business and thus increasing, not reducing, people's long-term vulnerability to malaria.[31] Or, indeed, the many occasions in Iraq and Afghanistan—chronicled by Rajiv Chandrasekaran, Tom Ricks, George Packer, Linda Robinson, and (with a certain unconscious irony) Paul Bremer—when our efforts had tragic unintended consequences because we just didn't get how things were supposed to work.[32]

But here's the thing: just because you live in New York, London, Sydney, or Tokyo—let alone Lagos, Karachi, Rio, or Cairo—doesn't guarantee that you understand how these giant coastal cities work, either. You can be a complete local, live your whole life in a place, yet still not understand what's driving the problems that affect it—because you only have a partial view, because your perspective is skewed by your own interests or affiliations, because living there limits your access to certain kinds of technical or functional knowledge that you'd need to understand the problem, or because where you live is just too big and complex and variegated for any one person to fully grasp what's going on. To paraphrase Neil Gaiman and Terry Pratchett, someone standing in Trafalgar Square can't see greater London, let alone all of England.[33] Likewise, a crack addict on the streets of a big American city, a social worker in the neighborhood, a nurse in the local emergency room, or a police officer on the beat may all have a profound understanding of a particular set of hyperlocal issues and conditions, but that doesn't mean they grasp the overall pattern in their city as a whole, or understand how to fix the problems they inhabit, any more than outsiders do.

It also doesn't mean they can form a consensus on a way forward. In fact, their intimate involvement with a set of local problems makes it, if anything, *less* likely that they'll agree. Each of them is looking at a gigantic (and constantly morphing) complex system through a soda straw. For this reason a pure bottom-up approach, which privileges local insight over outside knowledge, where you "just ask a local," isn't the answer, either. It can be just as problematic as a top-down technocratic approach that brings in outside "experts" who ignore local perspectives. How do you decide which local to ask, for a start? And what if they disagree, suck you into local disputes, or just have no clear idea what's going on? This is the perpetual challenge that confronts researchers in a fieldwork environment. It also bedevils aid workers, social workers, police, emergency services personnel, and military leaders who intervene in complex emergencies, and there are no easy answers. At a more basic level, as we saw in Chapter 1, the data on international interventions suggest that if outsiders understood local problems, the dozens of interventions that happen every year would probably have a greater success rate; if locals understood their own problems and could agree on how to fix them, those interventions wouldn't be needed. Clearly, neither is the case. I think there *is* an approach that can work, a structured co-design technique that combines local and outsider inputs, but I'll come to that in due course.

A further general observation is that the normative systems we've observed in action in Kingston and Mogadishu, in remote areas of Afghanistan, and in Libya, Syria, Lebanon, and Iraq—what I've called the theory of competitive control—seem to recur across rural and urban environments of all kinds, and are therefore probably hardwired into human nature, rather than habitat-dependent. This in turn means that competitive control is probably an enduring feature of human behavior, making it broadly applicable to many kinds of nonstate violence and thus potentially useful beyond narrowly defined counterinsurgency theory. Whether the group we're examining is a militia like the Somali National Alliance or Arkan's Tigers, a street gang like the Shower Posse or MS13, an organized crime network like the Sicilian mafia or the Honduran *narcos*, a soccer club like the Ultras or Red Star Belgrade, a mass movement like Hezbollah, an insurgency like the Taliban, a terrorist group like al Qaeda in Iraq, or a government, the same principles seem to hold. A group that creates predictability and consistency by establishing a normative system of rules and sanctions is thereby defining a safe behavioral space for people afflicted by terrifying uncertainty, and the safety that system creates will attract that population. In a conflict situation, people's uncertainty arises from the presence of armed groups targeting the population; in a city that's growing exponentially—constantly outgrowing itself—the same terrifying lack of predictability can arise simply from the pace of change. Thus a megacity under stress can offer the same opportunities for conflict entrepreneurs to control populations, provided they create a predictable rule set that makes people feel safe in the face of instability.

This occurs—and this is the critical point—because of the *predictability* inherent in the rules, whether people like the group or not, and regardless of the content of those rules. As we saw in Chapter 3, you don't have to like the cops, or agree with the speed limit, for the road rules to make you feel safe. Eventually, provided the group builds consistency and order, through a wide spectrum of persuasive, administrative, and coercive measures, it may gain the subjective loyalty and support of a population. But the coercive end of the spectrum is the foundation for a normative system, since in a competitive control environment, a group that can't fight off other groups or discipline its own members will be swept away. Support follows strength, and strength flows from the ability to enforce the rules (Mao's "barrel of the gun"); this applies to any group seeking to control a population.

One related insight from the Arab Awakening (and the San Francisco protests) discussed in Chapter 4 is that people feel attacked when their connectivity is disrupted. In both these examples, when governments turned off cellphone networks, this alone was enough to bring people onto the streets to support previously marginalized activists. Suddenly a minority cause became a mass protest, because people felt a shared sense of grievance and indignation when the authorities pulled the plug. I think this is about more than just the convenience of electronic connectivity, though. Constant access to the digital world, letting people upload images or tweet what's happening to them, creates a sense of security. There's always an actual or potential witness to what's going on: someone's watching, ready to blow the whistle if the authorities pull something brutal or repressive. It's as if there were always a media crew of reporters and cameramen watching out for you—but a virtual, digital, distributed crew enabled by constant connectivity. This idea of "Web as witness"— the protection that comes from virtual monitoring by independent outsiders, and the restraint this imposes on governments—is the flip side of the privacy concerns that go with our ever-connected environment. In a sense, it allows remote actors to extend their normative system into places where they can't physically be. This idea of the permanent, universal witness is a new element in conflict, politics, and human rights advocacy alike, it's entirely an artifact of the connected, urban world, and it's mostly a good thing.

This leads me to a final general observation, which is that things are not all bad. I admit I've painted a pretty dismal picture here, and indeed, there *are* daunting challenges in a world that will add three billion new city dwellers over the next generation, mostly in low-income countries that were already short of resources and lacking in governance capacity. Jacques Attali, in the bleak passage from his *Brief History of the Future* that I quoted at the beginning of this chapter, summarizes this dystopian vision very well.[34]

But there are upsides, too. For one thing, population growth and urbanization tend to coincide with gains in prosperity, health, and education, so by midcentury another billion people—many in emerging markets like India and China—could be lifted out of poverty and into the global middle class, creating massive opportunities for trade and industry, unleashing immense human capital, and giving them the prospect of better lives.[35] For another, there's evidence that when population, settlement, agriculture, and energy production are concentrated in denser areas (like multistory buildings in urban zones), this reduces carbon footprint and ecological impact for a given population.[36] As Robert Bryce has argued, the organizing principle for a green future is density.[37]

I mentioned resiliency earlier, and in a broader sense, cities throughout history have shown enormous capacity for innovation, reinvention, and self-renewal. We saw this in the case of Lagos in Chapter 1, as people adapted to the city's lack of infrastructure and its horrendous traffic by developing their own, self-synchronized system of traffic alerts. In fact, as Andrew Zolli and Ann Marie Healy argue in *Resilience: Why Things Bounce Back*, increases in the size of cities tend (on average) to make them more efficient and faster, increasing innovation and prosperity, enabling more growth even as they also bring problems. "The bigger the city," Zolli and Healy report, quoting a 2011 study, "the higher the wages were for the residents, the more patents produced there but also the greater the number of violent crimes, the more traffic, etc. 'When you double the size of the city, you produce, on average, fifteen percent higher wages, fifteen percent more fancy restaurants, but also fifteen percent more AIDS cases, and fifteen percent more violent crime. *Everything* scales up by fifteen percent when you double the size.'"[38]

The key phrase here is "on average"—Zolli and Healy's research reveals that growing cities, even struggling ones, have within themselves the adaptive resources they need to address their problems, provided they can unleash and apply them. But these resources aren't evenly distributed, and it's the unequal (or, more accurately, the perception of *unjust*) allocation of resources that creates conflict. Their research highlights the danger of exclusionary growth: if some subset of people is excluded from the general gain as a city grows, this creates relative deprivation and a sense of injustice that leads to violence, as we saw in Benghazi. Inequality per se might not be the problem—indeed, some argue that a certain amount of inequality, as long as it comes with opportunity, can spur people to better themselves, creating achievable, aspirational goals, and thus becoming an engine of economic growth and societal stability.[39] But inequality *without* opportunity—permanent exclusion, marginalization without hope of improving one's circumstances—can create lethal, city-killing resentments, when people who realize they can never join the party decide to burn the house down instead. Likewise, "cities that become overly reliant on just a few forms of value creation," excluding parts of their population, economy, and territory from the wealth and capital they create, "can find themselves enjoying a golden age followed by catastrophic decline. (Think Detroit)."[40] Conversely, if cities can generate enough carrying capacity quickly enough, they can build resiliencies that help them bounce back from crises. If cities have metabolisms, they also have immune systems—ways to deal with internal challenges, absorb toxins, and neutralize threats. Thinking of resiliency in this way makes more sense than focusing on stability, I think.

All this implies that it's possible to "bend the curve": that the linear projections I've outlined in this book need not automatically result in mass conflict and chaos, provided we figure out ways to unlock the adaptive resources that already exist in major cities. Cities are (or can be) engines of peace, justice, innovation, and prosperity, even as they also create violence, injustice, exclusion, and poverty. And actions that communities and governments take in their own cities can bend the curve toward resiliency.

## III. Co-Design in Cities Under Stress

If the first part of this chapter is a description of the complex of problems that are affecting cities on a crowded, coastal, connected planet, then what are the appropriate governance, economic, and civil society responses to these challenges? Here, to be frank, the picture is much brighter, and this is where I believe the most exciting opportunities lie, as we seek to bend the curve away from the bleak vision suggested in a straight-line projection from current data. The problems are real enough, as are the difficulties in addressing them using traditional top-down, technocratic, outsider-led, state-based frameworks. But there are other approaches. Let's consider three of these: Women of Liberia Mass Action for Peace, which ended that country's civil war; CeaseFire Chicago, which seeks to prevent violent crime in U.S. cities; and Crisis Mappers, which brings together a community of online analysts and observers to build reliable maps of conflict-or disaster-affected areas in real time.

### Women of Liberia Mass Action for Peace

In 2003, Liberia's civil war was in its fourteenth year, with two rebel groups fighting the regime of President Charles Taylor, heavy civilian casualties, and no end in sight. Taylor's National Patriotic Front, which was backed (among others) by Muammar Gaddafi in Libya, had cemented its rule over most of Liberia's population and territory, through the exact kinds of competitive control techniques we've been discussing. These ranged from terror and coercive violence against individuals and whole communities to administrative measures designed to keep communities quiet, to rigged elections in 1997. Two hundred thousand people had been killed in the conflict, with many more wounded or horribly mutilated. Rebel and government fighters had raped enormous numbers of women and forcibly recruited young boys and girls as child soldiers, porters, and sexual slaves. A tide of refugees fleeing this horror had swamped Liberia's capital, Monrovia, and large squatter camps had formed on the city's outskirts. These camps lacked food and water and were horribly overcrowded and disease-ridden, putting an already stressed and barely functioning city infrastructure under unbearable pressure.[41]

In March of that year, Leymah Gbowee, a social and trauma worker at St. Peter's Lutheran Church in Monrovia's coastal district of Sinkor, and the mother of four children, began a protest movement calling for peace in Liberia. The movement she started began organizing mass demonstrations and prayer vigils in a local fish market, and occupied a soccer field near the route used by President Taylor's motorcade on Tubman Boulevard, Sinkor's main road. Muslim women organized by Asatu Bah Kenneth joined forces with Gbowee's group, creating a multifaith women's protest movement. The movement attracted international media attention, forcing Taylor to meet with its leaders in April 2003. Taylor challenged the women (now calling their movement Women of Liberia Mass Action for Peace) to find the rebel leaders, which they did—sending a delegation to Freetown, Sierra Leone, where rebel commanders were meeting, and convincing them through a series of nonviolent protest actions to agree to peace talks. The movement maintained its occupation of the soccer field and its prayer vigil throughout this period, which saw significant violence in Monrovia's refugee camps and across Liberia.[42] Peace talks began in June 2003 in Accra, Ghana, and on August 11 these talks resulted in a comprehensive peace agreement, President Taylor's exile to Nigeria, and the entry of United Nations peacekeepers into Liberia. The women's movement, led by Gbowee, remained closely engaged during the peacekeeping operation, helped ensure the peaceful disarmament of rebel and government fighters, and worked with transitional authorities and peacekeepers to organize free elections.[43] They set up polling stations, registered voters, and scrutinized the electoral process. The poll resulted in the election of President Ellen Johnson Sirleaf on November 23, 2005, began the process of transition to democracy, and brought a sharp (though not total) reduction in violence. Leymah Gbowee and President Sirleaf were jointly awarded the 2011 Nobel Peace Prize for their work.[44]

The Liberian women's movement has been rightly praised as an example of nonviolent protest, women organizing for peace, and civil society influencing the political process through mass action. All this is true, but what's also true is that this wasn't solely a bottom-up, local movement. Local people (including women's groups) had tried to oppose violence before, but they'd been brutally crushed—in 1990, many of them were killed in the same church in Sinkor where Gbowee began her movement in 2003. This time things were different, because Gbowee's passion, courage, and insight into the hyperlocal context of the war were matched by technical and functional expertise from outsiders. Gbowee had trained as a trauma worker in a UNICEF program early in the war. At St. Peter's, she was mentored as a peace activist by Sam Gbaydee Doe, leader of West Africa Network for Peace (WANEP), a regional peace-building network founded in 1998 in Ghana that was funded by the U.S. Agency for International Development, the British Department for International Development, the British and Dutch branches of Oxfam, and the Catholic Organization for Relief and Development Aid, and which drew heavily on Internet and cellphone connectivity among activists. Thelma Ekiyor, a Nigerian lawyer specializing in alternative dispute resolution, was a particularly important mentor and sponsor of Gbowee's efforts.[45] Both Ekiyor and Doe had been formally trained in techniques of peace building, mass action, and conflict resolution when they attended Eastern Mennonite University's Center for Justice and Peacebuilding (CJP) at Harrisonburg, Virginia. Ekiyor trained and advised Gbowee, gained WANEP funding for her initiative, and mentored her as Gbowee founded the Liberian women's movement. The movement's Ghanaian and Nigerian connections may also have played a role in the peace process, with Ghana hosting the peace talks and Nigeria accepting Charles Taylor as the conflict ended.[46] The World Bank and several United Nations organizations also played roles in ending the conflict—not to mention the 15,000 soldiers and 1,115 police and civilian staff of the UN peacekeeping mission, supported by 4,350 U.S. Navy and Marine Corps personnel of

Joint Task Force Liberia, who enforced an end to hostilities and maintained peace during the transition and elections process.[47]

Does this mean that an American university is responsible for Liberia's transformation from conflict, or that U.S. and British government development agencies, international NGOs, the UN, or U.S. and West African militaries can take credit for what happened? Of course not—but Gbowee could not have done it on her own, either. The external players brought what Gbowee lacked, including training for her and her colleagues, technical knowledge, and functional skill, while she brought what they lacked, including local context, insight, and the legitimacy and grass-roots organizing ability to build a local movement and forge collaboration between Christian and Muslim communities. Most important, she also brought charismatic leadership, wisdom, will and courage. Outsiders didn't tell Gbowee to sit down and shut up, nor were they passive funders and enablers—this was a collaborative, two-way process of *co-design*.

### CeaseFire Chicago

In a completely different setting, on the other side of the world, the same year Gbowee was starting at St. Peter's Church, Dr. Gary Slutkin was launching CeaseFire, a violence prevention and crime control program based on his insight that because violence follows biological (epidemiological) patterns in a population, it can therefore treated like an epidemic and can be prevented by stopping the behavior at its source.[48]

CeaseFire trains, mentors, and puts into the field outreach workers (known as "violence interrupters") drawn directly from local communities. Their role is to detect, prevent, and mitigate conflict on the street before it leads to violence. Being drawn from the local community, interrupters are often former gang members, respected older women or men, or other influential members of local society.[49] They rely on force of personality, street cred, relationships with key players in the community, and hyperlocal understanding of the territorial logic of their own district (how things work, what drives violence, and how the neighborhood flows). They focus on detecting and intervening in acts of violence before they occur, changing the behavior of individuals who are influential in the neighborhood system of violence or who are at risk for violent behavior, and changing community norms about violence.[50] Interrupters attend a formal training program designed by Slutkin and form part of a network (both physical and online) that supports their work, helps them track progress of situations and individuals, and links them to a broader movement. After being launched in 2000 in West Garfield, then Chicago's most violent neighborhood, the program has spread throughout Chicago, and offshoots of the program are now active in Baltimore, Kansas City (Missouri), New Orleans, New York, Phoenix, and several cities in California, as well as in Britain, South Africa, and the Caribbean.[51] The program expands by proliferating small projects with a common but flexible methodology and adapting to local conditions in each new area, rather than by imposing rigid controls or attempting to create a large, monolithic, one-size-fits-all model. The movement is funded by a combination of private philanthropy and donations from local and national businesses; for a time it was also supported by government money from the city of Chicago.

Gary Slutkin grew up in Chicago, but I suspect he would be the first to admit that he's not exactly an insider in the tight-knit, violent, low-income, marginalized, and excluded communities and social networks where CeaseFire works. He's a doctor, a specialist in internal medicine and infectious disease control, and an academic—professor of epidemiology and international health at the University of Illinois at Chicago School of Public Health. He did his initial medical training in Chicago, and his internship and residency at San Francisco General Hospital, learning infectious disease control methods (and getting intimately acquainted with street crime, gang violence, and public health) in the tuberculosis program of the San Francisco Health Department. He then spent several years working in Africa for the World Health Organization, where he specialized in reversing epidemics, including tuberculosis, cholera, and AIDS, "including being principally responsible for supporting Uganda's AIDS program—the only country to have reversed its AIDS epidemic."[52]

Thus CeaseFire, like the Liberian women's peace movement, is an example of co-design. Slutkin is an outsider in the communities where his program is succeeding so well (in fact, he *is* the proverbial white guy with a clipboard, maybe even a lab coat as well). He couldn't, and doesn't, succeed by trying to go into other people's communities, telling them what their problems are, making them stand aside, and then imposing his own technocratic solutions. Clearly, though, local people weren't doing too well solving their own problems before his program arrived. What Slutkin brings to this collaborative, co-designed effort is training and mentoring, technical skill, functional (not locally specific) knowledge, a scientifically developed methodology, and a perspective on how these kinds of problems work in many different places. It's the local community that brings the insight, hyperlocal context, and spatial understanding of the systems logic and day-to-day flow of their own districts, and who ultimately hit the streets to implement the program in their own way, with support and technical assistance from Slutkin, but bringing their own insights and leadership talents to the effort. Ultimately, too, there is a police force, mostly offstage and out of mind but with the ability to bring lethal force to bear in a complex urban environment, to prevail in a close fight, and thus to enforce a normative system (in this case, that of an elected government), upholding the coercive end of the spectrum in the districts where CeaseFire works. The enlightened and informed support of police, and in some cases integration with community-oriented policing programs, is a key external enabler, framing the program's success.

## Crisis Mappers

If the Liberian women's movement and CeaseFire are examples of street-level co-design in dangerous urban areas under stress, then Crisis Mappers is the virtual, remote-observation analog to these local physical programs. Crisis Mappers—formally, the International Network of Crisis Mappers—was co-founded by Jen Ziemke and Patrick Meier in 2009, at the first International Conference on Crisis Mapping. The network describes itself as "the largest and most active international community of experts, practitioners, policymakers, technologists, researchers, journalists, scholars, hackers and skilled volunteers engaged at the intersection between humanitarian crises, technology, crowd-sourcing, and crisis mapping." Crisis mapping, in this context, means applying a huge variety of techniques—mobile and Web-based smartphone apps; participatory maps (where local communities work with a tech platform or an outside expert to record their perception of their own environment, for their own use); crowd-sourced data on events such as tsunamis, earthquakes, and conflict; aerial and satellite imagery; geospatial platforms such as

Open Street Map or Google Earth; advanced visualization tools; live simulations; and computational and statistical models—to provide early warning and to support rapid responses to complex humanitarian emergencies. It is a fundamentally multidisciplinary endeavor that combines local field insight from affected communities or researchers on the ground with remote observation, visualization, and analysis by people far from the scene of a crisis.

This is quite a mouthful, but what in means in practice is a network of about five thousand people spread across the world in more than four hundred organizations (private companies, academic institutions, and NGOs)—not to mention quite a few talented individuals in basements and coffee shops—who combine their efforts to monitor developing humanitarian crises and to produce accurate, up-to-the-minute, geospatially referenced visualizations of events on the ground as they unfold. Humanitarian NGOs, first responders, or local communities can then use these visualizations to shape their response to developing crises in real time. Partners on the ground can contribute data, validate what's being reported, and update inaccurate information in real time. Crisis mappers work, like Anonymous or Telecomix in the Arab Awakening examples we looked at in Chapter 4, as an "adhocracy": nobody gets paid, everyone contributes out of personal commitment or passion for the tech or humanitarian concern, and the ultimate outcome is the organizational manifestation of the "Web as witness" phenomenon that I described earlier—someone *is* watching, and she and five thousand others are making and updating a map in real time.

The map matters—because everything that happens, happens somewhere—and knowing where things are occurring is the first step toward understanding them and responding to them. In urban metabolism terms, mapping the flow requires an understanding of what's happening where, and you need that knowledge before you can understand why it's occurring, as we saw in the Kingston and San Pedro Sula examples. In terms of the networking between the virtual and human domains, mapping human social networks and understanding how they intersect with electronic ones is critical if you want to make them work together, as we saw in the Tunisian, Egyptian, and Libyan examples in the Arab Awakening. And in cases of major natural disaster or conflict—such as the January 2010 Haiti earthquake, the April 2011 Japanese earthquake and tsunami, or the efforts to map the flow and needs of refugees and displaced persons during the Libyan and Syrian civil wars—crisis mappers can provide essential information by ensuring that help can get to the right people quickly.

Crisis Mapping is an example of co-design in two different ways. First, it's a voluntary, ad hoc, free association of motivated individuals who get together in a self-synchronized, self-directed way and swarm onto specific projects and events that interest them. Group hackathons and crowd-sourced code are used to build open-source, open-architecture systems that anyone can use, add to, and refine. Data are shared and resources are pooled. Second, the crisis mapper in a remote location is analogous to the outsider, while local civil society organizations, individual researchers and field teams, and local communities on the ground provide the insider inputs. Without the field component, a crowd-sourced crisis map is just an unverified guess; without the crowd-sourced map, the field team can only produce unstructured data. Together, though, they represent an unparalleled solution to an incredibly difficult problem—remote mappers build the apps and create the frameworks and the initial data cut (the base map, if you like), which local teams and on-the-ground partners validate, add to, and refine. Working together, these two components can produce an incredibly detailed and workably accurate map in near-real time as a crisis unfolds.

## Co-Designing for Resilience

Together, as I mentioned, these examples are as hopeful for me as the military projection is daunting. They suggest that the same factors that make the future conflict environment so problematic—rapid urbanization, crowded spaces, the dramatic expansion of connectivity, the emergence of technically skilled and networked populations across the planet—also suggest the outlines of potential solutions. We talked earlier about resilience, about making actors in a system better able to handle and bounce back from shocks within it, rather than grasping to reclaim a mythical "stability" that was probably never there in the first place. We noted the work of Andrew Zolli and Anne Marie Healy, whose research suggests that as cities grow, even as they run into massive problems of urban overstretch, they also carry within them the adaptive resources needed to overcome these problems. We noted that the same factors that will swamp the world's poorest and least-governed cities with three billion new people in the next generation will also bring unprecedented health, education, and prosperity to many of them, unleashing enormous new human potential. Part of the key to unlocking this potential may well have something to do with the idea of co-designing for resilience.

What I mean by this should be clear from the preceding examples. The co-design approach is something we seek to use in chaotic, complex environments—particularly cities under stress—where there exist problems (often involving intense violence) that local communities have been unable to solve, and that outsiders lack the knowledge or commitment to understand. The methodology tries to avoid fetishizing external, technocratic, top-down, white-guy-with-clipboard knowledge. At the same time, it also tries to avoid the magical thinking associated with treating local people as the fount of all knowledge and insight. If locals could understand and agree on the problem, let alone fix it, there'd be no need for outside intervention. If outsiders understood and could fix the problem, their interventions wouldn't be failing so often. Both outsiders and locals need to come together, in defined spheres of expertise and in a defined process, to jointly design approaches to their problem—which, in the modern connected world, where problems in one place rapidly spread to and affect others, is a joint problem, too, not something wholly owned by a local community.

These spheres of expertise are clear. What insiders bring (what some anthropologists call the emic perspective) is insight into their own environment, an understanding of their own social and spatial system in its own terms and in their own words and images—what drives what, what matters and what doesn't, how things work, how their district flows and breathes, what has been tried before, what typically works there, what doesn't usually work there, and why. They also bring leadership, initiative, motivation, and a genuine desire to make a change, without which nothing else, however cleverly designed, can work. What outsiders bring is a technical understanding of relevant disciplines, functional skills, knowledge of what usually works and what doesn't work in other places where similar problems have occurred, a large-$n$ perspective (one that draws on a large number of examples), access to knowledge, networks, supporting data and expertise, connectivity to international public opinion, and of course access to funding and resources. They also bring humility, skepticism about the brilliance of their own insights, conscious and continuous awareness of how little they know about a local environment, and a willingness to experiment—starting small, testing hypotheses, and figuring out what works by trying things out.

There's a third sphere of expertise, one that we can be clear-eyed about, whether we like it or not—the security sphere, the category of action that's ultimately founded on coercion. For insiders and outsiders to sit down together and jointly work on problems, or for different groups of insiders to come together, build consensus, and figure out a way forward, there has to be a modicum of security, safety, and predictability. Someone has to guarantee that predictability, and whoever that is, they have to be able to prevail in a close fight if necessary. We're talking about a normative system here: creating rules of acceptable behavior that give people predictability and allow them the feeling of safety that makes everything else possible. Who it is that provides that security depends on the situation. Better an insider than an outside intervener, obviously, for all the reasons discussed in the last few chapters. Better a civil society organization than an external police force, and better a police force than the military. Far better a local military than an intervening one, and so on. But ultimately, *someone* has to set conditions for the meeting of minds, or nothing can happen. The paradox is that although there are no purely military solutions, there are also no solutions without the ultimate sanction of coercion to enforce the order that makes joint action possible.

This is all starting to sound very theoretical and philosophical, but in practical terms it's actually pretty straightforward. First, create a secure enough environment with enough predictability and sense of safety that locals can get together and begin to work towards a consensus on the nature of their problems. Then, provided locals have the necessary leadership and desire, bring in an external team—the smaller and less intrusive the better—with specific functional and technical knowledge relevant to the problem. The external team has to explicitly acknowledge that it has no right to tell the locals what to do, no privileged knowledge about their circumstances, and no legitimate opinion about what they should or must do. But it shares what it knows, provides data and expertise that fill the gaps in locals' knowledge, builds the maps and visualizations that help locals understand the whole of the system they inhabit (not just their own little bit), and acts as a research and support team as the locals decide what to do next—if anything—about their problem. Then the external team takes a backseat, except perhaps if asked to facilitate, answer specific research questions, or help mediate disputes. The locals, armed with the knowledge of what has worked elsewhere, and secure in the protective bubble provided by a security system that gives them safety and predictability, take what they want from the outside perspective, discard what they don't need, build on it, change it as they see fit, and come out at the end (perhaps) with new ideas and an agreed way forward. If appropriate, they pitch their idea to their own communities, without the outsiders in the room. And then . . . well, it's their city, it's their problem set, and they handle it.

What I've described isn't theory. It's what our teams do, all over the world, in conflicts and crises in half a dozen different cities. They focus on resilience rather than stability, on enhancing connectivity and building predictability, on helping local communities figure things out themselves. Is it perfect? Absolutely not: it doesn't always work, it depends utterly on local commitment and talent, and it's imperfect, like any other approach. But when it fails, it fails quickly and cheaply, it doesn't involve turning someone else's society upside down because of things that seemed to us like a good idea at the time, and it doesn't invoke Colin Powell's "Pottery Barn rule" of international intervention: "if you break it, you own it." Most important, the co-design methodology isn't an answer to a problem: it's just a set of ways to think toward solutions. Can it work in a high-threat, chaotic, urban conflict environment? Absolutely—and, in fact, when I think back to times when what we've done *has* worked in conflict zones, including in very high-threat counterinsurgency environments such as Baghdad, it's always been because of something akin to this approach. Locals bring the leadership and the insight that outsiders lack, outsiders bring the technical support that fills the locals' gaps, and someone (the less coercively, the better, but nonetheless)—someone provides the security that lets the whole thing work.

Given the dense, urban, coastal, networked environment where populations will live, and where governments, businesses, communities, and military and police forces will operate in the future, we're really going to need these kinds of participatory design-based approaches to solving strategic problems. That is, external interveners in these environments—whether "external" in the sense that they're foreign governments, or merely in the sense that they come from a different part of town or are members of a different community—need to begin with a conscious acceptance of their own ignorance about the environment. Outsiders need to accept that, initially at least, they don't understand exactly what is going on, and therefore they have few useful insights about what needs to be done.

To me, the co-design approach that I've outlined here makes vastly more sense than trying to bring in state-based, government-driven solutions to every problem—to govern every piece of ungoverned space on the planet, or to turn every society into a mirror of our own. Quite apart from being authoritarian and coercive, that kind of unilateralism is just too expensive, time-consuming, and difficult to be achievable. Even if it did work, this sort of approach would be problematic—it would turn Western governments, in particular, into a global version of Baron Haussmann—but the fact is that it doesn't work anyway: we simply don't have the money, the persistence, or the military will to make it happen.

The alternative, the kind of co-design approach I've described here, involves local people directly and intimately in a participative way, designing solutions to their own problems, but not left to sink or swim on their own. It looks for ways to combine local insights with outside expertise, and recognizes that neither outsiders nor locals alone can solve (or even understand) many of these problems.

In the crowded, complex, connected urban environment of the future, instead of what James C. Scott has called the "high modernist" absolutism of centralized planning or the unilateral and ill-informed prescriptions of outside designers or (worse) outside military interveners, there's a clear need to apply collaborative methods: approaches that seek the hypercontextualized insight only locals can bring, yet also draw on outsider knowledge from fields such as urban planning, geosocial information systems, user experience design, big-data analysis, and industrial systems design. These methods can help us treat the coastal city as a system and allow people to look for intervention or impact points to move that system in a positive, more resilient direction. The same sensing methods can also stimulate, illuminate, reveal, and map the "dark networks" that nest within the dense human and political thickets of the urban environment, and can provide the international monitor, the "Web as witness," that gives people an essential sense of security.

## IV. Conclusions

We've covered an enormous amount of ground here, not all of it bad, but much of it complex and confronting. This isn't the place to summarize what I've written, since you can always turn back and look at each section or chapter for relevant insights. But I do want to make three very brief, concluding points.

First, none of what I've written about in describing the future environment is a prediction. This is not how the future world will be or has to be. There will be unexpected shocks, black swans, and events (both good and bad) that will change this projection. And that's all it is: just a straight-line projection of current trends, based on data currently available, that suggest where conflict on the planet may be heading, given its current course. This projection suggests a high degree of continuity in the things that militaries, aid agencies, diplomatic services, city governments, and other organizations in this space will be expected to do. But it also suggests a very sharp discontinuity in the environment, which will be increasingly, and intensively, urban, coastal, crowded, and connected. Because we have the data, because we can see the projection, we can change the outcome—we can bend the curve, ideally in the direction of greater resilience, unlocking the adaptive resources that are already present in the cities under stress that we have discussed here. But if we can't prevent violence—and history suggests that, at least some of the time, we won't be able to—then we need to be ready to prevail in the complex, messy, lethal business of irregular warfare in urban, networked littorals: not as an end in itself, but as a means to create the predictability and order, the feeling of safety, that can allow collaborative problem solving to have some chance of success.

The second concluding insight, and forgive me for sounding a little Zen here, is that the project isn't the project. The *community* is the project. In David Lean's classic 1957 movie *The Bridge on the River Kwai*, a demoralized unit of British prisoners is building a bridge over a river in Thailand, part of a strategic Japanese railroad. They're laboring, under atrocious conditions, beneath the murderous tyranny of the prisoner-of-war camp commandant, Colonel Saito. Saito and the British battalion commander, Colonel Nicholson (played, in his greatest-ever role, by Alec Guinness), engage in a near-fatal struggle for control over working conditions. Having won the struggle against authority and—in essence—regained command of his men, Nicholson then proceeds to design a new and better bridge, moves the site to a more suitable spot, reorganizes the labor shifts to make the work more efficient, and begins demanding hard work and dedication from the men. He has essentially taken over the project. The medical officer, Major Clifton, puzzled that Nicholson, who so nearly died resisting Saito, is now working the battalion so hard in order to help Saito achieve his mission, confronts him. I paraphrase, but in essence Clifton says, "What the hell is going on? What we're doing is helping the Japanese. Why are you working the men so hard, doing such a good job, on a project that's only helping the enemy?" Nicholson replies, and again I paraphrase: "You don't get it: the project isn't the bridge, the project is the *battalion*. The men are demoralized, prisoners, without hope, without morale. The bridge is just a means to an end: we're using the bridge to rebuild the battalion. If we didn't have the bridge to hand, we'd have to make up some other project—but we're using what we have, as a way to recover the cohesion and morale that we'd lost."

Now, life is not a Hollywood movie, nor yet the excellent French novel by Pierre Boulle on which David Lean's movie is based. But in this one respect, I do believe that life imitates art. In societies under stress, where basic systems have broken down and the very social compact that binds people together is under strain, the project we need to undertake is not the bridge—or the road, or the banking system, or the sanitation system, or whatever. The project is the community. The specifics of projects that people undertake in the chaotic coastal slums we've been discussing are actually less important than the community cohesion, sense of solidarity, and common purpose that those projects generate. These are not side effects of a successful project—they *are* the project.

The war in Afghanistan is not yet over, and even when Western troops leave, it won't truly end: we will need to remain engaged, not least because we have friends there who have committed to us, and vice versa. But as we turn our attention back to the world after Afghanistan and Iraq, and as the dust of the last decade settles, we need to remember what we were doing before 9/11. At that time, a whole community of people was thinking hard and writing extensively about the civil and military problems of conflict in urbanized, complex, heavily populated littorals. The military dropped out of this conversation sometime after 2003, when the wars in Afghanistan and Iraq really kicked off. For a decade since then, the discussion has gone on without much input from those who have been fighting the war. Companies like IBM, Google and McKinsey, several universities, and a number of think tanks have thought through most of the problems of urban growth, littoralization, and connectivity—but often without enough well-informed thought on the implications for conflict, or a systems perspective on how that conflict will affect, and in turn be affected by, the emerging environment of coastal megacities.

It's time for the generation who fought the war to take what they learned in the hills and valleys of a landlocked conflict, and apply it to a challenging new environment; it's time to think about the implications of the coming age of urban, networked, guerrilla war in the mega-slums and megacities of a coastal planet. It's time to drag ourselves—body and mind—out of the mountains.

# Appendix

## On War in the Urban, Networked Littoral

I'VE SAVED MUCH OF the most specific and technical discussion about future war for this appendix, which talks about how military organizations might find themselves getting sucked into conflict in urban, networked littoral areas, what things may be like when they do, and how they'll need to organize, equip, and operate so as to prevail there. These ideas aren't just relevant to military leaders and planners, though—as previous chapters have shown, this sort of thing is unfortunately going to be everyone's business, in one way or another.

As we think about war in the urban, networked littoral, it's essential to first recognize the rather obvious point that many future problems will have no purely military solutions. Rapid unplanned urbanization, lack of governance capacity, limited economic opportunity, youth unemployment, or shortages of energy, water, and sanitation—all of which, as we've seen, can be city-killers—can't be fixed simply by the judicious application of some magic formula of kinetic force. Armies, in particular, have a tendency to destroy cities, as we saw in Chapter 2, and bringing large numbers of troops or police into places like Tivoli Gardens or La Rocinha may just give people more opportunities to be shaken down and intimidated. Many threats in future cities will be what have been called "threats without enemies"—there'll be nobody to fight, nothing to kill.

But that doesn't mean armed forces (and, by extension, armed law enforcement, including constabulary, gendarmerie, border security, and coast guard organizations) don't have a critical role. On the contrary: as our discussion of competitive control theory showed in Chapter 3, the ability to prevail at the coercive end of the spectrum is the foundation for everything else, since without that ability, administrative and persuasive efforts (however excellent) are moot. To paraphrase the Vietnam War adviser John Paul Vann, security might only be 10 percent of the problem, or it might be 90 percent, but whichever it is, it's the *first* 10 percent, or the *first* 90 percent. If you fail to create a basic minimum level of security and predictability for ordinary people on the street, it doesn't matter what else you try to do, because none of it is ever likely to happen.[1] Likewise, unless you can control surface problems of violent conflict, it's impossible (or at least dramatically more difficult) to get to the underlying issues that need to be addressed in order to build a city's resilience.

And because, as we've seen, cities disaggregate combat—reducing even large battles to a series of small, fleeting, short-range engagements—dominating the coercive end of the spectrum implies the ability to prevail in *close combat*. (Close combat—sometimes called close-quarter battle—can occur on land, at sea, or in the air, and involves two-way fights that happen well within maximum visual or sensor distance. If you can shoot farther than you can see, and someone's shooting back, you're in a close-combat situation.) Another way of putting it is that to do anything in a contested, urbanized environment, you must first establish *persistent presence*, and to establish that presence you have to prevail (or deter, by proving you *can* prevail) in a fight. That fight, by definition, will be a close fight because of the way cities create close-range, distributed, fleeting engagements. Before we break this idea down in more detail, it's worth explaining how the military might—despite everyone's best intentions—be dragged into this kind of combat.

### Getting Drawn In

It's tempting to focus on *conflict prevention* to the exclusion of conflict as such. We like to think of ways to prevent problems, to stop tensions from spiraling into open conflict or to defuse limited conflicts before they escalate into larger ones. Military officers, in particular (probably because they know exactly how ugly war can be), have a strong tendency to prefer prevention. Prevention is important and valuable: military planners, diplomats, and peace workers have produced excellent programs in this field in recent years, covering issues including border security, rule of law, security sector reform, law enforcement assistance, dispute resolution and mediation, and human rights advocacy. All Western countries and many international institutions engage in these efforts, which deserve continued support from policy makers and the public. Prevention is far better than cure, and often vastly cheaper.

But ultimately, conflict prevention is like fire prevention. Preventing fires is important, and any city government would be insane not to focus a lot of attention on hazard reduction and risk mitigation. But we pay firefighters to *fight* fires. Fire departments have valuable roles in prevention, but their core business isn't prevention, it's response: fighting fires when they break out, putting them out as quickly and safely as possible, stopping them from spreading. Likewise, we pay militaries to fight when prevention fails, and to win when they fight. Armed forces have valuable preventive and deterrent roles, but their core business is war. Thus, the rest of society expects the military to think carefully about how to fight—even, or perhaps especially, in the most extreme and awful circumstances—and for this reason it's not acceptable to just look at the complex future environment and mutter, "Well, conflict in coastal cities is messy and complex, so our plan is to avoid it."

Unfortunately, for too long that *was* the preferred response—ground forces planned to bypass cities, navies focused on blue-water operations against peer adversaries, air forces liked to think about strategic air interdiction (although air planners such as John Warden did develop a systems modeling approach for cities), and amphibious operations revolved around bypassing strongpoints and going where the enemy wasn't. That won't be an option in the future, when the coastal zone of an entire continent may be one giant megaslum, when most of the world's population will be concentrated in coastal cities, and when the enemy will be wherever we go, in part because it will be our very presence that turns some locals into enemies. We need to be thinking hard and unsentimentally about what to do when we find ourselves in an urban, networked, littoral conflict.

There are literally dozens of ways in which militaries might get pulled into conflicts like this, but here are just a few scenarios to consider. First, armed forces may find themselves in humanitarian assistance, disaster relief, or noncombatant evacuation operations (pulling civilians out of conflict or disaster zones) that escalate into conflict. Think of the work of the United States, Australian, and allied forces, with thousands of troops and dozens of aircraft and ships (including the aircraft carrier USS *Abraham Lincoln*) providing water, electricity, medicine, and food to coastal cities damaged in the 2004 Indian Ocean tsunami, working closely with civilian aid agencies and NGOs, and remaining in place for months to help societies rebuild. Ships remained alongside for lengthy periods, providing electricity and water to stricken towns, and ships (including the hospital ship USNS *Mercy*) provided emergency medical care.[2] In some places—Sri Lanka, for example, and Aceh—this brought Western forces into preexisting conflicts, where local governments were fighting globally networked insurgencies. No major conflict erupted between interveners and local militants in this case, but it's easy to see how such humanitarian missions might escalate into combat. That's exactly what happened in Mogadishu in 1993, for example. Humanitarian assistance in conflict zones is never neutral: in helping one group, we always hurt another, and this can lead to violence—as in the Afghan ambush I described in the introduction. Likewise, pulling civilians out of combat zones (as the U.S. Navy did in 2006, evacuating almost fifteen thousand Americans from Lebanon during the Israel-Hezbollah conflict discussed in Chapter 3) brings Western forces into ambiguous conflict environments where mistakes can escalate quickly into lethal combat.[3]

A second scenario can arise when governments are giving long-term assistance (sending military advisors, special operations forces, law enforcement support, or civilian development aid) to cities that are experiencing conflict. There are many examples of foreign advisors being kidnapped, held for ransom, or used as bargaining chips in local conflicts, and of special operations forces having to go in and rescue them. In remote, rural settings, these operations are dicey enough, but in crowded urban environments there's immense potential for things to go wrong, creating noncombatant casualties that provoke further conflict, or resulting in a rescue force getting pinned down or captured, prompting another, larger rescue, and thus creating an escalating spiral of conflict.[4]

A third scenario is peacekeeping or peace enforcement. As urbanization continues, and the populations of developing countries continue to concentrate in coastal cities, any kind of population-centric operation—including peacekeeping, peace enforcement, and mass atrocity response—is by definition going to be urban and coastal, too. Even where policy makers' intent is to resolve a conflict, monitor a truce, or police a cease-fire, putting peacekeepers into an urban conflict zone amounts to laying out an attractive array of targets for terrorist groups, local insurgents, street gangs, organized crime, or just commercial kidnapping networks, and this can force peacekeepers into combat at short notice. In fact, the very idea of peacekeeping becomes problematic when there's no structured peace to keep, no stable peacetime environment to return to, and no consistent set of actors to work with—meaning that peacekeeping probably needs a rethink for the future conflict environment. Likewise, military forces may find themselves dragged into messy urban conflicts after state collapse or civil war, as the international community intervenes to prevent loss of life or ensure a particular outcome (as we saw in Libya in Chapter 4).

Of course, armed forces may find themselves in urban littoral conflicts in conventional state-on-state war, too. As discussed in detail in Chapter 2, just because a conflict starts out conventional doesn't mean it will stay that way (think Iraq), and several scenarios—including the more or less hypothetical cases of war with China, North Korea, or Iran—involve urbanized terrain, coastal cities, and constricted littoral sea space. It's unrealistic to imagine that an enemy in this scenario would stick to the open sea and air, where it will be easy for an advanced navy or air force to detect targets and apply its complete range of high-tech weapons systems. Rather, such an enemy would almost certainly try to suck opposing forces into the complex, urbanized littoral, where the presence of noncombatant civilians would impose restraints on the kinds of weapons they could use, an enemy's local knowledge would become a key advantage, and a cluttered littoral environment would allow enemy forces to hide and strike at will.

Finally, because of the increasingly dense networks of connectivity among cities and populations across the planet, expeditionary operations (where the military goes overseas to fight) may bring retaliatory attacks in home territory—most probably, again, in major cities—that will draw public safety organizations and military forces into lethal situations in urban areas. There have been several instances where members of immigrant communities engaged in attacks against

Western cities—either ordered or indirectly inspired by nonstate armed groups in their countries of origin.[5] Enhanced connectivity has led to the spread of networked diaspora populations and the emergence of dark networks (discussed in Chapter 2) such as the Shower Posse's transnational extortion racket. This points to an increasing threat that we might call "diaspora retaliation," where adversaries hit back at an expeditionary military through diaspora networks—striking the homeland directly as a means of influencing political leaders to call the troops off. Any country that engages in military operations in a part of the world from which it has an immigrant population now needs to take this possibility into account. At the same time, of course, democracies mustn't tar all immigrants with the same brush, or deny due process to citizens of foreign descent—and countries can leverage the talents, local knowledge, and connections of diaspora networks to help conduct more effective engagements overseas. All this will demand careful and balanced handling, and may dissuade some governments from overseas interventions altogether. But it clearly means that expeditionary operations bring with them a risk of domestic insecurity and increased threat to major cities.

## The Multidomain Challenge

Thus, there are many ways in which military and law enforcement organizations might be drawn into crowded, coastal, urbanized conflicts. What will the environment be like when they get there? Well, it will be maddeningly complex, for a start.

In 1997, the Commandant of the United States Marine Corps, General Charles C. Krulak, coined the idea of "three-block war" to describe the complexity and danger of urban asymmetric fighting, where Marines would engage simultaneously in combat, peacekeeping, and humanitarian operations, all within three city blocks.[6] As I noted in the acknowledgments at the start of this book, Krulak's notion was briefly influential in the Marines but was thrust aside by concepts such as counterinsurgency and stabilization operations as the wars in Iraq and Afghanistan escalated.[7] Three-block war has been criticized on conceptual and practical grounds by thinkers including Frank Hoffman, John Agoglia, Walter Dorn, and Michael Varey because it doesn't cover the full range of operations in complex urbanized environments or because it's ill suited to be an overarching strategy (which, as Dorn and Varey note, Krulak never intended it to be).[8] I would offer a different comment: three-block war does a great job in underlining how complex, ambiguous, and rapidly changing the urban conflict environment will be (which was clearly Krulak's intent), but it mainly covers the ground tactical domain; an urbanized, littoral conflict will be vastly more complex even than this.

In Chapter 1, I gave a general definition of a littoral zone as an area where the influences of land, sea, airspace, and cyberspace overlap. But when you start thinking about conflict in this zone in practical terms, it's clear that there are in fact nine intersecting spaces in which military maneuver needs to take place, perhaps simultaneously or in close synchronization. These include the seabed, the submarine environment, the sea surface, and naval airspace (airspace over the sea), which together make up the maritime domain; the land surface, subterranean space, and supersurface space (to include tunnel systems, canals, sewers, basements, exterior street-level surfaces, building interiors, high-rise structures, and rooftops), making up the land domain; the airspace domain; and the domain of cyberspace. All these domains are in play in a littoral operation, and not just in state-on-state conflict: nonstate armed groups have fielded weapons and forces in all nine of these spaces, too. Colombian drug cartels, for example, have used submarines and semisubmersibles for narcotics trafficking (and possibly people smuggling); the Tamil Tigers built a fleet of small, fast attack boats; several insurgent groups have created air capabilities including drones and remote-controlled aircraft; terrorists employed vessel-borne bombs against the USS *Cole* in 2000 and the MV *Limburg* in 2002; and subterranean operations have long been common in urban fighting. Likewise, in Chapter 2 we noted that Lashkar-e-Taiba's raid on Mumbai was only one of several sea-based raids of this kind, and by no means the first.

The intersection of these nine spaces—each with complex problems in its own right—poses intricate coordination challenges and creates an enormously cluttered environment that hampers intelligence, surveillance, and reconnaissance. This exponentially increases the difficulty for commanders in understanding and maneuvering through littoral zones. It also makes it harder to integrate the effects of the remote warfare capabilities discussed in Chapter 4 (such as drones, cyberwarfare, or special operations) that are virtually, rather than physically, in theater. When we consider the different, often conflicting legal authorities that apply to civilian populations and combatants, to traffic within and outside territorial seas and airspace, and to military, law enforcement, emergency management, customs, and border security agencies, the challenges are even more complex.

Second, the littoral battlespace will be extremely heavily populated. This is obvious enough in the land domain, with civilians living (in their millions) in megaslums or large cities. But it's also true of seaspace and airspace. I frequently hear army officers (and sometimes marines) comment that since people live on land, the land domain is populated, while the maritime and airspace domains are not. That's true in one sense—obviously enough, *Homo sapiens* is a terrestrial mammal, so if you want to decisively defeat a human enemy or control a population, you need to engage people where they live, on land. But if you look at the stunning satellite images of global air, land, and sea traffic patterns produced by Felix Pharand-Deschenes for the Cartography of the Anthropocene project, it's clear that air and sea space—with thousands of coastal ships and small boats, hundreds of aircraft, and permanent installations such as offshore terminals and oil rigs—is densely inhabited.[9]

This imposes severe constraints on targeting, the use of weapons systems as well as radar and sonar, and rules for stop-and-search. It also makes fast littoral maneuver extremely difficult. The Sri Lankan navy, for example, during the Tamil insurgency, found itself in a densely populated coastal environment. Dozens of small, fast, heavily armed Sea Tiger raiding craft were able to hide among the thousands of fishing boats, cargo vessels, and passenger ferries operating along Sri Lanka's coastline.[10] This allowed the Tigers to move people, weapons, and supplies from point to point along the coast, extract forces from encirclement, insert raiders to strike population centers at will, run smuggling operations, and position mother ships far out at sea as mobile bases. It proved extremely difficult to defend large warships against small, fast-moving vessels that could dart in and out of coastal coves and inlets, hide in civilian traffic, and approach within striking distance without detection.[11] In order to defeat this threat, ultimately the Sri Lankan navy had to develop innovative new tactics, deploy a swarm of small craft of its own (the 4th Fast Attack Flotilla), acquire a new radar system to distinguish Tiger vessels from fishing boats by their speed and acceleration, and target the Sea Tigers' mother ships.[12]

This need to operate in heavily trafficked coastal waterways isn't unique to counterinsurgencies. For example, as land routes from Mexico into the United States have become harder to use over the past several years, smugglers have begun to bypass the land border, using small boats to smuggle people and drugs into California. This has required greater U.S. Coast Guard activity, as well as riverine and harbor security operations in large coastal cities such as San Diego.[13] Police forces in Los Angeles County and even farther north have had to account for this littoral threat.[14] Likewise, in 2011, Brazilian police were forced to form a new antipiracy task group, to operate on the Amazon basin in Brazil's northern Pará province. The task group is a rapid-response force that includes fifty police officers and eight armed vessels, aimed at a growing pattern of piracy in inland waterways.[15] While Pará is primarily rural, attacks have occurred in urban canals and harbors, including the port of Manaus, capital of Amazonas province—a city of almost two million that lies several hundred miles inland on the Amazon, the world's largest hydrographic basin.[16] Similar police and coast guard forces have been created in cities around the world, reflecting another aspect of the environment: the urban riverine.

Most coastal cities include inland waterways—rivers, canals, and inlets, as well as harbors, offshore terminals, and docks. This overlap between sea and land environments means that riverine capabilities—such as U.S. Special Operations Command's special boat teams (SBTs), and naval special warfare capabilities in general—are vital for expeditionary forces that need to maintain themselves in a littoral city for any length of time. SBTs represent the high end of the spectrum, with their ability to quickly deploy swarms of small, armored, shallow-draft, extremely heavily armed attack craft known as special operations craft–riverine (SOC-R). These are fast, quiet, highly maneuverable mini-gunboats that can move at up to forty knots in as little as twenty-six inches of water and can be carried and air-dropped by C-130 cargo aircraft, to be inserted anywhere in the world at short notice. This gives SBTs an ability to insert and extract teams, provide supporting fire, gather intelligence, act as a command and communications platform, evacuate wounded, bring in supplies, and move forces along shallow, restricted waterways.[17] All these capabilities are needed in urban riverine environments, where buildings typically come right to the water's edge (giving adversaries hard cover and letting them overlook waterways from concealed and elevated firing positions) and where small boats and other river traffic pose constant hazards. SOC-Rs and their special warfare combatant–craft crewmen (SWCCs) saw considerable urban combat in Iraq, including on the Tigris and Euphrates Rivers in and around Baghdad and in Basra.[18] SEALs and SWCCs worked closely together, often with helicopters and drones in support, and sometimes with combat swimmers and mini-submersibles (known as SEAL delivery vehicles), creating a highly effective but small and agile integrated sea-air-ground team.[19]

Many military forces have realized that to operate in an urban littoral they'll need similar capabilities. In Basra, British Special Boat Service (SBS) teams and members of 539 Assault Squadron Royal Marines operated rigid-hulled inflatable boats (some of which were armored) in urban canals and harbors, getting into many close-combat fights in the city's inland waterways.[20] The SBS also operates SEAL delivery vehicles, and U.S. Marines (who also maintain a special operations riverine capability) formed a special task force that operated riverine assault craft in engagements on Iraq's inland lakes and rivers. Across the world, in Scandinavia's heavily indented coastline, Swedish coastal forces have long operated armored fast combat craft known as CB-90s, which can maneuver in restricted fjords and around coastal islands and ports; provide suppressive fire, surveillance, and radio communications; and insert or extract up to twenty-one fully armed infantry.[21] Several countries (including Malaysia, Mexico, Brazil, Greece, Norway, Germany, and the United States) have acquired CB-90s for coastal operations, including constabulary and law enforcement. Many of these countries field CB-90s in urban canals and harbors.

Harbors point to another major challenge in the urban littoral: the risk posed by industrial zones that contain hazardous materials or destructive forces. These include chemical plants, power stations (sometimes nuclear), petroleum refineries, fuel storage areas, and bulk loading terminals. Hazards can occur accidentally—before or during a conflict—or be deliberately triggered by an adversary. The most notorious example of this kind of accidental hazard, and the worst industrial disaster in history, was the December 1984 Bhopal disaster, in which a pesticide factory in the city of Bhopal, capital of India's Madhya Pradesh province, released thirty-two metric tons of toxic gas into urban shantytowns and slums, killing more than fifteen thousand people and leaving half a million with long-term health problems.[22] Emergency services were overwhelmed, and public safety across Madhya Pradesh was compromised, with refugee flows disrupting neighboring towns. Public unrest due to dissatisfaction with the government's response prompted a security crackdown that triggered further violence.[23] Almost thirty years later, the cause of the disaster has still not been fully settled—an investigation sponsored by the plant owner, Union Carbide, concluded that a disgruntled worker could have sabotaged a pesticide storage tank, while another theory is that poor maintenance procedures by a cleaning crew led to the release.[24]

Whatever the cause, it's clear that this kind of disaster can both trigger military involvement (in a cleanup, humanitarian response, or security operation in the aftermath of an incident), and dramatically exacerbate the difficulty of such an intervention. It can also occur during an ongoing military operation, after a force is already in place, putting both local civilians and intervening military personnel in grave danger. In a harbor city, there are also risks from seaborne cargo (ships carrying explosives, fuel, or other dangerous goods) that can cause immense damage not only to ports but also to the wider city—as in the devastating 1917 Halifax explosion or the 1947 Texas City disaster, each of which involved cargo explosions on ships in harbors that killed thousands of people and devastated enormous urban areas.[25] These accidents occurred outside combat zones; the risk may be even worse in a conflict, in cities experiencing crises that prevent industrial workers from conducting maintenance or attending to safety issues, or simply in places that lack appropriate infrastructure. This means that armed forces in the urbanized littoral will need to be able to protect and decontaminate themselves, help the public, manage mass population movement and possible panic, and continue operations under conditions of chemical, biological, radiological, or nuclear contamination, even if there's no clear enemy present or the only likely adversary is a nonstate armed group.

Indeed, in this environment, nonstate armed groups will be both the most likely enemies and the most likely allies for an intervening force. The enemy part is obvious, the alliance aspect perhaps less so. As discussed in Chapter 3, competitive control isn't a one-way process in which armed actors dominate a passive, supine population—on the contrary, unarmed populations intensively manipulate the armed groups in their midst. Intervening forces in chaotic environments quickly receive offers of help from a variety of local people, who offer logistical support, suggest themselves as guides or auxiliaries, or offer to organize the population. This is even more common in urban areas, with educated populations, than in rural settings. Of course, local alliances aren't necessarily bad, but they do impose an obligation to be wary of being manipulated or used to settle local scores, and to carefully vet potential allies. Any outside intervener who takes on a local partner becomes tainted by that partner's baggage—local feuds going back over generations, things that happened in the immediate run-up to intervention, or family affiliations all now attach, inadvertently and perhaps unconsciously, to the outside actor. In every operation of this kind in which I've been involved, we've always developed relationships early on that we regretted later, once we came to understand local players' backgrounds. The entire Human Terrain System was established to address this problem in Iraq and Afghanistan, but in each case we'd already allied ourselves with local actors with negative baggage, or summarily rejected offers of help from others (such as the Iraqi tribal sheikhs who offered to work with the coalition in 2003) who later proved crucial to our efforts.

This suggests that *pre-conflict sensing*—trying to understand as much as possible about a given environment before it gets into crisis, so that we know the relationships among different actors in the society, understand the extent of different groups' territorial control or popular support, and can track flows and patterns in cities and towns that explain their systems logic—will be critically important. Hyperlocal context, the sort of open-source (but denied-area) information that relies on insider insights, will be essential here, and this information will need to be time-stamped and geospatially located in order to make sense. It will be too late to surge knowledge and understanding, or the trust that comes from it, once a crisis is already under way. In a connected world, this kind of pre-conflict sensing need not involve anything intrusive or underhand—no nefarious sneaking around or spying—since most of what we need to know is open-source information, is already being gathered and published by local people and civil society organizations, or is well known to diasporas in our own countries. Triangulating among various groups' perceptions and gathering on-the-ground information to correlate with and corroborate remote sensing data will still be a requirement, but this is vastly easier today than at any time in the past.

When nonstate armed groups in urban areas do become our enemies, we can expect to see the same kinds of swarm tactics discussed in Chapter 2, as well as the networked collaboration between online and street-level groups examined in Chapter 4. We will encounter small, lightly equipped, fast-moving groups of adversaries who can operate on water, on land and possibly in the air, can move through the city by "infesting" it (as discussed in Chapter 2), and can synchronize actions across multiple groups and wide areas using cellphones, text messages, Twitter feeds, and visual signals. They will engage superior forces using hit-and-run tactics, will hide in the complex physical terrain of a city, will target the population rather than security forces, and will exploit complex human and informational terrain to avoid getting pinned down in a straight fight that they might lose. Thus, one of the main frustrations of operating in this environment will be the fleeting and distributed nature of combat engagements, where the enemy is rarely if ever seen, fights can be over in seconds, and you always seem to get to the scene of an incident just a little too late. In Krulak's terms, this will be three-block war, but on one block.

How, then, will military forces need to organize and operate for this environment? In the first instance, they'll need to get there.

### Getting Ashore . . .

Getting into the littoral zone will involve amphibious operations, but these probably won't look much like *Saving Private Ryan*, with massed naval gunfire stonking a heavily defended beach, and troops wading ashore from flat-bottomed boats, under intense fire from dug-in positions protected by obstacles underwater and on the shore. This may be a depiction of amphibious assault in conventional war, but there are many types of amphibious operations—including amphibious raids, demonstrations and withdrawals, and amphibious support to other operations.[26] And, as we saw in Chapter 4, naval forces can help ground troops maneuver along coastlines (using the sea as a maneuver space, embarking them to avoid encirclement, and reinserting them to outflank an adversary), while ground forces can land to protect the flanks of a naval force operating in a constricted coastal waterway.

The last large-scale opposed amphibious assault in which U.S. forces were engaged was sixty-three years ago, during the Korean War, at the battle of Incheon in September 1950, mentioned briefly in Chapter 1. Incheon involved an opposed landing in urban terrain, followed by extremely slow and heavy house-to-house fighting, as U.S. forces advanced from the port of Incheon into the contiguous city of Seoul, which had a population of roughly one million at that time (its population today is almost ten million). The city had been depopulated and damaged during its capture by North Korean forces that July, but still represented a tough challenge. The operation entailed a difficult approach through constricted coastal channels, with little sea room, an enormous tidal range, and no opportunity for ships to maneuver. Underwater obstacles and defended islands hampered the attack. The landing force had to assault into an urban harbor, landing across seawalls and docks. Once the port was secured there was an urgent need to put it back into service so that other forces could be brought ashore to advance into Seoul. General Douglas MacArthur's bold move to cut off North Korean forces by landing at Incheon is widely regarded as a strategic masterstroke, but as Russell Stolfi has argued, it was "followed by a ground advance to Seoul so tentative that it largely negated the successful landing."[27] The urbanized littoral terrain undoubtedly contributed to the slowness of this advance: the Marines secured Incheon in only twelve hours, but it took another twelve days to secure Seoul.

The most recent world (as distinct from U.S.-only) example of an opposed amphibious assault was in 2003, when British forces seized the Faw Peninsula in southern Iraq. The aim was to capture Iraq's oil infrastructure intact and protect the landward flank of a naval task group that was clearing sea mines in the Khawr Abd Allah waterway. This was an essential part of the coalition effort to open the estuarine approach to Umm Qasr, Iraq's only deepwater port. It was a joint (sea-air-land) operation involving 3 Commando Brigade, 40 and 42 Commando groups, helicopters, artillery, engineers, and the U.S. 15th Marine Expeditionary Unit (MEU), supported by U.S. Air Force bombers and AC-130 Specter gunships, U.S. Navy F/A-18 fighters, and naval gunfire support from one Australian and three British warships.[28]

Unlike Incheon (but in common with most amphibious operations since the mid-1950s), this operation relied on air strikes and helicopters rather than battleships and surface landing craft. On the night of March 20, 2003, an assault force in helicopters launched from amphibious ships at sea after a short but intense air bombardment by land-based and carrier-based aircraft. Royal Marines from 40 Commando (a battalion-sized unit) air-assaulted directly onto their objectives just after 10:00 p.m. and seized oil infrastructure on the eastern side of the Khawr Abd Allah waterway. They bypassed the beach entirely. Simultaneously, U.S. Navy SEALs captured the Mina al-Bakr offshore oil terminal, and Polish GROM special forces captured the Khawr al-Amaya terminal (both of these were offshore oil platforms in the Faw Peninsula area). One hour later, the Royal Marines' 42 Commando, supported by Cobra attack helicopters, ground-based artillery, and naval gunfire support, tried to land just north of the town of Al Faw but had to abort due to bad weather and an aircraft crash. They completed their assault landing in a different location the next morning. At the same time, on the western side of the waterway, 15th MEU left its staging area in Kuwait, crossed the land border into Iraq, bypassed the city of Umm Qasr, seized the port area intact, and then drove northward up the western coastline of Khawr Abd Allah. The Marines met heavy resistance from Iraqi irregular fighters in the urbanized terrain along the coastline, but soon reached their objectives.

Meanwhile, combat engineers and mine clearance divers, inserted by hovercraft from the sea, worked frantically to clear a beach wide enough to land British Army light armored vehicles, but they had to abandon this attempt due to large-scale mining by the Iraqis. The armor had to return to Kuwait, and ended up entering Iraq by land twenty-four hours later.[29] As the British after-action review commented, the "co-operation between the Commando Groups and the MEU, the ships and helicopters from the Amphibious Task Group, the tanks and other elements of 1 (UK) Armoured Division, and the AC-130 Specter gunships and coalition Close Air Support sorties that supported the amphibious operation provided useful lessons for the all-arms approach to littoral operations."[30] Both Incheon and Al Faw, of course, also underline the incredible complexity of amphibious operations in urbanized littorals, and the difficulty of conducting a Normandy-style beach landing against a prepared enemy.

This type of operation will almost certainly happen again (and it would be extremely unwise to rule it out in conventional state-on-state operations), but a more likely scenario in the irregular operations that are the historical norm is that an advance force might have to seize a port, harbor, or airfield as a sea or air point of entry for follow-on forces, perhaps against light irregular opposition, then put it back into service as a base of operations. In fact, seizing a lodgment area large enough to cover both a seaport and an airfield will probably be a prerequisite for virtually any long-term operation in a littoral environment. As in the Faw Peninsula, this may involve a combination of helicopter-borne or air-landed forces as well as amphibious forces.

For example, on the first day (D-Day) of the Australian-led intervention in East Timor in September 1999, my company's parent battalion had the objective of securing Komorro airport on the edge of Timor's capital city, Dili, then immediately advancing into the city, through a densely urbanized littoral environment (parts of which happened to be on fire) to secure the harbor. We were a light infantry unit specializing in helicopter air assault, but for this operation we air-landed in C-130 transport aircraft directly onto the airstrip, then pushed out on foot and in light vehicles to seize the harbor. We had control of the port by nightfall on D-Day, allowing follow-on forces (armored vehicles) to land from the sea in navy amphibious ships that came into the harbor and docked under cover of darkness. The whole city was secured by sundown on D+1. The initial lodgment perimeter was quite large: it had a frontage of about four miles and covered the airfield, the port, and a critical road bridge over the Comoro River, which separated the two. The air assault troops had to hold the bridge for just over twenty-four hours, until armored units landing by ship were able to move inland and link up with them. Air traffic controllers, airfield operations units, and a harbor terminal operations group landed the first night and put the port and airfield back into operation as bases for further expansion of the foothold. The landing was only lightly and sporadically opposed—the enemy melted away once they realized the scale and speed of what was happening, though they returned after recovering from their initial shock. Similar initially unopposed landings occurred in the Falklands in 1982, in Somalia in 1993, and in Sierra Leone in 2000; this seems to be a fairly normal pattern in littoral operations against irregular opponents, or where (as in the Falklands) the task group achieves operational surprise by landing in an unexpected place. These kinds of joint air-land-sea insertions are known in Australian parlance as "entry from air and sea" (EAS) and in U.S. doctrine as "joint forcible entry operations." They'll probably be more common than Incheon-style surface assaults in future conflicts.[31]

As in the Faw Peninsula, modern thinking tends to focus on bypassing coastal defenses using helicopters and airborne forces. But in the cluttered and fully urbanized environment of the future, even without organized enemy defenses, finding unobstructed places to land will be highly problematic, and exits from landing areas surrounded by megaslums will be even harder to find. That said, there's little mention of urbanized littorals in amphibious doctrine as it stands today. Indeed, the words *urban* and *city* don't appear at all in the current (2009) U.S. joint publication on amphibious operations, which states that "the preferred tactic against coastal defenses is to avoid, bypass, or exploit gaps whenever possible."[32] Neither is littoral urbanization discussed in doctrine for joint forcible entry operations, published as recently as November 2012.[33] In contrast, the August 2011 version of the capstone U.S. Marine Corps doctrine, *Marine Corps Operations*, talks extensively of "complex expeditionary operations in the urban littorals" and the difficulty of moving in restricted sea-space in coastal environments, suggesting that Navy and Marine thinking is further along in this regard than joint doctrine—although even Marine doctrine doesn't engage with the challenges of dramatically enhanced connectivity that were described in Chapter 4 and will be present to an even greater degree in the urban, networked littorals of the future.[34]

The previous (2001) version of *Marine Corps Operations* also talked about littoral urbanization in detail, but subscribed to a then-current concept of coastal envelopment known as "operational maneuver from the sea" (OMFTS). Under OMFTS, Marines would launch from ships over the horizon (about twenty-five miles offshore) directly onto objectives up to two hundred miles inland, using a technique called "ship-to-objective maneuver" to bypass shore defenses, and thus avoiding the traditional pause to build up forces and supplies at a beachhead.[35] Helicopters and MV-22 Osprey tilt-rotor aircraft would move troops ashore, while surface vessels (including amphibious armored vehicles and hovercraft) might move to undefended or lightly defended points on the coast. The idea was to deploy forces through both vertical and surface means but keep the command, aviation, and logistics components afloat and well offshore, through a concept known as "sea basing."[36]

This suite of concepts was never fully implemented, in part because (as we've already seen) the wars in Afghanistan and Iraq took Marines into landlocked environments, and in part because of resource shortfalls occasioned by those wars and the subsequent recession. As a result, much of the equipment for OMFTS wasn't purchased, and capabilities that *were* acquired (such as the MV-22 Osprey) were used for quite different tasks in Iraq and Afghanistan. As these wars end, thinkers across the world are reengaging with a changed environment. In the decade since OMFTS was first proposed, it's become even clearer that rapid urbanization in the littorals, the development of advanced antiaccess/area-denial (A2AD) technologies (such as sea mines and area-denial munitions) by some adversaries, and the lack of funding for OMFTS may render the idea of bypassing urban coastal areas moot. When the entire coastal strip is one giant urbanized area—Mike Davis's "planet of slums"—there may be nowhere to bypass *to*, and thus no option but to enter the complex and dangerous environment of coastal cities.

### . . . And into the Fire

Once they've navigated the complex littoral approach, landed from air and sea, and established themselves in an urbanized area, military forces may find they've jumped out of the frying pan and into the fire. The first, most critical issue will be expeditionary logistics.

The idea behind sea basing, obviously enough, was to sustain forces ashore directly from ships at sea, rather than creating a land base (by seizing a port or bringing ships close to land to conduct logistics over the shore) in the traditional manner. The advantage of sea-based logistics was that it avoided the need to capture and hold a port, and kept vulnerable and expensive ships at sea and out of the littoral clutter. In deep water, away from coastal shipping traffic, ships would be safer from land-based attack, could stay out of the complex hydrography of the shoreline, avoid the threat of mines in shallow waters, and be better protected against submarines. The sea base would carry fifteen days' worth of combat supplies (food, fuel, ammunition, and spare parts) for a battalion-sized marine expeditionary unit on board an amphibious readiness group, which would comprise a large helicopter assault ship or similar "big-deck" amphibious ship plus several smaller landing ships.[37]

Sustainment from the sea base could be vertical (using helicopters and tilt-rotor aircraft) or surface (using landing ships and hovercraft). The preference was for vertical sustainment, of course, because surface sustainment would mean bringing hovercraft and ships close inshore on a regular basis, and might also entail holding a land-based port or dock to enable ship-to-shore transfer of supplies. (Either event, of course, would negate the advantages that led the U.S. Navy to pursue sea basing in the first place.) In practice, exclusively vertical sustainment is rarely feasible for more than the first few days of an operation: there's stiff competition for limited air and sealift, ships have trouble carrying enough fuel to operate aircraft from far offshore for long periods, and most supply vessels lack a capacity for selective offload—the entirely nontrivial ability to find and offload a particular item, perhaps deeply buried in a ship's hold or a stack of containers, without having to unpack the entire ship's cargo (a complicated activity that can't be done at sea and which would probably require a secure beachhead).[38] This suggests that sea-based logistics needs further thought (and possibly new equipment and software) if it's to work in an urbanized littoral, and that most operations in the near future will involve seizing some kind of land base, ideally including a port and an airfield, as a logistics hub.

But that will invoke another, much bigger problem: urban overstretch. Remember that the reason military forces might be going into urban littorals, in this scenario, is precisely because cities are under stress, lacking capacity, overwhelmed, and unable to meet their people's needs. So seizing a city's port and airport and drawing logistical support—water, fuel, food, labor, construction materials, and so on—from the local economy via contract (the standard method of the last two decades) is not going to work. It will just exacerbate the very problems the force is trying to fix, making the military a parasite on an already stressed urban metabolism. To avoid this, we'll need to bring all our own stuff. Self-contained expeditionary logistics is extremely expensive, but that's what may be needed—at least initially. It follows that a force may also need to assist local communities under stress (as in the 2004 tsunami example mentioned earlier). Repairing and maintaining urban infrastructure (roads, bridges, and buildings) as well as operating ports, docks, and airfields will be important needs. So will bulk water purification, energy generation, and public health support—including the ability to handle mass-casualty situations and evacuate or decontaminate people after an industrial disaster or disease outbreak. Like most aspects of logistics, all this is much easier said than done.

Lightening the logistical footprint—in particular, reducing demand for fuel, water, and electricity—will be important, to minimize the expense and danger of bringing in bulk commodities, and to extend the "dwell time" before a force is forced to either transition to standard ground lines of communication or leave an area. Solar, biofuels, and wind energy, individual recharging systems, well-drilling capabilities, and so on—a complete suite of technologies for reducing the burden that expeditionary forces place on their environment—are being examined as ways to address this issue, through programs such as the Department of Defense Operational Energy strategy and the USMC Expeditionary Energy program.[39] This isn't just a problem for forces that are actually on the coastline—Marines' experience of the difficulty and danger of supplying fuel and water to remote inland areas led to the USMC Energy Summit in 2009 and the Experimental Forward Operating Base (ExFOB) program.[40] In 2010, the U.S. defense department created the Office of the Assistant Secretary of Defense for Operational Energy Plans and Programs, under the leadership of Sharon Burke, an extremely well-regarded expert in energy and natural resource security.[41] These efforts show that the military (in the United States, at least) is recognizing the importance of expeditionary energy. Besides just focusing on reducing their own footprint, militaries may find that the ability for expeditionary forces to transfer technologies to a local community in a sustainable way, as a leave-behind capability, and to bring in technolog-ically appropriate energy systems for populations becomes important as part of an exit strategy from coastal cities under stress.

I've discussed logistics before tactics, in part because in real-world operations, logistics issues are often the most important. Moreover, as this discussion makes clear, logistical challenges in the urban littoral will be immense, and overcoming them will be a prerequisite for being in these environments at all. But assuming the military can surmount these diffi-culties, the challenge of urban close combat will be just as hard. The main issues will revolve around organization and protection.

*Organization*

The ability to quickly aggregate and disaggregate (mass and disperse) forces and fires is the critical aspect of organizing for urban combat. Like the Somali fighters described in Chapter 2, ground forces will need to move dispersed (perhaps in the same swarming style, with semiauton-omous teams moving independently along multiple pathways through an urban environment) but then fight concentrated (massing their fires, or moving rapidly to join each other, piling on to reinforce success or recover from a setback). This implies a modular structure, perhaps down to a much lower level than in the past. The U.S. Army's modular force concept, for example, considered the need to mix and match units, creating flexible organizations that can bring to bear a variety of different capabilities depending on the environment, but brought this modularity down only to the level of the brigade combat team, which remains a fixed organization.[42] Clearly, a BCT (which, depending on type, can be around four thousand people, with hundreds of vehicles) is a huge organization for urban operations, even though in practice brigades are task-organized, with battalions, companies, and sometimes platoons allocated among headquarters based on mission.

The British Royal Marines' Commando 21 structure, designed in 2000, went three levels below the brigade, organizing for modularity at the battalion, company, and troop (platoon) levels. Commando 21 is worth discussing in detail, since it was a considered response to the demands of littoral warfare at the turn of the century and was tested in battle during the 2003 Faw Peninsula operation. Commando 21 gave the Commando (a battalion-sized unit) a modular structure of six companies, each of which could be broken down and reassembled in various ways to create a flexible mix of firepower and maneuver.[43] The six companies included a command company, a logistics company, two close-combat companies, and two standoff companies. The command company had a headquarters, a reconnaissance troop (a platoon-sized unit with patrols and snipers), communications teams, an antitank guided weapon (ATGW) troop with Milan or Javelin missiles, an 81 mm mortar troop, and a heavy machine-gun troop with .50-caliber machine guns. This capable organization was intended not to fight as a single group but rather to distribute its elements among the other companies while keeping a reserve of firepower, ammunition, and personnel. Close-combat companies had three troops, each with three close-combat sections (squads) and a maneuver support section (a heavy-weapons squad).[44] Close-combat sections comprised a pair of four-man fire teams, so the basic building block of the commando group remained the team or "brick." Standoff companies had one close-combat troop (for local protection, to help carry ammunition, and as a limited assault capability), one ATGW troop with Milan missiles, and a machine gun troop with .50 caliber heavy machine guns. One of the two standoff companies was mounted in tracked Viking armored vehicles, the other in Wolf (armored) Land Rovers, later replaced by the Jackal armored all-terrain wheeled vehicle; close-combat companies moved on foot, in helicopters, or on landing craft from supporting ships.[45]

This structure (which was how 40 and 42 Commando were organized for the Faw operation) gave the Commando enormous flexibility in urbanized terrain, letting it disaggregate fires and forces down to a low level but quickly reaggregate them. It could be fought as two half battalions, by pairing each close-combat company with a standoff company and giving each a portion of command company assets. It could also be fought as four company groups, as eight half-company groups, or in troop and section groups. Thus the Commando had the ability to mass fires and fighters at decisive points; it could disperse to pass through broken terrain, and concentrate to overwhelm an enemy. The Commando 21 structure also represented a very significant increase in firepower over the previous organization, with numerous new heavy weapon systems and an extra fighting company. The structure's major weakness was its lack of protected mobility for logistics and personnel and its dependence on external airlift, sealift, and ground transport.[46] Commando 21 is still officially in force, but it was operationally short-lived: once the invasion phase ended in Iraq, the Royal Marines' next deployment was to Afghanistan, where the need to be interchangeable with army battalions in a rural, landlocked theater led Commandos to regress to their previous organization (essentially the same as a British Army light-role infantry battalion) while on counterinsurgency operations. (Indeed, Commando 21 is a microcosm of the broader pattern we've seen already: creative thinking about urbanized littorals, which flourished in several organizations at the turn of the century, was side-lined by the urgent need to fight guerrillas in the land-locked Afghan mountains after 9/11.)

That said, experiments conducted in Australia, the United States, and Great Britain in 2003–8 suggest that even the Commando 21 level of modularity may not be enough in the future: there may be a need to go down to four-person teams (even pairs, as in Mumbai) that can operate independently, group themselves around a mobility platform (in the manner of a Somali technical), and aggregate into larger units for specific tasks.[47] Each team will need a mix of weapons and communications systems so that it can control remote fires from ships, artillery, drones, or aircraft, gather surveillance data, collect and report electronic intelligence, and call for assistance as needed. These "splinter teams" will often operate within a larger organization, and also occasionally provide a framework for small interagency teams including diplomats, aid workers, police, intelligence personnel, or medical specialists. Logistically, teams will need to be self-sufficient for at least the first seventy-two hours of an operation, because it usually takes that long for the chaos of a contested air-sea entry to settle down and for regular resupply to begin. In Timor, for example, I had my first hot meal (of dehydrated combat rations) about thirty-six hours into the operation, which was a pretty typical lag time for infantry troops in the first wave. Our first resupply was on D+3, after the operation had begun to settle down; air and sea assets began to be freed up from the task of moving troops into theater and started running logistic support missions instead. The first fresh food got to us in our new operational area, out on the jungle border between East and West Timor, on D+42, six weeks into the operation. Troops who stayed in the urban area around Dili got their first fresh food on about D+14 (indicating that the logistics system was fully up and running by then).

After the initial chaos of the landing, the main challenges will be physiological and psychological. Teams may need to operate on a twenty-four-hour cycle of low- and high-tempo operations. As groups become exhausted or suffer casualties, they may be rotated through tasks to allow for rest and refit. Selected individuals (snipers, reconnaissance and surveillance specialists, or intelligence operators) may need to operate alone for extended periods. In the environments we've described, this will be both extremely wearing and potentially very dangerous. The psychological and physiological pressures of continuous operations in the urban environment—with constant sensory overload, 360-degree combat, no rear area, and operations around the clock—mean that teams are likely to run out of physiological and psychological "puff" before they run out of supplies, and there may need to be a continuous cycle of groups into and out of action (much as the Egyptian demonstrators did during the bridge battle described in Chapter 4). Several militaries are considering (or already undertaking) physiological and cognitive enhancement programs to allow sustainable high-tempo operations in this environment.[48] Some have also studied how adversaries might apply performance enhancements.[49]

Perhaps equally confronting for some armed forces will be the need to task-organize around different types of units than in the past. Infantry, cavalry, and tank battalions and brigades have traditionally formed the basis for combined-arms teams. But in the urban littoral, engineers (both combat and construction) and civil affairs battalions may be more appropriate as organizations around which to build task forces. The Israel Defense Forces already organize around armored engineer units for urban operations, and have gained experience with this in battles such as Jenin (2002), Ramallah (2002), Bint Jbeil and the Litani Offensive (2006), and Gaza (2008–9).[50] Likewise, engineer battalions formed the basis for Canadian and Australian task forces in Afghanistan, and U.S. engineer and artillery battalions formed maneuver task forces in Iraq. Civil Affairs battalions, on the other hand, are normally broken up into small teams and allocated as specialists to larger units. In the future environment, given the need to keep footprints small, restart stalled urban systems, and deal with governance and capacity problems in a high-threat environment, Civil Affairs units may find themselves acting as the parent organization for task forces. These would need to include more than just civil-military coordination, however: they would also need naval gunfire support and tactical air control elements, intelligence support teams, law enforcement support units, construction engineers, and the ability to rapidly draw on a wide variety of high-readiness individual augmentees to fill particular specialist roles. Thus an organization such as the Marine Corps Force Headquarters Group, a Marine Civil Affairs Group, a naval mobile construction battalion (Seabee) unit, or an army Civil Affairs Brigade (Airborne) might find itself forming the core of a joint interagency task force.[51] Something like this has already been tried in the Horn of Africa, where a composite Civil Affairs battalion based in Djibouti forms the main ground unit in a joint task force that operates across fifteen African countries.[52]

I mentioned police just now, and it's worth touching briefly on police-oriented programs in urban operations. As Chapter 3 made clear, there's a huge overlap between crime and war when nonstate armed groups are involved, and thus a great deal of commonality between policing and military operations. Police have learned from military population security techniques, and several police jurisdictions in urban areas within the United States are applying techniques or concepts drawn from operations overseas. Meanwhile the U.S. military has studied policing approaches, and has brought along law enforcement advisers on expeditionary operations across the world. Special operations forces and coast guards work closely with foreign police in counterterrorism missions worldwide, and deployable field police (on the model of the Australian Federal Police International Deployment Group, an innovative organization created in 2004 to support security and stability operations both domestically and overseas) or along traditional constabulary or gendarmerie lines, have worked in many war zones.[53] Likewise, the Italian Carabinieri, with long experience operating alongside military forces, sponsors the NATO Center of Excellence for Stability Policing Units at Vicenza, Italy, which trains students from police forces and constabularies of many developing nations in stability and community-oriented policing techniques, as well as in human rights and rule of law.[54]

One way in which the military could learn even more from police and emergency services, however, is in the use of jurisdictional rather than hierarchical command and control. By definition, in a disaggregated battlefield where forces operate in small teams, most firefights begin with a junior officer or NCO in charge of the team that makes initial contact with the enemy. In a hierarchical command-and-control system, this junior leader is sidelined as soon as the commander of a larger unit turns up, that commander in turn is sidelined when a higher commander arrives, and so on. Thus, if a sergeant in charge of a squad initiates a firefight, it's quite possible that within fifteen or twenty minutes he will have been superseded by a lieutenant, then a captain, then a colonel. Each of these new arrivals brings greater firepower and more troops but less situational awareness. None of them, except possibly the first, may have a clear idea of the circumstances under which the firefight began, or the locations of noncombatant civilians or key terrain. This system makes authority inversely proportional to knowledge. Meanwhile, the same enemy commander who began the firefight is still in charge (and probably scratching his head in puzzlement at his enemies' periodic loss of focus as new commanders take over), and new swarms of fighters are self-synchronizing, slotting themselves into position without orders as they arrive. Thus, the hierarchical command system imposes a significant (and entirely self-inflicted) risk of poor or slow decision making, killing innocent bystanders, or even a blue-on-blue fratricide incident, because of a lack of command continuity.

Contrast this with the jurisdictional or incident-command method used by some police and emergency services. Under this model, the commander first on the scene is designated as incident commander. As other units arrive, their commanders place themselves (regardless of rank) under control of the incident commander, who continues to run the incident until it comes to a natural break point or he hands it off—which he may do at any time by choice, or procedurally when the incident reaches a certain size and complexity. This approach preserves operational continuity and situational awareness, and it allows higher commanders to avoid getting sucked into the current fight and keep their attention on the broader battle and the next and subsequent moves. But in order to work, this approach relies on implicit trust between commanders at different levels and demands a high level of training, reliable communications systems, and a common operating picture down to the NCO level. This in turn implies that junior officers and NCOs must be correctly selected and trained—and then trusted—by more-senior commanders. Many units achieved exactly this level of trust, training, and flexibility through long operational tours in Iraq and Afghanistan over the past decade. In a coastal urban setting, the complexity of the environment will demand this level of trust and initiative right from the outset.

*Protection*

However they're organized and commanded, ground forces will have to protect themselves in heavily populated urban environments. In this context, we can think of protection in two modes: direct and indirect. Direct protection is the ability to survive a hit; indirect protection is the ability to avoid being hit in the first place. Heavy armored vehicles such as tanks rely on direct protection: they have enough armor to sit in a street, take a certain number of hits, and keep functioning without needing to leave the area in order to survive, and without having to fire back. In contrast, light armored vehicles rely on indirect protection: they need good enough surveillance and target acquisition systems to detect a threat first, mobility and speed to avoid being hit, and firepower to neutralize the threat by shooting (or launching countermeasures) before they can be hit. Dismounted light infantry and special operations forces, for their part, rely even more heavily on indirect protection—stealth, night operations, speed, deception, and cover from aircraft and artillery—in order to survive.

While indirect protection might seem smarter, in fact what's mostly needed in a populated urban environment is direct protection. The 1993 battle of Mogadishu, discussed in Chapter 2, illustrates this very clearly. Light forces (SEALs and Rangers) operating on foot or in soft-skinned vehicles, were dependent on air support in order to remain mobile, suppress threats, and gain situational awareness. When the two Black Hawks were shot down, the lightly equipped ground forces became pinned down in one spot. They lost broad-area situational awareness and had to call in heavy airborne firepower (and make very extensive use of their own weapons) to survive. As well as suffering significant losses of their own, this compelled Task Force Ranger to inflict heavy casualties on the Somali irregular fighters (militia and armed civilians alike) who attacked them, contributing to the shock effect of the battle on U.S. public opinion. Even then, airborne firepower alone wasn't enough to extricate the force from its encircled position. It was only when the rescue force, in tanks and armored personnel carriers, made its way into the Black Sea that TF Ranger was able to extract. In several cases, tanks sat in the street and took close-range RPG hits without firing back, acting as mobile cover and communications relays for the ground troops.

Indirect protection (because of the need to see and shoot first, or else risk being destroyed) can be very damaging in an urban area. Lightly armored vehicles may have to suppress suspected enemy positions just in case, or fire their main weapons before positively identifying a threat, because they can't afford to wait until they're certain. These weapons (typically heavy machine guns or quick-firing cannons with explosive shells) can easily penetrate walls and structures in flimsy slums and shantytowns. They may travel a very long way through several homes, killing noncombatants or setting fire to an entire area. Alternatively, light vehicles may carry so-called active defense systems designed to detect incoming missiles with radar and shoot them down with a shotgun-like blast (as in the Israeli Trophy or U.S. Quick Kill system).[55] Despite the small danger zone of these systems, they're problematic in a crowded street full of noncombatants (say, at a checkpoint or a humanitarian relief distribution point). Fragment-free systems such as the European AMAP-ADS offer some improvement—but defeating an incoming missile, while minimizing risk to surrounding civilians or dismounted infantry, is still a daunting technical challenge when it comes to RPGs and (even more so) improvised explosive devices (IEDs).[56]

I sometimes hear people express the hope that the IED threat will diminish as Western forces pull out of Afghanistan. Unfortunately, nothing could be further from the truth—the IED has now entered the standard repertoire of irregular forces in urban areas across the planet, and there are no signs this threat is shrinking; on the contrary, it seems to be growing. As Mike Davis points out in *Buda's Wagon*, his excellent history of the car bomb, vehicle-borne IEDs have a long history and have been steadily increasing in sophistication and lethality for decades.[57] The wars in Iraq and Afghanistan created a generation of technically adept and combat-experienced bomb makers with skills for hire, and brought together criminal and extremist networks with a common interest in smuggling bomb components. Most adversaries can be expected to quickly field IEDs in the event of new conflict. And, as discussed in Chapter 4, urban populations that have basic familiarity with industrial tools and consumer electronics, plus Internet connectivity, can quickly pick up the necessary knowledge and skills to produce IEDs from scratch. This can be seen in trends in IED usage, which averaged 260 incidents per month *outside* Iraq and Afghanistan in 2010.[58] From January to November 2011, also outside Iraq and Afghanistan, there were 6,832 IED events globally, averaging 621 per month—a huge increase from the previous year.[59] These incidents caused 12,286 casualties in 111 countries and were perpetrated by forty regional and transnational threat networks. This isn't just an international trend: of those totals, 490 events and 28 casualties were in the United States, according to the U.S. government's Joint IED Defeat Organization.[60]

In urbanized areas, IEDs are extremely effective in denying access to strongholds, creating urban no-go areas, or blocking specific routes a force may wish to use. They can be used to channel ground forces into an ambush or lead them into a sniper's killing area, bog them down so that an adversary can escape, or provoke troops hit by an IED to retaliate by shooting into surrounding buildings (colloquially known in Baghdad as the "Iraqi death blossom"), killing or wounding—or at the very least, radically pissing off—local people. More strategically, IEDs can defeat a force by targeting commanders and bases in the field, or political leaders at home (whose will and confidence can be undermined through loss of public support after a major bombing). There have been dozens of examples of all of these uses of the IED in Iraq and Afghanistan, but it isn't unique to these countries, or to counterinsurgency: the October 1983 suicide truck bombing of a U.S. Marine barracks and a French compound during peacekeeping operations in the urbanized, littoral environment of Beirut is a case in point. The bombing, carried out by Islamic Jihad (later Hezbollah), killed 299 U.S. and French soldiers and six Lebanese civilians, as well as the two bombers, and led to the withdrawal of international peacekeepers from

Lebanon.[61] Criminal organizations have also used IEDs (including in several cities in Mexico).[62] In February 2013 President Obama issued a National Counter-IED Policy directing U.S. military and law enforcement agencies to work together both domestically and overseas to counter this threat, and in the aftermath of the Boston Marathon bombing of April 2013, the emphasis on IEDs as a domestic threat is only likely to increase.[63]

To protect themselves, small teams in a future urbanized environment will need to move inside a "triple bubble" comprising three layers of defense: organic capabilities and techniques that reside in the team itself (including counterambush and countersniper capabilities), resources it can draw from its parent unit (mortar and artillery fire, counter-IED, high-risk search, and signals intelligence), and force-level capabilities (including shipborne counterbattery fire, air defense, and cybersecurity). Six defensive disciplines will define these bubbles: counter-IED, counterambush, countersniper, counterfires (i.e., protection against mortars and rockets), counterdrone (increasingly necessary as nonstate groups field their own uninhabited aerial systems), and cyberdefense. Engineering capabilities (for hardening structures, building defensive strongpoints, clearing routes, designing obstacles to counter enemy mobility, and civil engineering) will probably be held at the force level, but like other capabilities they will need to be modular and readily distributable to teams as needed.

Because the dense urban maze of the future environment will make observation very difficult, fire support will need to be networked, with every team linked into a communications and location-tracking system that lets it call for fire from its parent organization, tie into overhead systems (drones, piloted aircraft, or blimp-like aerostats), and direct the fire of every other small team that's in range and can support. This may look something like the mesh networks that emerged during the uprisings in Syria and Egypt, mentioned in Chapter 5. Redundant mesh-network communications systems (perhaps with the ability to rapidly deploy mobile secure cellphone networks) will be particularly important, since radio signals in cities tend to suffer from multipath propagation and attenuation (they bend around buildings, get absorbed by structures, and don't travel as straight or as far as in open areas). Fires will need to be jointly coordinated, including naval gunfire, ground-based artillery and mortars, and air strikes, and besides precision (the ability to hit what you aim at) they'll need much greater discrimination (the ability to know what you're aiming at and decide whether or not to shoot). Less-lethal systems (such as the variable-explosive bomb and low-collateral-damage bomb the U.S. Navy developed for Iraq) will most likely require further refinement, so that air forces can engage targets in flimsily constructed areas without harming innocent bystanders.[64]

Lest we think that the main role for air power in urban warfare is solely for tactical close air support, however, I should point out that air forces bring critically important capabilities to the urban littoral that no other service can provide. We've already discussed the difficulties of sea-based logistics and surface amphibious warfare and the importance of air assets in modern littoral operations. Air power can compensate for these difficulties by allowing rapid, large-scale troop movement into air points of entry and by providing long-range resupply. Unlike surface forces, aircraft can exploit the third dimension to gain an overhead view of complex urban terrain, letting them escape the tyranny of short-range, disaggregated engagements that afflicts ground and (sometimes) naval forces. Aircraft aren't subject to the constraints of coastal hydrography and can range across the coast at will, while providing intelligence, surveillance, and reconnaissance support to surface forces. In urban areas where communications are attenuated by the density of buildings and structures, air forces can provide overhead command, control, and communications, and preserve situational awareness. They can isolate an urban area (or a portion of a larger city) from outside reinforcement, conduct precision strikes, and run battlefield air interdiction operations. Most important, they can control the airspace over a littoral operation, providing air superiority over the landing area—a critical prerequisite for surface operations.

For both air and surface forces, many capabilities described above have been in service for some time or are already in an advanced stage of development. Not all armed forces have access to them, however, and as nonstate armed groups continue to develop better capabilities (driven by the democratization of weapons and communications technologies discussed in Chapter 4) there will be a need for innovative technologies, new techniques, and fresh tactics if military forces are to prevail against the evolved irregular threat.

Most important, military forces that have gotten used to standard-length operational tours in Afghanistan or Iraq will need a change of attitude. In a complex fight in the urbanized littoral, there will be none of the fixed installations, lavish intelligence infrastructure, or constant cell-phone and Wi-Fi coverage of counterinsurgency operations. The garrison mind-set, with its short-duration operations and frequent access to bases with hot showers, air-conditioned dining halls, and sleeping cots, will need to give way to a mobile, improvisational, expeditionary mentality. Troops will have to become hikers again, not campers.

# NOTES

## Introduction

1. This account draws on my field notes for September 10, 2009, written the morning after the ambush from personal observation during the firefight, discussions with patrol members and a film crew at the landing zone approximately forty-five minutes after the ambush, and a conversation with civilian and military members of the patrol the following night at the United States Embassy compound, in Kabul.

2. Mine-resistant ambush-protected vehicles (MRAPs) were introduced into Iraq and Afghanistan beginning in 2006, in response to the escalating threat of roadside bombs. There are several variants; our patrol had four Category 2 MRAPs, each with a crew of two plus eight fully equipped infantry in the troop-carrying compartment, and three Category 1 vehicles, with smaller capacity but marginally less atrocious maneuverability.

3. Rocket-propelled grenades (RPGs) are Soviet-designed shoulder-launched rockets intended to destroy buildings and lightly armored vehicles. The weapon is recoilless, directing its blast backward through a rear-facing venturi. Unless carefully sited with a clear area behind the firer, this back-blast can kick up a large cloud of dust, giving away the weapon's position. These disadvantages are more than compensated for, however, by the RPG's low weight, low cost, and rapid rate of fire. Along with the Kalashnikov assault rifle, the RPG is one of the most common weapons used worldwide by guerrillas and those who fight them.

4. Winston Churchill, *The Story of the Malakand Field Force: An Episode of Frontier War* (Edinburgh: Thomas Nelson and Sons, 1898), 199–200.

5. This characteristic was something the Taliban shared with the mujahideen of the Soviet-Afghan War, who, as Ali Jalali and Les Grau showed, had a strong tendency to set patterns and repeat the same maneuvers in the same places over and over again. See Ali Ahmad Jalali and Lester A. Grau, *The Other Side of the Mountain: Mujahideen Tactics in the Soviet-Afghan War* (Fort Leavenworth, KS: Foreign Military Studies Office, 1998). For a detailed explanation of pattern setting in the Afghan approach to conflict, see also Rob Johnson, *The Afghan Way of War: Culture and Pragmatism, a Critical History* (London: Hurst, 2011).

6. The *delgai*, or small group, is the basic operational unit of main-force (i.e., regular, full-time) Taliban in eastern and southern Afghanistan. It comprises eight to twenty guerrillas under a commander, and may—for reconnaissance, or in an urban environment—be further broken down into cell groups (*otaq*). Several *delgai* may loosely cooperate under a regional commander for a specific operation such as a large-scale ambush or major ground assault.

7. The battle of Wanat, which occurred in July 2008, has been extensively discussed in print and in the electronic and online media, and is likely to be seen as one of the defining battles of the Afghan war, at least in the eastern part of the country. The most comprehensive accounts of the battle are Douglas R. Cubbison's untitled working paper on the battle, completed in 2009, and Combat Studies Institute, *Wanat: Combat Action in Afghanistan 2008* (Fort Leavenworth, KS: Army Command and General Staff College Press, 2010).

8. See Alissa Rubin and Sharifullah Sahak, "Taliban Attack Afghan Guards in Deadly Raid," *New York Times*, August 20, 2010.

9. Ibid.

10. Combat Studies Institute, *Wanat*, 49.

11. Ibid., 4–5.

12. Author's discussion with German officers, Kabul, March 2008. This story was confirmed by General Kasdorf, head of the German Army and former Bundeswehr commander in Afghanistan, in discussion with the author in Washington, DC, October 2011.

13. Author's interview with Aegis RLT, Baghdad, June 30, 2007.

14. Analysts including Hilton Root, Paul Collier, Anke Hoefflery, and others have described this phenomenon for African development and in the historical patterns of civil war, while Andrew Wilder, Sarah Chayes, Clare Lockhart, Anand Gopal, and Carl Forsberg have noted its prevalence in Afghanistan. See Hilton Root, *Alliance Curse: How America Lost the Third World* (Washington, DC: Brookings Institution Press, 2008); Paul Collier and Anke Hoefflery, "Greed and Grievance in Civil War," *Oxford Economic Papers* 56, no. 4 (August 2004): 563–95; Sarah Chayes, *The Punishment of Virtue: Inside Afghanistan After the Taliban* (New York: Penguin, 2007); Clare Lockhart, "Learning from Experience," *Slate*, November 2008; Anand

Gopal, *Battle for Afghanistan: Militancy and Conflict in Kandahar* (Washington, DC: New America Foundation, 2010); and Carl Forsberg, *Power and Politics in Kandahar* (Washington, DC: Institute for the Study of War, 2010).

15. U.S. Army and U.S. Marine Corps, FM 3–24/MCWP 3–33.5, *Counterinsurgency* (Washington, DC: Headquarters Department of the Army, 2006), paragraph I-2, page 1–1.

16. See David J. Kilcullen, "Counterinsurgency Redux," *Survival* 48, no. 4 (December 2006), and "Countering Global Insurgency," *Journal of Strategic Studies* 28, no. 4 (August 2005).

17. I draw this formulation from Jeffrey Gettleman, "Africa's Forever Wars: Why the Continent's Conflicts Never End," *Foreign Policy*, March/April 2010.

## Chapter 1

1. For a cogent set of criticisms, see Stephen Graham, "Olympics Security 2012: Welcome to Lockdown London," *Guardian*, March 12, 2012.

2. Victor Hugo, *Les Misérables*, trans. C. E. Wilbour (New York: Carleton, 1862), 134.

3. Some parts of this chapter and the next appeared in David Kilcullen, "The City as a System: Future Conflict and Urban Resilience," *Fletcher Forum of World Affairs* 36, no. 2 (Summer 2012): 19–39.

4. For a comprehensive survey of the role of war in contemporary geopolitics—and a strong argument that interstate war is becoming increasingly rare—see Christopher J. Fettweis, *Dangerous Times? The International Politics of Great Power Peace* (Washington, DC: Georgetown University Press, 2010).

5. Since the mid-nineteenth century the United States has engaged in only six conventional wars. But over the same period, interventions involving irregular warfare, stability operations, or counterinsurgency have included the Mexican War of 1846–48, the Indian Wars against Native American peoples throughout the second half of the nineteenth century; the Philippine Insurrection of 1899–1902; the 1916–17 punitive expedition into Mexico; the intervention in Russia in 1918–20; the banana wars in the Caribbean (including interventions in Panama, Honduras, Nicaragua, Mexico, Haiti, and the Dominican Republic) during the 1920s and 1930s; the post–World War II occupation and reconstruction of Japan and Germany; several wars in Indochina, including Laos, Cambodia, and Vietnam; engagements in Thailand, Lebanon, Panama, Pakistan, Grenada, Somalia, Liberia, El Salvador, and Colombia; peace operations in the Balkans; and of course the wars in Iraq and Afghanistan. Long though it is, this list is only a small selection of dozens of such engagements over the past 150 years.

6. For a detailed study of these operations, see the excellent account in Brian McAllister Linn, *The U.S. Army and Counterinsurgency in the Philippine War, 1899–1902* (Chapel Hill: University of North Carolina Press, 2000).

7. See Roy E. Appleman, *South to the Naktong, North to the Yalu* (Washington, DC: U.S. Army Center for Military History, 1992), 722–24.

8. More broadly, a Defense Science Board summer study in 2004 found a long-standing five-to-seven-year cycle of repeated interventions in small and medium-scale stabilization operations since the end of the Cold War, imposing an increasing burden on the U.S. military. See Defense Science Board, *2004 Summer Study on Transition to and from Hostilities*, online at www.acq.osd.mil/dsb/reports/ADA430116.pdf, 14.

9. I am of course aware that there are many competing definitions of *irregular warfare*. In this book, I use the term simply to mean any conflict where one or more of the actual or potential protagonists is a nonstate armed group.

10. United States Department of Defense, *Sustaining U.S. Global Leadership: Priorities for 21st Century Defense* (Washington, DC: Department of Defense, January 2012), 3 (emphasis in the original).

11. See Nick Turse, "The New Obama Doctrine," *Nation*, June 14, 2012, and Leon Wieseltier, "Welcome to the Era of the Light Footprint: Obama Finally Finds His Doctrine," *New Republic*, January 29, 2013.

12. A total of forty-nine coalition members participated in Operation Iraqi Freedom under the command of Multi-National Force—Iraq between 2003 and 2010; of these, however, a much smaller number (between three and five, depending on the year of the conflict) provided actual combat troops at battalion scale or larger, and at the height of the fighting (in October 2007) the U.S. troop presence of 171,000 accounted for 94 percent of the total coalition troop presence of 182,668. See *US-Iraq War: Coalition Forces in Iraq*, Procon.org, available online at http://usiraq.procon.org/view.resource .php?resourceID=000677. By contrast, fifty coalition members participated in Afghanistan under the NATO-led International Security Assistance Force between 2001 and 2012, and of these, between eight and ten (again, depending on the year concerned) provided battalion- or larger-sized combat units, all of which operated outside the capital city. See ISAF, *Troop Numbers and Contributions*, online at www.isaf.nato.int/troop-numbers-and-contributions/index.php.

13. See Iraq Body Count, "Civilian Deaths from Violence in 2007," figures in final table, online at www.iraqbodycount.org/analysis/numbers/2007.

14. David Kilcullen, "Don't Confuse the 'Surge' with the Strategy," *Small Wars Journal*, January 19, 2007.

15. Nassim Nicholas Taleb, *The Black Swan: The Impact of the Highly Improbable* (New York: Random House, 2007).

16. Harry Holbert Turney-High, *The Military: The Theory of Land Warfare as Behavioral Science* (North Quincy, MA: Christopher, 1981), 34, quoted in Lawrence H. Keeley, *War Before Civilization: The Myth of the Peaceful Savage* (New York: Oxford University Press, 1997), 47–48. Likewise, the historian Philip Bobbitt considers warfare to be one of the three key influencers (along with law and commerce) upon the formation and shape of the

state throughout history. And Lawrence Keeley argues convincingly, in *War Before Civilization*, that "a society's demography, economy, and social system provide the means for, and impose limits on, military technique." See Philip Bobbitt, *The Shield of Achilles: War, Peace and the Course of History* (New York: Knopf, 2002).

17. Keeley's groundbreaking 1997 study integrates research from several different statistical sources to suggest that somewhere between 90 and 95 percent of all known societies throughout history have regularly engaged in organized warfare. See Keeley, *War Before Civilization*, Chapters 2 and 3.

18. Even piracy, an apparent exception to this general pattern, turns out on closer observation to be a phenomenon that clusters in and around coastal towns and on the sea routes between such towns.

19. See Micheal Clodfelter, *Warfare and Armed Conflicts: A Statistical Reference to Casualty and Other Figures, 1618–1991* (Jefferson, NC: McFarland, 1992); see also Mark Mazower, *Dark Continent: Europe's Twentieth Century* (New York: Viking, 2000). Mazower estimates total battle deaths in the range of 48 million for both world wars; some estimates range as high as 76 million.

20. This estimate represents the median prediction of the United Nations population progression model, as reported in United Nations, Department of Economic and Social Affairs, *World Population Prospects: The 2010 Revision*, online at http://esa.un.org/wpp/Documentation/publications.htm.

21. See Qiu Aijun, *How to Understand the Urbanisation Rate in China?*, Cities Development Institute for Asia, online at www.cdia.asia/wp-content/uploads/How-to-understand-the-urbanisation-rate-in-China.pdf.

22. See "Concrete Jungles: A Mainly Rural Country Is Ill-Prepared for Its Coming Urban Boom," *Economist*, September 29, 2012.

23. Quoted in Casey Kazan, "Sprawl! Is Earth Becoming a Planet of Super-Cities?" *The Daily Galaxy*, June 24, 2009.

24. United Nations, Department of Economic and Social Affairs, *World Urbanization Prospects: The 2009 Revision*, 1, online at http://esa.un.org/unpd/wup/Documents/WUP2009_Highlights_Final.pdf (emphasis added).

25. Ibid.

26. For a discussion of these factors as they apply to rapid urbanization and slum growth in one African city, see Emmanuel Mutisya and Masaru Yarime, "Understanding the Grassroots Dynamics of Slums in Nairobi: The Dilemma of Kibera Informal Settlements," *International Transaction Journal of Engineering, Management, and Applied Sciences and Technologies* 2, no. 2 (March 2011): 197–213.

27. See United Nations Environment Program, *Cities and Coastal Areas*, online at www.unep.org/urban_environment/issues/coastal_zones.asp.

28. See Ethan Decker, Scott Elliott, Felisa Smith, Donald Blake, and Sherwood Rowland, "Energy and Material Flow Through the Urban Ecosystem," *Annual Review of Energy and the Environment* 25 (2000): 690–91. Decker and colleague list the top twenty-five megacities as Karachi, Cairo, Teheran,

Tianjin, Beijing, Seoul, Moscow, New York, Delhi, London, Buenos Aires, Shanghai, Osaka, Tokyo, Los Angeles, Mexico City, São Paulo, Rio de Janeiro, Lagos, Jakarta, Dhaka, Manila, Bangkok, Calcutta, and Mumbai. Of these, only Delhi, Moscow, Teheran, and Beijing are inland cities—all the others lie within 100 miles of a coastline or on a major coastal river delta.

29.  Central Intelligence Agency, *World Factbook 2012*, field listing for "Urbanization," online at https://www.cia.gov/library/publications/the-world-factbook/fields/2212.html. This entry lists the ten largest cities on the planet as Tokyo, 36.7 million; Delhi, 22.1 million; São Paulo, 20.3 million; Mumbai, 20 million; Mexico City, 19.5 million; New York–Newark, 19.4 million; Shanghai, 16.6 million; Kolkata, 15.6 million; Dhaka, 14.6 million; and Karachi, 13.2 million. Of these, only Delhi and Mexico City are not littoral cities.

30.  This definition is similar in some respects to that used by the United States and British Commonwealth navies. It is adapted from the definition applied by the Australian Army's Directorate of Future Land Warfare, where the author worked in 2003–5, in developing Australia's future operational concepts for *Manoeuvre Operations in the Littoral Environment* and *Complex Warfighting*. For the equivalent U.S. Navy definition, see U.S. Department of the Navy, *Naval Warfare*, Naval Doctrine Publication 1 (Washington, DC: U.S. Department of the Navy, 1994).

31.  United States Marine Corps, Task Force 58, "Execution 25 November to 25 December" (after-action review), *Strategy Page*, online at www.strategypage.com/articles/tf58/execution.asp.

32.  French Republic, Parliamentary Office for Scientific and Technical Assessment, *The Pollution in Mediterranean: Current State and Looking Ahead to 2030*, summary of the report by M. Roland Courteau, online at www.senat.fr/fileadmin/Fichiers/Images/opecst/quatre_pages_anglais/4p_mediterranee_anglais.pdf.

33.  Olivier Kramsch, "Towards a Mediterranean Scale of Governance: Twenty-First Century Urban Networks Across the 'Inner Sea,'" in Barbara Hooper and Olivier Kramsch, eds., *Cross-Border Governance in the European Union* (London: Routledge, 2007), 200.

34.  Iginio Gagliardone and Nicole Stremlau, *Digital Media, Conflict and Diasporas in the Horn of Africa* (London: Mapping Digital Media Program of the Open Society Foundations), December 2011, 9–10.

35.  World Bank, *Migration and Remittances Factbook 2011*, quoted in Gagliardone and Stremlau, *Digital Media*, 12.

36.  Rasna Warah, Mohamud Dirios, and Ismail Osman, *Mogadishu Then and Now: A Pictorial Tribute to Africa's Most Wounded City* (Bloomington, IN: Author House, 2012), 3.

37.  In fact, it's worth speculating that there may be a critical mass for the size of a diaspora relative to the home population, a kind of quantum effect threshold, above which flows of money, information, and people suddenly jump to a much greater level and home populations and diaspora populations begin

to move in a synchronized manner despite the geographical distance between them. Several researchers have examined this issue in passing, but it's unclear how big a diaspora is needed to generate a critical mass of connectivity. Still, what is very clear is that there is a link between conflict at home and diaspora size, and that some populations—including Somalis, Tamils, Tunisians, Libyans, and perhaps Jamaicans, Haitians, and Filipinos—have reached this tipping point. See Dilip Ratha and Sonia Plaza, *Harnessing Diasporas*, International Monetary Fund, September 2009, online at www.imf.org/external/pubs/ft/fandd/2011/09/pdf/ratha.pdf. See also Yevgeny Kuznetsov, ed., *Diaspora Networks and the International Migration of Skills* (Washington, DC: World Bank Institute, 2006), and Rodel Rodis, "The Tipping Point of the Filipino Diaspora," *Global Nation Inquirer*, September 23, 2011, online at http://globalnation.inquirer.net/13403/the-tipping-point-of-the-filipino-diaspora.

38. See Nicholas Van Hear, Frank Pieke, and Steven Vertovec, *The Contribution of UK-Based Diasporas to Development and Poverty Reduction*, ESRC Centre on Migration, Policy and Society (COMPAS), University of Oxford, April 2004, online at www.compas.ox.ac.uk/fileadmin/files/People/staff_publications/VanHear/NVH1_DFID%20diaspora%20report.pdf. See also "Sri Lankan President Calls Influential Tamil Diaspora to Invest in Post-War Progress," *People's Daily*, November 30, 2011.

39. See "UN Bans Trade in Charcoal from Somalia," *East African*, February 25, 2012, online at www.hiiraan.com/news4/2012/feb/22927/un_bans_trade_in_charcoal_from_somalia.aspx.

40. Sean Everton, *Disrupting Dark Networks: Structural Analysis in the Social Sciences* (London: Cambridge University Press, 2012).

41. See Gordon H. Hanson, "Regional Adjustment to Trade Liberalization," *Regional Science and Urban Economics* 28 (1998): 419–44, quoted in Zhao Chen, Ming Lu, and Zheng Xu, "Agglomeration Shadow: A Non-Linear Core-Periphery Model of Urban Growth in China (1990–2006)," paper presented at Global Development Network 13th Annual Conference, June 16–18, 2012, online at http://cloud2.gdnet.org/~research_papers/Agglomeration%20shadow:%20A%20non-linear%20core–periphery%20model%20of%20urban%20growth%20in%20China%20(1990–2006).

42. Josh Eells, "Chaosopolis: A Wild Week in Lagos," *Men's Journal*, May 2012, online at www.mensjournal.com/article/print-view/chaosopolis-20120504.

43. Ibid.

44. Ibid.

45. See Asian Development Bank, *Climate-Induced Migration in Asia and the Pacific*, September 2011, online at http://beta.adb.org/features/climate-induced-migration-asia-and-pacific.

46. Ibid.

47. See Independent Evaluation Group, *Facts and Figures on Natural Disasters* (Washington, DC: World Bank, 2006), online at www.worldbank.org/ieg/

naturaldisasters/docs/natural_disasters_fact_sheet.pdf; see also
PPRD South, *Tackling Floods, the Most Common Natural Disaster in the
Mediterranean*, February 9, 2011, online at www.euromedcp.eu/index
.php?option=com_content&view=article&id=706%3Atackling-floods-the-
most-frequent-natural-disaster-in-the-mediterranean&catid=199%3Agen
eral-news&Itemid=881&lang=en, and Patrick Cronin and Nora Bensahel,
*America's Civilian Operations Abroad: Assessing Past and Future Require-
ments* (Washington, DC: Center for a New American Security, 2012),
online at www.cnas.org/files/documents/publications/CNAS_
AmericasCivilianOperationsAbroad_BensahelCronin_0.pdf.

48. See T. B. C. Alavo, A. Z. Abagli, M. Accodji, and R. Djouaka, "Unplanned
Urbanization Promotes the Proliferation of Disease Vector Mosquitoes,"
*Open Entomology Journal* 4 (2010): 1–7.

49. See Colleen Lau, "Urbanisation, Climate Change, and Leptospirosis:
Environmental Drivers of Infectious Disease Emergence," conference paper
presented at Universitas 21 International Graduate Research Conference:
Sustainable Cities for the Future, Melbourne and Brisbane, November
29–December 5, 2009.

50. David M. Bell et al., "Pandemic Influenza as 21st Century Urban Public
Health Crisis," *Emerging Infectious Diseases* 15, no. 12 (December 2009):
1963–9.

51. See N. Sarita Shah et al., "Worldwide Emergence of Extensively Drug-
Resistant Tuberculosis," *Emerging Infectious Diseases* 13, no. 3 (March
2007): 380–87. See also Joshua M. Epstein et al., "Controlling Pandemic
Flu: The Value of International Air Travel Restrictions," *PLOS One* 2,
no. 5 (2007): 401.

52. Decker et al., "Energy and Material Flow Through the Urban Ecosystem," 710.

53. See Muhammad Hayat, "Fishing Capacity and Fisheries in Pakistan," in
S. Pascoe and D. Greboval, eds., *Measuring Capacity in Fisheries*, Food and
Agriculture Organization , Fisheries Technical Paper no. 445, 2003, online
at ftp://ftp.fao.org/docrep/fao/006/y4849e/y4849e00.pdf.

54. Stephen Graham, "Urban Metabolism as Target: Contemporary War as
Forced Demodernization," in Nik Heynen, Maria Kaika, and Erik Swinge-
douw, eds., *In the Nature of Cities: Urban Political Ecology and the Politics of
Urban Metabolism* (London: Routledge, 2006), 236.

55. See Dominic Wabala, "65 Criminal Gang Members Arrested in Nairobi
Major Swoop," *Nairobi Star*, March 23, 2012, online at http://allafrica.com/
stories/201203231381.html; Kenfrey Kiberenge, "Saccos Bring Sanity to
Public Transport," Kenya *Standard*, May 5, 2012, online at www
.standardmedia.co.ke/index.php/business/mag/radio-maisha/?articleID=
2000057647&;pageNo=1; County Team, "Fears of Mungiki-Like Gangs
Disrupt Transport Sector," Kenya *Standard*, September 6, 2012, online at
www.standardmedia.co.ke/index.php?articleID=2000065490&;story_
title=Fears-of-Mungiki-like-gangs-disrupt-transport-sector.

56. Mutisya and Yarime, "Understanding the Grassroots Dynamics of Slums," 197–99.
57. Christopher Eastwood, "Identifying Sustainable Water Supplies: A Preliminary Assessment of Sustainable Water from an Urban Metabolism Perspective," master's thesis, Queensland University of Technology, Brisbane, 2007, 5.
58. Yan Han, Shi-guo Xu, and Xiang-zhou Xu, "Modeling Multisource Multiuser Water Resources Allocation," *Water Resource Management* 22 (2008): 911–12.
59. Decker et al., "Energy and Material Flow Through the Urban Ecosystem," 697–700.
60. Sheela Patel, founding director of the Society for the Promotion of Area Resource Centers, Mumbai, interviewed by Gary Hustwit in the documentary film *Urbanized*, Plexifilm, New York, 2012.
61. Kees Koonings and Dirk Kruijt, "Conclusions: Governing Exclusion and Violence in Megacities," in Kees Koonings and Dirk Kruijt, eds., *Mega-Cities: The Politics of Urban Exclusion and Violence in the Global South* (London: Zed Books, 2009), 174–75.
62. Jamaican garrison communities such as Tivoli Gardens are discussed later in this book. See also "Witness Provides Compelling Account of Jamaican 'Garrisons,'" *Caribbean News Now*, online at www.caribbeannewsnow.com/news/newspublish/home.print.php?news_id=11049.
63. Widespread rioting and civil unrest in outlying and periurban areas struck Paris (and several other French cities) in 2005 and again in 2007 and 2010, while large-scale rioting and looting occurred in parts of London in 2011.
64. See (among many other works) Mike Davis, *Planet of Slums* (New York: Verso, 2007); Stephen Graham, *Cities Under Siege: The New Military Urbanism* (New York: Verso, 2011); Diane E. Davis, *Cities and Sovereignty: Identity Politics in Urban Spaces* (Bloomington: Indiana University Press, 2011); and Saskia Sassen, *Global Networks, Linked Cities* (London: Routledge, 2002).
65. The Australian Army published its operational concepts *Manoeuvre Operations in the Littoral Environment* and *Complex Warfighting* in 2002 and 2004, respectively, and the Royal Marines developed the *Commando 21* concept in 2003. Like these military concept papers, the U.S. Marine Corps *Vision and Strategy 2025* and the U.S. Department of Defense *Joint Operating Environment 2010* discuss the implications of urbanized littoral areas on modern warfare. See Department of Defence (Australia), *Future Warfighting Concept* (Canberra: Headquarters Australian Defence Force 2002), online at www.defence.gov.au/publications/fwc.pdf; Australian Army, *Complex Warfighting* (Canberra: Australian Army Headquarters 2005), online at www.quantico.usmc.mil/download.aspx?Path=./Uploads/Files/SVG_complex_warfighting.pdf; United States Department of

Defense, *Joint Operating Environment 2010*, online at www.fas.org/man/
eprint/joe2010.pdf; and United States Marine Corps, *Marine Corps
Vision and Strategy 2025* (Quantico, VA: Headquarters USMC, 2009),
online at www.onr.navy.mil/~/media/Files/About%20ONR/usmc_vision_
strategy_2025_0809.ashx.

66. For a useful review of the literature on this approach, see Elizabeth Rapo-
    port, "Interdisciplinary Perspectives on Urban Metabolism: A Review of the
    Literature," University College London Environmental Institute Working
    Paper, October 27, 2011, online at www.ucl.ac.uk/environment-institute/
    forthcoming-events/urbanlitreview.

67. Joel Tarr, "The Metabolism of the Industrial City: The Case of Pittsburgh,"
    *Journal of Urban History* 28, no. 5 (July 2002): 511.

68. We should note that this is a contested approach that includes a range of
    perspectives. Some view biological systems as useful metaphors for the
    physical and sociopolitical dynamics of urban space, while others view
    the interdependent subsystems that overlap within this space as organic
    elements of a material flow system that is *truly* (not just metaphorically)
    biological.

69. Tarr, "Metabolism of the Industrial City."

70. See John Bellamy Foster, "Marx's Theory of Metabolic Rift: Classical Foun-
    dation for Environmental Sociology," *American Journal of Sociology* 105,
    no. 2 (September 1999): 366–405.

71. Ibid.; Abel Wolman, "The Metabolism of Cities," *Scientific American* 213
    (July-December 1965): 179–93.

72. Rapoport, "Urban Metabolism," 5.

73. I am grateful to officials of the Colombian government for insights into the
    concept of "territorial logic," which I extend in this context to the notion of
    "systems logic." Author's discussions with Colombian National Police and
    the Presidency of the Republic of Colombia, Bogotá, Colombia, December
    2011.

74. David J. Kilcullen, "Countering Global Insurgency," in *Small Wars Journal*,
    November 22, 2004, 22–23.

75. See "Honduran City Is World Murder Capital; Juarez Drops for Second
    Year in a Row," Fox News Latino, February 6, 2013.

76. James Bargent, "Latin America Dominates World's Most Dangerous Cities
    List," *Insight Crime*, February 8, 2013, online at www.insightcrime.org/
    newsbriefs/latin-america-dominates-worlds-most-dangerous-cities-list.

77. See Mark Kukis, "Is Baghdad Now Safer than New Orleans?" *Time*, May 1,
    2009; Citizens Report, "All London Murders, 2006–2013," online at
    www.citizensreportuk.org/reports/london-murders.html.

78. This section draws on original research produced by a Caerus Associates
    field team led by Stacia George and Dr. Christopher Johnson, which con-
    ducted fieldwork in 2012–13 in San Pedro Sula. See Caerus Associates, "The
    City as a System: Understanding Illicit and Licit Networks in San Pedro
    Sula, Honduras," Washington, DC, February 6, 2013.

## Chapter 2

1. The following account draws on multiple sources, including contemporaneous media accounts, published analyses of the Mumbai terrorist attacks, and testimony at the trials of the sole surviving attacker, Mohammed Ajmal Kasab, and of David Coleman Headley (a Pakistani American allegedly involved in the support network for the attack).

2. Testimony by Willi Brigitte, quoted in Sebastian Rotella, "On the Trail of Pakistani Terror Group's Elusive Mastermind Behind the Mumbai Siege," *Washington Post*, November 10, 2010.

3. Saikat Datta, "Terror Colours, in Black and White: Outlook Accesses the Dossier India Has Sent to Pakistan and Its Unabridged Version That Proves the Pakistani Link," in *Outlook* (India), January 19, 2009.

4. Jedburgh Corporation, "Mumbai Attack Timeline and Order of Battle," online at http://jedburgh-usa.com/wp-content/uploads/Mumbai%20 Reconstruction.pdf.

5. Sebastian Rotella, "Mumbai Case Offers Rare Picture of Ties Between Pakistan's Intelligence Service, Militants," ProPublica.org, May 2, 2011.

6. "Mumbai Attacks 2008: '40 Indians Involved in Terror Plot,'" One India News, July 2, 2012, online at http://news.oneindia.in/2012/07/02/ mum-26-11-2008-attacks-40-indians-involved-terror-plot-1027835.html.

7. "Serving Major Among 4 Pak Nationals Behind 2008 Mumbai Attacks: US Chargesheet," *Times of India*, May 9, 2011.

8. Gordon G. Chang, "India's China Problem," *Forbes*, August 14, 2009.

9. The inclusion of these items of escape-and-evasion gear have led some to speculate that the raiding team intended to survive the attack and exfiltrate by blending in with the city afterward.

10. Damien McElroy, "Mumbai Attacks: Terrorists Took Cocaine to Stay Awake During Assault," *Daily Telegraph*, February 9, 2009.

11. S. Ahmed Ali, "26/11: Kuber Skipper Didn't Re[s]ist When Militants Used Ship," *Times of India*, January 6, 2009, online at http://articles.timesofindia .indiatimes.com/2009-01-06/mumbai/28005435_1_vinod-masani- kuber-amar-narayan.

12. S. Ahmed Ali and Vijay V. Singh, "Terrorists Used Code Words to Evade Suspicion," *Times of India*, December 6, 2008.

13. In an uncharacteristic error, the LeT raiding party failed to sink the *Kuber*, which seems to have been their original intention. As a result the ship drifted, abandoned, until it was discovered along with Solanki's body several days after the attack. A GPS unit and satellite phone on board provided valuable intelligence to Indian investigators, showing the team's origin in Karachi, a fact later confirmed by Mohammed Ajmal Kasab, the sole surviving terrorist.

14. Richard Watson, "Mumbai: What Really Happened," *Telegraph*, June 28, 2009.

15. A hard compromise occurs when a raiding team is detected and attacked by security forces; a situation (as in this case) where local civilians detect the team's presence but no security forces are engaged is usually defined as a soft compromise.

16. Jedburgh Corp., "Mumbai Attack Timeline."

17. Onook Oh, Manish Agrawal, and H. Raghav Rao, "Information Control and Terrorism: Tracking the Mumbai Terrorist Attack Through Twitter," *Information Systems Frontiers* 13 (September 2011): 33–43.

18. "Mumbai Attacks 2008: '40 Indians Involved in Terror Plot.'"

19. Datta, "Terror Colours."

20. Watson, "Mumbai: What Really Happened."

21. "Saving the Patients and the Babies Was Our First Duty," Rediff News, December 26, 2008, online at http://specials.rediff.com/news/2008/dec/26sld3-how-the-cama-nurses-saved-their-patient.htm.

22. Vinay Dalvi, "Hemant Karkare Thanked for Exposing Saffron Terror," *Mid-Day* (Mumbai), November 17, 2011.

23. Amitav Ranjan, "Ashok Chakra for Only Two: Karkare and Omble," *Indian Express*, January 21, 2009.

24. Much of what we know about the internal workings of the raid comes from the interrogation and trial of Mohammed Ajmal Kasab. Kasab was tried on eighty-six terrorism-related offenses. He was found guilty and sentenced to death on May 6, 2010; he was hanged at Pune, Maharashtra State, on November 21, 2012. See Ashutosh Joshi, "India Hangs Gunman from Mumbai Attacks," *Wall Street Journal*, November 21, 2012.

25. Wilson John et al., *Mumbai Attacks: Response and Lessons*, Observer Research Foundation, 23–24, online at www.orfonline.org/cms/export/orfonline/modules/report/attachments/Mumbai%20attack_1230552332507.pdf.

26. Damien McElroy, "Mumbai Attacks: Foreign Governments Criticize India's Response," *Telegraph*, November 28, 2008.

27. John et al., *Mumbai Attacks*, 24.

28. Ibid.

29. Ibid., 25–27.

30. Watson, "Mumbai: What Really Happened."

31. Ibid.

32. "How Mumbai Attacks Unfolded," BBC News, November 30, 2008.

33. Author's discussion with a U.S. counterterrorism analyst, Washington, DC, November 29, 2008.

34. John et al., *Mumbai Attacks*.

35. Nobhojit Roy, Vikas Kapil, Italo Subbarao, and Isaac Ashkenazi, "Mass Casualty Response in the 2008 Mumbai Terrorist Attacks," *Disaster Management and Public Health Preparedness* 5, no. 4 (April 2011): 273–79.

36. Ibid., 275.

37. Ibid.

38. Fred de Sam Lazaro, "Karachi and Mumbai: A Tale of Two Megacities," *PBS NewsHour*, July 15, 2011.

39. See Port of Karachi official website, at www.kpt.gov.pk/pages/default.aspx?id=39, accessed October 27, 2012.

40. Roy et al., "Mass Casualty Response," 273.

41. Watson, "Mumbai: What Really Happened."

42. Ibid., 275.

43. John P. Sullivan and Adam Elkus, "Postcard from Mumbai: Modern Urban Siege," *Small Wars Journal*, February 16, 2009.

44. Richard Norton-Taylor and Owen Bowcott, "'Mumbai-Style' Terror Attack on UK, France and Germany Foiled," *Guardian*, September 28, 2010.

45. Discussion with an officer from U.S. Naval Special Warfare Command, at U.S. Naval Amphibious Operations Base Coronado, November 14, 2012; discussion with officers and enlisted operators from Naval Special Warfare Development Group, September 9, 2010.

46. Gwyn Prins's 1993 notion of "threats without enemies" was originally formulated to describe environmental challenges of exactly the type discussed in this book, although the concept has since been more widely appropriated by nontraditional security analysts. See Gwyn Prins, *Threats Without Enemies: Facing Environmental Insecurity* (London: Routledge, 2009 [1993]).

47. Richard J. Norton, "Feral Cities," *Naval War College Review* 66, no. 4 (Autumn 2003): 98.

48. Ibid.

49. M. V. Bhagavathiannan, "Crop Ferality: Implications for Novel Trait Confinement," *Agriculture, Ecosystems and Environment*, 127, nos. 1–2 (August 2008): 1–6.

50. Author's personal experience hunting wild pigs in northern Australia, and discussions with animal-culling experts, Townsville, Queensland, 1998.

51. Author's personal observation of feral dogs, pigs, cats, and horses during operations in the destroyed or conflict-affected cities of Nicosia (Cyprus), 1997; Arawa (Bougainville), 1998; Dili (East Timor), 1999–2000; Kabul, Khost, Kandahar, Jalalabad, and Asadabad (Afghanistan), 2006–12; and Baghdad (Iraq), 2007.

52. Central Intelligence Agency, *World Factbook 2012*, field entry for "Urbanization," online at https://www.cia.gov/library/publications/the-world-factbook/fields/2212.html.

53. As the anthropologist Graham St. John observes, "'Feral' designates an Australian youth milieu connected with grassroots resistance.... Adherents express dissonance from 'the parent culture' and, in acts of local defiance and identification, seek anarchist and ecological alternatives." See Graham St. John, "Ferality: A Life of Grime," *UTS Review* 5, no. 2 (1999): 102.

54. Richard Littlejohn, "The Politics of Envy Was Bound to End Up in Flames," *Daily Mail*, August 12, 2011.

55. See, among many examples, the discussion of urban exclusion in Susan Parnell and Owen Crankshaw, "Urban Exclusion and the (False) Assumptions of Spatial Policy Reform in South Africa," in Kees Koonings and Dirk Kruijt, eds., *Mega-Cities: The Politics of Urban Exclusion and Violence in the Global South* (London: Zed Books, 2009), 161–67.

56. See, for example, Charles Murray's discussion of super-zips and self-segregation (often also referred to as internal secession) in the United States, in Charles Murray, *Coming Apart: The State of White America, 1960–2010* (New York: Crown Forum, 2012).

57. The same core/gap or core/periphery split that strategists such as Thomas P. M. Barnett (or theorists such as Immanuel Wallerstein) have identified at the global level thus also arguably exists at lower fractal levels including cities, districts, blocks, or streets. What Barnett describes as "gap countries" and world-systems analysts call "semiperiphery" or "periphery" countries equate to marginalized or excluded populations and periurban settlements at the city level. See Thomas P. M. Barnett, *The Pentagon's New Map: War and Peace in the Twenty-First Century* (New York: Berkley, 2005), and Immanuel Wallerstein, *The Modern World-System* (New York: Academic Books, 1974).

58. See, for example, the discussion in Tim Nieguth, "'We Are Left with No Other Alternative': Legitimating Internal Secession in Northern Ontario," *Space and Polity* 13, no. 2 (August 2009): 141–57.

59. Aristotle argued that "it is evident that the state is a creation of nature, and that man is by nature a political animal." See Aristotle, *Politics*, trans. Benjamin Jowett (Kitchener: Batoche Books, 1999), book 1, ch. II, 5.

60. Graham argues that "as societies urbanize and modernize, so their populations become ever-more dependent on complex, distanciated systems for the sustenance of the political ecological arrangements necessary to sustain life (water, waste, food, medicine, goods, commodities, energy, communications, transport, and so on) . . . [therefore] the collapse of functioning infrastructure grids now brings panic and fears of the breakdown of the functioning urban social order." Stephen Graham, "Urban Metabolism as Target: Contemporary War as Forced Demodernization," in Nik Heynen, Maria Kaika, and Erik Swyngedouw, eds., *In the Nature of Cities: Urban Political Ecology and the Politics of Urban Metabolism* (London: Routledge, 2006), 252–53.

61. Quoted in Graham, "Urban Metabolism as Target."

62. Rasna Warah, Mohamud Dirios, and Ismail Osman, *Mogadishu Then and Now: A Pictorial Tribute to Africa's Most Wounded City* (Bloomington, IN: Author House, 2012), 3.

63. Mark Bowden, *Black Hawk Down: A Story of Modern War* (New York: Grove Press, 1999), 7.

64. President George H. W. Bush, "Towards a New World Order," address to a joint session of the United States Congress, Washington, DC, September 11, 1990. Full video of the speech is at www.youtube.com/watch?v=Chm7vStGV5I.

65. Human Rights Watch, "Somalia: Human Rights Developments," *Human Rights Watch World Report 1994*, online at www.hrw.org/reports/1994/WR94/Africa-08.htm.

66. Bowden, *Black Hawk Down*, 158.

67. David J. Morris, "The Big Suck: Notes from the Jarhead Underground," *Virginia Quarterly Review* 83, no. 1 (Winter 2007): 144–69.

68. Bowden, *Black Hawk Down*, 328.

69. Ibid., 21.
70. See Marc Lacy, "Amid Somalia's Troubles, Coca-Cola Hangs On," *New York Times*, July 10, 2006.
71. J. F. C. Fuller, *Plan 1919*, May 24, 1918, online at www.alternatewars.com/WWI/Fuller_1919.htm.
72. Colonel John A. Warden, "Air Theory for the Twenty-first Century," *Air and Space Power Journal*, September 1995.
73. Nuruddin Farah, "Country Cousins," *London Review of Books* 20, no. 17 (September 1998), 1.
74. Ibid., 1–2.
75. Hanna Batatu, "Some Observations on the Social Roots of Syria's Ruling Military Group and the Causes for Its Dominance," *Middle East Journal* 35, no. 3 (Summer 1981): 337.
76. Malise Ruthven, *Encounters with Islam: On Religion, Politics and Modernity* (London: I. B. Tauris, 2012), 95.
77. Ibid., 2.
78. U.S. State Department Cable Kingston 00682, dated 242332May2010, online at www.mattathiasschwartz.com/wp-content/uploads/2012/06/tny-cable.pdf.
79. Matthias Schwartz, "As Jamaican Drug Lord Is Sentenced, U.S. Still Silent on Massacre," *New Yorker*, June 8, 2012.
80. See Wayne Robinson, "Eradicating Organized Criminal Gangs in Jamaica: Can Lessons be Learnt from a Successful Counterinsurgency?" dissertation, U.S. Marine Corps Staff College, Quantico, VA, online at http://cdn.bajanreporter.com/wp-content/uploads/2010/06/Jamaica-Tivoli.pdf.
81. Richard Drayton, "From Kabul to Kingston: Army Tactics in Jamaica Resemble Those Used in Afghanistan—and It's No Mere Coincidence," *Guardian*, June 14, 2010.
82. Horace Helps, "Toll from Jamaica Violence Rises to 73," Reuters, May 27, 2010.
83. Benjamin Weiser, "Jamaican Drug Lord Gets Maximum Term," *New York Times*, June 8, 2012.
84. See "Witness Provides Compelling Account of Jamaican 'Garrisons,'" Caribbean News Now, May 25, 2012, online at www.caribbeannewsnow.com/news/newspublish/home.print.php?news_id=11049.
85. Obika Gray, *Demeaned but Empowered: The Social Power of the Urban Poor in Jamaica* (Kingston: University of the West Indies Press, 2004), 73–74.
86. Ibid., 151.
87. Christopher A. D. Charles and Orville Beckford, "The Informal Justice System in Garrison Constituencies," Department of Sociology, Psychology, and Social Work, University of the West Indies, online at www.academia.edu/1438587/The_Informal_Justice_System_in_Garrison_Constituencies.
88. Ibid.
89. Ibid., 16.

90. "Witness Provides Compelling Account of Jamaican 'Garrisons.'"
91. Charles and Beckford, "The Informal Justice System in Garrison Constituencies," 18.
92. See Ken Menkhaus, "Governance Without Government in Somalia: Spoilers, State Building, and the Politics of Coping," *International Security* 31, no. 3 (Winter 2006–7): 74–106.
93. Gray, *Demeaned but Empowered*, 25.
94. Ibid.
95. See Enrique Desmond Arias, "The Structure of Criminal Organizations in Kingston, Jamaica and Rio de Janeiro, Brazil," presentation delivered at the conference "Drug Trafficking, Violence, and Instability in Mexico, Colombia, and the Caribbean: Implications for US National Security," Ridgeway Center for International Security Studies, University of Pittsburgh, October 30, 2009.
96. See Enrique Desmond Arias, "The 2010 Emergency and Party Politics in Kingston, Jamaica: Towards a Less Violent Democracy," *Revista*, Winter 2012, online at www.drclas.harvard.edu/publications/revistaonline/winter-2012/2010-emergency-and-party-politics-kingston-jamaica.
97. Desmond Arias, personal communication via email, November 22, 2012.
98. Ibid.
99. Anonymous witness at the trial of Christopher Coke, May 2012, reported in "Witness Provides Compelling Account of Jamaican 'Garrisons.'"
100. Sullivan and Elkus, "Postcard from Mumbai," 10.
101. See David J. Kilcullen, *Counterinsurgency* (New York: Oxford University Press, 2010), xi–xii.
102. Nora Bensahel and Patrick M. Cronin, *America's Civilian Operations Abroad: Understanding Past and Future Requirements* (Washington, DC: Center for a New American Security, 2012).
103. Angel Rabasa, Robert D. Blackwill, Peter Chalk, Kim Cragin, C. Christine Fair, Brian A. Jackson, Brian Michael Jenkins, Seth G. Jones, Nathaniel Shestak, and Ashley J. Tellis, *The Lessons of Mumbai* (Santa Monica, CA: RAND Corporation, 2009), 13.
104. Ben Connable and Martin C. Libicki, *How Insurgencies End* (Santa Monica, CA: RAND Corporation, 2010), xviii.
105. See "DIY Weapons of the Syrian Rebels," *Atlantic*, February 2013.
106. Ibid.
107. For detailed descriptions of the battle, see Richard S. Lowry, *New Dawn: The Battles for Fallujah* (New York: Savas Beatie, 2010), and Bing West, *No True Glory: A Frontline Account of the Battle for Fallujah* (London: Bantam Press, 2006).
108. Qiao Liang and Wang Xiangsui, *Unrestricted Warfare* (Beijing: PLA Literature and Arts Publishing House, 1999).
109. See Richard Dobbs, Jaana Remes, James Manyika, Charles Roxburgh, Sven Smit, and Fabian Schaer, *Urban World: Cities and the Rise of the Consuming*

*Class*, McKinsey and Company, June 2012, online at www.mckinsey.com/insights/urbanization/urban_world_cities_and_the_rise_of_the_consuming_class; IBM, "Smarter Cities," online at www.ibm.com/smarterplanet/us/en/smarter_cities/overview/index.html.

110. See Scott Nelson et al., "Charlie Company 1/5 Marines: Lessons Learned, Operation Hue City," operational after-action review, 1968, online at www.au.af.mil/au/awc/awcgate/lessons/hue.pdf. For a general description of the battle, see Erik Villard, *The 1968 Tet Offensive Battles of Quang Tri and Hue City* (Washington, DC: U.S. Army Center for Military History, 2008).

111. See Olga Oliker, *Russia's Chechen Wars 1994–2000: Lessons from the Urban Combat* (Washington, DC: Rand Publishing, 2001).

112. See Amnesty International, *Israel and the Occupied Territories: Under the Rubble: House Demolition and Destruction of Land and Property*, May 2004, online at www.amnesty.org/en/library/info/MDE15/033/2004; "Israel Levels Palestinian Homes: Israel Ignores UN Calls to Halt Destruction of Palestinian Properties in East Jerusalem," Al Jazeera, October 28, 2009, online at www.aljazeera.com/news/middleeast/2009/10/2009102822111496109.html.

113. Eyal Weizman, "The Art of War," *Frieze*, no. 99 (May 2006), online at www.frieze.com/issue/article/the_art_of_war.

114. Ibid.

115. Peter Arnett, "Major Describes Move," *New York Times*, February 8, 1968.

116. Mark Owen and Kevin Maurer, *No Easy Day: The Firsthand Account of the Mission That Killed Osama Bin Laden* (New York: Penguin, 2012), ch. 4.

117. Paula Broadwell, "Travels with Paula (1): A Time to Build," at Thomas E. Ricks, *Best Defense (Foreign Policy)* blog, January 13, 2011, online at http://ricks.foreignpolicy.com/posts/2011/01/13/travels_with_paula_i_a_time_to_build.

118. See Jonathan Rugman, "UN Food Stolen from the Starving in Somalia: Fake Camp Fraud," *Times* (London), June 15, 2009, online at www.hiiraan.com/news4/2009/jun/11095/un_food_is_stolen_from_the_starving_in_somalia_fake_camp_fraud.aspx.

119. Matt Potter, *Outlaws Inc.: Under the Radar and On the Black Market with the World's Most Dangerous Smugglers* (New York: Bloomsbury, 2001), 139–44.

120. See David J. Kilcullen, "Counterinsurgency: The State of a Controversial Art," in Paul B. Rich and Isabelle Duyvesteyn, eds., *The Routledge Handbook of Insurgency and Counterinsurgency* (London: Routledge, 2012).

121. For a recent comprehensive study of insurgency outcomes, see Connable and Libicki, *How Insurgencies End*.

## Chapter 3

1. Our partner unit at this time was the reconnaissance platoon of the 2nd Battalion, Pacific Islands Regiment, part of the Papua New Guinea Defence Force (PNGDF).

2. See Leonid Zalizynak, "The Ethnographic Record, and Structural Changes in the Prehistoric Hunter-Gatherer Economy of Boreal Europe," in Marek Zvelebil and Robin Dennell, eds., *Harvesting the Sea, Farming the Forest: The Emergence of Neolithic Societies in the Baltic Region* (Sheffield, UK: Sheffield Academic Press, 1998), ch. 5.

3. For the "fishers of men" quote, see Matthew 4:19 and Mark 1:17 in the New Testament.

4. "Random Stuff to Think About," *Life in Rocinha*, April 2, 2012, online at http://lifeinrocinha.blogspot.com.

5. This case study, though presented as a hypothetical example here in order to protect sources, is based on actual participant observation and interviews in the field conducted in Kandahar between March 2008 and May 2011. Where appropriate, individual interviews and sources are noted.

6. According to the CIA World Factbook, 43.6 percent of the Afghan population is age fourteen or younger. See "Afghanistan Demographic Profile 2010," at www.indexmundi.com/afghanistan/demographics_profile.html, accessed January 21, 2011

7. See Thomas Ruttig, "How Tribal Are the Taleban?" Thematic Paper 04/10, Afghanistan Analysts Network, online at http://aan-afghanistan.com/index.asp?id=865, accessed December 20, 2010.

8. In the Afghan context, the Sunni Muslim honorific *mullah* usually refers to a local religious leader, who may or may not have completed formal religious studies. The term *maulawi* normally refers to someone who has completed a full course of study at a recognized madrassa, or Islamic seminary.

9. Presentation by Dr. Carter Malkasian during pre-deployment training for 1st Marine Expeditionary Force, U.S. Naval Base Point Loma, San Diego, November 2011.

10. During a tour on Cyprus in 1997 with the United Nations Peacekeeping Force in Cyprus, I regularly observed Greek Cypriot Orthodox priests taking a leading role in organizing demonstrations in Eleftheria Square, Nicosia, and at major crossing points across the Green Line that divides Greek and Turkish Cypriots. On the similar roles of Catholic clergy during the uprising in East Timor, see David J. Kilcullen, "The Political Consequences of Military Operations in Indonesia, 1945–99," Ph.D. dissertation, University of New South Wales, 2001, 115, 146–50.

11. For an outstanding account of Afghan warlord state-building behavior during this period, see Antonio Giustozzi, *Empires of Mud: Wars and Warlords in Afghanistan* (London: Hurst, 2009).

12. See Mullah Abdul Salam Zaeef ['Abd al-Salam Za'if], with Alex van Linschoten and Felix Kuehn, *My Life with the Taliban* (New York: Columbia University Press, 2010), xxii.

13. Anand Gopal, "The Battle for Afghanistan: Militancy and Conflict in Kandahar," New America Foundation, Washington, DC, 2010, 7, online at http://security.newamerica.net/sites/newamerica.net/files/policydocs/kandahar_0.pdf.

14. For one of several versions of this story in wide circulation in Kabul in late 2009, see Miles Amoore, "Taliban Bring Order, Say Afghans," *Sunday Times* (London), December 14, 2009.

15. Interviews with Afghan respondents SP in Jalalabad, September 2009; RP and RSP in Kabul, December 2009; and FA in Kabul, October 2010.

16. Interview with Afghan respondent RP, a Taliban-aligned businessman from Kandahar, in Kabul, December 2009.

17. See Hernando de Soto, *The Mystery of Capital: Why Capitalism Triumphs in the West and Fails Everywhere Else* (New York: Basic Books, 2000).

18. Stathis N. Kalyvas, *The Logic of Violence in Civil War*, Cambridge Studies in Comparative Politics (Cambridge, UK: Cambridge University Press, 2006), 12.

19. Ibid.

20. C. E. Callwell, *Small Wars: Their Principles and Practice* (London: HMSO, 1906), 21. The familiar notion of "nonstate actors" is too broad to be useful here, because in modern conflict there may be dozens of nonstate actors in any given space, including humanitarian NGOs, local or international businesses, development contractors, bilateral and multilateral aid donors, the news media, and local or international civil society organizations. Many of these are not armed, do not apply violence, and do not prey on population groups. Likewise, the concept of "illegal armed groups" (like the related concept of "illicit networks") has extremely limited applicability in failed or failing states, where there is no clear sovereign legal authority. Also, in civil wars where sovereignty is fragmented and legal frameworks are contested, the construct of "legal" and "illegal" armed groups lacks real-world meaning. Under my definition, a nonstate armed group may or may not be formally structured, it may or may not have an overt political motivation or an explicit ideology, and its actions may or may not serve a broader purpose than the self-interest of its members. But equally, the violence it applies is not merely random, psychotic, or bestial (though atrocious cruelties can and do occur) but rather *purposeful*—it is violence that supports a wider goal, that shows a pattern of rational intent.

21. For example, members of the Islamic Defenders Front (Front Pembela Islam) in Indonesia or the Zeta Killers in Mexico would fall into the category of vigilantes or armed public defender groups.

22. I am indebted for this last insight to Professor Tammy S. Schultz of the United States Marine Corps Command and Staff College, Quantico, Virginia.

23. David Witwer, "'The Most Racketeer-Ridden Union in America': The Problem of Corruption in the Teamsters Union During the 1930s," in Emmanuel Kreike and William Chester Jordan, eds., *Corrupt Histories* (Rochester, NY: University of Rochester Press, 2004), 200.

24. Ibid., 212–13.

25. See, for example, Philip Selznick, *The Organizational Weapon: A Study of Bolshevik Strategy and Tactics* (Glencoe, IL: Free Press of Glencoe, 1960), 27–28, 72–73.

26. Ibid., 26.

27. Ilse Derluyn, Eric Broekaert, Gilberte Schuyten, and Els De Temmerman, "Post-traumatic Stress in Former Ugandan Child Soldiers," *Lancet* 363 (May 2004): 861–63.

28. Diego Gambetta, *Codes of the Underworld: How Criminals Communicate* (Princeton, NJ: Princeton University Press, 2009), 17.

29. See United Nations, *Final Report of the United Nations Commission of Experts*, Annex IV, "The Policy of Ethnic Cleansing," United Nations, New York, December 28, 1994, online at www.ess.uwe.ac.uk/comexpert/ANX/IV.htm#0-VI.

30. See Lijepa Nasa Domovina Hrvatska, "Brcko BC001-EA," online at www.lijepanasadomovinahrvatska.com/dokumenti-mainmenu-70/79-iskazi/433-br-bc001ea.

31. Author's interview with British officers recently returned from service in Bosnia with UNPROFOR and SFOR, British Army training area, Copehill Down, UK, September 8, 1997.

32. Author's interviews and personal observation in the Balibo, Maliana, Batugade, and Ermera areas of East Timor, September 1999 to February 2000.

33. Interview with a U.S. diplomat serving in rural areas of Peru during the early period of the Shining Path uprising, Washington, DC, February 20, 2012.

34. Bernard B. Fall, "The Theory and Practice of Insurgency and Counterinsurgency," *Naval War College Review*, Winter 1998 [1965].

35. See the Appendix for a more detailed explanation of the theoretical basis for this discussion, which draws on the theory of normative systems and in particular on the work of Carlos Alchourron and Eugenio Bulygin in legal theory, David Dressler in sociology, and Thomas Agotnes et al. in computer science.

36. In taking this definitional approach, I draw in part on Hans Kelsen, *General Theory of Law and State* (Cambridge, MA: Harvard University Press, 1943), 110ff., and in part on Carlos E. Alchourron and Eugenio Bulygin, *Normative Systems* (New York: Springer Verlag, 1971), 53–59.

37. Max Weber, *The Theory of Social and Economic Organization* (New York: Simon and Schuster, 2009), 154.

38. Mao Zedong, "Problems of War and Strategy," *Selected Works of Mao Tse Tung*, vol. 2 (Peking: Foreign Languages Press, 1967).

39. Simon Neville, "U.S. Road Deaths at Lowest Levels for 60 years . . . but Still One Killed Every 16 Minutes," *Daily Mail*, April 1, 2011.

40. Joseph Conrad, *Heart of Darkness* (New York: New American Library, Signet Classics,1959), 121–22

41. For instance, Adam Hochschild argues that the character of Kurtz is drawn from Conrad's direct observation of colonial officials in the field, in particular Captain Leon Rom of the Belgian Force Publique. Adam Hochschild, *King Leopold's Ghost* (New York: Mariner Books, 1999), ch 9.

42. Joseph Conrad, "An Outpost of Progress," in *Tales of Unrest*, 1898, online at http://ebooks.adelaide.edu.au/c/conrad/joseph/c75ta/chapter3.html

43. Author's personal observation in Baghdad and surrounding areas, January to March 2006, and February to September 2007.

44. Author's observation; see also "Informant Led U.S. to Strike Zarqawi Dead," *Courier* (James Logan High School, Union City, CA), June 9, 2006, online at http://jameslogancourier.org/index.php?itemid=365.

45. See Nir Rosen, *Aftermath: Following the Bloodshed of America's Wars in the Middle East* (New York: Nation Books, 2010), 257.

46. David Kilcullen, "Reading al-Anbar," *American Interest*, September/October 2010.

47. For a detailed description of these events, see United States Marine Corps, *Al-Anbar Awakening*, 2 vols. (Quantico, VA: USMC, 2010).

48. Kilcullen, "Reading al-Anbar."

49. See Human Rights Watch, "Flooding South Lebanon: Israel's Use of Cluster Munitions in Lebanon in July and August 2006," February 17, 2008; BBC News, "Million Bomblets in S Lebanon," September 26, 2006.

50. Robert Fisk, "Hizbollah's Reconstruction of Lebanon Is Winning the Loyalty of Disaffected Shia," *Independent*, August 24, 2006.

51. "Israel's Barak Says Hezbollah Stronger than Ever," Agence France-Presse, January 7, 2008,

52. Fisk, "Hizbollah's Reconstruction of Lebanon."

53. Roula Khalaf, "Hezbollah Hopes to Engineer a Quick Recovery," *Financial Times*, August 27, 2006.

54. Ibid.

55. See, for example, Benjamin S. Lambeth, *Air Operations in Israel's War Against Hezbollah: Learning from Lebanon and Getting It Right in Gaza* (Santa Monica, CA: RAND Corporation, 2011); David E. Johnson, *Military Capabilities for Hybrid War: Insights from the Israel Defense Forces in Lebanon and Gaza* (Santa Monica, CA: RAND Corporation, 2011); Avi Kober, "The Israel Defense Forces in the Second Lebanon War: Why the Poor Performance?" *Journal of Strategic Studies* 31, no. 1 (2008): 3–40.

56. "Israel's Barak Says Hezbollah Stronger than Ever."

57. Quoted in Physicians for Human Rights, *The Taliban's War on Women: A Health and Human Rights Crisis in Afghanistan* (Boston: Physicians for Human Rights, 1998), 117–18.

58. Nushin Arbabzadah, "The 1980s Mujahideen, the Taliban and the Shifting Idea of Jihad," *Guardian*, April 28, 2011.

59. Ibid.

60. Quoted in Roy Gutman, "We've Met the Enemy in Afghanistan, and He's Changed," McClatchy Newspapers, March 14, 2010.

61. Interviews with schoolchildren, teachers, and school principals in the Jalalabad, Kunduz, and Kunar regions, September and December 2009.

62. Ray Rivera, "Taliban Challenge U.S. in Eastern Afghanistan," *New York Times*, December 25, 2010.

63. Joel S. Migdal, *Strong Societies and Weak States: State-Society Relations and State Capabilities in the Third World* (Princeton, NJ: Princeton University Press, 1988). Migdal's work develops a functional model of state effectiveness,

drawing on previous work by Gabriel Almond, G. Bingham Powell, Harry Eckstein, and others.

64. Ibid., 3.

65. William Maley, *The Afghanistan Wars* (London: Palgrave Macmillan, 2002), 13.

66. Robert Kemp, "The District Delivery Program in Afghanistan: A Case Study in Organizational Challenges," *Small Wars Journal*, June 26, 2012.

67. Author's discussion with Afghan provincial government official, Kabul, December 2009.

68. Steve Bowman and Catherine Dale, *War in Afghanistan: Strategy, Military Operations, and Issues for Congress* (Washington, DC: Congressional Research Service, 2009), 5ff.

69. Jerome Starkey, "Former Warlord Blames UK for Breakdown in Security," *Independent*, June 9, 2008.

70. James C. Scott, *The Moral Economy of the Peasant: Rebellion and Subsistence in Southeast Asia* (New Haven, CT: Yale University Press, 1976), 1, 3–4.

71. Ibid., 5.

72. Ibid.

73. See James C. Scott, *Domination and the Arts of Resistance: Hidden Transcripts* (New Haven, CT: Yale University Press, 1992).

74. Obika Gray, *Demeaned but Empowered: The Social Power of the Urban Poor in Jamaica* (Kingston: University of the West Indies Press, 2004), 60.

75. Karl D. Jackson, *Traditional Authority, Islam, and Rebellion: A Study of Indonesian Political Behavior* (Berkeley: University of California Press, 1980).

76. David J. Kilcullen, *The Accidental Guerrilla: Fighting Small Wars in the Midst of a Big One* (New York: Oxford University Press, 2009), 76.

77. Author's personal observations and discussions with community elders in Sadr City, Abu Ghraib, Dora, and Kadhimiya districts of Baghdad, March to July 2007.

78. Ibid.

79. For a discussion of this concept, see C. Boggs, *Gramsci's Marxism* (London: Pluto, 1976), 39.

Chapter 4

1. John Pollock, "People Power 2.0: How Civilians Helped Win the Libyan Information War," *MIT Technology Review*, April 20, 2012, 1.

2. Ibid.

3. See Pollock's reporting in *MIT Technology Review*, including "Watching a Digital 'Jasmine Revolution' Unfold: Using Facebook and Twitter to track trouble on the streets of Tunisia," June 21, 2011; "Play It Again, King Mohammed: Oldest Arab Monarchy Uses Classical Tactics to Stifle Latest Protests," June 22, 2011; "Streetbook: How Egyptian and Tunisian Youth Hacked the Arab Spring," August 23, 2011; and "The Voice of Libya: An Inspiring Story of Citizen Journalism," September 5, 2011.

4. In this chapter, as throughout this book, I use the term "connectedness" to describe the general phenomenon of increasingly dense informational, financial, human and electronic linkages among populations across the planet, and the term *connectivity* or *network connectivity* to describe the narrower subset of those linkages that is associated with access to mobile communications technology and, especially, the Internet.

5. *Department of Defense Dictionary of Military and Associated Terms*, United States Government Joint Publication 1–02 (Washington, DC: Department of Defense, 2001), 533.

6. Ibid.

7. Obviously, there's a lot more to the international law of armed conflict than just this territorial aspect, and lawyers generally recognize that a person's combatant status "travels" with that person if he or she leaves an area of conflict. My point here is merely that the "theater of war" construct, which drives part of this legal regime, is a spatial one.

8. Australian Army, *Future Land Warfare Operating Concept: Complex Warfighting* (Canberra: Australian Army Headquarters, Directorate-General of Future Land Warfare, 2004), 8–9.

9. Karoun Demirjian, "Creech Drone Pilot, Instructor Feted in White House Dinner Honoring Iraq Veterans," *Las Vegas Sun*, March 2, 2012.

10. Elisabeth Bumiller, "A Day Job Waiting for a Kill Shot a World Away," *New York Times*, July 29, 2012.

11. Relevant Supreme Court judgments include *Hamdi v. Rumsfeld* (2004), *Hamdan v. Rumsfeld* (2006), and *Boumedienne v. Bush* (2008). See also David Rivkin and Lee Casey, "Within His Rights," *American Lawyer*, February 9, 2013.

12. See James Gordon Meek and David Saltonstall, "Pakistani Taliban Leader Hakimullah Mehsud Is Brutal Mastermind Behind Thwarted Times Square Bombing," New York *Daily News*, May 9, 2010; United States Department of State, Rewards for Justice Program, wanted poster for Hakimullah Mehsud, online at www.rewardsforjustice.net/index.cfm?page=mehsud.

13. Akbar Ahmed, *The Thistle and the Drone: How America's War on Terror Became a Global War on Tribal Islam* (Washington, DC: Brookings Institution Press, 2013).

14. Siobhan Gorman, Yochi Dreazen, and August Cole, "Insurgents Hack U.S. Drones," *Wall Street Journal*, December 17, 2009.

15. Ibid.

16. Ibid.

17. Noah Schachtman, "Computer Virus Hits U.S. Drone Fleet," *Wired*, October 7, 2011.

18. David Sanger, *Confront and Conceal: Obama's Secret Wars and Surprising Use of American Power* (New York: Random House, 2012).

19. David Sanger, "Obama Order Sped Up Wave of Cyberattacks Against Iran," *New York Times*, June 1, 2012.

20. Ibid.
21. Elisabeth Bumiller and Thom Shanker, "Panetta Warns of Dire Threat of Cyber-attack Against U.S.," *New York Times*, October 11, 2012.
22. Mikko Hypponen, "Cyber Pearl Harbor," *F-Secure* blog, October 18, 2012, online at www.f-secure.com/weblog/archives/00002446.html.
23. Thomas Rid, "CyberFail: The Obama Administration's Lousy Record on Cyber-Security," *New Republic*, February 4, 2013.
24. Pollock, "Streetbook," 2.
25. Ibid.
26. Olivier Kramsch, "Towards a Mediterranean Scale of Governance: Twenty-First Century Urban Networks Across the 'Inner Sea,'" in Barbara Hooper and Olivier Kramsch, eds., *Cross-Border Governance in the European Union* (London: Routledge 2007), 200.
27. Ibid., 4.
28. Paul Wood, "Gangster's Life of Serb Warlord," BBC News, January 15, 2000.
29. Dave Fowler, "Football, Blood and War," *Observer*, January 18, 2004.
30. Author's participant observation and discussions with community elders in Dili, Balibo, Ermera, and Batugade districts, East Timor, September 22–23, 1999, November 15, 1999, and January 2, 2000. See analysis in Chapter 4 of David J. Kilcullen, "Political Consequences of Military Operations in Indonesia, 1945–1999," Ph.D. dissertation, University of New South Wales, 2000.
31. James M. Dorsey, "Pitched Battles: The Role of Ultra Soccer Fans in the Arab Spring," *Eurasia Review*, December 24, 2012.
32. Ibid.
33. Ibid.
34. Ibid.
35. Ibid.
36. Robert F. Worth, "How a Single Match Can Ignite a Revolution," *New York Times*, January 21, 2011.
37. Jonathan Adams, "Tunisian Protests Escalate, Reflecting Widespread Discontent," *Christian Science Monitor*, January 10, 2011.
38. See the Web portal of the democracy activist group Nawaat for screenshots of Amamou's smartphone post, at http://nawaat.org/portail/2011/01/06/tunisia-blogger-slim-amamou-arrested-today.
39. Peter Beaumont, "The Truth About Twitter, Facebook and the Uprisings in the Arab World," *Guardian*, February 24, 2011.
40. Ibid.
41. Ibid.
42. Pollock, "Streetbook," 6.
43. Ibid.
44. Quinn Norton, "How Anonymous Picks Targets, Launches Attacks, and Takes Powerful Organizations Down," *Wired*, July 3, 2012.
45. Evan Hill, "Hackers Hit Tunisian Websites," Al Jazeera, January 3, 2011.

46. See Open Net Initiative at https://opennet.net, WikiLeaks at http://wikileaks .org, Cryptome at http://cryptome.org, and Nawaat at http://nawaat.org.

47. Kramsch, "Towards a Mediterranean Scale,"

48. See "Egypt Population Reaches 91 Million, Grows 18 Percent in Eight Years," *Ahram Online*, August 30, 2012, online at http://english.ahram.org .eg/News/51634.aspx.

49. Andrew McLaughlin, "Egypt's Big Internet Disconnect," *Guardian*, January 31, 2011.

50. Ibid.

51. David Kirkpatrick and David Sanger, "A Tunisian-Egyptian Link That Shook Arab History," *New York Times*, February 13, 2011.

52. Kamel Labidi, "Ben Ali and Mubarak: Brothers in Arms," Index on Censorship, February 8, 2011, online at www.indexoncensorship.org/2011/02/ben-ali-and-mubarak-brothers-in-arms.

53. Kirkpatrick and Sanger, "A Tunisian-Egyptian Link."

54. Ibid.

55. Pollock, "Streetbook," 6.

56. Quinn Norton, "2011: The Year Anonymous Took On Cops, Dictators and Existential Dread," *Wired*, January 11, 2012.

57. Chavala Madlena, "Telecomix: Tech Support for the Arab Spring," *Guardian*, July 7, 2011.

58. John Naughton, "How Twitter Engineers Outwitted Mubarak in One Weekend," *Observer*, February 6, 2011.

59. Kirkpatrick and Sanger, "A Tunisian-Egyptian Link."

60. Jenna Krajeski, "The Taking of Kasr Al Nil," *Newsdesk* blog, *New Yorker*, January 28, 2011.

61. Ibid.

62. Kareem Fahim, "Egyptian Hopes Converged in Fight for Cairo Bridge," *New York Times*, January 28, 2011.

63. Kirkpatrick and Sanger, "A Tunisian-Egyptian Link."

64. Krajeski, "The Taking of Kasr Al Nil."

65. Fahim, "Egyptian Hopes Converged in Fight for Cairo Bridge."

66. Kirkpatrick and Sanger, "A Tunisian-Egyptian Link."

67. See "Egyptian Activist Shares Evolution of a Revolution," *UCLA Today*, n.d., online at http://today.ucla.edu/portal/ut/PRN-activist-ahmed-maher-on-campus-219353.aspx.

68. Labidi, "Ben Ali and Mubarak."

69. "Who Are the Pro-Mubarak Supporters?" Euronews, February 3, 2011, online at http://www.euronews.com/2011/02/03/who-are-the-pro-mubarak-supporters.

70. "Who Are the Pro-Mubarak Protestors?" MSNBC News, February 2, 2011.

71. "Gunfire Breaks Out as Mubarak's Allies and Foes Clash," MSNBC News, February 2, 2011.

72. Ibid.

73. Ibid.
74. Timothy Phelps and Laura King, "Hosni Mubarak Supporters Attack Protestors in Cairo's Tahrir Square," *Los Angeles Times*, February 2, 2011.
75. Kirkpatrick and Sanger, "A Tunisian-Egyptian Link."
76. Hassan Aly, "Reflections on the Libyan Uprising," Ohio State University College of Arts and Sciences, February 16, 2011, online at http://artsandsciences.osu.edu/news/reflections-on-the-libyan-uprising.
77. Simon Shuster, "The Tyrant of Belarus: Gaddafi's Friend Far, Far to the North?" *Time*, March 2, 2011.
78. Matthew Weaver, "Muammar Gaddafi Condemns Tunisia Uprising," *Guardian*, January 16, 2011.
79. Ian Black, "Gaddafi Urges Violent Showdown and Tells Libya 'I'll Die a Martyr,'" *Guardian*, February 22, 2011.
80. See Osama Kh. Ali, Noorazuan Hashim, Katiman Rostam, and Hamzah Jusoh, "Population Growth in the Region of Tripoli, Libya," *Australian Journal of Basic and Applied Sciences* 5, no. 11 (November 2011): 1609–15; Central Intelligence Agency, entry for Libya in *The World Factbook, 2012*, online at https://www.cia.gov/library/publications/the-world-factbook/geos/ly.html
81. Hassan Aly, "Reflections on the Libyan Uprising."
82. For example, Benghazi's only sewage treatment plant was four decades old and raw sewage was regularly pumped into the sea. See Andrew Lee Butters, "Dispatch from Libya: Why Benghazi Rebelled," *Time*, March 3, 2011.
83. Black, "Gaddafi Urges Violent Showdown."
84. Nick Meo, "Libya Protests: 140 'Massacred' as Gaddafi Sends In Snipers to Crush Dissent," *Daily Telegraph*, February 20, 2011.
85. John Hooper and Ian Black, "Libya Defectors: Pilots Told to Bomb Protestors Flee to Malta," *Guardian*, February 21, 2011.
86. Ibid.
87. Martin Chulov, "Inside Libya's First Free City: Jubilation Fails to Hide Deep Wounds," *Guardian*, February 23, 2011.
88. Ibid.
89. Beaumont, "The Truth About Twitter."
90. Pollock, "People Power."
91. Ibid.
92. Ibid.
93. See Pollock, "People Power" and Andy Carvin, "Munitions in Misrata: A Virtual Investigation by @acarvin's Twitter Followers," Storify, online at http://storify.com/acarvin/munitions-in-misurata.
94. See Pollock, "Streetbook" and the Anonymous #OpLibya IRC Channel, online at http://irc.lc/Anonops/OpLibya
95. Audrey Kurth Cronin, "Cyber-mobilization: The New Levee en Masse," *Parameters* 36, no. 2 (Summer 2006): 77–87.
96. Ibid., 77–78.

97. Ibid., 79.

98. Ibid., 81.

99. Marshall McLuhan, *Culture Is Our Business* (New York: Ballantine Books, 1970), 66.

100. Chulov, "Inside Libya's First Free City."

101. Dorsey, "Pitched Battles."

102. Ibid.

103. Ibid.

104. Gaddafi's mercenaries were not all black—there were eastern Europeans, Pakistanis, and a few white South Africans among them—but many allegedly came from Chad, Ghana, Kenya, Sudan, and other black African countries. This led to protests by the African Union that the rebels were indiscriminately targeting black migrant workers and people from Libya's black ethnic groups.

105. Ibid.

106. Ibid.

107. Ibid.

108. Ian Black, "As Libya Uprising Reaches Tripoli Gaddafi Vows to 'Open Up the Arsenals,'" *Guardian*, February 25, 2011.

109. Ibid.

110. "ICC to Probe Gaddafi over Violence," Al Jazeera, March 3, 2011.

111. United Nations News Centre, "Security Council Authorizes 'All Necessary Measures' to Protect Civilians in Libya," March 17, 2011.

112. Author's interview with a member of the Libyan National Transitional Council, Oslo, Norway, June 29, 2011.

113. See Portia Walker, "Qatari Military Advisers on the Ground, Helping Libyan Rebels Get into Shape," *Washington Post*, May 12, 2011.

114. Pollock, *People Power 2.0.*

115. Indeed, these problems are perhaps an inevitable downside of the light-footprint, limited-ground-presence approach, since with extremely few NATO boots on the ground, target identification and coordination with rebel forces were more difficult than they might otherwise have been.

116. Martin Chulov, "Gaddafi's Last Moments: 'I Saw the Hand Holding the Gun and I Saw It Fire,'" *Guardian*, October 20, 2011.

117. Media analysis by Nathaniel Rosenblatt, Caerus Associates, Middle East North Africa Analysis team, March-April 2012.

118. Andrei Netto, "Muammar Gaddafi's 'Trophy' Body on Show in Misrata Meat Store," *Guardian*, October 21, 2011.

119. Butters, "Dispatch from Libya."

120. Ibid.

121. Ibid.

122. For a description of this enormous project, see MEED, "The Great Man-Made River Project," December 2011, online at www.meed.com/Journals/1/Files/2011/12/11/Sample%20Chapter.pdf.

123. Butters, "Dispatch from Libya."
124. Joseph Felter and Brian Fishman, *Al Qaeda's Foreign Fighters in Iraq: A First Look at the Sinjar Records* (West Point, NY: Combating Terrorism Center, 2007), 11–12.
125. Butters, "Dispatch from Libya."
126. Ibid.
127. Amr Hamdy, *Survey of ICT and Education in Africa: Libya Country Report* (Washington, DC: World Bank, 2007).
128. African Economic Outlook, *Libya Country Note*, African Development Bank, 2012, 11.
129. Ibid.
130. Ibid., 13.
131. In part, the restraint shown by the army in Egypt was perhaps a result of attempts—by the United States, in particular—over several decades of military assistance and advisory effort, to professionalize the Egyptian army. This professionalization effort was aimed at helping the army become less politicized, more cognizant of human rights and international law, and more focused on external threats rather than internal repression. When the crisis hit, phone calls between senior U.S. military officers and their Egyptian counterparts (who, in some cases, had attended professional training courses in the United States) may have helped encourage Egyptian military leaders, at the moment of crisis, to refuse to attack their own people. Obviously, no such cooperation or professionalization effort existed for Libya.
132. "Gaddafi Survival Means Weak Army, Co-opted Tribes," Associated Press, February 23, 2011.
133. "Libya—130 Soldiers Executed," Agence-France Press, February 23, 2011.
134. Nick Lockwood, personal communication via email from Benghazi, March 2011.
135. Personal observation and interviews by a Caerus field team, Benghazi, February–May 2011.
136. See "DIY Weapons of the Libyan Rebels," *Atlantic*, June 14, 2011.
137. Pollock, "Streetbook".
138. Stéphanie Plasse, "Libya: Gaddafi and his Mali-Chad Tuareg Mercenaries," *Afrik News*, March 24, 2011.
139. "Gaddafi Hires Separatist Militants from Niger, Mali, Algeria and Burkina Faso to Fight Rebels in Libya," Agence-France Presse, March 4, 2011.
140. Michael Gunning, "Background to a Revolution," *N Plus One Magazine*, August 26, 2011.
141. Author's interview with Nathaniel Rosenblatt, Caerus senior analyst, Washington, DC, March 11, 2013.
142. Suzanne Saleeby, "Sowing the Seeds of Dissent: Economic Grievances and the Syrian Social Contract's Unraveling," *Jadiliyya*, February 16, 2012.
143. Kareem Fahim and Hwaida Saad, "A Faceless Teenage Refugee Who Helped Ignite Syria's War," *New York Times*, February 8, 2013.

144. Katherine Marsh, Matthew Taylor and Haroon Siddique, "Syria's Crackdown on Protesters Becomes Dramatically More Brutal," *Guardian*, April 25, 2011.

145. See Yassin al-Haj Salih, *The Syrian Shabiha and Their State* (Berlin: Heinrich Böll Stiftung, 2012).

146. Ibid.

147. Helmi Noman, "The Emergence of Open and Organized Pro-Government Cyber Attacks in the Middle East: The Case of the Syrian Electronic Army," *Information Warfare Monitor*, May 30, 2011.

148. Rosenblatt, interview, March 11, 2013

149. Marcus F. Franda, *Launching into Cyberspace: Internet Development and Politics in Five World Regions* (Boulder, CO: Lynne Rienner Publishers, 2002), 70.

150. Ibid.

151. See "Asad's Wife," uploaded by XxHAMSHOURExX, April 3, 2007, www.youtube.com/watch?v=wRfs1qJQ_J8.

152. Nathaniel Rosenblatt, personal communication via email to the author, March 11, 2013.

153. Ibid.

154. Ibid.

155. Interview with researcher studying Libyan and Syrian anti-regime networks, Washington, DC, March 11, 2013.

156. Ibid.

157. "Rebels in Syria's Largest City of Aleppo Mostly Poor, Pious and from Rural Backgrounds," Associated Press, October 16, 2012.

158. For a discussion on youth unemployment and social exclusion in Syria's cities, see Nader Kabbani and Noura Kamel, *Youth Exclusion in Syria: Social, Economic, and Institutional Dimensions* (Dubai: Wolfensohn Center for Development, 2007).

159. Nour Ali, "Assad's Forces Pound Syrian Port City of Latakia," *Guardian*, August 14, 2011.

160. See "DIY Weapons of the Syrian Rebels," *Atlantic*, February 20, 2013.

161. Ibid.

162. Ibid.

163. David Ronfeldt, John Arquilla, Graham E. Fuller, and Melissa Fuller, *The Zapatista Social Netwar in Mexico* (Santa Monica, CA: RAND Corporation, 1998), 7.

164. Author's field notes, Baghdad, January–March 2006.

165. Peter Harling, *Popular Protest in North Africa and the Middle East (VII): The Syrian Regime's Slow-Motion Suicide* (Damascus: International Crisis Group, 2011), 9.

166. "BART Officials Blocked Cell Phones During Transit Protest," Associated Press, August 12, 2011.

167. Ibid.

168. Michael Cabanatuan, "BART Admits Halting Cell Service to Stop Protests. Move to Disrupt Protesters' Plans Blasted as Violation of Free Speech," *San Francisco Chronicle*, August 12, 2011.

169. Paul Elias and John S. Marshall, "'Anonymous' Hackers Protest San Francisco's BART Cellphone Blocking," Associated Press, August 15, 2011.

170. Zusha Ellison, "After Cellphone Action, BART Faces Escalating Protests," *New York Times*, August 20, 2011.

171. Ibid.

172. Pollock, *People Power 2.0.*

## Chapter 5

1. "DIY Weapons of the Syrian Rebels," *Atlantic*, June 14, 2011.

2. See Caitlin Dewey, "Are Syria's Pro-Assad Hackers Up to Something More Nefarious?" *Washington Post*, March 1, 2013; Max Fisher, "Syria's Pro-Assad Hackers Infiltrate Human Rights Watch Web Site and Twitter Feed," *Washington Post*, March 17, 2013.

3. Abigail Fielding-Smith, "Alawite Heartland on Syria's Coast Remains Loyal to Assad Regime," *Washington Post*, March 15, 2013.

4. See Spencer Ackerman, "Syria Fires Scud Missiles, Burning Bombs and Even Sea Mines at Rebels," *Wired*, December 12, 2012; Joby Warrick, "Intelligence on Syrian Troops Readying Chemical Weapons for Use Prompted Obama's Warning," *Washington Post*, December 13, 2012.

5. See Ken Dilanian and Brian Bennet, "CIA Begins Sizing Up Islamic Extremists in Syria for Drone Strikes," *Los Angeles Times*, March 15, 2013; Press TV (Iran), "US Drone Strikes in Syria 'Dangerous Escalation,'" online at http://www.presstv.ir/usdetail/293911.html

6. Author's interview with Nathaniel Rosenblatt, Washington, DC, March 19, 2013.

7. Associated Press, "Opposition Activists Set Off Small Bombs During General Strike in Bangladesh's Capital," *Washington Post*, March 18, 2013.

8. For a discussion of groundwater arsenic poisoning and fecal contamination of surface water in Bangladesh, see Andrew Zolli and Ann Marie Healy, *Resilience: Why Things Bounce Back* (New York: Free Press, 2012), 110ff.

9. Sirajul Haq Talukder, "Managing Megacities: A Case Study of Metropolitan Regional Governance for Dhaka," Ph.D. dissertation, Murdoch University, Perth, 2006, iii.

10. Economist Intelligence Unit, "The Liveability Ranking and Overview," August 2012, online at https://www.eiu.com/public/topical_report .aspx?campaignid=Liveability2012.

11. "Dhaka Reels Under High Population Growth," New York *Daily News*, January 1, 2013.

12. Saleemul Huq and Mozaharul Alam, "Flood Management and Vulnerability of Dhaka City," in Alcira Kreimer, Margaret Arnold, and Anne Carlin, eds., *Building Safer Cities: The Future of Disaster Risk* (Washington, DC: World Bank, 2003), 126.

13. Jo Beall, Basudeb Guha-Khasnobis, and Ravi Kanbur, *Creating Place for the Displaced: Migration and Urbanization in Asia*, paper presented at the 13th Annual Conference of the Global Development Network, 16–18 June, 2012, p.1–5, online at http://www.gdn.int/admin/uploads/editor/files/2012Conf_Papers/Paper_Basudeb%20Guha_1_1.pdf

14. United Nations Human Settlements Programme (UN-HABITAT), "Dhaka's Extreme Vulnerability to Climate Change," State of the World's Cities, 2008/2009, online at http://www.unhabitat.org/downloads/docs/presskitsowc2008/Dhaka%20extreme.pdf.

15. Ibid., 122; Munich Re, *Megacities—Megarisks: Trends and Challenges for Insurance and Risk Management*, online at http://www.preventionweb.net/files/646_10363.pdf, p. 21.

16. GRID-Arendal Centre, "Potential Impact of Sea-Level Rise on Bangladesh," online at www.grida.no/publications/vg/climate/page/3086.aspx.

17. For Hurricane Sandy, see Hal Needham, "Hurricane Sandy Produces Record-Breaking Storm Surge," Southern Climate Impacts Planning Program, online at www.southernclimate.org/index.php/main/news/451. For Hurricane Katrina, see Richard D. Knabb, Jamie R. Rhome, and Daniel P. Brown, *Tropical Cyclone Report Hurricane Katrina 23–30 August 2005* (Washington, DC: National Hurricane Center, 2005 [updated 2011]), online at www.nhc.noaa.gov/pdf/TCR-AL122005_Katrina.pdf.

18. See, for example, the connections and partners listed on the highly socially networked blog *Life in Rocinha*, online at http://lifeinrocinha.blogspot.com.

19. See "Police Occupation and UPP," *Life in Rocinha*, October 15, 2012, online at http://lifeinrocinha.blogspot.com.

20. "Destroying Makoko," *Economist*, August 18, 2012.

21. Ibid.

22. Ibid.

23. Adam Nossitter, "Cholera Epidemic Envelops Coastal Slums in West Africa," *New York Times*, August 22, 2012.

24. Mike Davis, *Planet of Slums* (London: Verso, 2006), 26.

25. United Nations News Centre, "Deputy UN Chief Calls for Urgent Action to Tackle Global Sanitation Crisis," March 21, 2013.

26. Antonio Giustozzi, *Empires of Mud: Wars and Warlords in Afghanistan* (New York: Columbia University Press, 2012).

27. Of course, this is true of the natural landscape, too, which is shaped by war in a similar manner. But this happens, if anything, on a much longer time scale even than for urban areas, which are distinguished by the constant and intensive human interaction with the built environment of a densely inhabited landscape.

28. For a seminal description of hegemonic stability theory and its problems, see Duncan Snidal, "The Limits of Hegemonic Stability Theory," *International Organization* 39, no. 4 (Autumn 1985): 579–614.

29. Population growth figures drawn from Mongabay, online at http://population.mongabay.com.

30. Sara V. Flanagan et al., "Mitigation of Arsenic in Tube Well Water in Bangladesh," *Bulletin of the World Health Organization*, September 14, 2012.

31. See, for example, Jenny Stefanotti, "Fighting Malaria: The Bed Net Controversy," *Developing Jen* (blog), April 26, 2009, online at www.developingjen .com/blog/fighting-malaria-the-bed-net-controversy.

32. See Rajiv Chandrasekaran, *Imperial Life in the Emerald City: Inside Iraq's Green Zone* (New York: Knopf, 2006), and his *Little America: The War Within the War for Afghanistan* (New York: Vintage, 2012); Thomas E. Ricks, *Fiasco: The American Military Adventure in Iraq* (New York: Penguin, 2006); George Packer, *The Assassin's Gate: America in Iraq* (New York: Farrar, Straus, and Giroux, 2006); L. Paul Bremer, *My Year in Iraq: The Struggle to Build a Future of Hope* (New York: Threshold Editions, 2006).

33. Neil Gaiman and Terry Pratchett, *Good Omens* (London: Gollancz, 1990), 146.

34. Jacques Attali, *A Brief History of the Future: A Brave and Controversial Look at the Twenty-First Century*, trans. Jeremy Leggatt (New York: Arcade, 2011), 132.

35. Richard Dobbs, Jeremy Oppenheim, Fraser Thompson, Marcel Brinkman, and Marc Zornes, *Resource Revolution: Meeting the World's Energy, Materials, Food, and Water Needs* (Washington, DC: McKinsey Global Institute, November 2011), 2.

36. See Witold Rybczynski, "The Green Case for Cities," *Atlantic*, October 2009; Robert Bryce, "Get Dense," *City Journal* 22, no. 1 (Winter 2012).

37. Bryce, "Get Dense."

38. Zolli and Healy, *Resilience*, 98.

39. See, for example, Charles Murray's argument in *Coming Apart: The State of White America 1960–2010* (New York: Crown Forum, 2012).

40. Zolli and Healy, *Resilience*.

41. See Kylin Navarro, "Liberian Women Act to End Civil War, 2003," case study at Swarthmore College Global Nonviolent Action Database, October 2010, online at http://nvdatabase.swarthmore.edu/content/liberian-women-act-end-civil-war-2003.

42. Ibid.

43. United States Institute of Peace, *Women's Role in Liberia's Reconstruction* (Washington, DC: U.S. Institute of Peace, May 2007).

44. The Yemeni journalist Tawakkol Karman was separately honored with a Nobel Peace Prize in 2011 for her part in the peaceful overthrow of President Ali Abdullah Saleh during Yemen's 2011 uprising, mentioned briefly in Chapter 4.

45. For a description of Gbowee's experience, including her mentoring by Doe and Ekiyor and the support of external organizations and expertise, see her memoir: Leymah Gbowee and Carol Mithers, *Mighty Be Our Powers* (New York: Beast Books, 2011).

46. Ibid.

47. For a description of JTF Liberia, see Blair A. Ross, "The U.S. Joint Task Force Experience in Liberia," *Military Review*, May-June 2005, 60–67; for the UN peacekeeping mission, see http://unmil.unmissions.org.

48. For a street-level description of this program, see Beth Cohen, "On the Street with Violence Interrupters," Pop!Tech, June 7, 2010, online at http://poptech.org/blog/on_the_street_with_violence_interrupters.

49. Alex Kotlowitz, "Blocking the Transmission of Violence," *New York Times Magazine*, May 4, 2008.

50. Ibid.

51. See Cure Violence's website at http://cureviolence.org for details of the program.

52. Gary Slutkin biography at Cure Violence website, online at http://cureviolence.org/staff-member/gary-slutkin.

## Appendix

1. John Paul Vann, quoted in Neil Sheehan, *A Bright Shining Lie: John Paul Vann and America in Vietnam* (New York: Random House, 1988), 67.

2. See Bruce Elleman, *Waves of Hope: The U.S. Navy's Response to the Tsunami in Northern Indonesia* (Newport, RI: Naval War College Press, 2007).

3. See United States, Government Accountability Office, "State Department: The July 2006 Evacuation of American Citizens from Lebanon," memo dated July 7, 2007, online at www.gao.gov/new.items/d07893r.pdf.

4. See "France Confirms Failed Somalia Hostage Rescue Attempt," Al Jazeera, January 13, 2013.

5. As we noted in Chapter 4, there have been instances where nonstate armed groups, attacked by powerful expeditionary militaries, have mounted retaliatory attacks against those forces' homelands. The Pakistani Taliban-sponsored attempt to bomb Times Square in New York City is one such example; the London bombing of July 7, 2005, shows a similar pattern, in that three of the four bombers were of Pakistani immigrant descent (the fourth was a Jamaican immigrant) and their expressed motivation was retaliation for Western (including British) support of actions—including expeditionary operations in Iraq and Afghanistan—they deemed as "anti-Islamic."

6. See Charles Krulak, "The Three Block War: Fighting in Urban Areas," *Vital Speeches of the Day* 64, no. 5 (December 15, 1997): 139–41; Charles Krulak, "The Strategic Corporal: Leadership in the Three Block War," *Marine Corps Gazette* 83, no. 1 (January 1999): 18–23.

7. See, for example, Walter Dorn and Michael Varey, "Fatally Flawed: The Rise and Demise of the 'Three-Block War' Concept in Canada," *International Journal* 63, no. 4 (Autumn 2008): 967–78, and Hans de Marie Hengoup, "Tactique et stratégie dans la guerre nouvelle: place du caporal stratégique," *Revue Défense National* (Paris) 128 (2011): 1–5.

8. Dorn and Varey, "Fatally Flawed."

9. See the Cartography of the Anthropocene images by Felix Pharand-Deschenes at Globaia, online at http://globaia.org/en/anthropocene/#Maps.

10. Author's interview with Admiral Thisara Samarasinghe, commander of the Sri Lanka Navy, Colombo, June 2, 2011.

11. Ibid.

12. Author's interview with officers of the 4th Fast Attack Flotilla, Sri Lanka, Colombo, June 1, 2011.

13. Public Radio International, "Maritime Immigrant, Drug Smuggling Picking Up Along California Coast," January 18, 2013.

14. Author's interview with John P. Sullivan, Los Angeles, November 9, 2012.

15. Tom Phillips, "Brazil Creating Anti-Pirate Force After Spate of Attacks on Amazon Riverboats," *Guardian*, June 17, 2011.

16. Ibid.

17. United States Special Operations Command, *U.S. SOCOM Factbook 2012* (Tampa, FL: U.S. Special Operations Command, 2012), 28.

18. See Louis Hansen, "New Riverine Force Will Take Fight Upriver in Iraq," *Virginian-Pilot*, April 10, 2006, and Erik Sofge, "Behind the Scenes with a Special Operations Boat Crew," *Popular Mechanics*, October 1, 2009,

19. Interviews with SWCC crews, SEAL officers, and navy intelligence support team, Baghdad, June 3, 2007.

20. See the official Royal Navy unit Web page at www.royalnavy.mod.uk/The-Fleet/The-Royal-Marines/3-Commando-Brigade/539-Assault-Squadron.

21. Information on the Stridsbåt 90H is at www.soldf.com/strb90h.html.

22. For a detailed timeline and description of the disaster, see Ingrid Eckerman, *The Bhopal Saga—Causes and Consequences of the World's Largest Industrial Disaster* (New Delhi: Universities Press, 2005).

23. Ibid.

24. For the company's version, see Union Carbide, "Statement of Union Carbide Corporation Regarding the Bhopal Tragedy," 2012, online at www.bhopal.com/~/media/Files/Bhopal/ucs_2012.pdf.

25. For an account of the Halifax disaster, see David Flemming, *Explosion in Halifax Harbour: The Illustrated Account of a Disaster That Shook the World* (Halifax, NS: Formac, 2004). For a description of the Texas City explosion, see Hugh Stephens, *The Texas City Disaster, 1947* (Austin: University of Texas Press, 1997).

26. U.S. Department of Defense, *Amphibious Operations*, JP 3–02 (Washington, DC: Department of Defense, August 2009), I-2.

27. See Russell Stolfi, "A Critique of Pure Success: Inchon Revisited, Revised, and Contrasted," *Journal of Military History* 68, no. 2 (April 2004): 505–25.

28. United Kingdom Ministry of Defence, *Operations in Iraq: Lessons for the Future* (London: DCCS, 2003), 11.

29. Ibid., 11–13.

30. Ibid., 13.

31. U.S. Department of Defense, *Joint Forcible Entry Operations*, JP 3–18 (Washington, DC: Department of Defense, 2012).

32. Department of Defense, *Amphibious Operations*, IV-1.

33. Department of Defense, *Joint Forcible Entry Operations*.

34. See United States Marine Corps, *Marine Corps Operations*, MCDP 1–0 (Washington, DC: HQ Marine Corps, 2011), I-15.

35. See United States Marine Corps, *Marine Corps Operations*, MCDP 1–0 (Washington, DC: HQ Marine Corps, 2001), 2–15ff.

36. Ibid., 5–23ff.

37. United States Marine Corps, *Marine Corps Concept Paper: Seabased Logistics*, n.d., online at www.fas.org/man/dod-101/sys/ship/docs/sbl.htm.

38. With the retirement from service in 2005 of the Navy's *Sacramento*-class fast combat supply ships (AOEs) and the decommissioning in 2004 of the remaining *Supply*-class fast combat supply ships (T-AOEs) and their transfer to Military Sealift Command (MSC), the principal supply vessel for afloat replenishment and support of amphibious operations is now the *Lewis and Clark*–class (T-AKE) dry cargo ship operated by the civilian-crewed Naval Fleet Auxiliary Force of MSC, of which only the last three ships (USNS *William McLean*, *Medgar Evers*, and *Cesar Chavez*) have a selective-offload capability allowing them to support amphibious operations using the sea-based logistics model.

39. See United States Marine Corps, *Expeditionary Energy Strategy and Implementation Plan* (Washington, DC: Headquarters USMC, 2010), and Department of Defense, *Operational Energy Strategy Implementation Plan* (Washington, DC: Office of the Secretary of Defense, 2012).

40. See U.S. Marine Corps Warfighting Laboratory, *Experimental Forward Operating Base*, online at www.mcwl.marines.mil/Divisions/Experiment/ExFOB.aspx.

41. For Burke's work on natural resource security and energy policy, see U.S. Department of Defense, "Sharon E. Burke: Assistant Secretary of Defense for Oeprational Energy Plans and Programs," www.defense.gov/bios/biographydetail.aspx?biographyid=259, and Center for a New American Security, "Sharon E. Burke," http://cnas.org/node/64.

42. U.S. Army, *The Modular Force*, FMI3–0.1 (Washington, DC: Headquarters, Department of the Army, 2008), vii.

43. For a detailed discussion of Commando 21, see Major H. J. White RM, "Future War: Commando 21, an Increase in Combat Power and Flexibility," master's thesis, U.S. Marine Corps School of Advanced Warfighting, Quantico, VA, May 5, 2002.

44. Ibid.

45. Ibid.

46. Ibid.

47. For a description of these initiatives, see Mark Unewisse, *Land NCW: An Australian Perspective* (Adelaide: Defence Science and Technology Organisation, 2010).

48. See Steven Kornguth, Rebecca Steinberg, and Michael D. Matthews, eds., *Neurocognitive and Physiological Factors During High-Tempo Operations*

(Farnham, UK: Ashgate, 2010), and North Atlantic Treaty Organization, *Human Performance Enhancement for NATO Military Operations (Science, Technology and Ethics)*, 2009.

49. See E. Williams et al., *Human Performance* (McLean, VA: Mitre Corporation, JASON, 2008).

50. For an assessment of the last two operations, see Daniel Helmer, "Not Quite Counterinsurgency: A Cautionary Tale for US Forces Based on Israel's Operation Change of Direction," *Australian Army Journal* 5, no. 2 (Winter 2008): 117–28.

51. Organizations such as the U.S. Marine Corps Force Headquarters Group or the U.S. Army's 95th Civil Affairs Brigade (Airborne) would seem ideally suited to this role, provided they were given appropriate command authority and resources. For descriptions of these organizations, see U.S. Army Special Operations Command, "95th Civil Affairs Brigade (Airborne)," www.soc.mil/Assorted%20pages/95th%20CAB.html, and U.S. Marine Corps, "Force Headquarters Group," www.marforres.marines.mil/Major-SubordinateCommands/ForceHeadquartersGroup.aspx.

52. Author's interviews with civil affairs, commanders and planning staff, Combined Joint Task Force Horn of Africa, Djibouti, May-June 2011.

53. For a description of the IDG, established in 2004, see Australian Federal Police, "International Deployment Group," www.afp.gov.au/policing/international-deployment-group.aspx.

54. Author's interview with commanders and staff, COESPU, Vicenza, November 2012.

55. For a description of the Israeli system, see Israel Defense Forces, "Trophy," www.idf.il/1557-en/Dover.aspx.

56. For a description of AMAP-ADS, see ADS, "AMAP-ADS: The Active Defence System," http://ads-protection.org/amap-ads/active-defence-system.

57. Mike Davis, *Buda's Wagon: A Brief History of the Car Bomb* (London: Verso, 2007).

58. U.S. Government, Joint IED Defeat Organization, *JIEDDO Annual Report 2010*, 8, online at https://www.jieddo.mil/content/docs/JIEDDO_2010_Annual_Report_U.pdf.

59. U.S. Government, Joint IED Defeat Organization, *Counter Improvised Explosive Device Strategic Plan 2012–2016*, 2, online at https://www.jieddo.mil/content/docs/20120116_JIEDDOC-IEDStrategicPlan_MEDprint.pdf.

60. Ibid.

61. See Michael Petit, *Peacekeepers at War: A Marine's Account of the Beirut Catastrophe* (New York: Faber and Faber, 1986).

62. See David Kuhn and Robert Bunker, "Mexican Cartel Tactical Note #15: IED Recovered from Trunk of Car by Police Station in Ciudad Victoria, Tamaulipas (January 2012)," *Small Wars Journal*, January 14, 2013.

63. U.S. Government, White House, *Countering Improvised Explosive Devices*, February 26, 2013, online at www.whitehouse.gov/sites/default/files/docs/cied_1.pdf.

64. See "Bombs Behaving Oddly," *Strategy Page*, August 24, 2011, online at https://www.strategypage.com/htmw/htweap/articles/20110824.aspx.

# INDEX